PENNSYLVANIA COLLEGE OF TECHNOLOGY LIBR
5 0608 01063565 3

D1254419

AFFIRMATIVE ACTION :

CATALYST OR ALBATROSS?

AFFIRMATIVE ACTION :

CATALYST OR ALBATROSS?

S.N. Colamery

Nova Science Publishers, Inc.
Commack, N.Y.

Assistant Vice President/Art Director: Maria Ester Hawrys
Office Manager: Annette Hellinger
Graphics: Frank Grucci
Acquisitions Editor: Tatiana Shohov
Book Production: Ludmila Kwartiroff, Christine Mathosian, Maria A. Olmsted and Tammy Sauter
Editorial Production: Susan Boriotti
Circulation: Cathy DeGregory and Maryanne Schmidt

Library of Congress Cataloging-in-Publication Data available upon request

ISBN 1-56072-552-4

6080 Jericho Turnpike, Suite 207
Commack, New York 11725
Tele. 516-499-3103 Fax 516-499-3146
E-Mail: Novascience@earthlink.net
Web Site: http://www.nexusworld.com/nova

Printed in the United States of America

CONTENTS

Foreword

There seems to be fewer policy issues in Washington and around America which cause more hackles to rise than affirmative action.

Both sides in this debate are deeply entrenched and show little, if any, signs of movement. Is it a catalyst or an albatross?

In this book, we have gathered articles concerning the historical background of the legislation and its implementation, analyses of its effects and proposals for revision of various provisions of the law. We have tried to concentrate on issues of employment although two articles cover sexual harassment and one deals with American's with disabilities.

The heart of the affirmative action policy is, after all, an attempt toward fairness. One of the pillars which supports America's claim toward greatness is the idea that all of its citizens should have a fair chance. Action is surely required to realize this dream, but which action? We hope that the papers in the volume present a useful review of this crucial issue.

CHAPTER 1

Affirmative Action Law: A Brief Introduction

Charles V. Dale

Affirmative action is once again at the forefront of national debate as a consequence of legal and political developments at federal, state, and local levels. Early in the 104th Congress, minority and female preferences in federal contracting law, employment, and financial assistance programs surfaced on the agenda of the new Republican majority. Legislation proposed by congressional critics of affirmative action to end the use of racial, ethnic, or gender preferences by the Federal Government was met with a pledge by the Clinton Administration to "mend it, not end it." On Election Day 1996 California voters by a substantial margin approved Proposition 209, a ballot initiative designed to eliminate race, ethnicity, and gender as a basis for state governmental action. Concurrent judicial trends have further constrained the hands of government, as a constitutional matter, from imposing racial or ethnic preferences to achieve "diversity," or as a remedy for past discrimination, in education, employment or public contracting.

EVOLUTION OF FEDERAL AFFIRMATIVE ACTION LAW

The origins of affirmative action law may be traced to the early 1960's as first, the Warren, and then Burger Courts grappled with the intractable problem of racial segregation in the nation's public schools. Judicial rulings from this period recognized an "affirmative duty," cast upon local school boards by the Equal Protection Clause, to desegregate formerly "dual school" systems and to eliminate "root and branch" the last "vestiges" of state-enforced segregation.[1] These holdings ushered in a two decade era of "massive" desegregation--first in the South, and later the urban North--marked by federal desegregation orders frequently requiring drastic reconfiguration of school attendance patterns along racial lines and extensive student transportation schemes. School districts across the nation operating under these decrees have since sought to be declared in compliance with constitutional requirements in order to gain release from federal intervention. The Supreme Court eventually responded by holding that judicial control of a school system previously found guilty of intentional segregation should be relinquished if, looking to all aspects of school operations, the court determines that the district has complied with desegregation

---

1 *See e.g. Green v. County Board,* 391 U.S. 430 (1968); *Swann v. Board of Education,* 402 U.S. 1 (1971); *Keyes v. Denver School District,* 413 U.S. 189 (1973).

requirement in "good faith" for a "reasonable period of time" and has eliminated "vestiges" of past discrimination "to the extent practicable."[2]

Congress and the Executive Branch have crafted a wide range of federal laws and regulations authorizing, either directly or by judicial or administrative interpretation, "race-conscious" strategies to promote minority opportunity in jobs, education, and governmental contracting. The historical model for federal laws and regulations establishing minority participation "goals" may be found in Executive Orders which since the early 1960's have imposed affirmative minority hiring and employment requirements on federally financed construction projects and in connection with other large federal contracts. Executive Order 11246, as presently administered by the Office of Federal Contract Compliance Programs, requires that all employers with 50 or more employees, and federal contracts in excess of $50,000.00, file written affirmative action plans with the government. These must include minority and female hiring goals and timetables to which the contractor must commit its "good faith" efforts. Race and gender considerations--which may include numerical goals--are also a fundamental aspect of affirmative action planning by federal departments and agencies to eliminate minority and female "underrepresentation" at various levels of agency employment.[3]

Federal contract "set-asides," and minority subcontracting goals, have been basic components of the § 8(a) and § 8(d) programs conducted by the Small Business Administration to expand participation by "socially and economically disadvantaged" entrepreneurs in the federal procurement process.[4] Minority group members and women are presumed to be socially and economically disadvantaged under the Small Business Act. "Goals" or "set-asides" for minority groups, women, and other "disadvantaged" individuals, have also been routinely included in federal funding measures for education, defense, transportation and

---

[2] *Dowell v. Board of Education*, 498 U.S. 237 (1991). *See also Freeman v. Pitts*, 503 U.S. 467 (1993)(allowing incremental dissolution of judicial control) and *Missouri v. Jenkins*, 115 S.Ct 2038 (1995)(directing district court on remand to "bear in mind that its end purpose is not only 'to remedy the violation' to the extent practicable, but also 'to restore state and local authorities to the control of a school system that is operating in compliance with the Constitution.'").

[3] 42 U.S.C. § 2000e-16(b)(1); 5 U.S.C. § 7201. The EEOC and the Office of Personnel Management have issued rules to guide implementation and monitoring of minority recruitment programs by individual federal agencies. Among various other specified requirements, each agency plan "must include annual specific determinations of underrepresentation for each group and must be accompanied by quantifiable indices by which progress toward eliminating underrepresentation can be measured." 5 C.F.R. § 720.205(b).

[4] 15 U.S.C. § 637(a),(d).

other activities over much of the last decade and a half.[5] Currently, each federal department and agency must contribute to achieving a government-wide, annual procurement goal of at least 5% with its own goal-oriented effort to create "maximum practicable opportunity" for minority and female contractors.[6]

The *Bakke* ruling in 1978 launched the contemporary constitutional debate over state-sponsored affirmative action.[7] One five-Justice majority there invalidated on equal protection grounds a state medical school special admissions program which set-aside sixteen of one hundred positions in each incoming class for minority students where the institution itself was not shown to have discriminated in the past. But another five Justices would have found that institutional interests in student diversity and academic freedom nonetheless warranted nonexclusive consideration of race in educational admissions. Justice Powell, who cast the deciding vote, found that neither the state's asserted interest in remedying "societal discrimination" nor of providing "role models" for minority students was sufficiently "compelling" to warrant the use of a "suspect" racial classification in the admission process. But the attainment of a "diverse student body" was, for Justice Powell "clearly a permissible goal for an institution of higher education" since diversity of minority viewpoints furthered "academic freedom," a "special concern of the First Amendment."[8] Accordingly, race could be considered by a university as a "plus" or "one element of a range of factors"--even if it "tipped the scale" among qualified applicants--as long as it "did not insulate the individual from comparison with all the other candidates for the available seats."[9] The "quota" in *Bakke* was infirm, however, since it defined diversity only in racial terms and absolutely excluded nonminorities from a given number of seats.

Bakke was followed by *Wygant v. Jackson Board of Education*,[10] where a divided Court ruled unconstitutional the provision of a collective bargaining agreement that protected minority public school teachers from layoff at the expense of more senior white faculty members. While holding the specific layoff

---

[5] *See "Compilation and Overview of Federal Laws and Regulations Establishing Affirmative Action Goals or Other Preference Based on Race, Gender, or Ethnicity,"* CRS Memorandum, February 17, 1995 (Dale), *reprinted at* 141 *Cong. Rec.* S 3929 (daily ed. 3-15-95).

[6] 15 U.S.C. § 644(g)(1). The Federal Acquisition Streamlining Act of 1994 permits federal agency heads to adopt restricted competition and a 10% "price evaluation preference" in favor of "socially and economically disadvantaged individuals" to achieve the government-wide and agency contracting goal requirements. Pub. L. 103-355, 108 Stat. 3242, § 7104 (1994).

[7] *Regents of the University of California v. Bakke*, 438 U.S. 265 (1978).

[8] *Id.* at 311-12. [9] *Id.* at 317. [10] 476 U.S. 267 (1986).

preference for minority teachers unconstitutional, seven *Wygant* Justices seemed to agree in principle that a governmental employer is not prohibited by the Equal Protection Clause from all race-conscious affirmative action to remedy its own past discrimination. Another series of decisions approved of congressionally mandated racial preferences to allocate the benefits of contracts on federally sponsored public works projects,[11] and in the design of certain broadcast licensing schemes,[12] while condemning similar actions taken by local governmental entities to promote public contracting opportunities for MBEs.[13] However, in each of these cases, the Justices failed to achieve a consensus on most issues, with bare majorities, pluralities, or--as in *Bakke*--a single Justice, determining the "law" of the case.

By the mid-1980's, the Supreme Court had approved the temporary remedial use of race- or gender-conscious selection criteria by private employers under Title VII of the 1964 Civil Rights Act.[14] These measures were deemed a proper remedy for "manifest racial imbalance" in "traditionally segregated" job categories, if voluntarily adopted by the employer,[15] or for entrenched patterns of "egregious and longstanding" discrimination by the employer, if imposed by judicial decree.[16] In either circumstance, however, the Court required that affirmative action "goals" or "quotas" be sufficiently flexible, of temporary duration, and so hedged with safeguards as to prevent "reverse discrimination" against white male employees. Similarly, the Justices approved of affirmative action by public employers to increase promotional opportunities for women and minorities, either as a voluntary measure or pursuant to Title VII court decree.[17]

RECENT LEGAL AND CONSTITUTIONAL DEVELOPMENTS

In *Adarand Constructors, Inc. v. Pena* [18] the Supreme Court invoked the same "strict scrutiny" standard of constitutional review for racial preferences adopted by the federal government as it had previously applied to state and local

---

11 *Fullilove v. Klutznick*, 448 U.S. 448 (1980).

12 *Metro Broadcasting, Inc. v. FCC*, 497 U.S. 547, *reh'g denied*, 497 U.S. 1050 (1990).

13 *City of Richmond v. J.A. Croson, Co.*, 488 U.S. 469 (1989).

14 42 U.S.C. §§ 2000e *et seq.*

15 *United Steelworkers v. Weber*, 443 U.S. 193 (1979).

16 *Local 28 Sheet Metal Workers v. EEOC*, 478 U.S. 421 (1986).

17 *United States v. Paradise*, 480 U.S. 149 (1987); *Johnson v. Transportation Agency*, 480 U.S. 616 (1987).

18 115 S. Ct. 2097 (1995).

affirmative action programs. Although the Court refrained from deciding the constitutional merits of the particular program before it, and remanded for further proceedings below, it now appears that all "racial classifications" by government at any level must be justified by a "compelling governmental interest" and "narrowly tailored" to that end. *Adarand* suggests that the federal government still has a "compelling" interest in remedying past discrimination against racial or ethnic minorities evidenced by "particularized" and "specific" findings. However, racial line-drawing by Congress or federal agencies in the future may have to be a "finely tuned" response to demonstrable racial exclusion affecting particular programs rather than an antidote for "societal discrimination" or to promote "diversity" for nonremedial purposes.

In effect, *Adarand* advances a unifying principle from the Court's earlier rulings that racial preferences, whether imposed by the legislature or judicial decree, are a remedy of last resort reserved for "extreme cases" of "systematic" discrimination or deliberate "patterns" of racial exclusion. Accordingly, at a minimum, Congress may now bear a far weightier burden of justification for any distinctions along racial or ethnic lines. All "explicit" classifications in federal laws, benefitting or burdening any racial or ethnic group, must be "narrowly tailored," a constitutional standard demanding exhaustion of all race-neutral solutions before resorting to race-conscious remedies. Consequently, all racial preferences in federal statute or regulation may stand on more precarious constitutional footing after *Adarand*.

In response to *Adarand*, the Justice Department on May 23, 1996 proposed regulations setting stricter certification and eligibility requirements for minority contractors claiming "socially and economically disadvantaged" status under the § 8(a) and other federal affirmative action programs.[19] The plan would suspend for two years set-aside programs in which only minority firms may bid on contracts and would establish "benchmarks" for federal contracting in various industries to assess when preferential treatment is no longer necessary. Where minority participation in an industry falls below the benchmark, a price or evaluation credit--not set-asides--would be authorized for the evaluation of bids by socially and economically disadvantaged firms and prime contractors who commit to subcontract with such firms. The new system would be monitored by the Commerce Department, using data already collected to evaluate the percentage of federal contracting dollars awarded to minority-owned businesses, and would rely more heavily on "outreach and technical assistance" to avoid potential constitutional pitfalls. The comment period for the proposed changes closed after 60 days, but the final version of the regulations has not been issued to date.

On the closing day of its October 1995 Term, the U.S. Supreme Court denied review of the Fifth Circuit decision in *Hopwood v. State of Texas*[20]

---

[19] 61 *Fed Reg.* 26042, Notices, Department of Justice, Proposed Reforms to Affirmative Action in Federal Procurement, Part IV (May 23, 1996).

[20] 95 F.3d 53 (5th Cir.), *cert. denied* No. 95-1773, 116 S.Ct 2581 (1996).

which invalidated an affirmative action program of the University of Texas Law School. A three judge appellate panel there held that the desire to admit a diverse student body never provides a "compelling" justification for the consideration of race in student admissions, and that despite its early history of racial exclusion, the Law School had failed to demonstrate sufficient continuing effects of its own prior illegal acts to warrant remedial affirmative action. The *Hopwood* court rejected the diversity rationale proposed by Justice Powell in *Bakke* as "not binding precedent," since his opinion was not formally joined by any other Justice. Race and ethnicity can never be used for nonremedial purposes as a "proxy for other characteristics" valued by an educational institution since that would inevitably lead to racial "stereotyp[ing]" and "stigmatization" forbidden by *Croson* and *Adarand*. Instead,

> For the admissions scheme to pass constitutional muster, the State of Texas, through its legislature, would have to find that past segregation has present effects; it would have to determine the magnitude of those present effects; and it would need to limit carefully the "plus" given to applicants to remedy that harm. A broad program that sweeps in all minorities with a remedy that is in no way related to past harms cannot survive constitutional scrutiny.[21]

A recent Title VII case, *U.S. v. Board of Education of the Township of Piscataway*,[22] also held that a school board's desire to promote faculty "diversity" could not justify its decision to protect a black teacher from layoff, while dismissing an equally qualified white colleague, where there was no showing of past discrimination or minority underrepresentation in the district's hiring practices. *Hopwood* and *Piscataway* join an earlier Fourth Circuit ruling, *Podberesky v. Kirwan*,[23]--which invalidated a race-based scholarship program administered by the University of Maryland for the exclusive benefit of black students.

Collectively, these rulings marginalize the constitutional value of academic or workplace diversity as support for racial or ethnic preferences which are not "narrowly tailored" to correcting the present-day effects of historical discrimination for which the institution is itself responsible. The Supreme Court's refusal to hear *Hopwood* has had an unsettling impact on academic affirmative action policies nationwide. In early November of 1996, however, the Piscataway School Board filed for Supreme Court review of the Third Circuit's ruling on the permissible role of race as a factor in employment decisions. As noted in its petition for certiorari, "[t]his case has become a lightening rod in a stormy national debate over whether Title VII permits school officials to consider race in employment decisions to foster a diverse learning environment."

---

[21] *Id.* at 13.

[22] 91 F.3d 1547 (3d Cir. 1996).

[23] 38 F.3d 147 (4th Cir. 1994), *cert denied,* 115 S.Ct. 2001 (1995).

If it grants review in the case, the Supreme Court may clarify the legality of affirmative action plans set up solely to promote diversity under Title VII's prohibition on racial discrimination.

CHAPTER 1A

Affirmative Action: Yesterday, Today and Beyond*

Reginald Wilson
American Council on Education

1. Introduction

> ... Discrimination because of race, creed, color or national origin is contrary to the Constitutional principles and policies of the United States...
>
> President John F. Kennedy
> Executive Order 10925
> March 6, 1961

Affirmative action has had a long and contentious history dating back many years in the United States. It began haphazardly without a clear sense of its final scope or full intent and evolved into the present complex of laws and executive orders. However, the purpose always was clear: to overcome the history of America's past of slavery, peonage, racism, and, finally, legally sanctioned segregation, that barred blacks (and other minorities and women of all races) from full participation in the work force and in America's educational institutions. The segregation was systemic and nearly complete. Such exclusion, especially of blacks, contradicted the lofty statements of the Constitution and Declaration of Independence and was a blot on the conscious of many Americans. These barriers have been deeply embedded in the attitudes and institutional structures of American society since the founding of the nation. Although many attempts have been made to eradicate these barriers, their attempted removal has been met with equally fierce resistance. What follows is the history of such attempts, in brief, from the past to the present.

II. History

> Eight decades into the twentieth century and more than a dozen decades following the end of legalized slavery in the United States, the nation has not achieved equality of educational opportunity for all its citizens.

---

* This paper was presented at the U.S. Senate Hearing on Affirmative Action

> Although there is significant evidence that progress has been made toward the realization of equal opportunity in education, much more has to be accomplished before educational parity is attained.
>
> James E. Blackwell[1]
> Professor of Sociology (retired)
> University of Massachusetts Boston

It is important to begin this history with African Americans because from the time of the nation's founding their status as slaves was legally sanctioned by the Constitution and codified into the laws of the United States. As a result, the laws to redress segregation and discrimination have been aimed primarily at them and secondarily at others.

Although the Freedman's Bureau and jobs for the freed slaves were established in 1865 immediately after Emancipation, these were reduced considerably by 1875, following great resistance by white southerners and the removal from the South of federal troops that were protecting the freed slaves. This resistance, plus many cumulative regional restrictions, was finally codified into national law by the infamous Supreme Court decision in *Plessy v. Ferguson* (1896), which legally sanctioned segregation of the races.

Plessy was followed immediately by the passage of Jim Crow laws in the South that prevented blacks from voting and restricted other areas of black life. By 1890, blacks were strictly segregated in every facet of life from public transportation to schools, and would remain so for half a century.

Although significant restrictions were imposed on other ethnic groups and on white women, most of the references in this part will be confined to African Americans because the strictures applied to them were so pervasive and confining, and all were sanctioned by law in the South and by custom in the North, thus providing the initial impetus of the civil rights movement and the struggle for affirmative action. [The next section will deal with the impact of affirmative action on other ethnic groups and on white women.]

Despite the restrictions on black education, some strides were made, but they were limited. For instance, from 1876 to 1929, only 51 blacks were awarded the doctorate from American universities. It was not until 1930 that black colleges were given a special "approved" designation by the Southern Association of Colleges and Schools, and they were granted full membership only in 1957.[2]

Black scholars, however brilliant, were restricted to teaching at the historically black colleges (HBCUs). Yet, some of them were famous: W.E.B. DuBois, Harvard Ph.D., organized the first international Pan-African conference in London; Rayford W. Logan, who graduated Phi Beta Kappa from Williams College and earned a Ph.D. from Harvard, was head of the history department at Howard University; Charles Drew earned his M.D. degree from McGill University, headed the American Red Cross Blood Bank, and eventually taught at Howard.3 Only five black colleges had graduate schools, and by 1933 they had awarded 76 master's degrees. Most southern blacks who wanted graduate education beyond the master's were paid by their state to go North to secure their degrees at white universities.

The black schools not only suffered from restrictions on their scholastic offerings but were underfunded as well. For example, one white school in 1943 had laboratory equipment valued at $2,500 while the school for blacks had no equipment, and the white male teachers were paid $2,508 per year while the black teachers were paid $1,850 (even though over 50 percent of the black teachers had higher degrees than the whites).[4] In Mississippi, another example, as late as 1950, black schools received $32.55 in education funding per pupil, whereas white schools received $122.93.[5]

In 1941, a survey of the predominantly white colleges and universities conducted by the Julius Rosenwald Fund found only two black faculty—both in non-teaching laboratory positions—in all of these institutions. That year, Dr. Allison Davis, the eminent black sociologist, was appointed to a full-time faculty position at the University of Chicago, at the urging of, and with his salary partially subsidized by, the Rosenwald Fund.[6]

These few facts are cited to stress two things: 1) that black education was strictly segregated race until about 40 years ago; and 2) that it was not only segregated but systematically limited in curriculum and underfunded as well, restricting access and opportunity in various fields.

African Americans were equally restricted and segregated in the economic sphere. Blacks were confined by and large to unskilled jobs requiring physical labor—picking cotton, working as domestics, etc. With the advent of the First World War, the boll weevil's decimation of the cotton industry, and the subsequent migration of millions of blacks to the North, African Americans for the first time got factory and industrial jobs, albeit still mostly unskilled. However, it is instructive to remember that by 1917, on the threshold of World War I, 89 percent of blacks still lived in the South and still were confined mainly to agricultural and domestic work.[7]

The dramatic rise in racism in the United States ironically presaged the nation's entry into "the War to end all Wars." In the first decade of this century, Thomas Dixon published *The Clansman* (1905), Charles Carroll published *The Negro as Beast* (1900), Robert W. Shufeldt wrote *The Negro, a Menace to American Civilization* (1907).[8] The Republican Party platform of 1912 called for citizens "to condemn and punish lynching." The Democratic platform was silent on this issue. Between 1901 and 1910, 754 blacks were lynched.[9]

> Slavery was our original sin, just as race remains our unresolved dilemma.
>
> Senator Bill Bradley (D-NJ)
> 1994

The history described above continued until 1940, the eve of World War II. At that time, 79 percent of African Americans still resided in the South. Of those blacks in college, 85 percent attended the HBCUs, and only a little over 1 percent of blacks possessed a college degree. Life for African Americans was still very segregated, despite the nation being on the verge of "the War for Democracy."

In 1940, A. Philip Randolph, a prominent black labor leader, met with President Franklin D. Roosevelt along with other lack leaders to protest discrimination in the burgeoning defense industry that was gearing up at the time. Randolph warned the president that if blacks continued to be refused jobs in these plants, he would organize a march on Washington of thousands of blacks in protest. The threat convinced Roosevelt to issue Executive Order 8802, which barred discrimination by race or national origin in industries with government contracts. This led in turn to the second massive migration of millions of blacks from the South, many of whom sought jobs in the defense industries, which were located mainly in the North.

Following the war, the Servicemen's Readjustment Act of 1944 (popularly called the "G.I. Bill of Rights") granted every veteran a free college education or job training as well as a loan to purchase a home. Over one million African Americans had served in the armed forces in World War II, and thousands of them eagerly went to college—most of them to the HBCUs in the South, but many to predominantly white universities in the North, which welcomed all veterans with their government vouchers. Many colleges waived or lowered entrance requirements, gave extra points on entrance examinations, and provided extra help for veterans who had been out of school for three to five years (the first affirmative action in college admissions!). And the veterans prospered. "There has not been a college class that accomplished as much academically before or since."[10] Subsequently, the armed forces were desegregated by President Truman in 1946.

These two measures of the 1940s—Executive Order 8802 and the G.I. Bill—provided the first significant opening of employment and education for blacks since Reconstruction. It was from this threshold that the momentum was generated that led to the civil rights movement and eventually to affirmative action.

This brief recapitulation of history is cited to stress three issues: 1) affirmative action grew out of a continuous history of racial oppression of a group, not of individuals; 2) that history not only oppressed blacks but restricted their opportunity for education and employment; and 3) that history was accompanied by a virulent racism that continues, albeit in diminished form, up to the present. (The continuing effects of discrimination to the present day will be documented later in this paper.)

> I say unequivocally, that the job of integrating African Americans, who were isolated generation after generation by official action and unofficial practice, into the American mainstream isn't done by any stretch of the imagination.
>
> Hugh B. Price, President, National Urban League
> February 10, 1995

III. Other Minorities and White Women

> Bringing the unique experience of women, particularly white women, a group of unparalleled size, into the discussion of affirmative action, is itself an important contribution. Race and racism have obscured the extraordinary role that affirmative action has played in moving women from their customary low tiers in the workplace.
>
> Eleanor Holmes Norton
> Delegate to Congress
> District of Columbia
> (Clayton & Crosby, 1992, p. ix)

As previously stated, this paper recognizes the racial oppression of other ethnic groups and the legal restrictions on white women. Those circumstances are described briefly in this section.

American Indians, of course, were the most oppressed. After all, they were the original occupants of this land. Over the course of American history, tribes were ravaged by disease, defeated in battle, and subjected to constant violations of the treaties into which they were forced. Many American Indians were restricted to reservations, sent to boarding schools where they were beaten if they spoke their native languages, and denied educational and occupational opportunities.[11]

In much of the United States, Hispanic women and men, particularly those of Mexican ancestry, for long periods were restricted mostly to jobs as manual laborers and provided few educational opportunities. Now, although some can trace their roots in this country back generations or centuries, Hispanics of Latino origin have become the target of renewed anti-immigrant sentiment, exemplified most particularly in California by the passage of Proposition 187. That draconian measure is designed not only to discourage new immigration, but to withhold many benefits from legal as well as illegal immigrants.[12] The impact of affirmative action on Hispanics—the nation's largest minority group except for African Americans (and soon to overtake them)—has been profound.

Asian men first were imported to work on the railroads in the West. Asian women followed and were employed in menial positions. Later, Asians were denounced for "taking white men's jobs," and the fear of the "Yellow Peril" led to restrictions on Asian immigration in the Exclusion Act of 1924, which was not lifted until 1945. Additionally, Japanese Americans were illegally confined to detention camps during World War II as a "national security measure" (though the U.S. Supreme Court upheld their relocation) and lost much of their property while they were incarcerated.

White women were not restricted because of their race, of course, but were denied many higher education and employment opportunities because of sex discrimination. For example, women of all races did not win the right to vote until 1920. Additionally, many of the more prestigious universities accepted only white males for many years. However, white women had their own female institutions such as Barnard and Radcliffe, and began to make inroads into the white male universities early in the century. Still, women, though a majority of the population (53 percent), are not proportionately represented in higher education or in most occupations. Also, they continue suffer pay inequity as well as discrimination in the workplace and underrepresentation in elective offices.

However, white women's status is quantitatively as well as qualitatively different from that of other underrepresented groups because of their race. Thus, in looking at factors such as education, employment, and income, it is important in most instances to disaggregate white women and women of color, lest minority women be obscured in the limbo between "minority" and "women".[13] Such disaggregation in no way denigrates the injustices still suffered by white women but recognizes the fact that minority women often face different obstacles to advancement.

Table 1
Percentage of White Women and Other Underrepresented Groups in Selected Professions

Occupation	White Women	Minority Men and Women: Blacks	Minority Men and Women: Latinos
Doctors	22	4	5
Lawyers	24	2	3
Scientists	31	3	1

Source: Department of Labor, 1994.

A May 1994 study by the National Rainbow Coalition of the National Broadcasting Corporation (NBC) showed these patterns of disparity in the company's racial and gender hiring practices in its New York headquarters division: "Out of 645 employees of the News Division, 354 were white males, 261 were white females (a total of 96%), 8 were black males, 7 black females, 7 Latino females, 1 Latino male, 3 Asian males, 3 Asian females, and 0 Native Americans."[14]

> Affirmative action is good for America, good for business, and good for working people because it promotes values of inclusion, fairness, and merit. Affirmative action does not mean quotas or arbitrary preferential treatment.
>
> Women United for Equality
> Press Release
> March 15, 1995

Table II
Income Disparities of Underrepresented Groups (*% of white men's salaries*)

	Black Men	Black Women	LatinoMen	Latino Women	White Women
1975	74	55	72	49	58
1985	70	57	68	52	63
1993	74	53	64	NA	70

Source: Department of Labor, 1994.

Hispanics and American Indians first were identified for specific melioration of their situation following the Supreme Court decision in *Brown v. Board of Education* in 1954, which desegregated public schools. These groups also were found to suffer from school segregation, particularly in those southern states where they represented a large segment of the population—Texas and Oklahoma. They, and all other minorities, later were covered by the Civil Rights Act of 1964. The Adams decision of 1973 also covered Hispanics in Texas higher education.

Asian Americans are, at present, not considered underrepresented in higher education or employment as a group. However, particular subgroups of Asian immigrants—Vietnamese, Hmong, Laotians—had a high incidence of illiteracy and poor job skills. Where these populations were concentrated, they benefited from affirmative action programs. Singly they were treated as other Asian Americans needing no protecting.

Women first were covered under anti-discrimination laws by Executive Order 11375, issued by President Lyndon B. Johnson on 1967, which added "sex" to the categories of protected classes. That coverage was expanded in 1972 under Title IX of the Education Amendments of that year.

Subsequently, the Age Discrimination Act was passed in 1975. In 1968, the Architectural Barriers Act had been enacted, requiring employers to modify buildings to make them accessible to the handicapped. This was followed in 1973 by Section 504 of the Rehabilitation Act, requiring affirmative action in the employment of people with disabilities

It is evident that what began in 1941 as a prohibition opposing employment discrimination against blacks in World War II defense plants has evolved into an increasingly complex and multi-layered set of laws and sanctions covering other minorities, women of all races, the elderly, and the handicapped. What began simply as a concern with fair hiring increased in complexity as knowledge and awareness of the problems of society grew. The laws and sanctions then proliferated to cover modification of buildings, recruitment of black and Hispanic students into predominantly white universities, more equitable funding for minority educational institutions and women's programs, and increased hiring of women and minority faculty and administrators. All of these directives fall under the heading of "affirmative action" although, strictly speaking, the term applies only to the Executive Orders.[15]

But what also is conspicuously evident is that these various laws and rules grew without a strong governmental or legal theory binding them coherently together. Therefore, some of the laws are conflicting and contradictory and exceedingly difficult to interpret, adding to the confusion and frustration of both those who oppose them and those who support them, and thus weakening their effectiveness and giving the courts unclear direction in interpreting them.

In the next section, we examine the various laws, acts, and court decisions regarding affirmative action.

IV. The Laws, Court Decisions, and Executive Orders

> [T]here is now little dispute over the power of courts to order remedial affirmative action plans, or the right of parties to settle their case with consent decrees incorporating such plans.
>
> Deval L. Patrick
> Assistant Attorney General for Civil Rights
> Testimony to Congress
> March 24, 1995

The following annotated cases are meant not to be exhaustive but to illustrate the legal history of affirmative action and how opinions change over time.

Executive Orders

1941 – Order 8802 (Roosevelt)
No discrimination by race in defense plants.

1961 – Order 10925 (Kennedy)
Encouraged affirmative action but had no enforcement procedures.

1965 – Order 11246 (Johnson)
Ordered all government contractors to take affirmative action.

1967 – Order 11375 (Johnson)
Added "sex" to protected classes of persons.

1978 – Revised Order No. 4 (Nixon)
Detailed specific goals and timetables for effective plans.

Laws

1964 – Civil Rights Act - Title VII
Prohibited all forms of discrimination in public and private sector hiring. (Did not apply to higher education faculty until 1972.)

1968 – Architectural Barriers Act
Ordered that buildings be modified to give access to the handicapped.

1972 – Educational Amendments – Title IX
Prohibited sex discrimination in any "federally assisted education program."

1973 – Rehabilitation Act – Section 504
Required affirmative action in employment of the handicapped.

1975 – Age Discrimination Act
Barred discrimination in hiring or firing of older persons.

1991 – Civil Rights Act
Corrected some Supreme Court decisions (*Wards Cove, Martin*) that Congress felt had been decided wrongly.

Federal Court Decisions

1954 – *Brown v. Board of Education*
Ended segregation in the public elementary and secondary schools; *de jure* in the South, *de facto* in the North.

1971 – *Griggs v. Duke Power*
Prohibited denial of employment opportunities to minorities even if not intentional discrimination.

1973 – *Adams v. Richardson*
Ended segregation of higher education where there were dual systems. Ordered recruitment of students and faculty to other-race institutions.

1978 – *Regents of the University of California v. Bakke*
Declared race specific quotas in medical school admissions impermissible, but approved taking race into account as a factor in admissions.

1979 – *United Steelworkers of America v. Weber*
Upheld a minority set-aside provision entered into voluntarily as meeting a "compelling interest" in ending industry-wide discrimination that exhibited "manifest racial imbalance."

1984 – *Firefighters Local 1784 v. Stotts*
1986 – *Wygant v. Jackson Board of Education*
Both cases affirmed two principles: 1) affirmative action in hiring minorities is allowable without proof of specific discrimination; and 2) layoff plans cannot protect minorities with less seniority.

1986 – *Local 93 v. City of Cleveland*
Approved a voluntary consent decree that established hiring goals for minorities even though they suffered no prior discrimination.

1986 – *Local 28 of Sheetmetal Workers v. EEOC*
Permitted a 29 percent race-conscious hiring goal where "a labor union has engaged in... egregious discrimination"; minorities hired need not be the actual victims of discrimination.

1987 – *Johnson v. Transportation Agency*
Approved hiring of a qualified woman whose score was two points lower than the rejected male when there was "manifest gender imbalance" but no findings of discrimination.[16]

1989 – *Richmond v. J.A. Croson Co.*
Disallowed state-ordered set-aside programs, even where intent is remedial, if plans do not meet "strict scrutiny" standard.

1989 – *Wards Cove Packing Co. v. Atonio*
Shifted burden of proof of discrimination to minorities despite demonstrable disparity in jobs.

1989 – *Martin v. Wilks*
Ruled that whites may challenge affirmative action policies that they previously agreed to, with no deadlines for such challenges.

1993 – *Hopwood v. Texas*
Ruled that while recruitment of minorities for law school was a "lawful objective," a process that excluded certain students was unconstitutional. (Under appeal.)

As can be seen, little clear-cut legal reasoning runs through these court decisions. They start out liberal and, as the composition of the Supreme Court changes in the 1980s, they become more narrowly construed and require affirmative action plans to meet "strict scrutiny" standards. President Clinton has had the opportunity to appoint two justices, but it is uncertain how the present Court, with its liberal/conservative balance, will rule in individual cases. For example, its refusal to hear an appeal of the recent case of *Kirwan v. Podberesky*, in which the Fourth Circuit Court of Appeals found a scholarship program at the University of Maryland targeted at high-achieving blacks to be illegal, gives no guidance on how the Court will rule in other, similar cases.

However, one thread does run clearly through all of these decisions—the one articulated by Assistant Attorney General Deval Patrick. The Supreme Court has held consistently that the principle of affirmative action could be upheld if the plan to implement it was narrowly tailored, met the "strict scrutiny" standard, was intended to remedy a specific wrong and (presumably) was intended as a temporary measure. These standards are difficult to meet but nevertheless, if they still obtain, may be the best that supporters of affirmative action have to hold on to in these perilous times.

V. Affirmative Action: Victories and Promise

> Affirmative action is first and foremost a legitimized constitutional remedy for past discrimination. It is a remedy in keeping with the basic principle that where there is a constitutional violation, there must be a remedy appropriate in scope to that violation.
>
> Vernon Jordan
> Former President
> National Urban League
> 1986

Affirmative action has had dramatic and measurable results in moving minorities and women into meaningful employment in industry and increasing their participation in higher education as students, faculty, and administrators. This progress has not come without difficulty and has been challenged by lawsuits and filings of reverse discrimination appeals with the Equal Employment Opportunity Commission.

Table III
Construction Firms Owned by Minorities and Women

	1972	1987
Minorities	39,875	107,650
Women	14,884	94,308

Source: Census Bureau, 1992.17

In private industry, minority and female-owned construction firms have gained a foothold in this most homogeneous of industries, and mostly through affirmative action. Previously, minority firms were too small to bid on competitive contracts and white-owned firms seldom took them on as subcontractors. As a result, their firms got only an infinitesimal share of the construction business. With affirmative action, however, cities and local governments began to set aside a portion of their construction business or required large white-owned firms to subcontract with firms owned by minority men and women of all races. However, the *Croson* decision may hamper progress in this area, and President Clinton has hinted that minority set-asides may be eliminated after his review of federal affirmative action programs.

Other areas of employment also have shown dramatically measurable results through aggressive implementation of affirmative action plans or their enforcement by the courts. For example, a consent decree obtained in an AT&T case increased the number of black women in skilled clerical positions by 65 percent in 1978-79. Large jumps in minority and female employment among sheet metal and electrical workers also were recorded.[18]

Table IV
Percentage of Minority and Women
Police Officers In 50 Largest Cities

	1983	1992
Blacks	12.4	17.3
Hispanics	6.8	8.3
Women	NA	11.6

Source: University of Nebraska, 1994.

In 1973, the Los Angeles Fire Department was 100 percent male and 94 percent white. A federal court secured a consent decree from the LAFD with specific affirmative action targets. Today, 1995, the LAFD is 26 percent Hispanic, 13 percent African American, 6 percent Asian and 4 percent women. This is a good beginning in a city that is 66 percent minority. However, the top officers, at the rank of battalion commander and above, remain virtually all white.[19]

Nevertheless the examples in Table IV (and others like it from some of the nation's large cities) refute the charge by some critics that affirmative action benefits only middle-class minorities. Studies show minorities have made gains in occupations not usually associated with advantaged states, such as law enforcement, fire fighting, and skilled construction work. Moreover, other studies show that of "the increased enrollment of minority students in medical school..., significant numbers were from families of low income and job status."[20]

VI. Minorities and Women in Higher Education

The impact of affirmative action on the employment and enrollment of underrepresented groups in higher education is the principal focus of this essay. However, we cannot discuss this issue meaningfully outside of the context of the difficult history described heretofore and the racial and sexual oppression that led up to the present. Some limited progress has been made by minority men and women of all races in higher education despite the many obstacles to their advancement and the continuous resistance they have encountered.

As can be seen in Table V, even white women, who constitute 40 percent of the population, have been moving up slowly in faculty numbers but have yet to reach parity. While 30.3 percent of faculty members in 1989 were women, 26 percent were white women. All minority women faculty members combined represented 4 percent. Neither group is proportionately represented. Ending affirmative action would seriously impede the progress of white women, but it would have a devastating impact on the precarious hold minority women have on faculty positions.

Table V
Percentage of Women Faculty and Ph.Ds
1890-1989

Year	Faculty	Ph.Ds Awarded
1890	19.6	1.3
1900	19.8	6.0
1910	20.1	9.9
1920	26.3	15.1
1930	27.2	15.4
1940	27.6	13.0
1950	24.5	9.6
1960	22.0	10.5
1970	23.1	13.3
1980	29.0	29.7
1989	30.3	37.7

Sources: 1890-1980: *Digest of Education Statistics 1989* (Washington, DC: National Center for Education Statistics, 1989), p. 166, 1989: *Minorities in Higher Education* (Washington, DC: American Council on Education, 1991), pp. 59-63.

Figure I Number of Full-Time Faculty in Higher Education by Race/Ethnicity, 1981 and 1991

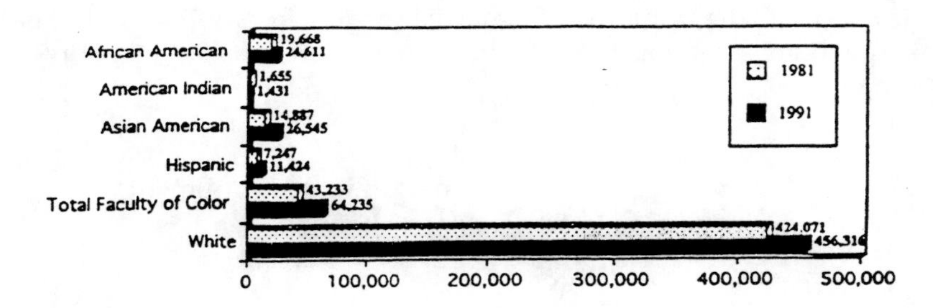

Source: U.S. Equal Employment Opportunity Commission. "EEO-6 Higher Education Staff Information Survey," 1981 and 1991.

Figure I indicates that *while minority faculty (men and women) have made some limited gains, again due mostly to affirmative action, they still represent collectively a minuscule percentage of the total.*

Student Enrollment

Table VI
Minorities as Percentage of Student Enrollment in Higher Education

	1981	1993
Four-Year Institutions	14	20
Two-Year Institutions	20	27
Total	17	23

Source: American Council on Education, 1995.[21]

Minority student enrollment at colleges and universities increased modestly but steadily from 1981 to 1993, as shown in Table VI. However, enrollment has increased slightly more in two-year institutions than in four-year institutions. The downturn in the economic circumstances of some minorities (American Indians and African Americans) and the rapid escalation of tuition during the past decade may have resulted in a "bumping down" of students into lower cost community colleges. While community colleges serve an important purpose, increased enrollment in two-year rather than four-year institutions by minority students lowers their likelihood of attaining a bachelor's degree. Moreover, this "bumping down" phenomenon may have led to fewer highly qualified minority students applying to the more expensive and prestigious universities, making the affirmative action competition for these students even more fierce. It is ironic that the topic of affirmative action in admissions is heating up while the number of black students at many of our leading universities is declining.

Table VII
Percentage of Black Undergraduate Enrollment at Selected Research Universities

Institution	1980	1992	Percent Change
Brown University	6.2	5.8	-6.5
University of Chicago	4.1	3.7	-9.8
Stanford University	6.1	5.2	-14.8
Columbia University	6.2	5.0	-19.4
Cornell University	5.0	4.0	-20.0
Northwestern University	8.2	6.1	-25.6
Princeton University	7.5	5.3	-29.3
Dartmouth College	7.7	5.4	-29.9
Mass. Inst. of Technology	5.4	3.5	-35.2

Source: *Journal of Blacks in Higher Education*, 1994.[22]

In their recent controversial book, *The Bell Curve*, Richard Hernstein and Charles Murray claim that "black students become Harvard dropouts instead of University of Texas graduates," and that "getting discouraged about one's capacity to compete in an environment may be another cost of affirmative action."[23] Regrettably, Hernstein and Murray never checked their facts. Table VIII shows the relevant black student graduation rates at a number of the nation's most selective schools and at the University of Texas.[24]

Table VIII
Black Graduation Rates at
Selected Institutions (%)

Institution	Graduation Rate
Harvard University	92
Wesleyan University	90
Yale University	88
Williams College	88
University of Texas	44

Source: *Journal of Blacks in Higher Education*, 1994/95.

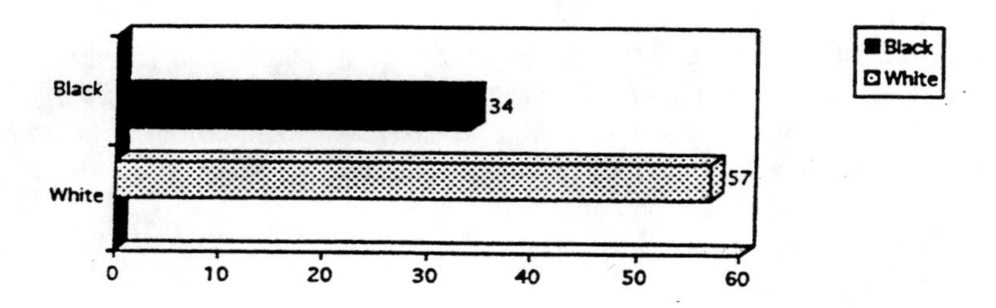

Source: *Journal of Blacks in Higher Education*, 1994.

Not only do black students do very well at the nation's most selective colleges and universities, but in most cases their graduation rate, compared with that of white students, is better at the most selective schools than at less selective institutions.[25]

Justice Lewis Powell, in his controlling decision in the *Bakke* case, cited Harvard's student admission policies as a particularly exemplary way a college could take various factors into consideration to achieve a racially diverse student body. An ideal college admission policy would weigh all these factors in considering the makeup of its freshman class: SAT (or ACT) scores, high school GPA, leadership and community service, special talents (music, athletics, etc.), geographic diversity, and racial diversity. Then any students needing academic help would receive it regardless of race or gender.

As Powell understood, without affirmative action, minority students might not be admitted into many colleges and universities. Yet, while affirmative action might be necessary, it is not a sufficient change mechanism for effectively serving all students.

An example of what to do and what not to do in college admissions is illustrated by two cases. Georgetown University Law Center has an excellent record in minority admissions, but never publicized its admission policies.[26] The school was embarrassed when a white student leaked information that the scores of Georgetown's black law students on average were somewhat lower than those of its white students. The story received wide publicity. Georgetown's dean, in an eloquent letter to the editor published in the *Washington Post*, defended the school's admission policies, but the damage had been done.

In contrast, Rutgers University Law School widely publicized its Minority Student Program (which accepts marginally qualified whites as well). Minority students with good records must compete in the regular admission pool. Students and faculty take pride in being in the MSP, and graduation rates are good. Some of the top black lawyers in the State of New Jersey are graduates of the MSP.[27]

The moral of the story is to take pride in a school's affirmative action policies, publicize the goals of the program widely, and aggressively educate all students about the program and how it enriches the school and adds to its reputation. Hiding or under-publicizing a program only will lead to the suspicion that it is less than worthy.

White Male Anger

In higher education, as in other areas, it is the *perception* of lost position rather than the reality that fuels white male anger. In 1973, there were 18,873,000 white Americans between the ages of 18 and 24 who were high school graduates. By 1993, due to falling birthrates among whites, this figure had declined to 16,196,000. However, in 1973, only 30 percent of white high school graduates entered college, whereas in 1993, that share had grown to 42 percent. Thus, despite a substantial drop in their overall numbers, *more* white high school graduates are going to college. The pattern of increased college participation holds true for every ethnic group—African Americans, Hispanics, Asian Americans, and American Indians. Nearly 15 million students now are enrolled in college, and *participation by every racial group has increased*.[28] That is partly what the anger on campuses is about—not that minorities are taking white places, but that whites, and everyone else, want even more spaces! Yet, whites nationally constitute 75 percent of the student body, earn 88 percent of the Ph.Ds awarded to U.S. citizens, are 87 percent of the college administrators, and hold 87 percent of the full-time faculty positions.

The growth of minority participation in higher education has been modest at best, but it is the perception of the loss of majority privilege that politicians have seized upon and irresponsibility whipped into a frenzy. That fact makes it exceedingly difficult to hold a dispassionate discussion about affirmative action.

Business Acceptance of Affirmative Action

On the other hand, business and industry leaders are well ahead of the higher education elites in accepting affirmative action as sound policy. A study based on data from 1966 to 1992 shows that "companies that implement quality affirmative action programs benefit economically through a higher evaluation of their company stock by investors. Discriminatory practices are viewed negatively by investors, which means lower stock prices," according to the study.[29]

Nor are local governments scrambling to eliminate affirmative action. A survey for the U.S. Conference of Mayors revealed that 40 percent of the city officials believed that affirmative action programs contributed to improved job efficiency and productivity. In addition, 60 percent of the cities had fewer employee grievances, 45 percent reported declines in employer turnover rates, and 40 percent had less absenteeism. The mayors' report concluded that the pursuit of a color-blind society to achieve fairness in hiring and promotion was "ideal but unrealistic."[30] Or as Gery Chico, Mayor Richard M. Daley's chief of staff, stated succinctly, "We don't care what Clinton does. We're not going to change a thing."[31]

VII. Affirmative Action: Failure and Resistance

> The only way we will ever get to a color-blind society is for government... to stop discriminating on the basis of race. A ban on racial preference will go a long way to remove the venom from race relations.
>
> Clint Bolick
> Institute for Justice
> April 1, 1995

Affirmative action has had its share of failures, either through inadvertence (as with any new program), overzealousness in enforcement of its many complex rules, or intent, as a result of deliberate efforts to embarrass its supporters or to make the program fail. In addition, opponents of affirmative action advance a number of arguments that should be answered forthrightly. Among the latter are these:

• *Affirmative action has not helped minorities.* This statement is repeated often. Citing black unemployment rates, which have remained twice as high as those of whites, Farrell Bloch, an economist, argues that "the evidence demonstrates that affirmative action has not significantly enhanced the employment prospects for the most disadvantaged African Americans."[32]

The unemployment rates of low-skilled blacks have remained disastrous since assembly line jobs began disappearing from Rustbelt factories. While some low-skill jobs are available in the suburbs, most urban blacks have no way of getting to them. In addition, to be employable, these blacks will have to be retrained—a massive undertaking for which neither the federal government nor state governments have much enthusiasm in these fiscally stringent times. Thus, these people are out of reach of help from affirmative action; it is irrelevant to their circumstances. Nonetheless, the considerable improvement in minority employment in law enforcement, firefighting, and construction, as well as in medicine and law, can be cited as a signal victory of affirmative action. Moreover, minorities have made measurable strides in employment in business and industry due to aggressive targeted hiring.

• *Affirmative action has caused reverse discrimination against whites.* Mortimer B. Zuckerman, editor-in-chief of *U.S. News and World Report*, stated in a recent editorial that "A program to end discrimination in the name of justice became a program to visit injustice on a different set of people."[33]

A 1995 analysis by the Labor Department found that affirmative action programs do not lead to widespread reverse discrimination claims by whites, and a high proportion of such claims that are filed are found to lack merit. The findings contradicted charges that affirmative action has helped minorities at the expense of white males. The analysis found that fewer than 100 out of 3,000 discrimination cases filed involved reverse discrimination and in only six cases were such claims substantiated. "The paucity of reported cases casts doubt on the dimension of the reverse discrimination problem," the report said.[34]

• *Persons should be selected for positions based on merit alone.* Usually, when people say "merit," they mean the scores on a test or examination or some other quantitative ranking. However, as the spokesperson for the University of California Medical School said recently: "Medical school is not a reward for high test scores or grades. Medical schools have to decide who is going to fulfill the most pressing needs of society, and that doesn't correlate extremely well with test results and grades."[35] Cultural sensitivity toward persons from different backgrounds, interpersonal skills, the ability to communicate effectively—all these are "meritorious" qualifications that relate to an individual's performance on the job.

Moreover, the case of *Johnson v. Transportation Agency*, the federal courts held that a woman with slightly lower scores than a white male's, if qualified, should be selected for a job where women were conspicuously absent from the work force. Finally, in *The Bell Curve*, Hernstein and Murray imply that minorities in the District of Columbia would be better served by well-trained police officers who scored high on selection tests. It is questionable whether the citizens of the District of Columbia (or Los Angeles) would feel better served by police officers who were selected only for their high scores. "Merit" involves much more than the ability to perform well on paper and pencil tests.

• *Affirmative action produces a feeling of inferiority in minority men and women of all races and creates a negative stereotype in the mind of white males.* Both of these statements have been repeated over and over until they have assumed the permanence of fact. However, the fact is that no national survey of affirmative action recipients ever has been done, and the stories are mostly anecdotal or speculative.

One black sociology professor, reacting to the anecdotal thesis that affirmative action harms blacks, stated forcefully, "I have never felt stigmatized, nor have I concerned myself with whether or not whites viewed my presence or success as undeserved."[36] The contention that affirmative action creates a negative stereotype in the minds of whites implies naively that whites had no negative stereotypes of minorities in their minds before. That theory goes counter to the nation's history. "Any stigma or negative stereotypes associated with race have existed in this country long before affirmative action was ever thought of."[37] Moreover, no stigma seems to be felt by the sons and daughters of alumni or athletes who are admitted to college with less than competitive qualifications.

• *We should have a color-blind society. That's what Martin Luther King wanted.* Justice Harry Blackman's opinion in the *Bakke* case is the most eloquent response to this contention:

> I suspect that it would be impossible to arrange an affirmative action program in a racially neutral way and have it successful. To ask that this be so is to demand the impossible. In order to get beyond racism, we must first take account of race. There is no other way. And in order to treat some persons equally, we must treat them differently. We cannot—dare not—let the Equal Protection Clause perpetuate racial supremacy.[38]

While the foregoing provides answers to the criticisms often leveled at affirmative action, a number of charges have arisen based on recent cases that are more serious and must be faced squarely. These are some of the more troubling ones:

• *Affirmative action allows minorities to buy something under a minority set-aside and sell it at a profit.* The purpose of a minority set-aside is to create more minority businesses, not to be used as a conduit to turn a quick profit. The case cited is the purchase of a TV station license by a minority male who then sold it to a white person four months later at a substantial profit. This is an abuse of the set-aside.[39]

• *A minority person can be used as a front for a white controlled firm.* The case cited is a construction firm ostensibly owned by a minority that in actuality was a front for a white firm that did the work and "kicked back" some of the profits to the minority. They were prosecuted and paid heavy fines. Such abuses are widespread in both minority- and women-owned firms and cast a cloud over all set-asides.[40]

- *Young minorities joining the work force expect that affirmative action will get them promoted.* The case cited involves young minority police officers who expect to get promoted without trying because of affirmative action. This is one of the most serious charges because it deals with an attitude that destroys the effectiveness and purpose of affirmative action. The program is intended to get one in the door, but one has to prove oneself after that.[41] It is not clear how pervasive this attitude is, but if it is widespread, it would have damaging consequences for the perception of affirmative action.

The critics of affirmative action constantly raise such charges to attack the entire principle. The defenders of affirmative action will be more credible if they admit that some programs have serious flaws that will have to be addressed. This will require better monitoring of setaside programs and putting minorities on notice that they will have to prove themselves once on the job. Such improvements may not be enough to save all programs that have been enacted in the name of affirmative action. Though it may be painful, some parts may have to be excised to save the body of the principle.

The difficulty of defending affirmative action is compounded by the fact that minority individuals are among its most vocal critics (and, as a result, are given excessive media attention). Shelby Steele, Stephen Carter, Thomas Sowell, Linda Chavez, Armstrong Williams, and Richard Rodriguez are some of the most well known. The media assault on affirmative action, plus the prominence given minority critics, has resulted in the minority community giving it only tepid support (51 percent of blacks in favor, according to one poll; 77 percent of white women opposed, according to another)

As Secretary of Labor Robert Reich has argued, *"angry white males" are venting their frustrations at minorities and women when the real problem they face (along with everyone else) is an increasingly competitive global economy that has produced massive changes in the domestic economy and drastically altered the nature and demands of the job market.*

VIII. Is Affirmative Action Still Necessary?

> We hope that race and other minority status will be much less of a distinguishing feature of American society in the future as we overcome the consequence of past discrimination in education and elsewhere. Race or other minority status would thus become less germane to achieving diversity in student bodies and to ensuring prospective service to the public... Significant progress has already been made within higher education, but there is still a substantial way to go.
>
> Carnegie Commission on Higher Education, 1977

That statement of nearly two decades ago shows how naively optimistic we were about the possibility of rapid change in the field of higher education. The following illustrations demonstrate that resistance to such change is characteristic of other areas of society as well.

• In 1990, an Urban Institute study utilizing pairs of black and white job applicants with identical credentials found that in 476 hirings in Washington, DC and Chicago "unequal treatment of black job seekers was entrenched and widespread, contradicting claims that hiring practices today either favor blacks or are effectively color blind. In 20 percent of the audits, whites were able to advance further through the hiring process than equally qualified blacks... [A] similar study using Hispanic job applicants found them discriminated against 29 percent of the time in San Diego and 33 percent of the time in Chicago."[42]

• In 1994, the Chevy Chase Federal Savings Bank agreed to an $11 million settlement of a lawsuit in which they were charged with "redlining" in mortgage lending by refusing to serve minority neighborhoods in Maryland.[43]

• In 1992, New York Manufacturers Hanover Trust rejected 18 percent of loan applications from high income whites, but rejected more than twice as many—43 percent and 45 percent—from high income African Americans and Hispanics.[44]

• A study of faculty hiring practices found that once a minority hiring goal was met, departments stopped seeking out minority applicants and, indeed, pulled their ads from minority publications, regardless of the number of vacancies that occurred subsequently.[45]

Figure III
Number of New Black Ph.Ds Awarded in the Natural Sciences and Number of Graduates Recruited to the Faculties of the Highest-Ranked Universities

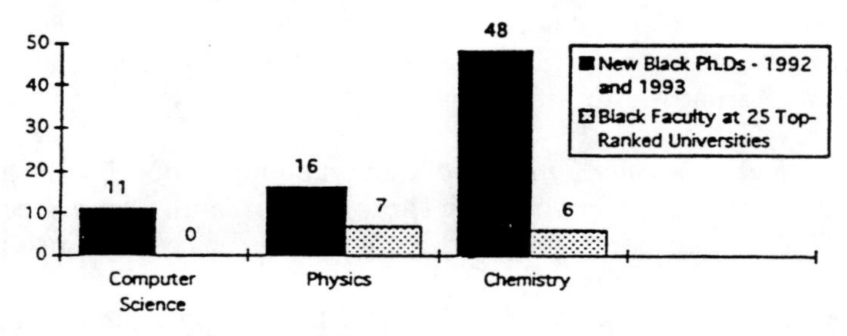

Source: *Journal of Blacks in Higher Education,* 1995.

These examples illustrate how institutions slip into old practices even when those practices are strictly forbidden by law (for example, redlining). In spite of affirmative action, employers tend to favor whites, particularly white males, over equally qualified African-American or Hispanic applicants. As Crosby and Clayton have pointed out:

> Much white males resistance to affirmative action may spring from an unwillingness on the part of any given white man to recognize the true extent to which his gender and his ethnicity, and not simply his own individual merit, have won him rungs on the ladder of success.[46]

Minorities—particularly minority females—on average are clustered on the lower rungs of the professiorate as assistant professors and non-tenure track lecturers, and their presence is tenuous at best. The possibility of their developing a critical mass and thereby becoming self-perpetuating can be assured only with a continuation of some form of affirmative action.

IX. Conclusion

> Negro political rights cannot be widely won through court actions until the white community is at least no longer violently hostile to their exercise by Negroes. No legislation can bring about overnight changes in peoples' morals, nor can any decisions of the Supreme Court do so.
>
> Supreme Court Justice Hugo Black

House Minority Leader Richard Gephardt (D-MO) has spoken out strongly in favor of affirmative action, noting, "there may be abuses that should be corrected, but we should not abandon the effort to stop discrimination and to see that people are treated fairly."[47] Senator Bill Bradley (D-NJ) has spoken out just as forcefully. Business leaders are equally forthright. As Avon Products CEO James Preston put it, "managing diversity is not something we do because it's nice but because it's in our interest."[48]

Equally strong voices are needed in academia speaking in support of the principle of affirmative action, providing "teachable moments" to educate students and faculty as to why it is needed and why it is enriching to everyone, and criticizing those elements of the program that have not worked well.

Leaders also need to critique carefully those policies that have been advanced as alternatives to affirmative action but that will not work:

> *Race neutral or color blind*: a policy that sounds good in the abstract but never works in reality because 1) progress or failure cannot be measured; and 2) it degenerates into the practice of business as usual, favoring mostly white males.
>
> *Policies based on need rather than race*: as Representative Gephardt states, "The United States has never had a history of discrimination against people who are in poverty that is at all comparable to the barriers facing women and minorities."

Through they sound attractive, policies based on need would fundamentally shift the purpose of the program away from compensating for prior discrimination. Moreover, the federal government currently has programs that address need and that should be expanded: Head Start, Upward Bound, Talent Search, Pell Grants, etc.

Lastly, the defenders of affirmative action should be the first to criticize those programs that do not work: set-asides that are abused, quotas that are introduced illegally, hiring unqualified minorities to fill token slots, etc. Only if we criticize our mistakes will we retain our credibility. In the present climate of the political assault on affirmative action, it is all the more important to speak out with a strong voice to defend what is right and what is working well.

Despite all of the laws and arguments on behalf of and in opposition to affirmative action, in the final analysis, affirmative action is not a legal question but a political and societal one. The question facing American society is whether it wishes to achieve equality and fairness for all of its citizens, after years of injustices to minorities and women, and how it proposes to do it. The questions confronting the academy are whether diversity is a legitimate goal; whether achieving a diverse student body is an educational value; and what is the educational role and purpose of higher education.

Racism and sexism are currents that run deep in the American mainstream. They will not easily be diverted. They have a tenacious hold on people who go to extraordinary lengths to rationalize them with sophisticated intellectual arguments. Affirmative action is a limited tool of the courts and Congress that, with all its clumsy complexity, was created to deal with only limited aspects of racism and sexism. That it has achieved some modest amelioration is remarkable. That we should expect it to do much more would be wishful thinking. We must constantly devise new strategies for the even more difficult struggles ahead.

References

1. James E. Blackwell, "Demographics of Desegregation," in Reginald Wilson (Ed.), *Race and Equity in Higher Education* (Washington, DC: American Council on Education, 1982), p. 28.
2. John E. Fleming, et al, *The Case for Affirmative Action for Blacks in Higher Education* (Washington, DC: Institute for the Study of Educational Policy, Howard University, 1978), p. 24.
3. *Ibid*. pp. 30-31.
4. *Ibid*, p. 33
5. Hilary Herbold, "Never a Level Playing Field: Blacks and the G.I. Bill," *Journal of Blacks in Higher Education*, Winter 1994-95, p. 106.
6. Reginald Wilson, "Affirmative Action: Yesterday, Today and Tomorrow," *CUPA Journal*, July 1989.
7. Rayford Logan, *The Betrayal of the Negro* (New York: The Macmillan Company, 1954), p. 315.

8. James A. Banks, "The Historical Reconstruction of Knowledge About Race," *Educational Researcher*, March 1995, p. 17.
9. Logan, *Op. Cit.*, p. 348.
10. Reginald Wilson, "African Americans and the G.I. Bill," *Educational Record*, Fall 1994, pp. 32-39.
11. Michael Pavel, Karen Swisher, and Marlene Ward, "Special Focus: American Indian and Alaska Native Demographic and Educational Trends," in *Minorities in Higher Education*. Thirteenth Annual Status Report, 1994 (Washington, DC: American Council on Education, 1995), pp. 33-56.
12. Howard Fineman, "Race and Rage," *Newsweek*, April 3, 1995, p. 24.
13. Reginald Wilson, "The Undergraduate Years Plus One" (unpublished paper delivered at NACME Conference), October 1994.
14. Rev. Jesse Jackson, "Affirming Affirmative Action," statement read at the National Press Club, March 1, 1995.
15. Reginald Wilson, "Affirmative Action: The Current Status," *AGB Reports*, May/June 1985.
16. Susan D. Clayton and Faye J. Crosby, *Justice, Gender and Affirmative Action* (Ann Arbor: University of Michigan Press, 1992), p. 16.
17. Cited in Fineman, *Op. Cit.*, p. 31.
18. Phyllis A. Wallace, "Title VII and the Economic Status of Blacks," Alfred P. Sloan School of Management (MIT), Working Paper 1578-84, July 1984.
19. David C. Ruffin, "Affirmative Action and the LAFD," *Focus*, The Joint Center for Political and Economic Studies, March 1995.
20. William L. Taylor and Susan M. Liss, "Affirmative Action in the 1990s: Staying the Course," *The Annals (AAPSS)*, September 1992, p. 34.
21. Deborah J. Carter and Reginald Wilson, *Minorities in Higher Education*. Thirteenth Annual Status Report, 1994 (Washington, DC: American Council on Education, 1995), pp. 68-89.
22. "News and Views," *The Journal of Blacks in Higher Education*, Autumn 1994, p. 30.
23. Richard J. Hernstein and Charles Murray, *The Bell Curve: Intelligence and Class Structure in American Life* (New York: The Free Press, 1994), p. 473.
24. "News and Views," *The Journal of Blacks in Higher Education*, Winter 1994/1995, pp. 16-17.
25. *Ibid*, p. 17.
26. Leigh Ann Mort and Milton Moskowitz, "The Best Law Schools for Blacks," *The Journal of Blacks in Higher Education*, Summer 1994, p. 62.
27. Dale Russakoff, "Rutgers Proud of Law School's Set-asides," *The Washington Post*, April 10, 1995, p. A1.
28. Carter and Wilson, *Op. Cit*..p. 69.
29. Carol Kleiman, "Companies taking stock in Affirmative Action," *Chicago Tribune*, June 8, 1994, p. C6.
30. National Urban League, "Chronology of Events: 1986," *The State of Black America: 1987* (Washington, DC: National Urban League, 1987), p. 214.

31. Vern E. Smith, "The Contractor: Minority Businessmen need white escorts to get in the door," *Newsweek*, April 3, 1995, p. 32.
32. Farrell Bloch, "Affirmative Action Hasn't Helped Blacks," *The Wall Street Journal*, March 1, 1995, p. A15.
33. Mortimer B. Zuckerman, "Fixing Affirmative Action," *U.S. News and World Report*, March 20, 1995, p. 112.
34. Sonya Ross, "Affirmative Action," Associated Press, March 31, 1995.
35. Richard Bernstein, "Move Under Way in California to Overturn Higher Education's Affirmative Action Policy," *The New York Times*, January 25, 1995, p. B7.
36. Clayton and Crosby, *Op. Cit.*, p. 110.
37. "Exploding the Big Lie—The Truth About Affirmative Action," Minority Business Enterprise Legal Defense and Education Fund (March 14, 1995), p. 4.
38. *Regents of the University of California v. Bakke*, 438 U.S. 265 (1978).
39. Linda Chavez, "Rein in Affirmative Action," *USA Today*, March 1, 1995, p. 11A.
40. Gordon Witkin, "Trying to Beat the System" *U.S. News and World Report*, February 13, 1995, p. 42.
41. Paul Glastris, "Black and Blue," *U.S. News, Ibid.*, p. 43.
42. Margery Austin Turner, et al, *Opportunities Denied, Opportunities Diminished: Discrimination in Hiring* (Washington, DC: The Urban Institute), September 1991, pp. 91-99.
43. Minority Business Enterprise Legal Defense and Education Fund, *Op. Cit.*, p. 6.
44. Julianne Malveaux, "The Parity Imperative," *The State of Black America* (Washington, DC: National Urban League, 1992), p. 283.
45. Martin Finkelstein, *The American Academic Profession* (Columbus: Ohio State University Press, 1984), p. 193.
46. Faye J. Crosby and Susan Clayton, "Affirmative action and the issue of expectancies," *Journal of Social Issues*, (Vol. 46, 1990), pp. 61-79.
47. David Broder, "Gephardt Defends Affirmative Action," *The Washington Post*, March 14, 1995, p. A6.
48. Quoted in R. Hernandez, "Diversity: Don't go to work without it," *Hispanic Business*, September 18, 1990, pp. 18-22.

CHAPTER 2

Affirmative Action: Recent Congressional and Presidential Activity

Andorra Bruno

Background

The U.S. Commission on Civil Rights has defined affirmative action to encompass "any measure, beyond simple termination of a discriminatory practice, adopted to correct or compensate for past or present discrimination or to prevent discrimination from recurring in the future."[1] Affirmative action operates in areas including employment, public contracting, education, and housing. In recent years, congressional and presidential attention has been focused mainly on affirmative action employment and contracting programs.

Affirmative action in employment dates to the 1960s. Title VII of the Civil Rights Act of 1964 (P.L. 88-352) prohibited discrimination by private employers on the basis of race, color, religion, sex, or national origin. Under Title VII, a court that found that an employer had intentionally engaged in discrimination could order affirmative action remedies. Executive orders issued in the 1960s, including Executive Order 11246 issued by President Lyndon Johnson in 1965, required that federal government contractors take affirmative action toward employees and applicants for employment in areas such as

---

[1] U.S. Commission on Civil Rights, *Statement on Affirmative Action* (Washington: 1977), p. 2.

recruitment, employment, and promotion. Regulations issued by the Nixon Administration in 1970 and revised in 1971 required larger federal contractors to develop written affirmative action plans that included goals and timetables. In the early 1970s, federal agencies were authorized, though not required, to use employment goals and timetables.[2] During the Reagan Administration, the Justice Department attempted to revise E.O. 11246 to eliminate the requirement that contractors set numerical goals. This effort was abandoned, however, in the face of opposition from some administration officials and others.

Federal efforts to assist the development of small minority- and women-owned businesses include various contract set-aside programs. Prominent among them is the Small Business Administration's 8(a) program, which channels federal procurement contracts to small businesses owned by minorities or other "socially and economically disadvantaged" individuals.[3]

Actions of the 104th Congress

Following the November 1994 elections, in which Republicans gained control of both the House and the Senate, affirmative action emerged as a key legislative issue. Congressional activity on affirmative action began early in the 104th Congress, in February 1995, with the introduction of a bill (H.R. 831) to amend the Internal Revenue Code. H.R. 831 contained a provision repealing a Federal Communications Commission (FCC) program intended to encourage minority ownership of broadcast companies. The FCC program allowed companies selling broadcast stations or cable television systems to minority-owned businesses to defer capital gains taxes. Another provision of H.R. 831 sought to make permanent a tax deduction for self-employed individuals who buy their own health insurance. Savings from the repeal of the FCC tax break were to be used to help finance the health insurance deduction. The House and Senate approved the conference report on H.R. 831 in March 1995 and April 1995, respectively. Citing the health insurance tax deduction, President Clinton signed the measure into law on April 11, 1995 (P.L. 104-7).

Other bills to restrict affirmative action were introduced in the 104th Congress, but none were enacted. Of these measures, the proposal that saw the most legislative activity was the "Equal Opportunity Act" (S. 1085, H.R. 2128). The companion bills, introduced by Senate Majority Leader Bob Dole and Representative Charles Canady on July 27, 1995, sought to bar the federal government from intentionally discriminating against, or granting a preference to, any individual or group based on race, color, national origin, or sex, in federal contracting, federal employment, or federally conducted programs. The Constitution Subcommittee of the House Judiciary Committee, the Employer-Employee Relations Subcommittee of the House Economic and Educational Opportunities

---

[2] For additional information on affirmative action in employment, see U.S. Library of Congress, Congressional Research Service, *Affirmative Action in Employment*, by Andorra Bruno, CRS Report 95-165 GOV (Washington: Jan. 17, 1995).

[3] For additional information on affirmative action in federal contracting, see U.S. Library of Congress, Congressional Research Service, *Minority and Women-Owned Business Programs of the Federal Government*, by Mark Eddy, CRS Report 95-757 GOV (Washington: June 27, 1997).

Committee,[4] and the Senate Labor and Human Resources Committee held hearings on the companion bills in 1995 and 1996. In March 1996, the House Constitution Subcommittee marked up H.R. 2128. The subcommittee voted along party lines to approve the bill, as amended. Although H.R. 2128 was on the full Judiciary Committee's agenda for markup, it was never taken up and died at the end of the Congress.

Another measure that received some attention in the final months of the 104th Congress was the "Entrepreneur Development Program Act of 1996" (H.R. 3994). The bill, introduced by Representative Jan Meyers in August 1996, would have eliminated the Small Business Administration's 8(a) program. Despite some indications that House leaders would move H.R. 3994, no action occurred on the bill beyond a September 1996 hearing by the House Small Business Committee.

Actions of the 105th Congress

Civil Rights Act of 1997. On June 17, 1997, Representative Canady introduced the "Civil Rights Act of 1997" (H.R. 1909). The bill, which is similar to legislation he introduced in the 104th Congress (see above), would prohibit the federal government from intentionally discriminating against, or granting a preference to, any individual or group based on race, color, national origin, or sex, in federal contracting, federal employment, or federally conducted programs. H.R. 1909 was referred to the Committees on the Judiciary, Education and the Workforce, Government Reform and Oversight, and House Oversight.

The Constitution Subcommittee of the House Judiciary Committee held a hearing on H.R. 1909 on June 26, 1997. On July 9, the subcommittee marked up the bill. Seven amendments were offered by Democratic subcommittee members, but all were rejected. The panel approved H.R. 1909 by voice vote. On November 6, the Judiciary Committee met to mark up H.R. 1909. A motion to table the bill was offered and was approved by a vote of 17 to 9. The 17 committee members voting to table H.R. 1909 included 13 Democrats and four Republicans.

On June 23, 1997, Senator Mitch McConnell introduced the "Civil Rights Act of 1997" (S. 950) in the Senate.[5] It was placed on the calendar. On June 24, Senator McConnell introduced a second bill (S. 952), which contains some of the provisions of S. 950. S. 952 was referred to the Judiciary Committee. Senator McConnell also introduced an amendment to S. 952 (S.Amdt. 433) on June 24, consisting of the text of S. 950. The amendment would strike all after the enacting clause of S. 952 and insert the text of S. 950.

ISTEA Reauthorization Amendments. On October 23, 1997, Senator McConnell filed two amendments that he intended to propose during floor consideration of the bill (S. 1173) to reauthorize the Intermodal Surface Transportation Efficiency Act (ISTEA). The

---

[4] This committee has been renamed the House Education and the Workforce Committee.

[5] S. 950 differs from H.R. 1909 in that the Senate bill includes an additional section entitled "Findings and Purpose."

amendments (S.Amdt. 1435, S.Amdt. 1437) would eliminate the section of S. 1173 reauthorizing the Department of Transportation's disadvantaged business enterprises (DBE) program.[6] The DBE program requires that not less than 10% of federal transportation contract funds be expended with small disadvantaged businesses owned by minorities or women.[7] In addition to eliminating the DBE program, S.Amdt. 1437 would establish a race-neutral Emerging Business Enterprise program. This program would require states to engage in outreach to small businesses in the construction industry and to provide them with technical services and assistance. Neither of the McConnell amendments had been offered by the time Senate leaders pulled S. 1173 from the floor, following failure to invoke cloture on October 28. Floor consideration of S. 1173 is not expected to resume until 1998.

Other Measures and Actions. Other affirmative action-related measures before the 105th Congress include two identical Senate bills (S. 46, S. 188), known as the "Civil Rights Restoration Act of 1997." The bills, introduced by Senator Jesse Helms, would amend Title VII of the 1964 Civil Rights Act to make it an unlawful employment practice for an employer to grant preferential treatment on the basis of race, color, religion, sex, or national origin. S. 46 was placed on the calendar, and S. 188 was referred to the Labor and Human Resources Committee. The measures are similar to bills introduced by Senator Helms in the 104th Congress. In the House, Representative Tom Campbell introduced a bill (H.R. 2079) to require the implementation of an alternative program whenever a federal program granting a benefit or preference based on race, gender, or national origin is invalidated by a court. H.R. 2079, the "Racial and Gender Preference Reform Act," was referred to the Judiciary Committee.

The Senate Judiciary Committee held an oversight hearing on affirmative action on June 16, 1997. That Committee's Subcommittee on the Constitution, Federalism, and Property Rights held a hearing on the Transportation Department's DBE program on September 30, 1997.

Actions of the Clinton Administration

The Clinton Administration has shown support for affirmative action. In February 1995, the President ordered a review of all federal affirmative action programs. In a July 19, 1995, address, he discussed the results of the study. "This review concluded," he said, "that affirmative action remains a useful tool for widening economic and educational opportunity." According to President Clinton, "When affirmative action is done right, it is flexible, it is fair, and it works." At the same time, the President stated that "affirmative

---

[6] For a discussion of S. 1173 (Intermodal Surface Transportation Efficiency Act of 1997) and other ISTEA reauthorization bills before the 105th Congress, see U.S. Library of Congress, Congressional Research Service, *ISTEA Reauthorization: Highway Related Legislative Proposals in the 105th Congress*, by John W. Fischer, CRS Report 97-516 E (Washington: Oct. 23, 1997).

[7] For information about the Department of Transportation's DBE programs, see *Minority and Women-Owned Business Programs*, CRS Report 97-757 GOV, pp. 10-11.

action has not always been perfect" and "should not go on forever."[8] The review's written report made various recommendations. In the area of contract set-aside programs, it suggested a number of reforms to address shortcomings and abuses.

Prior to the President's speech, on June 12, 1995, the Supreme Court handed down its decision in *Adarand Constructors Inc. v. Pena,* a case concerning a federal highway funding program that awarded bonuses to contractors who subcontracted with small businesses owned by minorities or other disadvantaged individuals. The Supreme Court ruled that federal affirmative action policies to benefit minorities must meet the same strict standards that apply to state and local programs.[9] On June 28, 1995, the Justice Department issued a memorandum to federal agencies, which provided an overview of the *Adarand* decision and discussed, in general terms, application of the "strict scrutiny" standard to federal affirmative action programs.

During his address, President Clinton announced that he was directing federal agencies to comply with the *Adarand* decision. He also instructed agencies to apply the following four standards to affirmative action programs: "No quotas in theory or practice; no illegal discrimination of any kind, including reverse discrimination; no preference for people who are not qualified for any job or other opportunity; and as soon as a program has succeeded, it must be retired." The President called for the elimination or reform of any program not meeting these standards.

In July 1995, the Justice Department began working with agencies to review their race-conscious programs for compliance with *Adarand.* As part of this review, the Defense Department announced on October 23, 1995, that it was suspending a contracting rule known as the "rule of two." Under the rule of two, contracts are set aside for small disadvantaged businesses "when there is a reasonable expectation" that at least two such firms qualified to perform the work will offer bids; other conditions also apply.[10]

On February 29, 1996, the Justice Department issued a memorandum to federal agencies addressing the application of "strict scrutiny" to affirmative action in federal employment. The memorandum stated that "the application of strict scrutiny should not require major modifications in the way federal agencies have been properly implementing affirmative action policies" and set forth guidelines for such policies.[11]

---

[8] For the text of the President's speech, see "Address by President Clinton on Affirmative Action, July 19, 1995," in remarks of Sen. Edward Kennedy, *Congressional Record*, daily edition, vol. 141, July 19, 1995, pp. S10306-S10309.

[9] For further information on the Adarand case, see U.S. Library of Congress, Congressional Research Service, *Minority and Small Disadvantaged Business Contracting: Legal and Constitutional Developments*, by Charles V. Dale, CRS report 97-665 A (Washington: June 24, 1997).

[10] 48 C.F.R. 219.502-2-70

[11] U.S. Dept. Of Justice, Office of the Associate Attorney General. *Post-*Adarand *Guidance on Affirmative Action in Federal Employment*, by John Schmidt, memorandum to general counsels (Feb. 29, 1996) (on file with author).

With respect to federal procurement, the Justice Department proposed new rules for the use of affirmative action on May 22, 1996.[12] The proposal set forth guidelines to limit, as appropriate, the use of race-conscious measures in specific areas of procurement. Under the proposed rules, the Small Business Administration's 8(a) program would be retained but reformed. After receiving public comment, the Justice Department modified its proposal.[13] One modification concerned a provision in the initial proposal that federal agencies not be allowed to set contracts aside for bidding exclusively by small, disadvantaged businesses for at least two years. As stated in the May 1996 proposal, the Justice Department believed that such measures should be unnecessary under the reformed system. After two years, the new system would have been evaluated to determine whether to allow set-asides. In response to comments, the Justice Department eliminated the provision for a two-year evaluation period. The proposal, as modified, would base the "determination whether to consider reservation of contracts in any industry ... not on the lapse of any particular period of time, but on the amount and strength of the evidence regarding the effectiveness of the new system in that industry."[14]

The Justice Department proposal is expected to be implemented in several parts. On May 9, 1997, the Department of Defense, the General Services Administration, and the National Aeronautics and Space Administration published proposed amendments to the Federal Acquisition Regulation concerning programs for small, disadvantaged businesses.[15] On August 14, 1997, the Small Business Administration published proposed amendments to the regulations governing the 8(a) program.[16]

On June 14, 1997, President Clinton launched a national initiative to improve race relations in a commencement address at the University of California at San Diego. In the speech, the President reiterated his support for affirmative action, which, he said, "has given us a whole generation of professionals in fields that used to be exclusive clubs ...." He singled out the military as the "best example of successful affirmative action," describing it as "perhaps the most integrated institution in our society." President Clinton urged his fellow supporters of affirmative action to "continue to stand for it." At the same time, he challenged opponents "to come up with an alternative," saying that he would "embrace [an alternative] if I could find a better way."[17]

---

[12] See U.S. Dept. Of Justice, "Proposed Reforms to Affirmative Action in Federal Procurement," *Federal Register*, vol. 61, no. 101, May 23, 1996, pp. 26041-26063.

[13] See U.S. Dept. Of Justice, "Response to Comments to Department of Justice Proposed Reforms to Affirmative Action in Federal Procurement," *Federal Register*, vol. 62, no. 90, May 9, 1997, pp. 25648-25653.

[14] *Ibid.*, p. 25651.

[15] See U.S. Dept. Of Defense, General Services Administration, and National Aeronautics and Space Administration, "Federal Acquisition Regulation; Reform of Affirmative Action in Federal Procurement," *Federal Register*, vol. 62, no. 90, May 9, 1997, pp. 25786-25795.

[16] See U.S. Small Business Administration, "Small Business Size Regulations; 8(a) Business Development/Small Disadvantaged Business Status Determinations .... ," *Federal Register*, vol. 62, no. 157, Aug. 14, 1997, pp. 43584-43628.

[17] Excerpts from the President's speech are printed in "In 'Building One America All Citizens Must Serve,'" *Washington Post*, June 15, 1997, p. A8.

CHAPTER 3

Affirmative Action: Selected References, 1995-1997

Tangela G. Roe

This selected bibliography includes articles and reports on affirmative action selected from the Public Policy Literature File (PPLT) and the Congressional Research Service Products File (CRSP). References to Internet URLs (Uniform Resource Locator) have also been provided. Congressional researchers may order the full text of articles by calling 7-5700; others should consult their local libraries.

Selected CRS Products

Affirmative action: recent congressional and presidential activity, by Andorra Bruno. Updated July 10, 1997. 6 p. 97-527 GOV

Affirmative action and equal employment opportunity: a checklist of CRS products, by Tangela G. Roe. Updated Aug. 25, 1997. 2 p. 97-580 L

Affirmative action in employment, by Andorra Bruno. Jan. 17, 1995. 54 p. 95-165 GOV

Affirmative action law: a brief introduction, by Charles V. Dale. Updated Nov. 14, 1996. 7 p. 96-378 A

California Civil Rights Initiative, by Andorra Bruno. Updated Aug. 29, 1997. 5 p. 96-931 GOV

Minority and small disadvantaged business contracting: legal and constitutional developments, by Charles Dale. Updated June 24, 1997. 14 p. 97-665 A

Minority and women-owned business programs of the federal government, by Mark Eddy. Updated June 27, 1997. 17 p. 95-757 GOV

Published Literature

Affirmative action. A.E. Sadler, book editor. San Diego, Calif., Greenhave Press, 1996. 94 p. HF5549.5.A34A4 1996

Affirmative action: a course for the future. Looking ahead, v. 18, Aug. 1996: whole issue (27 p.). LRS96-9046

Affirmative action: fairness or favoritism? Los Angeles times, Feb. 19, 1995: A1 +; Feb. 20: A1 +; Feb. 21: A1 +; Mar. 28: A1 +; Mar. 29: A1+; Mar. 30: A1 +; Apr. 30: A1 +; May 1: A1 +; May 2: A1 +. LRS95-4939

"Explores facets of the debate over affirmative action nationally and in California."

Affirmative action: redistribution or equal opportunity? Pro & con. Congressional digest, v. 75, June-July 1996: whole issue: (161-192 p.) LRS96-3051

Affirmative action: thirty years later. American economic review, v. 86, May 1996: 285-301. LRS96-3329

The Affirmative action debate. Edited by George E. Curry; with contributions by Cornel West ... [et al.] Reading, Mass., Addison-Wesley [1996] 368 p. HF5549.5.A34A4628 1996

The Affirmative action debate. Philosophy & public policy, v. 17, winter-spring 1997: whole issue (38 p.). LRS97-1898

Ayres, Ian. Cramton, Peter.
Deficit reduction through diversity: how affirmative action at the FCC increased auction competition. Stanford law review, v. 48, Apr. 1996: 761-815. LRS96-9821

Barkan, Joanne.
Affirmative action. Dissent, fall 1995: 461-476. LRS95-9889

"Dissent asked a variety of writers to address .... Who benefits from affirmative action? What price does it exact? Can it be improved upon or is an alternative needed?"

Barone, Michael.
Racial preferences just died; what comes next? American enterprise, v. 8, Jan.-Feb. 1997: 37-38. LRS97-155

"The death knell for racial quotas was sounded in 1996--at the polls and in court. How should Americans approach race now?"

Bolick, Clint.
The affirmative action fraud: can we restore the American civil rights vision? Washington, Cato Institute, 1996. 170 p. JC599.U5B556 1996

Bork, Robert H. Tushnet, Mark.
Equality: do the concepts of our legal system hinder efforts to achieve a meritocracy? American Bar Association journal, v. 82, Nov. 1996: 80-81. LRS96-8678

"Robert H. Bork, now a fellow at the American Enterprise Institute in Washington, D.C., calls into question the very notion of equality as desirable social policy. . . Mark Tushnet, a professor of constitutional law at Georgetown University Law Center in Washington, D.C., rejects the argument that laws promoting equality undermine advancement on the basis of merit."

Bovard, James.
Here comes the goon squad. American spectator, v. 29, July 1996: 36-41, 83.
LRS96-8908
"With more than 200,000 companies and institutions (together employing more than 25 million people) that do business with the U.S. government, the OFCCP enjoys more coercive power and less judicial scrutiny than any other of the nation's quota police."

Carney, Dan.
Effort to ban racial preference at Federal level restarted. Congressional Quarterly weekly report, v. 55, June 21, 1997: 1454. LRS97-4382
"Days after President Clinton's speech in San Diego calling for an examination of race relations in the United States, a group of congressional Republicans restarted efforts to ban racial and gender preference programs affecting federal hiring and contracting."

CCRI will become law: Federal panel overturns injunction. Washington, Center for Equal Opportunity, 1997. 8 p. LRS97-1697
"On April 8, 1997, a three-judge panel of the 9th Circuit Court of Appeals held that the California Civil Rights Initiative (CCRI) passed by voters in a statewide ballot last November, does not violate the U.S. Constitution .... This Civil Rights Update briefly analyzes the 9th Circuit's reasoning, explains the larger significance of the case, and outlines the future schedule of the Proposition 209 litigation."

Citrin, Jack.
Affirmative action in the people's court. Public interest, no. 122, winter 1996: 39-48.
LRS96-1012
"A majority of Americans rejects explicit preferences, regardless of the particular group they are intended to assist."

Comments and papers from a symposium on affirmative action and the law. Annual survey of American law, v. 3, 1996: whole issue (p. 359-564). LRS96-8899

Congressional Research Service. American Law Division.
Congressional Research Service's compilation and overview of Federal laws and regulations establishing affirmative action goals. Daily labor report (Bureau of National Affairs), no. 36, Feb. 23, 1995: E15-E26 LRS95-927
"The compilation of law's included in this memorandum reflects our efforts to be as 'comprehensive' as possible .... Consequently, we have included any statute, regulation, or executive order uncovered by our research which appears, in any manner, to prefer or consider race, gender, or ethnicity as factors in federal employment or the allocation of federal contracts or grants to individuals or institutions."

Cose, Ellis.
The color bind. Newsweek, v. 129, May 12, 1997: 58-59. LRS97-3122
"Thanks to a court order, a law school discovers that without an affirmative-action program its student body will be too white for comfort."

Enemark, Christine E.
Adarand Constructors, Inc. v. Pena: forcing the Federal Communications Commission into a new constitutional regime. Columbia journal of law and social problems, v. 30, winter 1997: 215-266. LRS97-2257
While Congress had "directed the FCC to protect the ability of women and minority applicants to compete in the new spectrum auction process," the Supreme Court's Adarand decision "implied that any such federal preference would no longer be constitutional."

Holzer, Harry. Neumark, David.

Are affirmative action hires less qualified? Evidence from employer-employee data on new hires. Available Internet: http://www.psc.lsa.umich.edu/pubs/papers/rr96-373.pdf (as of May 14, 1997). [15,11] p. (PSC research report series no. 96-373) LRS96-11574

"Our results show some evidence of lower educational qualifications among blacks and Hispanics hired under Affirmative Action, but not among white women. Further, our results show little evidence of substantially weaker job performance among most groups of minority and female Affirmative Action hires."

Kahlenberg, Richard D.

Equal opportunity critics. New republic, v. 213, July 17 & 24, 1995: 22, 24-25. LRS95-9732

Defends the idea of basing affirmative action measures on class, not race or ethnicity.

Lynch, Michael.

Affirmative action in California's State civil service: who is really underrepresented and why. Available Internet: http://www.ideas.org/issues/civright/briefing/civil_brief.html (as of Mar. 25, 1997). [16] p. LRS96-11323

"The data show that after years of focused hiring efforts for women and minorities two of the groups most underrepresented are whites and men. Any increased push for ethnic proportionality that is inclusive of all groups must thus include good faith efforts to bring these groups up to parity, which would result in significant erosion of the representation of some minority groups, most notably blacks."

Makower, Joel.

Managing diversity in the workplace. Business and society review, no. 92, winter 1995: 48-54. LRS95-7153

Profiles companies, such as Reebok and Timberland, that have found that engendering diversity in the workplace makes business sense.

Marshall, Will.

From preferences to employment: a new program on affirmative action. Washington, Progressive Policy Institute, 1995. 20 p. (Policy report (Aug. 3, 1995)) LRS95-6782

"Proposes striking a new bargain on affirmative action, trading race and gender preferences for a specific empowerment agenda. It also preserves, with modifications, affirmative action in college admissions."

McGinnis, John O.

The peculiar institution. National review, v. 48, Oct. 14, 1996: 62, 64-67. LRS96-7425

"Preferential affirmative action is a grave affront to American principles of justice."

Mishkind, Charles S.

Reverse discrimination/affirmative action litigation update: where is it going? Employee relations law journal, v. 22, winter 1996: 107-123. LRSS96-11611

"Examines a number of important post-Adarand cases and suggests that if affirmative action is going to pass judicial scrutiny, there must be a history of past discrimination at that employer in the relevant job classifications."

Mosley, Albert G. Capaldi, Nicholas.

Affirmative action: social justice or unfair preference? Lanham, MD, Rowman & Littlefield Publishers, 1996. 140 p. (Point/counterpoint) KF3464.M67 1996

Contents.--Affirmative action: pro, by Albert G. Mosley.--Affirmative action: con, by Nicholas Capaldi.--Response to Capaldi.--Response to Mosley.

Myers, Samuel L., Jr.
Why diversity is a smoke screen for affirmative action. Change, v. 29, July-Aug. 1997: 24-32. LRS97-5349
Argues that "diversity--useful on its face--may be no more than an ingenious device for dismantling affirmative action."

Post, Katherine. Lynch, Michael.
Free markets, free choices: women in the workforce. Available Internet: http://www.ideas.org/issues/civright/gend-pay/index.html (as of May 1, 1997). [22] p. LRS95-14130
Issued by the Pacific Research Institute, Dec. 1995.
"Examining the so-called wage gap, we find that it is simply individual choice -- in levels and choices of educational fields, careers, and marriage -- as opposed to discrimination that the statisticians measure when they find wage disparity."

Question: is it time to end affirmative action for women? Insight (Washington times), v. 11, Apr. 24, 1995: 18-21. LRS95-2376
"Women do not need affirmative action to scale the corporate ladder and break the glass ceiling, claims Elizabeth Larson. Centuries of cultural bias and discrimination based on race and gender make affirmative-action programs a necessity, counters Elizabeth Toledo."

Race versus class: the new affirmative action debate. Edited by Carol M. Swain. Lanham, MD, University Press of America, 1996. 281 p. JC599.U5R23 1996

Stanfield, Rochelle L.
Affirmative inaction. National journal, v. 29, July 12, 1997: 1414-1417. LRS97-4963
"The debate over affirmative action has always been marked by a certain lack of candor on all sides. Contradictions prevail and inconsistencies abound."

Thomas, Stephen B. Hirschman, Judy L.
Minority-targeted scholarships: more than a Black and white issue. Journal of college and university law, v. 21, winter 1995: 555-590. LRS95-4382
"The authors conclude that many existing affirmative action programs in their current form may violate the Fourteenth Amendment, Title VI, or section 1981 of the Civil Rights Act of 1964, and that holistic assessment can meet effectively the institutional goals of diversity and equal opportunity."

Tierney, William G.
Affirmative action in California: looking back, looking forward in public academe. Journal of Negro education, v. 65, spring 1996: 122-132. LRS96-11827
Article's "discussion highlights data indicating that (a) representation of African Americans and other minorities in public postsecondary education increased while affirmative action was in force; and (b) minority representation is certain to decrease in the absence of affirmative action."

U.S. Glass Ceiling Commission.
A solid investment: making full use of the nation's human capital. Washington, The Commission, for sale by the Supt. of Docs., G.P.O., 1995. 61 p. LRS95-12774
Presents a range of recommendations to both private sector and government leaders that include diversity goals in all strategic business plans. See LRS95-6592 for Good for business: making full use of the nation's human capital: the environmental scan; a factfinding report of the Federal Glass Ceiling Commission.

U.S. Merit Systems Protection Board.
Fair & equitable treatment: a progress report on minority employment in the Federal Government. Washington, The Board, 1996. 87 p. LRS96-6352

"Overall minority employment in the Federal Civil Service now exceeds minority participation in the civilian labor force, and promotion rates in the Government are generally comparable for minorities and nonminorities."

U.S. White House Office.

Affirmative action review; report to the President. Washington, White House Office, Executive Office of the President, 1995. 136, 13 p. LRS95-6267

"Describes the evolution of affirmative action, as policymakers sought to make real the promise of the civil rights legal breakthroughs [and] . . . . summarizes the evidence of discrimination and exclusion today, followed by a brief review of the overall effectiveness of affirmative action and anti-discrimination measures." An addendum contains the President's July 19, 1995 remarks on affirmative action at the National Archives.

Volokh, Eugene.

The California civil rights initiative: an interpretive guide. UCLA law review, v. 44, June 1997: 1335-1404. LRS97-6737

"My general conclusion is that the CCRI has a dramatic impact within its scope of operation, but this scope covers only a limited, well-defined area of government action."

Weiss, Robert J.

"We want jobs": a history of affirmative action. New York, Garland Pub., 1997. 292 p. (Studies in African American history and culture) HF5549.5.A34W44 1997

"The central theme of this book is the rejection by civil rights groups of gradualism in favor of rapid, concrete gains and the coalescence of an opposition to this process."

White attitudes toward policies intended to eliminate discrimination. Social science quarterly, v. 77, Dec. 1996: 723-788. LRS96-10166

Partial contents.--Understanding differences in whites' opinions across racial policies, by Laura Stoker.--Whites' opposition to race-targeted policies: one cause or many? By Steven A. Tuch and Michael Hughes.

Wilkins, Roger.

Racism has its privileges. Nation, v. 260, Mar. 27, 1995: 409, 412, 414-416. LRS95-3468

"Affirmative action . . . . has not outlived its usefulness."

Yang, Catherine. McNamee, Mike.

'A hand up, but not a handout': with solid technical assistance, set-aside programs can work. Business week, no. 3417, Mar. 27, 1995: 70, 72. LRS95-1695

CHAPTER 4

The Equal Rights Amendment: A Chronology

Leslie W. Gladstone

Summary

Although some women believed that over time suffrage alone would lead to reform of sexist laws and practices, others argued that such a process would be both lengthy and uncertain, and that, without a constitutional guarantee of equal status, many additional years might pass before rights for women were comparable to those accorded to men. The Equal Rights Amendment, first proposed in 1923, was reintroduced in various forms in subsequent Congresses, finally winning passage in 1972. Under the resolving clause, a 7-year deadline was set for ratification. In 1978, when the Amendment had been approved by 35 states, three less than the necessary three-quarters or 38, Congress voted to extend the deadline to June 30, 1982. No additional states voted for approval before the new deadline expired. The measure was reintroduced almost immediately, however, and has been put forward in each subsequent Congress since 1982.

Introduction

Proposals to clarify the status and legal rights of women extend from 1776 and Abigail Adams' famous letter to her husband at the Second Continental Congress admonishing lawmakers to "remember the Ladies" to present-day efforts to add an Equal Rights Amendment to the Constitution. In the 19th century, an attempt was made to include equality for women in the Fourteenth Amendment, which had been designed to guarantee rights and privileges to newly liberated black males. In wording the Fourteenth Amendment, however, Congress departed from previous constitutional usage in referring to "persons" or "citizens" and in Section 2 referred three times to "male inhabitants" or "male citizens." Attempts to include rights for women under the Fifteenth Amendment were also unsuccessful. An amendment proposed in 1878 that specifically affirmed the right of women to vote became the "Suffrage" or Nineteenth Amendment upon its eventual ratification in 1920.

The text of the Equal Rights Amendment as proposed by Congress to the states on March 22, 1972 reads as follows:

> Section 1. Equality of rights under the law shall not be denied or abridged by the United States or any State on account of sex.

Section 2. The Congress shall have the power to enforce, by appropriate legislation, the provisions of this article.

Section 3. The amendment shall take effect two years after the date of ratification.

Chronology

1776 Abigail Adams writes to her husband, John Adams, during the drafting of the Articles of Confederation at the Second Continental Congress admonishing him to "remember the ladies" in the new code of laws that is being proposed. She promises that if "unlimited power" is accorded to husbands, "we are determined to foment a rebellion, and will not hold ourselves bound by any laws in which we have no voice or representation."[1]

1776 New Jersey enfranchises "all free inhabitants" who could meet property and residence requirements and uses the phrase "he or she" in referring to voters. In 1807, however, a new election law in New Jersey excludes women from the polls after a 10-year campaign to revoke suffrage. Opponents of women's right to vote claim that women who appear at the polls are unfeminine and that they are too easily manipulated by their husbands, fathers, or brothers.[2]

1840 At a World Slavery Convention in London, active abolitionists Lucretia Mott and Elizabeth Cady Stanton are excluded solely on the basis of sex. Meeting together later, they note the irony of their treatment by an anti-slavery gathering called to protest oppression and note a similarity between blacks and women in their common lack of legal status. Seeking some form of action on behalf of women, they discuss organizing a meeting in the United States for protest and discussion.[3]

1848 The first Women's Rights Convention meets in Seneca Falls, N.Y. A "Declaration of Sentiments" is drafted, along with resolutions calling for the removal of all forms of subjection of women, demanding the right to vote and to complete equality under the law.[4]

1866 A Fourteenth Amendment is proposed by Congress, guaranteeing rights and privileges to newly liberated black males. In wording Section 2 of the Amendment, Congress departs from its customary constitutional usage of

---

[1]*Familiar Letters of John Adams and His Wife Abigail Adams During the Revolution* New York, 1996. p. 286-287. Letter dated March 31, 1777.

[2]See Kerber, Linda K. "Ourselves and Our Daughters Forever:" Women and the Constitution, 1787-1876. *This Constitution*. Spring 1985, No. 2. p. 28-29.

[3]See Flexner, Eleanor. *A Century of Struggle*. Harvard University Press, Cambridge, MA 1959. p. 71-72.

[4]*Ibid*. p. 74-77.

the words "persons" or "citizens" in specifying the beneficiaries of the Amendment and refers three times to "male inhabitants" or "male citizens." Efforts by leaders of the women's rights movement to have included in the Amendment equality without discrimination on the basis of sex are unsuccessful, as are later attempts to include rights for women under the 15th Amendment. In both Amendments, the seeming limitation of the word "citizen" to males raises the question of whether women are actually citizens under the Constitution.

1866 The American Equal Rights Association is organized by a group of feminists-abolitionists with Lucretia Mott as president and Susan B. Anthony and Henry Blackwell as secretaries. The Association proposes to work for the rights of both freedmen and women but is quickly consumed by the debate over the 14th Amendment.

1868 A weekly advocating equality of rights for women called *The Revolution* begins publishing.

1869 The Territory of Wyoming enfranchises women, later carrying enfranchisement into statehood in 1890. Before the 19th Amendment is ratified in 1920, 29 other states enfranchise women.

1920 The women's suffrage amendment, adopted by Congress in 1919, becomes the 19th Amendment in 1920 upon ratification by the necessary three-quarters of the 48 states. Shortly after this victory, the campaign for complete legal equality for women is resumed.

1923 An Equal Rights Amendment (S.J.Res. 21/H.J.Res. 75)[5] is introduced in Congress by two Kansas Members, Senator Charles Curtis and Representative Daniel Anthony, Jr. From 1923 to 1938, hearings are conducted on several occasions before subcommittees of the House and Senate Judiciary Committees, and on three occasions the resolution is favorably reported to the full Committee. Apart from these hearings, no further action is taken.

1940 The Republican party supports the Equal Rights Amendment in its political platform, the first endorsement by a major party.

1943 The Senate Judiciary Committee alters the earlier language of the amendment, giving it the form used today.

1944 The Democratic party platform endorses the Equal Rights Amendment.

1946 The proposed amendment is debated on the Senate floor for the first time since its introduction in 1923. It fails to pass by 11 votes.

---

[5]In the 67th Congress, S.J. Res 21, December 10, 1923 and H.J. Res. 75, December 13, 1923.

1950 — The amendment is passed by the Senate. It is amended on the floor by the "Hayden[6] rider," providing that

> The provisions of this article shall not be construed to impair any rights, benefits, or exemptions now or hereafter conferred by law upon persons or the female sex. (S.J.Res. 25, as amended, 81st Congress.)

1953 — The amendment again is passed by the Senate, amended by the Hayden rider.

1964 — The Senate Judiciary Committee reports that "this [the Hayden] rider is not acceptable to women who want equal rights under the law. It is under the guise of so-called 'rights' or 'benefits' that women have been treated unequally and denied opportunities which are available to men."[7]

June 11, 1970 — Representative Martha Griffiths introduces a petition to discharge the amendment from the House Judiciary Committee and bring it to the floor for consideration. The House Judiciary Committee has held few hearings on the amendment since its initial introduction in 1923. The most recent hearing was in 1948.

July 20, 1970 — Although use of the discharge petition is rarely successful, within five weeks the petition receives the requisite number of signatures (half the total membership of the House, plus one).

Aug. 10, 1970 — The House passes the Equal Rights Amendment by a vote of 352-15.

Oct. 12, 1971 — The House again adopts the Equal Rights Amendment (H.J.Res. 208, 92nd Congress).

Mar. 17, 1972 — The Senate begins debate on H.J.Res. 208.

Mar. 20-21, 1972 — Senator Sam Ervin introduces 10 amendments in an effort to moderate the application of the Equal Rights Amendment.

Mar. 22, 1972 — The Senate rejects the Ervin amendments and adopts H.J.Res. 208 by a vote of 84-8. The debate on the Ervin amendments provides a basis for determining the intent of Congress in passing the Equal Rights Amendment. It also summarizes most of the concerns about the Amendment.[8]

---

[6]Senator Carl Hayden of Arizona.

[7]U.S. Congress. Senate. Committee on the Judiciary. *Equal Rights for Men and Women.* S.Rept. 1558, 88th Congress., 2nd Sess. Washington, U.S. Govt. Print. Off., 1964.

[8]*Congressional Record.* v. 118, Mar. 21, 1972. p. 9314-9336 and 9337-9370; Mar. 22, 1972. p. 9517-9523, 9524-9540, and 9544-9598.

Nov. 1977	Thirty-five of the necessary 38 states (out of 50) have ratified the Equal Rights Amendment.[9] With time running short, H.J.Res. 638 is introduced in the 96th Congress to extend the March 22, 1979 ratification deadline.
Aug. 15, 1978	H.J.Res. 638, extending the deadline to June 30, 1982, is approved by the House by a vote of 233-189.
Oct. 6, 1978	The extension resolution is approved by the Senate by a vote of 60-36.
Oct. 20. 1978	President Carter signs the measure, although his approval is not required.
Dec. 21, 1981	President Reagan, who opposes the sweeping effect of the proposed amendment, signs Executive Order No. 12336, establishing the Task Force on Legal Equity for Women. The Task Force is charged with overseeing presidentially ordered changes in certain discriminatory federal regulations, policies and practices of 21 executive departments and agencies. The Attorney General is to review federal laws, as well as regulations,

[9]Of the 35 states initially voting to ratify the proposed amendment, five (South Dakota, Kentucky, Tennessee, Nebraska, and Idaho) later voted to withdraw or rescind ratification. The validity of their withdrawal has been left an open question. In December 1981, the U.S. District Court of Idaho ruled in *Idaho* v. *Freeman* (Civil No. 79-1079) that "a rescission of a prior ratification must be recognized if it occurs prior to unrescinded ratification by three-fourths of the states." Since this ruling conflicted with a 1939 Supreme Court decision in *Coleman* v. *Miller* (307 U.S. 433) that rescission is a political matter for Congress to decide, the Supreme Court stayed the Idaho decision in January 1982. After the proposed Equal Rights Amendment died without being ratified, the Court ordered that the *Idaho* v. *Freeman* ruling be vacated.

policies and practices, "which contain language that unjustifiably differentiates, or which effectively discriminates on the basis of sex"[10] and to make quarterly reports to the President. (The final report is submitted to the President in April 1986.)

June 30, 1982 — The extended ratification deadline ends without the three additional states needed.

July 14, 1982 — The Amendment is reintroduced in Congress, but no further action is taken.

1983-1984 — The Senate Judiciary Committee holds a series of hearings on the impact of the ERA. The inquiry covers the following subject areas: private and parochial education, military law and policy, abortion rights, veterans programs, social security programs, the role of discriminatory intent and discriminatory impact, homosexual rights, family law, and the state experience.[11]

1983-present — The Amendment is reintroduced in each subsequent Congress.

1994 — Representative Robert Andrews introduces H.J.Res. 432 in the 103rd Congress to require the House to verify ratification of the proposed ERA when it is ratified by three additional states. The proposal would attempt to set aside deadlines established for ratification of the amendment passed by Congress in 1972 and extended in 1978.[12]

---

[10]Public Papers of the Presidents of the United States. Ronald Reagan. *Executive Order 12336—Task Force on Legal Equity for Women.* December 21, 1981. Washington, U.S. Govt. Print. Off., 1982. p. 1176-1177.

[11]U.S. Congress. Senate. Committee on the Judiciary. Subcommittee on the Constitution. *The Impact of the Equal Rights Amendment.* Hearings on S.J.Res. 10, 98th Cong., 1st and 2nd Sess., Parts 1 and 2, May 26, September 13, Nov. 1, 1983; January 24, February 21, March 20. April 23, May 23, June 22, August 7, and September 19, 1984. Washington, U.S. Govt. Print. Off., 1984.

Also published as U.S. Congress. Senate. Committee on the Judiciary, Subcommittee on the Constitution. *Summary of Hearings Before the Senate Subcommittee on the Constitution, on the Impact of the Proposed Equal Rights Amendment.* Committee Print, 99th Congress, 1st Sess., Washington, U.S. Govt. Print. Off., October 1985.

[12] For a discussion of issues relating to the Andrews proposal see U.S. Library of Congress. Congressional Research Service. *Equal Rights Amendment: Ratification Issues.* General Distribution Memorandum by David C. Huckabee, Mar. 18, 1996. Washington, 1996.

CHAPTER 5

California Civil Rights Initiative

Andorra Bruno

Summary

On November 5, 1996, California voters approved Proposition 209, popularly known as the California Civil Rights Initiative (CCRI), by a vote of 54% to 46%. The CCRI proposed to amend the California constitution to ban discrimination and preferential treatment based on race, sex, color, ethnicity, or national origin in the state's employment, education, and contracting systems. Following the CCRI's passage, its opponents and proponents took their battle to the courts. On November 3, 1997, the U.S. Supreme Court refused to hear a challenge to Proposition 209, leaving in place a lower court ruling that the measure is constitutional. Proposition 209 may have significant effects outside California. Some expect it to influence future congressional action on federal affirmative action policies.

Background

The CCRI was written by two academics in California, Glynn Custred and Thomas Wood. The main clause of the constitutional amendment reads:

> The state shall not discriminate against, or grant preferential treatment to, any individual or group on the basis of race, sex, color, ethnicity, or national origin in the operation of public employment, public education, or public contracting.

In congressional testimony to the Constitution Subcommittee of the House Judiciary Committee in April 1995, Custred explained that the CCRI was needed "in order to counter a growing trend of racial, ethnic and gender preferences in the public sector."[1]

Efforts by Custred and Wood to place the CCRI on the 1992 and 1994 California ballots failed. In 1994, a California legislator introduced a constitutional amendment similar to the CCRI in the state assembly, in an attempt to gain legislative approval

---

[1]Statement of Glynn Custred, in U.S. Congress, House Committee on the Judiciary, Subcommittee on the Constitution, *Group Preferences and the Law*, hearings, 104th Cong., 1st sess., April 3, June 1, and Oct. 25, 1995, p. 99.

to place the measure on the March 1996 primary ballot. The amendment was defeated in an assembly committee. Following the November 1994 elections, in which Republicans gained majorities in both Houses of the U.S. Congress and in one house of the California legislature, California legislators again attempted to place a CCRI-like constitutional amendment on the March 1996 ballot. They reasoned that opponents in the legislature might vote in favor of the measure, in order to keep the issue off the ballot in the November 1996 presidential election. In March 1995, however, a California Senate committee rejected the proposed amendment.

Failing to gain legislative approval, CCRI backers turned to the other avenue available for putting initiatives before the electorate, and began preparations for collecting the more than 693,000 valid signatures required to qualify the CCRI for the November 1996 ballot. On February 21, 1996, the deadline for filing signatures, CCRI backers turned in about 1.1 million signatures. In April 1996, the Secretary of State of California officially qualified the CCRI for the November ballot.

CCRI Campaign

The CCRI was the subject of hard-fought campaigns in California by initiative supporters and opponents. Supporters, who included California Governor Pete Wilson and the state Republican party, argued that preferential policies based on race and gender were unfair and discriminatory, and bred resentment among non-beneficiaries. Opponents, including a large number of civil rights and women's organizations, countered that affirmative action remained necessary to combat discrimination and ensure equal opportunity for all. They contended that the CCRI would have serious, negative consequences for women and minorities.

Debate Over the Impact of the CCRI

CCRI proponents and opponents debated the initiative's potential consequences for state affirmative action programs. Opponents of the initiative argued that it would eliminate all state-run affirmative action. They expressed concern that the term "preferential treatment" was not defined in the initiative and, thus, could be interpreted as prohibiting a wide range of programs, including outreach and recruitment programs designed to expand opportunities for minorities and women.

Leaders of the pro-CCRI campaign objected to the characterization of the initiative as an "anti-affirmative action measure." (Many of these leaders did agree, however, that the initiative would prohibit a large number of existing affirmative action programs.) They argued that the term affirmative action encompassed programs that used race- and gender-based preferences as well as nondiscriminatory programs, and that the latter would not be affected by the initiative. CCRI proponents maintained that race- and gender-neutral affirmative action, such as giving preferences in public college admissions to economically disadvantaged applicants, would be permissible under Proposition 209.

Much of the debate about the CCRI centered on clause (c) of the proposed amendment and its potential impact. Clause (c) reads:

> Nothing in this section shall be interpreted as prohibiting bona fide qualifications based on sex which are reasonably necessary to the normal operation of public employment, public education, or public contracting.

Some legal scholars have argued that this provision would lessen the current protection against gender discrimination under the California constitution. Other scholars have rejected this interpretation, maintaining that clause (c) would in no way modify existing protections against sex discrimination.

Election Results

On November 5, 1996, the California electorate approved Proposition 209 by a vote of 4,737,273 (54%) to 3,986,742 (46%).

Legal Actions

Following passage of the CCRI, opponents turned to the courts to block enforcement of the measure. On November 6, 1996, they filed a lawsuit in federal court, which argued, in part, that the CCRI violates the equal protection clause of the U.S. Constitution. On December 23, Chief U.S. District Judge Thelton Henderson issued a preliminary injunction blocking enforcement of Proposition 209.[2] His decision stated that "plaintiffs have demonstrated a probability of success on the merits of their equal protection claim."[3] The defendants in the case, who included California Governor Pete Wilson and the state's attorney general, appealed to the U.S. Court of Appeals for the Ninth Circuit. The Justice Department filed an *amicus* brief with the appeals court, urging the court not to lift Judge Henderson's injunction. On April 8, 1997, a three-judge panel of the appeals court ruled that Proposition 209 is constitutional and overturned the injunction.[4] CCRI opponents asked the appeals court to reconsider that decision, but on August 21, the court denied the request. The appeals court also refused to issue a stay to block enforcement of Proposition 209 while opponents petitioned the U.S. Supreme Court to hear the case. On November 3, the Supreme Court refused without comment to hear the challenge to Proposition 209, leaving the appeals court's April ruling in place.

Implementation of the CCRI

On August 28, 1997, Proposition 209 went into effect in California. Implementation of the measure, however, requires further actions by state courts, state agencies, and local governments.

---

[2] *Coalition for Economic Equity v. Wilson*, 65 U.S.L.W. 2421 (N.D. Cal. Dec. 23, 1996).

[3] 65 U.S.L.W. at 2423.

[4] *Coalition for Economic Equity v. Wilson*, 65 U.S.L.W. 2650 (9th Cir. April 8, 1997). This ruling is also available online at ftp://ftp.vcilp.org/pub/law/Fed-Ct/Circuit/9th/9715030.asc, visited April 17, 1997.

National Implications

Although Proposition 209 applies only to California state policies and programs, it is widely perceived as having broader implications. Since its passage, legislators in other states have indicated that they plan to press efforts to eliminate affirmative action programs in their states. Campaigns to put CCRI-like measures on the ballot are being organized in Washington state, Florida, and elsewhere. (In the city of Houston, voters rejected a CCRI-like initiative on November 4, 1997.) Many critics of affirmative action hope that approval of the CCRI will be a first step toward eliminating federal preferential policies.

Clinton Administration

During the 1996 presidential election campaign, President Clinton indicated that he opposed the CCRI. Although Republican nominee Robert Dole endorsed the initiative, the CCRI never became a major issue in the campaign. The Clinton Administration participated in the legal challenge to Proposition 209, as discussed above.

104th Congress

The 104th Congress showed interest in the CCRI and its potential national implications. As noted above, CCRI co-author Custred gave testimony at an April 1995 House hearing. In April 1996, the Senate Judiciary Committee held a hearing specifically on "California and affirmative action." Witnesses at the hearing included CCRI campaign chairman Ward Connerly and California Governor Wilson.

In March 1995, Senator Jesse Helms introduced a bill (S. 497) modeled on the CCRI. In introductory remarks on the Senate floor, he explained that he was "proposing to eliminate the same kinds of discriminatory, expensive, and counterproductive programs on the Federal level as California is attempting on the State level."[5] A House companion bill (H.R. 1764) was subsequently introduced. Another House bill (H.R. 1840), introduced in June 1995 by Representative George Radanovich, contained language similar to that in the main clause of the CCRI and sought to broadly ban preferential treatment. No actions other than committee referrals occurred on any of these measures.

---

[5]Sen. Jesse Helms, remarks in the Senate, *Congressional Record,* daily edition, v. 141, March 3, 1995, p. S3472.

The major affirmative action bill considered in the 104th Congress had some basic similarities to the CCRI. The Equal Opportunity Act (S. 1085/H.R. 2128), which was introduced in July 1995 by Senator Dole and Representative Charles Canady, sought to prohibit the federal government from intentionally discriminating against, or granting a preference to, any individual or group based on race, color, national origin, or sex in federal contracting, federal employment, or federally conducted programs. H.R. 2128 was marked up by the House Judiciary Committee's Constitution Subcommittee, but neither bill was reported out of a full committee. Both bills died at the end of the 104th Congress.

105th Congress

Some observers believe that the passage of Proposition 209 in California will encourage congressional action on federal affirmative action policies. In a press release issued the day after the November 1996 election, Representative Canady, House sponsor of the Equal Opportunity Act in the 104th Congress, said:

> In light of Proposition 209's success, further inaction by elected officials is simply unacceptable.... It is now up to those of us outside of California to learn the lessons of CCRI and to continue the noble battle they have begun to put an end to government policies that divide the American people into racial and gender groups.[6]

On June 17, 1997, Representative Canady introduced the "Civil Rights Act of 1997" (H.R. 1909). Like the Equal Opportunity Act he introduced in the 104th Congress, H.R. 1909 would prohibit the federal government from intentionally discriminating against, or granting a preference to, any individual or group based on race, color, national origin, or sex in federal contracting, federal employment, or federally conducted programs. The House Constitution Subcommittee approved the bill on July 9. On June 23, Senator Mitch McConnell introduced companion legislation (S. 950) in the Senate.[7]

---

[6]Press Release by Representative Charles Canady, Nov. 6, 1996.

[7]For further information about these and other affirmative action-related bills, see U.S. Library of Congress, Congressional Research Service, *Affirmative Action: Recent Congressional and Presidential Activity*, by Andorra Bruno, CRS report 97-527 GOV.

CHAPTER 6

Affirmative Action in Employment

Andorra Bruno

INTRODUCTION

Affirmative action in employment is a highly controversial public policy. The controversy encompasses the very definition of the term itself. One complicating factor is that the meaning of affirmative action has changed over the years, as have the obligations imposed on employers. As used in the Civil Rights Act of 1964, affirmative action referred to remedial steps required of employers who had engaged in discriminatory practices. In several executive orders issued in the 1960s, the term was also used to describe special efforts beyond strict nondiscrimination that Federal Government contractors were to undertake in areas such as employee recruitment and training. Affirmative action became unacceptable to many, however, when, beginning in the late 1960s, contractors were required to set goals and timetables in an effort to correct any "underutilization" of minorities and women. To some observers, goals, in effect, became quotas.

The United States Commission on Civil Rights has defined affirmative action to include "any measure, beyond simple termination of a discriminatory practice, adopted to correct or compensate for past or present discrimination or to prevent discrimination from recurring in the future."[1] Randall Kennedy offers a more succinct definition that highlights the controversial aspects of affirmative action, both as a concept and a current practice: "Affirmative action refers to policies that provide preferences based explicitly on membership in a designated group." Kennedy distinguishes between "'soft' forms [of affirmative action] that might include special recruitment efforts" and "'hard' forms that might include reserving a specific number of openings exclusively for members of the preferred group."[2]

---

[1]U.S. Commission on Civil Rights. *Statement on Affirmative Action*. Washington, 1977. p. 2.

[2]Quoted in Jones, James E., Jr. "The Origins of Affirmative Action." In *A Report of the Study Group on Affirmative Action to the Committee on Education and Labor,* U.S. House of Representatives. Committee Print, 100th Cong., 1st Sess. Washington, U.S. Govt. Print. Off., 1987. p. 163.

Affirmative action, or preferential treatment, raises fundamental questions about the nature of rights. As noted by Kennedy, underlying the concept of affirmative action is a notion of group rights. Individuals become eligible for affirmative action due to membership in a particular group. Some argue that group-based preferential treatment is antithetical to traditional values of fairness and merit. Moreover, some maintain that defining the main beneficiary groups by race, ethnicity, sex, and disability violates the constitutional principle of equal protection of the laws and statutory bans on discrimination. In response, proponents of affirmative action argue that group-based remedies are necessary to combat group-based discrimination. They believe that only special affirmative action measures can effectively overcome "group wrongs" that "pervade the social, political, economic, and ideological landscape" and "become self-sustaining processes."[3] Thus, in their view, fairness requires affirmative action.

Affirmative action, particularly in the form of goals or quotas, likewise raises questions about the meaning of equality and the proper role of government in helping achieve that equality. In a historic 1965 speech, President Lyndon B. Johnson took the position that reliance on strict equality of opportunity to overcome the effects of past discrimination was inadequate. "[I]t is not enough just to open the gates of opportunity," President Johnson said. "All our citizens must have the ability to walk through those gates." He went on to declare, "We seek ... not just equality as a right and a theory but equality as a fact and equality as a result."[4] To some critics, defining equality as equality of results—and requiring the use of goals and timetables—is tantamount to entitling groups to proportional shares of jobs, resources, or benefits. Affirmative action supporters reject the characterization of numerical goals as group entitlements. Rather, they argue that such measures are meant to be temporary remedies and that genuine equality of opportunity remains their ultimate aim.

Tensions among the above principles and values, and efforts to balance them, touch all aspects of the affirmative action debate covered in this report—government action, court decisions, scholarly and public opinion, alternatives, and future prospects. The Supreme Court, for example, has upheld judicial affirmative action quotas in cases of persistent discrimination, provided that the quotas do not impose unacceptable burdens on innocent third parties.

Much recent discussion of affirmative action has focused on its effects on its intended beneficiaries. A belief among some scholars that affirmative action policies have been harmful to recipients has reinvigorated the debate over affirmative action.

---

[3]U.S. Commission on Civil Rights. *Affirmative Action in the 1980s: Dismantling the Process of Discrimination*. Washington, Nov. 1981. p. 39. (Hereinafter cited as *Affirmative Action in the 1980s*)

[4]U.S. *Public Papers of the Presidents of the United States, Lyndon Johnson, 1965*, v. 2. Washington, U.S. Govt. Print. Off., 1966. p. 636.

I. HISTORY OF AFFIRMATIVE ACTION

Affirmative action in employment is rooted in a series of presidential, congressional, and court actions designed to make it easier for certain classes of Americans to achieve nondiscriminatory access to and treatment in the workplace. The term affirmative action appeared in the text of the 1935 Wagner Act,[5] a landmark labor relations statute that broadened employee rights to organize and bargain collectively. Under the Wagner Act, employers who were found to have engaged in unfair labor practices against union organizers and members had to take "affirmative action, including reinstatement of employees."[6]

In 1941, prior to U.S. entry into World War II, President Franklin D. Roosevelt issued an executive order affirming that it was U.S. policy "to encourage full participation in the national defense program by all citizens of the United States, regardless of race, creed, color, or national origin."[7] Announced under the threat of a black march on Washington,[8] E.O. 8802 called on employers and labor unions "to provide for the full and equitable participation of all workers in defense industries."[9] It required that all future defense contracts negotiated by the U.S. Government contain a nondiscrimination provision. E.O. 8802 differed from previous policy statements of nondiscrimination in that it established a mechanism—an advisory committee known as the Fair Employment Practice Committee—to process discrimination complaints.[10]

Executive orders issued over the next 20 years built on the nondiscrimination mandate of E.O. 8802.[11] These orders re-affirmed the Federal Government's commitment to equal opportunity and reorganized

---

[5]Act of July 5, 1935, ch. 372, 49 Stat. 449 (also known as the National Labor Relations Act).

[6]49 Stat. 454

[7]U.S. President, 1933-1945 (F. Roosevelt). Executive Order 8802, "Reaffirming Policy of Full Participation in the Defense Program by All Persons . . . ." *Federal Register*, v. 6, June 27, 1941. p. 3109. (Hereinafter cited as E.O. 8802)

[8]See Morgan, Ruth P. *The President and Civil Rights: Policy-Making by Executive Order.* Lanham, Md., University Press of America, 1987. p. 37-38.

[9]E.O. 8802, p. 3109.

[10]See Kellough, J. Edward. *Federal Equal Employment Opportunity Policy and Numerical Goals and Timetables.* New York, Praeger, 1989. p. 15.

[11]Among the most important were E.O. 9346 (1943), 9980 (1948), 10308 (1951), 10479 (1953), 10557 (1954), and 10590 (1955). See Morgan, *The President and Civil Rights*, p. 87-88.

administrative structures to implement nondiscrimination policies in Federal employment and employment under Government contract.

Civil Rights and Affirmative Action

President John F. Kennedy appeared to endorse a more proactive approach to equal employment opportunity in a 1961 executive order calling for affirmative action. E.O. 10925 replaced existing committees on Government employment policy and Government contracts with a new President's Committee on Equal Employment Opportunity. In the area of Federal employment, the Committee was directed "to consider and recommend additional affirmative steps which should be taken by executive departments and agencies to realize more fully the national policy of nondiscrimination within the executive branch of the Government."[12]

The order also required that Government contractors agree not to engage in employment discrimination based on race, creed, color, or national origin, and agree to "take affirmative action to ensure that applicants are employed, and that employers are treated during employment" without regard to these characteristics.[13] Although the order did list some areas in which affirmative action should be taken—such as employment, upgrading, transfer, recruitment, layoff, and pay rates—it left unspecified contractors' obligations in these areas. Historian Hugh Davis Graham has described the order as "classic nondiscrimination, however couched in positive new rhetoric." According to Graham, "affirmative action," as used in the order, "seemed self-defined to require more aggressive recruitment in hiring, and special training for minorities to encourage their advancement."[14]

Civil Rights Act of 1964

Relying on the President's constitutional authority and implied duties, the above executive orders addressed employment in the executive branch and by Federal Government contractors. Private employers who were not party to Government contracts were not covered.[15] Coverage of private employment was achieved by Title VII of the Civil Rights Act of 1964,[16] often cited as the most important piece of civil rights legislation enacted in this century.

---

[12]U.S. President, 1961-1963 (Kennedy). Executive Order 10925, "Establishing the President's Committee on Equal Employment Opportunity." *Federal Register*, v. 26, March 8, 1961. p. 1977.

[13]Ibid.

[14]Graham, Hugh Davis. *The Civil Rights Era.* New York, Oxford University Press, 1990. p. 42.

[15]See Morgan, *The President and Civil Rights,* p. 30-32.

[16]P.L. 88-352, July 2, 1964, 78 Stat. 241. Title VII is codified at 42 U.S.C. 2000e *et seq.*

Title VII of the Civil Rights Act, as amended,[17] broadly prohibits employment discrimination. Section 703(a) makes it is unlawful for employers subject to the act—

> to fail or refuse to hire or to discharge any individual, or otherwise to discriminate against any individual with respect to his compensation, terms, conditions, or privileges of employment, because of such individual's race, color, religion, sex, or national origin; or
>
> to limit, segregate, or classify his employees or applicants for employment in any way which would deprive or tend to deprive any individual of employment opportunities or otherwise adversely affect his status as an employee, because of such individual's race, color, religion, sex, or national origin.[18]

In the event that a court finds that an employer or other respondent has "intentionally engaged in ... an unlawful employment practice," Section 706(g) of the original 1964 act empowered the court to "order such affirmative action as may be appropriate, which may include reinstatement or hiring of employees, with or without back pay."[19] This language was broadened in 1972 to allow the court to "order such affirmative action as may be appropriate, which may include, but is not limited to, reinstatement or hiring of employees, with or without back pay ... or any other equitable relief as the court deems appropriate."[20]

Some Members of Congress raised concerns about the Civil Rights Act of 1964 that foreshadowed the quota debate over the 1991 Civil Rights Act. They contended that Title VII could be interpreted as requiring quota hiring based on the percentage of black people in a community. In response, the following provision (Section 703(j)) was included in Title VII:

> Nothing contained in this title shall be interpreted to require any employer ... to grant preferential treatment to any individual or to any group ... on account of an imbalance which may exist with respect to the total number or percentage of persons of any race, color, religion, sex, or national origin employed by any employer ... in comparison with the total number or percentage of persons of such race, color,

---

[17]Two of the amending statutes, the 1972 Equal Employment Opportunity Act and the 1991 Civil Rights Act, are also discussed below.

[18]42 U.S.C. 2000e-2(a) [19]78 Stat. 261 [20]42 U.S.C. 2000e-5(g)(1)

religion, sex, or national origin in any community ... or in the available work force in any community....[21]

Title VII also established the Equal Employment Opportunity Commission (EEOC), which was charged with working to eliminate "alleged unlawful employment practice by informal methods of conference, conciliation, and persuasion."[22]

Title VI of the Civil Rights Act of 1964 Act, as amended,[23] prohibits discrimination on the basis of race, color, or national origin in any program or activity receiving Federal financial assistance. Section 602 specifies that this discrimination ban applies to "Federal financial assistance to any program or activity, by way of grant, loan, or contract other than a contract of insurance or guaranty" and directs Federal agencies to issue rules and regulations to enforce the ban.[24] As explained by Graham, Title VI gave "statutory approval to the President's contract compliance authority."[25]

Further Executive Initiatives on Affirmative Action

A year after signing the Civil Rights Act, President Lyndon B. Johnson issued E.O. 11246, in which he reiterated President Kennedy's 1961 call for Government contractors not to discriminate and to take affirmative action.[26] Unlike the earlier order, however, E.O. 11246 applied these obligations to *all* a contractor's operations, not just those related to fulfilling a particular Government contract.

E.O. 11246 abolished the President's Committee on Equal Employment Opportunity and once again reassigned responsibilities for implementing nondiscrimination policies. It remodeled the contract compliance program, empowering the Secretary of Labor to enforce equal employment opportunity standards. In 1966, the Secretary established the Office of Federal Contract Compliance (OFCC) within the Labor Department to administer the policies, rules, and regulations of the compliance program. Under the terms of the

---

[21] 78 Stat. 257, 42 U.S.C. 2000e-2(j)

[22] 42 U.S.C. 2000e-5(b)

[23] 42 U.S.C. 2000d *et seq.*

[24] 78 Stat. 252, 42 U.S.C. 2000d-1

[25] Graham, Hugh Davis. "The Origins of Affirmative Action: Civil Rights and the Regulatory State." *Annals of the American Academy of Political and Social Science,* v. 523, Sept. 1992. p. 56.

[26] U.S. President, 1963-1969 (L. Johnson). Executive Order 11246, "Reassignment of Civil Rights Functions," Sept. 24, 1965. *Weekly Compilation of Presidential Documents,* v. 1, Sept. 27, 1965. p. 305. (Hereinafter cited as E.O. 11246)

executive order, however, primary responsibility for obtaining compliance was vested in the contracting agencies.[27]

Although E.O. 11246 did not use the term affirmative action in connection with Federal employment, it did require that each executive agency head "establish and maintain a positive program of equal employment opportunity for all civilian employees and applicants for employment within his jurisdiction."[28] The order reassigned supervisory responsibility for the Federal equal employment opportunity program to the Civil Service Commission (CSC).

E.O. 11375, which President Johnson issued in October 1967, amended E.O. 11246 to extend equal employment opportunity protections to women.[29]

Goals and Timetables

In implementing E.O. 11246, as amended, the Johnson Administration and later the Nixon Administration endorsed the use of numerical goals and timetables. The Nixon Administration's Philadelphia Plan, based on a plan developed by the Johnson Labor Department, required construction contractors bidding for Federal contracts in that city to submit affirmative action plans containing goals and timetables for minority employment. Under the plan, the invitation for bids would include target ranges for minority employment within which contractors could select goals.[30] Issued by the Department of Labor in 1969, the Philadelphia Plan was quickly challenged in Federal district court on a number of grounds, including that it violated Title VII and exceeded the Labor Secretary's authority under the executive order. A Federal district judge dismissed the suit, however, and that dismissal was affirmed by the U.S. Court of Appeals for the Third Circuit. The Supreme Court denied a request to review the case.[31]

---

[27]The OFCC was later renamed the Office of Federal Contract Compliance Programs (OFCCP). In 1978, in accordance with E.O. 12086, the contract compliance functions of 11 Federal agencies were consolidated into the OFCCP. See U.S. President, 1977-1981 (Carter). Executive Order 12086, "Equal Employment Opportunity Functions," Oct. 5, 1978. *Weekly Compilation of Presidential Documents*, v. 14, Oct. 9, 1978. p. 1714.

[28]E.O. 11246, p. 305.

[29]U.S. President, 1963-1969 (L. Johnson). Executive Order 11375, "Equal Opportunity for Women in Federal Employment and Employment by Federal Contractors," Oct. 13, 1967. *Weekly Compilation of Presidential Documents*, v. 3, Oct. 16, 1967. p. 1437.

[30]See Graham, *The Civil Rights Era*, p. 322-345.

[31]*Contractors Association of Eastern Pennsylvania v. Secretary of Labor*, 311 F. Supp. 1002 (E.D. Pa. 1970), 442 F.2d 159 (3rd Cir. 1971), cert. denied 404 U. S. 854 (1971); also see Graham, *The Civil Rights Era*, p. 341, 437-438.

In 1970, the Labor Department issued Order No. 4, which required Federal contractors with 50 or more employees and a contract of $50,000 or more to develop written affirmative action programs that included goals and timetables.[32] Revised Order No. 4 (1971), applicable to nonconstruction contractors, detailed the required contents of these affirmative action programs, which were to cover women as well as members of racial and ethnic minority groups.[33] According to the 1971 order, as later amended:

> An acceptable affirmative action program must include an analysis of areas within which the contractor is deficient in the utilization of minority groups and women, and further, goals and timetables to which the contractor's good faith efforts must be directed to correct the deficiencies and, thus to achieve prompt and full utilization of minorities and women, at all levels and in all segments of its work force where deficiencies exist.[34]

Current regulations enumerate factors which, at a minimum, the contractor has to consider in making separate utilization analyses for minorities and women. The contractor has to analyze the immediate labor area, as well as the availability of appropriately skilled minorities or women "in an area in which the contractor can reasonably recruit."[35] The contractor is likewise expected to consider possibilities for training.

The regulations stipulate that determinations of a contractor's compliance status are not to be based solely on whether or not the contractor achieves goals and meets timetables:

> Rather, each contractor's compliance posture shall be reviewed and determined by reviewing the contents of its program, the extent of its adherence to this program, and its good faith efforts to make its program work toward the realization of the program's goals within the timetables set for completion.[36]

---

[32]For a brief discussion of the circumstances surrounding the issuance of Order No. 4, see Graham, *The Civil Rights Era,* p. 342-343.

[33]U.S. Dept. of Labor. "Title 41—Public Contracts and Property Management." *Federal Register,* v. 36, Dec. 4, 1971. p. 23152.

[34]41 C.F.R. 60-2.10

[35]41 C.F.R. 60-2.11. In analyzing the immediate labor area, the contractor has to consider factors such as the "percentage of the minority [or female] work force as compared with the total work force in the immediate labor area" and the "general availability of minorities [or women] having requisite skills in the immediate labor area."

[36]41 C.F.R. 60-2.15

Contractors failing to comply with the regulations risk cancellation of their Government contracts.

Many argue that the endorsement of goals and timetables for minority and female employment marked a significant change in Federal equal employment opportunity requirements. According to sociologist Nathan Glazer:

> When color consciousness became a matter of setting statistical goals for employment, many involved in the fight against discrimination began to realize that something quite radical had happened.[37]

Numerical goals are often compared to quotas. In a 1981 statement on affirmative action, the U.S. Civil Rights Commission argued that goals and quotas are distinct concepts. It distinguished goals, which it defined as "means for assessing progress under an affirmative action plan," from quotas, which it described as "measures ... that some, but not all, plans use to reach these goals."[38] In the view of Glazer and others, however, goals and quotas are, for practical purposes, indistinguishable.

In 1971, the Civil Service Commission authorized the use of employment goals and timetables by Federal agencies, at their discretion. According to the CSC directive:

> Employment goals and timetables should be established ... in those organizations and localities and in those occupations and grade levels where minority employment is not what should reasonably be expected in view of the potential supply of qualified members of minority groups in the work force and in the recruiting area and available opportunities within the organization.[39]

By 1973, women were also officially covered by the directive.[40]

---

[37]Glazer, Nathan. *Ethnic Dilemmas, 1964-1982.* Cambridge, Mass., Harvard University Press, 1983. p. 160-161.

[38]*Affirmative Action in the 1980s,* p. 34. The Supreme Court has also distinguished between goals and quotas (see section below on judicial pronouncements on affirmative action).

[39]Robert Hampton, Chairman, U.S. Civil Service Commission, Memorandum for Heads of Departments and Agencies, May 11, 1971 (unpublished). Quoted in Rosenbloom, David H. "The Federal Affirmative-Action Policy." In Nachmias, David, ed. *The Practice of Policy Evaluation.* New York, St. Martin's Press, 1980. p. 171.

[40]Responsibility for the Federal equal employment opportunity program was subsequently transferred to the EEOC, which for a time required the use of numerical goals and timetables in certain cases of minority and female underrepresentation. EEOC regulations issued in 1987, however, changed this policy; they "permitted but no longer required agencies to utilize numerical goals." Kellough, J. Edward. "Affirmative Action in Government Employment." *Annals of the American Academy of Political and Social Science,* v. 523, Sept. 1992. p. 124.

Equal Employment Legislation

Since passage of the 1964 Civil Rights Act, Congress has enacted a number of provisions to proscribe various forms of employment discrimination and to promote equal employment opportunity. Some key provisions are summarized here.

In 1972, Congress enacted the Equal Employment Opportunity Act[41] to amend Title VII of the Civil Rights Act of 1964. The act expanded the powers of the EEOC. If the EEOC's efforts to conciliate private employment cases failed, it could bring civil actions in Federal court. The act also redefined "person" (whom the EEOC was empowered "to prevent ... from engaging in any unlawful employment practice"[42]) to include State and local governments and agencies.[43] Any civil actions against such entities, however, had to be brought by the Justice Department.

The Equal Employment Opportunity Act added to Title VII a new section 717, which forbade discrimination in Federal employment on the basis of race, color, religion, sex, or national origin. Section 717 required each executive branch agency to develop "a national and regional equal employment opportunity plan ... in order to maintain an affirmative program of equal employment opportunity." The plans, which were to include employee training and education programs, were to be submitted to the CSC (later, the EEOC) for annual review and approval.[44]

The Rehabilitation Act of 1973, as amended,[45] contains provisions to enhance employment opportunities for people with disabilities. Section 501(b) requires each executive branch agency to submit "an affirmative action program plan for the hiring, placement, and advancement of individuals with disabilities."[46] Under Section 503(a), Federal contractors are similarly required to "take affirmative action to employ and advance in employment qualified individuals with disabilities."[47]

---

[41]P.L. 92-261, Mar. 24, 1972, 86 Stat. 103, 42 U.S.C. 2000e *et seq.*

[42]86 Stat. 104, 42 U.S.C. 2000e-5(a)

[43]86 Stat. 103, 42 U.S.C. 2000e(a)

[44]86 Stat. 111-112 (CSC); 42 U.S.C. 2000e-16(b) (EEOC)

[45]P.L. 93-112, Sept. 26, 1973, 87 Stat. 355, 29 U.S.C. (various sections)

[46]29 U.S.C. 791(b)

[47]29 U.S.C. 793(a)

The Civil Service Reform Act of 1978[48] directed the Office of Personnel Management (OPM)[49] to establish a minority recruitment program. As part of the program, each executive branch agency was to "conduct a continuing program for the recruitment of members of minorities ... in a manner designed to eliminate underrepresentation of minorities in the various categories of civil service employment [such as GS grade or occupation] within the Federal service."[50] The act defined a minority group as underrepresented when its members constituted a smaller percentage of a category of civil service employment than of the national civilian labor force. The EEOC, which assumed responsibility for the Federal equal employment opportunity program in 1979,[51] was to establish guidelines for implementing the minority recruitment program.

The Americans with Disabilities Act of 1990, as amended,[52] broadly prohibits discrimination on the basis of disability. It bans discrimination by covered employers in "job application procedures, the hiring, advancement, or discharge of employees, employee compensation, job training, and other terms, conditions, and privileges of employment."[53]

The Civil Rights Act of 1991[54] sought to counter the effects of nine Supreme Court decisions that had restricted the scope of Federal protections against employment discrimination. Reversing the 1989 Supreme Court ruling in *Patterson* v. *McLean Credit Union*,[55] the Civil Rights Act prohibits racial discrimination in all phases of the making and enforcement of contracts. In

---

[48]P.L. 95-454, Oct. 13, 1978, 92 Stat. 1111, 5 U.S.C. (various sections)

[49]Effective January 1, 1979, the CSC's personnel management functions were transferred to the newly created OPM, and the CSC was redesignated as the Merit Systems Protection Board. U.S. President, 1977-1981 (Carter). Executive Order 12107, "Federal Civil Service Reorganization; Relating to the Civil Service Commission and Labor-Management in the Federal Service," Dec. 28, 1978. *Weekly Compilation of Presidential Documents,* v. 14, Jan. 1, 1979. p. 2292.

[50]92 Stat. 1152, 5 U.S.C. 7201(c)(1)

[51]U.S. President, 1977-1981 (Carter). Executive Order 12106, "Equal Employment Opportunity Enforcement; Transfer of Certain Equal Employment Enforcement Functions," Dec. 28, 1978. *Weekly Compilation of Presidential Documents,* v. 14, Jan. 1, 1979. p. 2290.

[52]P.L. 101-336, July 26, 1990, 104 Stat. 327, 42 U.S.C. 12101 *et seq.*

[53]104 Stat. 331-332, 42 U.S.C. 12112(a)

[54]P.L. 102-166, Nov. 21, 1991, 105 Stat. 1071

[55]491 U.S. 164 (1989)

response to a second 1989 Court decision, *Wards Cove Packing Co.* v. *Atonio*,[56] the act returns to employers the burden of proving that seemingly neutral employment practices that have a "disparate impact" on women and minorities are job-related and consistent with business necessity. Among its other provisions, the Civil Rights Act of 1991 enables victims of intentional discrimination based on sex, religion, or disability to recover previously unavailable compensatory and punitive damages.

The Civil Rights Act of 1991 ignited a national debate about quotas. The Bush Administration maintained that the bill, as introduced, would force employers to adopt numerical hiring and promotion quotas for women and minorities in order to avoid potential lawsuits. President Bush had vetoed a similar 1990 civil rights bill. Citing explicit anti-quota language in the 1990 and 1991 bills, proponents rejected the contention that the legislation would encourage institution of quotas.[57] President Bush signed a compromise version of the 1991 Civil Rights Act in November 1991. In his signing statement, the President described the measure as "historic legislation [which] strengthens the barriers and sanctions against employment discrimination." On the subject of quotas, he said, "This law will not lead to quotas, which are inconsistent with equal opportunity and merit-based hiring; nor does it create incentives for needless litigation."[58]

Judicial Pronouncements on Affirmative Action in Employment

The task of determining the permissible scope of affirmative action in employment has often fallen to the Supreme Court. Since the 1970s, the Court has heard challenges to programs designed to promote opportunities for women and minorities through the use of preferences, goals, and quotas. These affirmative action programs can be classified into two broad categories: court-ordered measures imposed to remedy violations of Federal law or the Constitution; and measures voluntarily adopted by public and private employers.[59]

---

[56]490 U.S. 642 (1989)

[57]See Cooper, Mary. "Racial Quotas." *Congressional Quarterly Researcher,* v. 1, May 17, 1991. p. 288, 290-293.

[58]U.S. President, 1989-1993 (Bush). "Statement on Signing the Civil Rights Act of 1991," Nov. 21, 1991. *Weekly Compilation of Presidential Documents,* v. 27, Nov. 25, 1991. p. 1701.

[59]The following discussion is based, in large part, on U.S. Library of Congress. Congressional Research Service. *Affirmative Action Revisited: A Review of Recent Supreme Court Actions.* Report No. 90-539 A, by Charles V. Dale and Kevin B. Greely. Nov. 2, 1990. Washington, 1990; also see Brooks, Roy L. "The New Law of Affirmative Action." *Labor Law Journal,* v. 40, Oct. 1989. Please note that several cases currently under consideration by the Supreme Court may change the law of affirmative action.

Court-Ordered Affirmative Action

The validity of judicially imposed affirmative action was addressed by the Supreme Court in 1986 in *Local 28, Sheet Metal Workers* v. *EEOC*.[60] By a vote of five to four, the Court upheld a Federal district court order reinstating a nonwhite membership goal of 29 percent for a union that had persistently refused to admit blacks. A plurality of Justices held that in cases of "persistent or egregious" discrimination, Title VII does not preclude race-conscious affirmative action remedies that benefit individuals who are not themselves identified victims of discrimination. The plurality opinion also noted the temporary and flexible nature of the membership goal. It characterized the numerical goal as a "benchmark" against which to measure the union's efforts, as opposed to a "strict racial quota" designed to achieve racial balance.

The following term, the Court again upheld a judicial affirmative action plan by a five-to-four vote, in *United States* v. *Paradise*.[61] It ruled that temporary one-black-for-one-white promotion quotas imposed by a district court on Alabama State troopers did not violate the Equal Protection Clause of the Fourteenth Amendment. The plurality opinion stated that the "narrowly tailored" quota was justified in view of the Government's "compelling interest" in both remedying the State's persistent discrimination against blacks and forcing State compliance with court orders. One component of the "narrowly tailored" requirement—and a recurrent issue in affirmative action cases—is the burden that race- or gender-conscious measures place on innocent nonbeneficiaries. The *Paradise* plurality determined that the burden imposed on whites was acceptable, since the quota postponed, but did not prevent, their advancement.

Voluntary Affirmative Action Programs

In *Wygant* v. *Jackson Board of Education*,[62] the Court considered an affirmative action plan voluntarily adopted by a public (State) employer. The 1986 case concerned a collective bargaining agreement between a school board and a teachers' union that gave hiring preferences and layoff protection to minority teachers. The plan was challenged as a violation of the Equal Protection Clause by a group of white teachers who had been laid off, while minority teachers with less seniority had been permitted to retain their positions.

The Court ruled that the minority layoff provision was unconstitutional. The plurality opinion cited the lack of evidence that the school board had discriminated, holding that general societal discrimination was insufficient to

---

[60] 478 U. S. 421 (1986)

[61] 480 U.S. 149 (1987)

[62] 476 U. S. 267 (1986)

justify race-based preferences. The plurality also found that the plan was not "narrowly tailored," since it imposed too heavy a burden on particular individuals.

When evaluating voluntary affirmative action plans adopted by employers to comply with Title VII of the Civil Rights Act, the Supreme Court has applied a different set of standards than in *Wygant,* a constitutional case. *United Steelworkers* v. *Weber* (1979)[63] concerned a voluntary affirmative action plan agreed to by the Kaiser Aluminum & Chemical Corporation, a private company, and the United Steelworkers of America. The plan sought to reserve 50 percent of openings in an in-plant craft training program for black employees, until the percentage of black skilled craft workers at the plant roughly approximated the level of blacks in the local labor force. Blacks, who represented 39 percent of the local labor force, held less than two percent of skilled jobs at the plant. Under the plan, separate seniority lists were compiled for white and black employees. A suit was filed by a white worker at Kaiser who had not been accepted into the training program, although he had more seniority than some of the black employees chosen.

The Court, in a five-to-two decision, ruled that the plan was a permissible remedy for "manifest racial imbalance in traditionally segregated job categories." The opinion addressed the issue of "whether Title VII *forbids* private employers and unions from voluntarily agreeing upon bona fide affirmative plans that accord racial preferences in the manner and for the purpose provided in the Kaiser-USWA plan" and decided that it did not. The Court found the plan to be consistent with Title VII's objective of opening up traditionally unavailable employment opportunities to blacks. At the same time, according to the Court, the plan was a temporary measure that did not "unnecessarily trammel the interests of white employees."[64]

The Court revisited the permissibility of affirmative action plans adopted under Title VII in a 1987 case, *Johnson* v. *Transportation Agency of Santa Clara County, California.*[65] In that case, the Court reviewed a voluntary program under which a public agency had promoted a qualified woman to road dispatcher over a somewhat-better-qualified male applicant. The agency's affirmative action plan permitted the consideration of race or gender as a factor in the promotion process, provided that there was proof of underrepresentation in a traditionally segregated job category. In the skilled craft worker category at issue in the case, women did not hold any of the 238 positions. The plan was

---

[63]443 U. S. 193 (1979)

[64]See Bell, Derrick A., Jr. *Race, Racism and American Law,* Second Edition. Boston, Little, Brown and Company, 1980. p. 647-651.

[65]480 U. S. 616 (1987)

flexible and did not include numerical quotas. The unsuccessful male applicant challenged the plan as a violation of Title VII.[66]

By a vote of six to three, the Justices ruled that the plan did not violate Title VII. Applying the *Weber* standard of "manifest imbalance," the Court concluded that the county agency's consideration of gender in the promotion process was a permissible way of addressing female underrepresentation. The Court noted that the measure did not unnecessarily trammel the rights of male employees nor bar their advancement.

II. THE DEBATE OVER AFFIRMATIVE ACTION IN EMPLOYMENT

Among academics and policymakers as well as the general public, there exists a wide spectrum of opinion on affirmative action in employment. This debate encompasses views on the need and rationale for affirmative action, questions about fairness, and assessments of the benefits and costs of affirmative action programs. The first section of this chapter presents arguments for and against affirmative action in employment as it is currently practiced. The second section describes the findings of public opinion polls.

---

[66]The plan was not challenged on equal protection grounds.

The Cases For and Against Affirmative Action

Much of the scholarly discussion of affirmative action has centered around minority groups, especially black Americans. As a consequence, the arguments presented below explicitly concern affirmative action in employment for black Americans and, in some cases, members of other minority groups. Some of the arguments, however, are likewise applicable to nonminority women. It should be noted that not all supporters or critics of affirmative action in employment necessarily agree with every pro or con argument included here.[67]

Rationale for Affirmative Action in Employment

Pro Arguments

- Affirmative action is deserved compensation for past injustice.
- Affirmative action is needed to combat the present effects of past discrimination.
- Affirmative action is a constitutional means to promote equality of opportunity.

Con Arguments

- Affirmative action cannot compensate for past injustice.
- Affirmative action is no longer needed to assure fair treatment of minorities.
- Affirmative action violates the constitutional guarantee of equal protection of the laws.

---

[67]Moreover, at least one scholar characterized here as an affirmative action supporter (Randall Kennedy) has been portrayed elsewhere as a critic. A 1991 article in *Chronicle of Higher Education* described Kennedy as a "new black dissenter" on affirmative action, citing his approach of weighing the costs and benefits of affirmative action in different settings. See Magner, Denise K. "Black Intellectuals Broaden Debate on Effects of Affirmative Action." *Chronicle of Higher Education*, v. 38, Oct. 16, 1991. p. A22-A23.

Supporters of affirmative action characterize it as "modest compensation"[68] for generations of past injustice. They argue that affirmative action remains necessary in light of the current economic and social situation of minorities, which, they believe, reflects the effects of past discrimination, among other factors. Proponents further contend that without affirmative action, discriminatory employment practices would likely increase and opportunities for women and minorities would narrow.

Critics respond that affirmative action can never compensate for historic injustices. And in the view of Shelby Steele, an English professor, it "indirectly encourages blacks to exploit their own past victimization as a source of power and privilege," rather than "look to present achievements."[69] Critics of affirmative action argue that the lower economic status of various minority groups may be due to many factors other than discrimination. As such, according to Nathan Glazer, identifying discrimination as "*the* cause of the economic differences between groups, even when it is extensive and pervasive, is a gross oversimplification."[70] Affirmative action opponents maintain that in the absence of preferential policies, minorities would receive fair, nondiscriminatory treatment. To ensure such nondiscriminatory treatment, some critics would favor enforcement measures, such as close monitoring of institutions.

Opponents further charge that affirmative action violates the constitutional guarantee of equal protection of the laws, by permitting discrimination based on race and ethnic origin. They argue that in making race and ethnic affiliation increasingly important, affirmative action programs betray the constitutional ideal of color blindness.

In response, Randall Kennedy, a law professor, argues that the colorblind theory of the Constitution is not the only way to interpret the Fourteenth Amendment's Equal Protection Clause. He offers the following reading of the Supreme Court decision in *Brown* v. *Board of Education in Topeka, Kansas,* and subsequent cases:

> *Brown* and its progeny do not stand for the abstract principle that governmental distinctions based on race are unconstitutional. Rather, those great cases, forged by the gritty particularities of the struggle against white racism, stand for the proposition that the Constitution prohibits any arrangements imposing racial subjugation—whether

---

[68]Kennedy, Randall. "Persuasion and Distrust." In Nieli, Russell, ed. *Racial Preference and Racial Justice.* Washington, Ethics and Public Policy Center, 1991. p. 51.

[69]Steele, Shelby. *The Content of Our Character.* New York, St. Martin's Press, 1990. p. 118.

[70]Glazer, *Ethnic Dilemmas*, p. 176.

> such arrangements are ostensibly race-neutral or even ostensibly race-blind.[71]

Rejecting the view that affirmative action programs aim to increase the importance of race and ethnicity in American society, supporters maintain that such programs seek to do the exact opposite—to reduce the degree of racial and ethnic consciousness.

Fairness of Affirmative Action

Pro Arguments

- Whites have historically enjoyed unfair employment advantages.

- Giving minorities some temporary advantage is fair.

Con Arguments

- Affirmative action unfairly harms individuals who are not guilty of discrimination.

- Affirmative action undermines the principle of merit selection.

Objections to affirmative action in employment are often raised on fairness grounds. Critics charge that preferential policies unfairly deny opportunities to individual white males who are not guilty of discrimination. According to Glazer, this practice amounts to "'reverse discrimination,' because the point of setting a goal is that one will hire more of one group, less of another, simply because individuals are members of one group or another."[72] More generally, Glazer maintains that group-based preferential treatment serves to undermine individual rights:

> The outrage an American feels when he (or she) is deprived of a job or a promotion because of his race or ethnic background is no less when that person is white than when he (or she) is black, or yellow, or brown.[73]

Affirmative action proponents reject the notion that the injury done to white males by preferential policies can be equated with the harm inflicted on black people by racial discrimination. According to English professor Stanley Fish:

---

[71]Kennedy, "Persuasion and Distrust," p. 54.

[72]Glazer, *Ethnic Dilemmas,* p. 161. [73]Ibid., p. 177.

> [B]lacks have not simply been treated unfairly; they have been subjected first to decades of slavery, and then to decades of second-class citizenship, widespread legalized discrimination, economic persecution, educational deprivation, and cultural stigmatization.[74]

Supporters defend affirmative action as being just. They argue that for years white workers were unjustly advantaged by discrimination against blacks. They maintain that fairness requires that discrimination against blacks and advantages for whites be ended. More controversially, they argue that it is fair to temporarily give blacks an advantage in the form of preferential employment policies. In Fish's view, "[T]he belated gift of 'fairness' in the form of a resolution no longer to discriminate against them [blacks] legally is hardly an adequate remedy for the deep disadvantages that the prior discrimination has produced."[75]

Opponents of affirmative action often invoke the experience of European immigrants who came to this country in search of greater opportunities. Russell Nieli traces the development of a "peculiarly American work and achievement ethic" during the immigrant influx after the Civil War. He describes the ethic and the role it played as follows:

> [T]he view that human beings are to be judged by their own characteristics and their own achievements, and not by their ethnic-tribal affiliations ... was a powerful ideal that generally had at least some effect in shaping people's attitudes and actions.[76]

In accordance with such an ethic, affirmative action critics argue that employment decisions should be based on colorblind merit selection, not group membership. It is a commonly held belief among opponents that affirmative action as currently practiced results in the hiring of unqualified members of minority groups.

Merit, in the view of affirmative action backers, has not traditionally determined the allocation of opportunities. They cite a range of other factors, including personal associations, social background, and ethnicity, that have often been key to employment decisions. Moreover, they argue that the historical exclusion of blacks from employment opportunities because of their race was a blatant violation of the merit principle. At the same time, affirmative action supporters maintain that they do not advocate the abandonment of merit or the mandated hiring of unqualified applicants. They reject the idea that affirmative

---

[74]Fish, Stanley. "Reverse Racism or How the Pot Got to Call the Kettle Black." *Atlantic Monthly*, v. 272, Nov. 1993. p. 130.

[75]Ibid.

[76]Nieli, Russell. "Ethnic Tribalism and Human Personhood." In Nieli, Russell, ed. *Racial Preference and Racial Justice.* Washington, Ethics and Public Policy Center, 1991. p. 79.

action and ability are mutually exclusively. Rather, they take the following position, as stated by Ira Glasser of the American Civil Liberties Union:

> [T]he rules should be the same for blacks as they have always been for whites. Standards should not be raised to higher levels when measuring black applicants. Merit should not be invoked in a new way to make it harder to end discrimination.[77]

Effects of Affirmative Action

Pro Arguments

- Affirmative action has opened up employment opportunities for minorities.
- Affirmative action helps eradicate racial stereotypes.
- Affirmative action produces role models, who serve as examples of opportunity.
- Affirmative action encourages the development of skills.

Con Arguments

- Affirmative action has not helped the underclass.
- Affirmative action stigmatizes recipients and provokes resentment on the part of nonbeneficiaries.
- Affirmative action engenders self-doubt in recipients.
- Affirmative action reduces incentives to work hard and perform well.

Much of the recent debate about affirmative action in employment has focused on benefits and costs. Supporters argue that affirmative action policies have succeeded in opening up opportunities for minorities in professional and blue-collar occupations. Critics counter that such policies have done little to improve the economic situation of those most in need and have, in fact, served to distract attention from their pressing problems.[78]

Advocates believe that affirmative action helps undermine racial stereotypes to the general benefit of society, by showing that blacks can perform jobs competently.

---

[77] Glasser, Ira. "Affirmative Action and the Legacy of Racial Injustice." In Katz, Phyllis A., and Dalmas A. Taylor, eds. *Eliminating Racism.* New York, Plenum Press, 1988. p. 350.

[78] The economic impact of affirmative action policies is discussed more fully in the next chapter.

By contrast, critics maintain that preferential hiring stigmatizes its beneficiaries by marking them as less capable, and as a consequence, leads co-workers to doubt the qualifications of all people hired under affirmative action programs. Far from eradicating stereotypes, critics argue, affirmative action serves to sustain them. According to Russell Nieli, "The inevitable effect of race- and ethnic-conscious hiring policies is to legitimate ethnic and racial stereotyping both as a way of thinking and as a manner of human beings relating to one another."[79] Glazer maintains that such policies necessarily arouse resentment on the part of those not in the beneficiary groups, creating tension in the workplace and the larger society.

Critics further argue that affirmative action leads its beneficiaries to doubt their own abilities and to question whether they have truly earned their positions. In their view, this self-doubt can have devastating effects. According to Shelby Steele:

> The effect of preferential treatment—the lowering of normal standards to increase black representation—puts blacks at war with an expanded realm of debilitating doubt, so that the doubt itself becomes an unrecognized preoccupation that undermines their ability to perform, especially in integrated situations.[80]

Supporters offer various responses to these stigma arguments. While many supporters allow that affirmative action does have some stigmatizing effect, they argue that such effects are limited mainly to professional occupations that require specialized training. The issue of qualifications, they maintain, is largely irrelevant to jobs requiring little or no prior training. More fundamentally, they argue that whites were discounting the abilities of blacks long before the advent of affirmative action. Proponents contend that *this* long-standing stigma, and the employment exclusion that supported it, was, in fact, a key reason why affirmative action was originally devised. Randall Kennedy seeks to resolve the stigma dilemma by weighing the stigmatization caused by affirmative action against the stigmatization that he believes affirmative action helps undermine. In his words:

> In the end, the uncertain extent to which affirmative action diminishes the accomplishments of blacks must be balanced against the stigmatization that occurs when blacks are virtually absent from important institutions in the society.[81]

Kennedy concludes that the latter stigmatization is worse.

---

[79]Nieli, "Ethnic Tribalism and Human Personhood," p. 87.

[80]Steele, *The Content of Our Character*, p. 117-118.

[81]Kennedy, "Persuasion and Distrust," p. 50.

Supporters reject the idea that beneficiaries of affirmative action commonly suffer self-doubt. They argue that in most cases, members of minority groups applying for jobs will assume that, if given the opportunity, they would be able to perform the jobs. "And," according to Ira Glasser, "they will perceive affirmative action goals as necessary to give them a fair chance...."[82] Supporters of affirmative action also identify a double standard under which only minority group members who receive preferences are said to experience self-doubt. As Philip Green has stated:

> Clearly implicit in this standard critique of affirmative action, is a notion that whereas it's never painful to be rewarded because you are in the majority or the established elite, it's always painful to be rewarded because you're in the minority, or a marginal group.[83]

Proponents maintain that a key benefit of affirmative action is the creation of valuable role models. They argue that affirmative action recipients provide concrete evidence of opportunity, motivating future generations to succeed. According to Glasser:

> Affirmative action will not today open up opportunities for the poor and the uneducated and the unskilled. But it will change how they look at the world, and it will say, by word and deed, that hard work pays off and that skills matter.[84]

For their part, critics discount the value of role models who achieve their positions through affirmative action. Contrasting "affirmative action role models" with "genuine role models," Nieli writes:

> The role that is actually modeled by affirmative action recipients is that of a patronized black, Hispanic, or female, who is of inferior qualifications in comparison to the best qualified applicant for a job or promotion.... Affirmative action role models ... serve only to perpetuate the prejudiced view that blacks, Hispanics, and women are ... incapable of competing with [Caucasian males] on an equal basis.[85]

Critics likewise reject the idea that affirmative action encourages hard work and skill development. They believe that it does just the opposite. Economist Thomas Sowell asks: "Is the arduous process of acquiring skills and discipline

---

[82]Glasser, "Affirmative Action and the Legacy of Racial Injustice," p. 354.

[83]Green, Philip. "The New Individualism." *Christianity and Crisis,* v. 41, March 30, 1981. p. 79.

[84]Glasser, "Affirmative Action and the Legacy of Racial Injustice," p. 356.

[85]Nieli, "Ethnic Tribalism and Human Personhood," p. 89.

supposed to be endured for years by people who are told, by word and deed, that skills are not the real issue?"[86]

Public Opinion

In an effort to discern public opinion on affirmative action in employment, pollsters have posed a variety of questions over the last several years.[87] A June 1991 NBC News/*Wall Street Journal* Poll asked, "All in all, do you favor or oppose affirmative action programs in business for blacks and other minority groups?" A majority of those polled (59 percent) said that they favored such programs, while 29 percent opposed them. The percentage of blacks expressing support was 82 percent, compared to 55 percent of whites. A survey conducted from July to September 1994 by L.H. Research for the National Conference of Christians and Jews found that 55 percent of white respondents supported affirmative action programs in hiring and promotion, while 31 percent opposed such programs. The percentages among black respondents were 71 percent and 20 percent, respectively.

Higher levels of public support have been expressed for Federal affirmative action policies that explicitly exclude quotas. A July 1991 Harris Survey found that 70 percent of all respondents favored "federal laws requiring affirmative action programs for women and minorities in employment and in education, provided there are no rigid quotas." Twenty-four percent opposed such laws.

Since the specific nature of the "affirmative action programs" at issue in the above poll questions was not specified, it is unclear what types of programs enjoy majority support. A Harris Survey of May 1991 identified at least one apparently acceptable form of affirmative action. More than three out of four people polled agreed that "[a]s long as there are no rigid quotas, it makes sense to give special training and advice to women and minorities so that they can perform better on the job."[88]

---

[86]Sowell, Thomas. "Black Progress Can't Be Legislated." *The Washington Post,* Aug. 12, 1984. p. B4.

[87]In interpreting this polling data, keep in mind that polls capture opinion at one particular point in time. Results of public opinion polls may vary considerably from one year or one month to the next. In addition, it is important to consider the way in which questions are worded, since, by framing an issue in a particular way, wording can influence responses. Most of the poll questions discussed here are contained in U.S. Library of Congress. Congressional Research Service. *Race Issues in the United States: National Public Opinion Polls (January 1988-March 1992).* Report No. 92-428 GOV, by Marc A. Aubin. May 9, 1992. Washington, 1992. Most of the polls, along with additional information about the surveys, can also be found in the POLLS database file on the Library of Congress's SCORPIO system.

[88]The percentages were 78 percent for all respondents, 85 percent for black respondents, and 77 percent for white respondents.

Whatever broad support exists for "affirmative action programs" and "special training and advice," however, does not extend to "hiring preferences." The June 1991 NBC News/*Wall Street Journal* Poll cited above, which found 59 percent overall support for affirmative action programs in business, also asked the following question:

> Do you think blacks and other minorities should or should not receive hiring preference to make up for past discrimination against them?

Eighteen percent of all respondents thought that minorities should receive such preferences, while 78 percent said that they should not. The "should/should not" split was 12 percent/84 percent among whites. Blacks were more evenly divided, with 51 percent supporting hiring preferences and 42 percent opposing them.

A June 1994 poll conducted by the ICR Survey Research Group for the Associated Press posed a similar question:

> Do you think blacks and other minorities should receive preference in hiring to make up for past inequalities, or not?

Seventeen percent of all respondents said that minorities should receive hiring preference, compared to 80 percent who said that they should not. Among whites, 12 percent supported minority hiring preferences and 86 percent opposed them. Among black respondents, 46 percent supported such preferences and 50 percent opposed them.

In addition, when given a choice between "preferential treatment" or "ability" as the basis for allocating opportunities, the public clearly favors ability. A June 1991 Gallup Poll asked:

> Some people say that to make up for past discrimination, women and members of minority groups should be given preferential treatment in getting jobs and places in college. Others say that their ability, as determined in test scores, should be the main consideration. Which point of view comes closer to how you feel on the subject?

Eighty-one percent of respondents said that test scores should be the main consideration, compared to 11 percent who believed that women and minorities should receive preferential treatment.[89] While percentages varied among whites and blacks, majorities of both groups (84 percent of whites; 60 percent of blacks) favored reliance on test scores over preferential treatment.

---

[89]Responses to this question have been very consistent over time. When asked in a March 1977 Gallup survey, for example, 83 percent of respondents chose test scores and 10 percent chose preferential treatment. See Gallup, George, Jr., and Dr. Frank Newport. "Blacks and Whites Differ on Civil Rights Progress." *The Gallup Poll Monthly,* no. 311, Aug. 1991. p. 55-56.

The findings of a March 1993 poll by the *New York Times* suggest that a greater percentage of the public, although not a majority, may be supportive of preferential employment policies specifically linked to past discriminatory behavior. Surveyed about whether they believed blacks should receive preference in hiring or promotion today "where there has been job discrimination against blacks in the past," 33 percent of respondents said "yes," 53 percent said "no," and 7 percent said (volunteered) that it depended.

As with affirmative action, higher levels of support for preferences were registered in response to a question which concerned government action and which stipulated that there would be no strict quotas. The question, in the July 1991 Harris Survey, read:

> Do you favor or oppose federal laws requiring racial preference for minorities in employment and education, provided there are no rigid quotas?

Respondents were nearly evenly split with 46 percent favoring such preferences and 48 percent opposing them.

Need for Affirmative Action

The May 1991 Harris Survey found that a majority of the public perceived a need for affirmative action programs to combat discrimination. Respondents were asked whether they tended to agree or disagree with the following statement:

> If there are no affirmative action programs helping women and minorities in employment and education, then these groups will continue to fail to get their share of jobs and higher education, thereby continuing past discrimination in the future.

Sixty-one percent of those polled agreed with the statement, while 36 percent disagreed. Among black respondents, the respective percentages were 76 percent and 23 percent, and among whites, 58 percent and 39 percent.

In a March 1991 NBC News/*Wall Street Journal* Poll, respondents were asked which of two statements about affirmative action came closer to their point of view. Sixty-one percent selected the following: "Affirmative action programs are still needed to counteract the effects of discrimination against minorities, and are a good idea as long as there are no rigid quotas." The remaining 28 percent making a choice believed, instead, that "[a]ffirmative action programs have gone too far in favoring minorities, and should be phased out because they unfairly discriminate against whites."

Fairness Issue

The fairness of affirmative action has been addressed more directly in other survey questions. The May 1991 Harris Survey asked respondents whether they tended to agree or disagree with the following statement about affirmative action programs:

> After years of discrimination, it is only fair to set up special programs to make sure that women and minorities are given every chance to have equal opportunities in employment and education.

Seventy-nine percent of all respondents said they agreed with the statement and 19 percent said they disagreed. Among blacks, 96 percent agreed and 3 percent disagreed with the statement. The percentages among whites were 76 percent and 22 percent, respectively.

Questions about fairness have often focused on the impact of affirmative action on white workers. A December 1990 *New York Times* Poll asked, "When preference in hiring or promotion is given to blacks, do you think that is fair to whites, or not fair to whites?" Twenty-four percent of respondents thought such preferences were fair to whites, 53 percent thought they were unfair, and 17 percent said that it depended. A May-June 1991 poll by ABC News/*Washington Post* posed the following question about the possible adverse effects of minority hiring preferences on whites: "Do you think giving preference in hiring to blacks and other minorities takes jobs unfairly from whites, or not?" Fifty-nine percent answered "yes," while 37 percent said "no." Opinions about the fairness of affirmative action to nonbeneficiaries appear to differ by race. In a September 1991 *Los Angeles Times* Poll, 33 percent of whites and 22 percent of blacks said that they thought affirmative action was often unfair to others.

III. IMPACT STUDIES

Has affirmative action benefitted its recipients? As the pro/con analysis in the previous chapter evidences, this question elicits many—and conflicting—responses. Addressing one aspect of the debate, economists have attempted to determine what, if any, impact affirmative action has had on minority and female employment and wages.

Affirmative Action and Federal Contractors

Since 1966, the EEOC has required that all private firms with 100 or more employees and all Federal contractors with 50 or more employees and with contracts worth at least $50,000 file annual EEO-1 reports, which contain employment and occupational data on women and minorities. As discussed in an earlier chapter, regulations issued by the Labor Department's Office of Federal Contract Compliance Programs (OFCCP) further required that Federal contractors meeting the above requirements develop affirmative action plans that included goals and timetables.

Employment Effects

Using EEO-1 reports filed by the same 68,690 firms for 1974 and 1980, Jonathan Leonard sought to assess the impact of affirmative action by comparing changes in the employment of women and minorities among contractors (subject to OFCCP regulations) and noncontractors. "If affirmative action is effective," he reasoned, "I expect the rate of change of protected groups' employment share to be higher in contractor establishments than in non-contractor establishments...."[90] Leonard found that the employment share of black men, black women, and white women did increase relatively more among contractors than among noncontractors during the period. For black men and black women, this relationship held true when he employed multivariate analysis and controlled for other factors, such as establishment size, industry, and region.[91] Leonard also investigated the importance of compliance reviews, in which the OFCCP audits a contractor's affirmative action program. He found that these reviews had likewise been effective in promoting black employment.

For nonblack minorities and white women, Leonard did not observe consistently greater employment gains at contractor firms than at non-

---

[90]Leonard, Jonathan S. *The Impact of Affirmative Action.* U.S. Department of Labor Report, July 1983. p. 101.

[91]Controlling for, or holding constant, other factors enables the researcher to better estimate the independent effect of the variable of interest (in this case, being a contractor or not being a contractor) on the dependent variable (in this case, the employment of selected groups).

contractor firms across statistical models.[92] He concluded that the "impact of affirmative action on non-black minorities and on white females has been mixed, and is sensitive to the specification of the statistical tests."[93] With respect to white women, Leonard cited their later coverage by affirmative action and the growth in the female labor supply during the period, which may have resulted in the increased employment of women at both contractor and noncontractor firms, as possible explanations for these results.[94]

Leonard also examined how employment changes under the contract compliance program[95] were distributed across occupations. For black males, who registered the greatest overall occupational gains, he discerned some evidence of a pro-skill bias. According to Leonard:

> The contract compliance program has not reduced the demand for black males in low skilled occupations. It has raised the demand for black males more in the highly skilled professional and technical occupations and in white-collar clerical jobs than in the blue-collar operative and laborer occupations.[96]

In other words, black males at all skill levels benefitted, but the highly skilled benefitted most. In addition, Leonard found an increased demand for black women across a range of white- and blue-collar occupations and training programs, and for Hispanic, Asian, and Native American men, in white-collar occupations and in training programs. Of the groups studied,[97] only white women did not share in these occupational gains. Leonard concluded that "with the puzzling exception of white females, affirmative action appears to have contributed to the occupational advance of members of protected groups."[98]

---

[92]In individual models reported in other work, however, he did obtain statistically significant, positive results for these groups. See Leonard, Jonathan S. "The Impact of Affirmative Action on Employment." *Journal of Labor Economics,* v. 2, Oct. 1984. p. 451.

[93]Leonard, *The Impact of Affirmative Action,* p. 385.

[94]See Leonard, Jonathan S. "The Impact of Affirmative Action Regulation and Equal Employment Law," June 1986. In *A Report of the Study Group on Affirmative Action to the Committee on Education and Labor,* U.S. House of Representatives. Committee Print, 100th Cong., 1st Sess. Washington, U.S. Govt. Print. Off., 1987. p. 269.

[95]Contract compliance program, as used in this discussion of Leonard's research, refers to the combined effects of being a contractor and undergoing a compliance review.

[96]Leonard, *The Impact of Affirmative Action,* p. 131-132.

[97]Leonard did not study the occupational advance of nonblack minority women.

[98]Leonard, *The Impact of Affirmative Action,* p. 135.

Authors of four earlier studies of affirmative action under the contract compliance program had reported weaker employment effects than did Leonard. Analyzing EEO-1 report data for different years within the 1966-1973 period, these economists generally found a positive significant relationship between contractor status and black male employment, as did Leonard. Yet, unlike Leonard, they found no evidence that black females made significant employment gains, or that any group registered occupational advances, under the contract compliance program. Only one of the three studies that investigated compliance reviews concluded that they were effective in promoting the employment of any beneficiary group.[99] Leonard suggested that timing helped explain the weaker findings of these earlier studies:

> These past studies are all based on data for a period that largely predates the beginning of substantial enforcement of regulations barring sex discrimination, the start of aggressive enforcement in the mid seventies, and the major reorganization of the contract compliance agencies into the OFCCP in 1978.[100]

James P. Smith and Finis Welch examined employment effects over the 1966-1980 period using information from EEO-1 reports and national employment data from the Current Population Survey. They explained their test of affirmative action's effectiveness, as follows:

> If affirmative action is effective and is adequately enforced, we anticipate that minority representation should expand more among firms that are required to report to the EEOC than among firms which are not. In addition, since federal contractors have more to lose, we also expect that the greatest relative gains will occur among EEO-1-reporting firms that are federal contractors.[101]

Smith and Welch found that the percentage of black workers, particularly black "officials and managers," employed at EEOC-covered firms increased greatly between 1966 and 1980.[102] Total employment gains for black women exceeded those for black men. The increase in black employment between 1970 and 1980 was concentrated at firms with Federal contracts.[103]

---

[99]For a review of these studies, see Ibid., p. 34-41.

[100]Leonard, "The Impact of Affirmative Action Regulation and Equal Employment Law," p. 264.

[101]Smith, James P., and Finis Welch. "Affirmative Action and Labor Markets." *Journal of Labor Economics*, v. 2, April 1984. p. 276.

[102]Please note that Smith and Welch did not use multivariate analysis, and therefore did not control for other variables that might have explained the employment changes they observed.

[103]Smith and Welch used data on contractor status beginning in 1970, rather than 1966, due to an error in the 1966 data.

According to the study, the percentage of white men at EEOC-covered firms fell during the 1966-1980 period. The percentage of white women working at covered firms also decreased, but to a lesser extent than white men. Among those white women employed, there was a shift from noncontractor firms to contractor firms during the 1970-1980 years. In addition, Smith and Welch reported that after 1970, white female "officials and managers" were more likely to be employed at contractor firms than at noncontractor firms.

On timing, Smith and Welch reported that the greatest growth in total black employment at covered firms occurred in the early years of affirmative action, between 1966 and 1970. They found that growth continued at a slower pace until 1974, at which time the proportion of black men in covered employment began to decline and the proportion of black women leveled off. The researchers had not expected to find such a trend, in light of "the limited financial and manpower resources available to [the EEOC and OFCC] during the 1960s, the inability of the EEOC to initiate suits before 1972, and the small volume of early litigation in the courts."[104] It raised concerns for them about the reliability of data in EEO-1 reports, although it did not lead them to dismiss their basic findings. They concluded:

> One can believe that affirmative action shifted black employment toward monitored firms and still register some skepticism about the magnitude of changes suggested by EEO-1 reports.[105]

Wage Effects

Employment shifts like those discussed above are not necessarily accompanied by increased wages. As Dave and June O'Neill explain, "Gains in employment of a minority group may reflect only a reshuffling from noncontractors to contractors without any relative wage gain."[106] Thus, the question arises as to whether affirmative action has increased the earnings of minorities and women. While there seems to be general agreement that nonwhite workers experienced real wage gains, relative to white workers, following passage of the Civil Rights Act of 1964, researchers disagree as to the causes of this improvement.[107]

---

[104]Smith and Welch, "Affirmative Action and Labor Markets," p. 276.

[105]Ibid., p. 289.

[106]O'Neill, Dave M., and June O'Neill. "Affirmative Action in the Labor Market." *Annals of the American Academy of Political and Social Science,* v. 523, Sept. 1992. p. 94.

[107]See Heckman, James J., and Brook S. Payner. "Determining the Impact of Federal Antidiscrimination Policy on the Economic Status of Blacks: A Study of South Carolina." *American Economic Review,* v. 79, March 1989. p. 138-139; Freeman, Richard B. "Black Economic Progress After 1964: Who Has Gained and Why?" In Rosen, Sherwin, ed. *Studies in Labor Markets.* Chicago, The University of Chicago Press, 1981. p. 247-248, 269-270.

Richard Freeman and others attribute these gains, in large part, to Federal antidiscrimination policies, including affirmative action. Based on a study of wage, income, and occupational data from the late 1940s through the mid-1970s, Freeman determined that nonwhite workers experienced significantly greater gains in earnings and occupational status (relative to white workers) after 1964 than before 1964.[108] According to his analysis, factors such as past trends in earnings and cyclical conditions could not account for these changes. Freeman argued that the evidence was "consistent with an explanation of black economic gains post-1964 that stresses the role of national antibias activity in raising the demand for black labor."[109] He found additional support for his "increased demand" theory in that those groups who experienced the greatest relative post-1964 gains were, in his view, those best positioned to take advantage of an increase in demand for black labor. These groups included young black men, highly educated and skilled black men, and black women.

Acknowledging the problems of inferring causality based on the coincidence of antibias activity and economic gains, Freeman looked to other sources for corroboration. He examined surveys and other studies to determine whether companies had changed their employment practices since 1964. "[I]n the absence of widespread changes in company personnel practices," he explained, "it is difficult to see how antidiscrimination policies could cause sizeable aggregative effects...." He found the evidence "overwhelming" that "personnel policies have, in fact, been greatly altered by federal equal employment opportunity and affirmative action pressures."[110]

Freeman's empirical analysis, coupled with his review of company employment studies, led him to the following, still-tentative conclusion:

> In sum, while by no means definitive, or ruling out other factors, the evidence on timing, on incidence, and on company personnel and employment practices suggests that at least some of the post-1964 black gains resulted from increases in demand for black labor induced, at least in part, by programs designed to accomplish that purpose. Imperfect though it is, the evidence suggests that the national antibias effort has contributed to black economic progress.[111]

---

[108]Freeman did not look separately at firms that were subject to affirmative action requirements and firms that were not. (EEO-1 reports do not contain wage data.)

[109]Freeman, "Black Economic Progress After 1964," p. 270.

[110]Ibid., p. 281. For an empirical study of the impact of affirmative action on the recruitment and hiring of women and black men for managerial positions, see Hyclak, Thomas, Larry W. Taylor, and James B. Stewart. "Some New Historical Evidence on the Impact of Affirmative Action: Detroit, 1972." *Review of Black Political Economy,* v. 21, fall 1992. Consistent with Freeman's conclusion, the results of this study suggest that firms subject to affirmative action requirements altered their hiring practices with respect to black men.

[111]Freeman, "Black Economic Progress After 1964," p. 283.

O'Neill and O'Neill offer a different explanation for the post-1964 black wage gains. They suggest that it was not affirmative action, but the 1964 Civil Rights Act, that was responsible for those gains.[112]

Smith and Welch briefly discussed affirmative action in a study of black economic progress during the period from 1940 to 1980 (although they did not include affirmative action in the statistical model they developed to explain the wage gains of black workers during those years). To assess the effectiveness of affirmative action, they compared the percentages by which the wage gap between black and white males narrowed in the 1940-1960 period, prior to affirmative action, and in the 1960-1980 period, during which affirmative action was implemented. Finding the percentages to be generally similar, they concluded that "affirmative action apparently had no significant long-run effect, either positive or negative, on the male racial wage gap."[113] Instead, they speculated that other factors investigated in their study, namely, education and migration, were "the primary determinants of the long-term black economic improvement."[114] Other researchers have challenged these conclusions.[115]

Smith and Welch did not completely discount the role of affirmative action in increasing black male wages. Rather, they maintained that its wage effects were temporary or limited. For example, they observed a significant increase in the wages of young black male workers (relative to the wages of young white male workers) between 1967 and 1972, which they attributed to affirmative action. By 1975-1976, however, they found that this "racial wage gap had returned to more normal levels."[116] Smith and Welch did isolate one subgroup of black men—young college graduates—whose wages "increased at a more rapid rate [after affirmative action] than was historically the case."[117] This finding led them to conclude that this group alone experienced positive wage effects of affirmative action.

---

[112]See O'Neill and O'Neill, "Affirmative Action in the Labor Market," p. 88-103.

[113]Smith, James P., and Finis R. Welch. *Closing the Gap: Forty Years of Economic Progress for Blacks.* Santa Monica, Calif., Rand Corporation, Feb. 1986. Prepared for the U.S. Department of Labor. p. 95.

[114]Ibid., p. 91.

[115]See Donohue, John J., III, and James Heckman. "Continuous Versus Episodic Change: The Impact of Civil Rights Policy on the Economic Status of Blacks." *Journal of Economic Literature,* v. 29, Dec. 1991. p. 1603-1643.

[116]Smith and Welch, *Closing the Gap,* p. 93.

[117]Ibid., p. 94-95.

Impact of Affirmative Action on Women

As illustrated by the preceding review of affirmative action studies, much research on the effectiveness of affirmative action has focused on the policy's impact on black employees relative to white employees. Some of these studies have included women, typically measuring effects on black women relative to white women. Other researchers, however, have more directly addressed the impact of Federal antidiscrimination measures, including affirmative action, on women.

Using economywide data from the U.S. Bureau of Labor Statistics and other sources, Augustin Kwasi Fosu investigated the occupational mobility (from "low-status" to "high-status" occupations) of black women during the 1958-1981 period. He noted that between 1960 and 1980, changes occurred in the "black female occupational structure," including a shift from private household employment to clerical employment. His study tested the hypothesis that "the relative occupational position of black women has improved since the mid-1960s, probably in response to the antidiscrimination measures of the era."[118]

Fosu found that the occupational mobility of black women, relative to white women and white men, did increase after 1964, controlling for pre-existing trends, cyclical economic conditions, education, and other factors. He attributed this increase to antidiscrimination measures, although, in light of his small sample, he stated that his findings "should be regarded as suggestive."[119] Since he observed no further upward trend as of the mid-1970s (when Leonard found affirmative action to be effective), Fosu further concluded that "the observed post-1964 trend was probably attributable to Title VII [of the 1964 Civil Rights Act]," rather than affirmative action measures.[120] In an effort to reconcile his findings with those of Leonard[121] and others, Fosu speculated that "the impact of Title VII on black female occupational mobility waned as of the mid-1970s, and that declines in the pre-existing trend might have been observed in the absence of affirmative action."[122]

Andrea Beller used Current Population Survey data for 1967 and 1974 to examine the impact of Federal equal employment opportunity enforcement on the probability of women entering male-dominated occupations. She reported

---

[118]Fosu, Augustin Kwasi. "Occupational Mobility of Black Women, 1958-1981: The Impact of Post-1964 Antidiscrimination Measures." *Industrial and Labor Relations Review,* v. 45, Jan. 1992. p. 282.

[119]Ibid., p. 290.

[120]Ibid., p. 289.

[121]As discussed above, Leonard found that affirmative action contributed to the occupational advance of black women between 1974 and 1980.

[122]Fosu, "Occupational Mobility of Black Women, 1958-1981," p. 290.

that the Federal contract compliance program significantly increased the probability that a female worker would be employed in a male-dominated occupation, controlling for education, experience, race, marital status, and a host of other factors.[123] Beller's research also has relevance for women's wages since, as she explained, "on the average, male occupations are more desirable in pecuniary terms for both sexes."[124]

In his study of the effectiveness of the contract compliance program, Paul Osterman looked at female quit rates. He explained his choice of dependent variable, as follows:

> Quits are a useful measure of people's perceptions about their opportunities, and effective affirmative action programs may improve intra-firm opportunities for advancement. As a result ... we expect that program effectiveness is captured by a reduction in quit rates from previous levels.[125]

Osterman used data for 1978 and 1979 and controlled for a number of factors in his model, including job tenure, education, race, marital status, and unemployment rate. He found that contract compliance program enforcement was associated with a lower female quit rate. He believed that the "most likely explanation" for this relationship was that affirmative action programs required by the contract compliance program "create better opportunities for women and hence increase their incentive to be stable employees."[126] Osterman identified the time frame of his study as a possible reason for his finding the contract compliance program to be more effective than had earlier researchers. As he explained, his data were for years following the centralization of the contract compliance program in the Department of Labor. He maintained that his results had potential long-term implications for women's wages, since, he argued, lower quit rates would likely reduce the male-female wage gap over time.

In an article on the male-female wage gap, Morley Gunderson reviewed studies on the impact of affirmative action, including a number of those cited above. He urged caution in interpreting the studies' empirical evidence about affirmative action's impact on female workers, however, in view of "data problems and difficulties in disentangling the pure legislative effect from the

---

[123]See Beller, Andrea. "Occupational Segregation by Sex: Determinants and Changes." *Journal of Human Resources,* v. 17, summer 1982. p. 371-392.

[124]Ibid., p. 374.

[125]Osterman, Paul. "Affirmative Action and Opportunity: A Study of Female Quit Rates." *Review of Economics and Statistics,* v. 64, Nov. 1982. p. 604.

[126]Ibid., p. 611.

myriad of other factors that have changed in the labor market for females over the same period."[127]

Affirmative Action and Public Sector Employment

In 1971, as explained in chapter 1, the Civil Service Commission gave Federal agencies the authority to use employment goals and timetables. To determine the effectiveness of this affirmative action approach, David Rosenbloom compared changes in the Federal employment of blacks and women[128] before and after the policy was implemented. Considering 1972 to be the first year of implementation, he compared changes in the employment of blacks across GS grade groups during the 1967-1971 preprogram period and the 1972-1976 postprogram period. He found that for all GS grade groups, employment changes were not very different during the preprogram and postprogram periods. His conclusion based on these results was that "affirmative-action (goals and timetables) policy has not had a substantial and intended impact on the employment of blacks in the general schedule component of the federal bureaucracy."[129]

Rosenbloom likewise found that changes in the Federal employment of women in grade groups at the low and high ends of the GS scale were fairly similar before and after the authorization of goals and timetables. In the middle GS 7-12 grade group, however, he observed that postprogram change for women "was substantially greater in the intended direction" than preprogram change. Between 1969 and 1970, the percentage of positions in the GS 7-12 group held by women fell by 4.8 percentage points; by comparison, women experienced a 7.0 percentage-point increase in this grade group between 1972 and 1976.[130]

---

[127]Gunderson, Morley. "Male-Female Wage Differentials and Policy Responses." *Journal of Economic Literature,* v. 27, March 1989. p. 63-64. For a discussion of changes in the female labor force since 1890, see Smith, James P., and Michael P. Ward. *Women's Wages and Work in the Twentieth Century.* Santa Monica, Calif., Rand Corporation, Oct. 1984. Prepared for the National Institute of Child Health and Human Development.

[128]Please note that *blacks* and *women,* as used in the following discussion of Federal employment, are not mutually exclusive categories. The category *blacks* includes both men and women, while *women* includes women of all racial groups. Thus, black women are included in both categories.

[129]Rosenbloom, David H. "The Federal Affirmative-Action Policy." In Nachmias, David, ed. *The Practice of Policy Evaluation.* New York, St. Martin's Press, 1980. p. 180.

[130]Please note that Rosenbloom used a shorter preprogram period for women (1969-1970) than for blacks (1967-1971) due to the unavailability of comparable data for women for the other years. In addition, his postprogram period for both groups (1972-1976) began prior to the explicit inclusion of women in the affirmative action program in 1973. According to Rosenbloom, however, "the original policy directive was not necessarily interpreted by all agencies as precluding the setting of goals and timetables for [women]." See Ibid., p. 181-182.

Rosenbloom concluded that "the policy of using goals and timetables may be somewhat more efficacious" in the case of women than blacks.[131]

Rosenbloom speculated that one reason for affirmative action's apparently greater success among women than blacks "may be that the underutilization of women has been based more upon discriminatory attitudes and practices than upon their economic and cultural distinctiveness."[132] As a result, he argued, women may be better positioned to take advantage of opportunities opened up by affirmative action than blacks and other minorities.

In a statistical study covering a longer time period, J. Edward Kellough generally confirmed Rosenbloom's findings. Focusing on the middle and higher grade levels of the Federal workforce, he compared trends in the employment of blacks and women before and after the authorization of goals and timetables.[133] Among blacks, Kellough found little change in the rate of employment increase between the prepolicy and postpolicy periods. He concluded:

> There is almost nothing to indicate that the availability of goals and timetables led to the more rapid correction of the under-representation of blacks in the top half of the general schedule.[134]

Among women, he observed an increase in the rate of employment growth in both the GS (and equivalent) 7-12 and 13-18 grade groups. He noted, however, that these increases were not very large and that "[w]omen remained significantly under-represented in general schedule and equivalent grades 13-18 as recently as 1984." Kellough concluded that "goals and timetables did not dramatically change patterns of employment for either group [blacks or women]."[135]

---

[131]Ibid., p. 181.

[132]Ibid., p. 182-183.

[133]Kellough, *Federal Equal Employment Opportunity Policy and Numerical Goals and Timetables*. Kellough examined data for blacks from 1962 to 1984 and data for women from 1968 (the first year comparable governmentwide data were available) to 1984.

[134]Ibid., p. 38. As explained below, Kellough evaluated "underrepresentation" based on the level of minority or female enrollment at institutions of higher education. For a discussion of this and other standards for determining underrepresentation, see Ibid., p. 5-7.

[135]Ibid., p. 38-39.

Although the CSC authorized Federal agencies to utilize goals and timetables in 1971, it did not require them to do so; decisions about whether, and how, to establish goals and timetables were left to the individual agencies. And research by Rosenbloom suggests that use of this form of affirmative action was uneven across the executive branch.[136] Thus, to more accurately assess the impact of the authorization of goals and timetables, Kellough examined agency-level employment data for blacks and women in grades 9-18.[137] He measured impact as the change in the time needed for blacks or women to achieve "parity" in an agency at the prepolicy (prior to the authorization of goals and timetables) rate of increase compared to the postpolicy rate. He defined parity as the level of black or female enrollment at institutions of higher education in 1971.[138]

Kellough found great variation in agency scores on his "proportional reduction in time to achieve parity" index. Some agencies significantly reduced the time needed to reach parity, while others did not. As an initial step toward explaining the differences in agency scores, Kellough examined the operation of a number of variables thought to influence equal employment opportunity, at two agencies. He concluded that four factors—"size of agency grade 9-18 work forces, the amount of resources applied to EEO, bureaucratic commitment to EEO, and the presence of goals and timetables in national EEO plans[—]appear to be associated with agency EEO progress."[139]

In summary, the evidence reviewed in this chapter on the effectiveness of affirmative action in employment is mixed. Some studies have credited affirmative action in the private sector with shifting employment, particularly black employment, from noncontractor firms to firms with Federal contracts. Whether affirmative action has simultaneously increased worker earnings is a matter of debate. Studies of the Federal Government's affirmative action program have found some increases in the employment of women, although they also report that women, like other beneficiary groups, are not well represented at the higher grade levels of Federal employment.

---

[136]See Rosenbloom, "The Federal Affirmative-Action Policy," p. 174-178.

[137]Data for blacks were from 1962 to 1980, and data for women were from 1966 to 1980.

[138]Kellough selected this parity standard because "[i]n most instances today, positions in the top half of the general schedule minimally require a college education." Kellough, *Federal Equal Employment Opportunity Policy and Numerical Goals and Timetables*, p. 7. For a more detailed description of Kellough's methodology, see p. 43-52.

[139]Ibid., p. 99.

IV. ALTERNATIVES TO AFFIRMATIVE ACTION

A variety of proposals have been put forth to supplement, modify, or replace affirmative action. They represent responses to the perceived shortcomings of affirmative action as an appropriate, effective, and politically feasible strategy for combatting discrimination and improving the economic circumstances of members of minority groups and women. A sampling of proposed alternative approaches and their policy implications, as relevant, are presented in this chapter.

Supplements to Affirmative Action

A growing number of private companies are supplementing affirmative action with "diversity management" programs. While affirmative action is credited, to varying degrees, with increasing the recruitment and hiring of minorities, its ability to achieve the retention and development of minority employees is seen as considerably weaker. And as the national workforce becomes increasingly diverse, the need to "keep, motivate and promote minorities," in an effort to fully utilize all employees, has become a priority for many corporate executives.[140] According to R. Roosevelt Thomas of the American Institute for Managing Diversity, the key to managing diversity is "enabling every member of your work force to perform to his or her potential."[141] The goal, in his view, is "to get from a heterogeneous work force the same productivity, commitment, quality, and profit that we got from the old homogeneous work force."[142] Although company approaches to diversity management differ, some elements, such as diversity workshops aimed at increasing awareness of racism and sexism, are common to many programs.[143]

Modifications to Affirmative Action

Writing in 1991, prior to enactment of the Civil Rights Act of that year, law professor David Strauss proposed a modified version of affirmative action, as part of a larger revamping of employment discrimination laws. Strauss

---

[140]Mabry, Marcus. "Past Tokenism." *Newsweek*, v. 115, May 14, 1990. p. 37.

[141]Thomas, R. Roosevelt, Jr. "From Affirmative Action to Affirming Diversity." *Harvard Business Review*, v. 68, March-April 1990. p. 112. In Roosevelt's view, affirmative action alone is unable to accomplish this, because it "fails to deal with the root causes of prejudice and inequality and does little to develop the full potential of every man and woman in the company." p. 117.

[142]Ibid., p. 109.

[143]For a discussion of individual company programs, see Ibid., p. 108-115; Mabry, "Past Tokenism." For additional materials on workforce diversity, see U.S. Library of Congress. Congressional Research Service. *Workforce Diversity in the 1990s: Bibliography-in-Brief, 1990-1994*. Report No. 94-63 L, by Robert Howe. Jan. 1994. Washington, 1994.

considered whether Title VII of the Civil Rights Act, with its emphasis on specific acts of discrimination, was the best way to address today's "mostly covert" forms of discrimination.[144] He concluded that it was not, that the focus of employment discrimination laws on individual discriminatory acts was "costly and ineffective" and "should become decidedly secondary."[145] Instead, he proposed a new arrangement aimed at "accomplish[ing] certain social purposes, such as deterring taste-based discrimination and avoiding racial stratification."[146] Under Strauss's proposal, all firms would be required to employ minorities in proportion to their percentage in the national population. Firms not complying with the numerical requirement would be fined.

Another proposal to modify affirmative action, which has been raised primarily in connection with college and university admissions, is to base preferences on social, economic, or cultural disadvantage, rather than race, ethnicity, or gender. Nieli has expressed qualified support for using these types of preferences in the employment area. He argues that a basic rationale for such an approach is that "all involuntarily disadvantaged people, commensurate with their degree of disadvantage," have an equal right to government help.[147] According to Nieli:

> While competency and ability should certainly be the main consideration for most job hiring, it would not seem to be inconsistent, either with our sense of justice or with the demands of economic efficiency, for government policy to encourage, at least on a voluntary basis, small deviations from the meritocratic principle in order to give a slight preference to those most in need of a job, or to those for whom a given employment position would represent the greatest step up the economic ladder.[148]

Limiting Affirmative Action

Some proposed modifications to affirmative action in employment retain race- or ethnicity-based preferences, but limit their scope. Lawrence Fuchs has suggested that the nature of the job in question is relevant to the extent to which preferences can reasonably be applied. He explains that affirmative action for occupations that "require a strict set of objective testing criteria to

---

[144]Strauss, David A. "The Law and Economics of Racial Discrimination in Employment: The Case for Numerical Standards." *Georgetown Law Journal,* v. 79, Aug. 1991. p. 1619.

[145]Ibid., p. 1657.

[146]Ibid., p. 1655. Strauss defined taste-based discrimination as "an antipathy to a racial minority group on the part of some relevant economic actor," such as employers, fellow employees, or consumers. p. 1621.

[147]Nieli, "Ethnic Tribalism and Human Personhood," p. 102.

[148]Ibid., p. 103.

determine merit"—such as navy fliers and ballet dancers—is "necessarily limited to special recruitment and training efforts."[149] He distinguishes these "merit" occupations from a second group of jobs requiring basic qualifications. He suggests that it is reasonable to set numerical goals for the hiring of fire fighters, machinists, computer operators, and others in the second occupational group, and once basic qualifications are met, to consider race, among many other factors, in an effort to fulfill these goals.

In a 1988 article, Nathan Glazer proposed limiting affirmative action in a different way—to certain groups. While acknowledging "the enormous political difficulties involved," he suggested changing Federal regulations to eliminate affirmative action for Asians and Hispanics.[150] He argued that both ethnic categories include many groups, some of which have made considerable economic progress. According to Glazer, restricting affirmative action in such a way "would begin to send the message that we view affirmative action as a temporary expedient, to be increasingly dispensed with, in various areas, for various groups, over time."[151] Even if affirmative action for other groups proved politically impossible to terminate, he believes that the relevant regulations should be reviewed regularly.

Alternatives to Affirmative Action

Those advocating the elimination of affirmative action as currently practiced offer a range of strategies to replace it. In many cases, their proposals explicitly provide for the continued enforcement or strengthening of civil rights laws to combat discrimination and promote equal employment opportunity. It should be emphasized that the alternative approaches presented here are not mutually exclusive and that, as indicated below, some authors favor pursuing a combination of them.

Self-Help Strategies

Roy Brooks, a law professor, has defined the American race problem as the "disparity in the distribution of societal hardships or burdens between Americans of different races who belong to the same socioeconomic class."[152] To address this problem, he proposes a combination of African American self-help and government assistance, with an emphasis on the former. His self-help

---

[149]Fuchs, Lawrence H. *The American Kaleidoscope: Race, Ethnicity, and the Civic Culture.* Hanover, N.H., University Press of New England, 1990. p. 452.

[150]Glazer, Nathan. "The Affirmative Action Stalemate." *Public Interest,* no. 90, winter 1988. p. 111.

[151]Ibid., p. 111.

[152]Brooks, Roy L. *Rethinking the American Race Problem.* Berkeley, University of California Press, 1990. p. 4.

prescription has two main components—support for African American institutions and support for African American households. In Brooks's scheme, institutional support may take the form of African American organizations or companies providing resources, including personnel, to largely African American public schools. He describes household support as a "program ... in which middle-class African Americans work one-on-one, long-term, with poorer families and individuals to impart and to coach the behaviors, values, and attitudes of mainstream society, as well as the survival techniques that African Americans have found essential in a racist society."[153] At these sessions, he foresees middle-class participants teaching poorer families life skills, such as budgeting, and informing them about employment opportunities and community resources. Brooks emphasizes, however, that "*no* amount of self-help alone can solve this problem [of intra-class racial disparity]." He argues that the Federal Government must provide legal and economic remedies.[154]

A modified form of self-help is advocated by sociologist Paul Starr. Starr perceives a need to bolster "'intermediate' institutions" in minority communities, such as community associations, schools, and media, which "provide the organizational foundation for collective development and effective public representation."[155] To that end, he calls for "communal self-development," supported by financial assistance from the larger society. Starr envisions a new private organization—National Endowment for Black America—which would "serve as a mechanism for receiving capital contributions and supporting a variety of social and cultural organizations in the black community." According to Starr, the endowment "could also support the development of minority businesses with programs aimed at fostering entrepreneurship."[156] Although he assumes the endowment would receive only private contributions initially, he believes that in time it might also become "a primary, legitimate mechanism for receiving public ... funds and providing capital support to black institutions."[157] Even if the endowment receives substantial funding, however, Starr argues that communal self-development efforts will necessarily be limited by larger social and economic problems and, thus, should be supplemented with broad, race-neutral social policies.

---

[153]Ibid., p. 14.

[154]Ibid., p. 150-151.

[155]Starr, Paul. "Civil Reconstruction: What to Do Without Affirmative Action." *American Prospect*, no. 8, winter 1992. p. 7.

[156]Ibid., p. 12. Although Starr uses the term "minority," the focus of his proposal is the black community.

[157]Ibid.

Individual and Community Empowerment

While supportive of minority self-help efforts, Clint Bolick of the libertarian Institute for Justice agrees with Brooks and Starr that self-help alone will be insufficient to overcome the problems facing minority Americans. Yet, unlike Brooks and Starr, Bolick does not favor government employment and social programs. Rather, he argues in a 1990 Heritage Foundation publication coauthored by Mark Liedl that self-help efforts should be supplemented by a program of "individual empowerment to control one's own life." Bolick and Liedl describe this approach as a "legislative strategy designed to remove government-imposed barriers that stifle economic opportunities for the poor."[158] Among the obstacles targeted are government regulations on business. According to Bolick and Liedl, laws at both the Federal and local level, such as minimum wage laws and local occupational licensing laws, limit entrepreneurial opportunities.[159] Viewing economic liberty as a fundamental right, they argue that such economic regulations should be challenged on civil rights grounds. They further call for enactment of "an Economic Liberty Act, which would require governmental entities to limit regulations restricting entry into trades or businesses to demonstrable public health, safety, or welfare objectives." In their opinion, these actions would "open the most important door to economic independence: self-employment and business creation."[160]

Bolick and Liedl also identify "substandard" public schools as barriers facing the poor. To increase educational opportunities, they advocate parental choice in education in the form of tax credits or vouchers. Welfare reform is a third component of their individual empowerment strategy. According to Bolick and Liedl, "[t]he federal government should encourage economic emancipation by reducing dependency on welfare and rewarding those who work."[161] To that end, they support such measures as mandatory work requirements for able-bodied welfare recipients and tenant management of public housing.

Robert Woodson, founder of a research institute called the National Center for Neighborhood Enterprise, also advocates a combination of self-help and "empowerment" to address the economic and social problems of the poor, particularly the black poor. Unlike Bolick and Liedl, however, he favors a distinctly community-based approach, which he argues is in the historical tradition of black America's self-help efforts. According to Woodson, private

---

[158]Bolick, Clint, and Mark B. Liedl. "Fulfilling America's Promise: A Civil Rights Strategy for the 1990s." Heritage Foundation *Backgrounder* No. 773, June 7, 1990. p. 3.

[159]For a discussion of these laws and their effects, see Bolick, Clint. *Changing Course: Civil Rights at the Crossroads.* New Brunswick, N. J., Transaction Books, 1988. p. 94-104. In these pages, Bolick draws on the work of economist Walter Williams. See Williams, Walter E. *The State Against Blacks.* New York, McGraw-Hill, 1982.

[160]Bolick and Liedl, "Fulfilling America's Promise," p. 14.

[161]Ibid., p. 16.

neighborhood groups and institutions are more effective than government bureaucracies at serving the needs of their communities. Thus, he calls for "new approaches that build on both the legacy of the free enterprise system and the strengths and resources already existing in our communities."[162] In Woodson's view, the "purpose of social policy should be to recognize the existence of [neighborhood] structures, to remove barriers that hinder them, and to use these structures more creatively."[163] Woodson is a strong proponent of tenant management of public housing. He likewise supports establishing an educational voucher system and giving black churches and other black institutions responsibility for coordinating certain social services in their communities, such as foster care and adoption.

Woodson emphasizes the need to promote economic development and entrepreneurship in poor areas. To attract capital investment, he proposes creating "business development districts," similar to enterprise zones, which would be "singled out for special treatment under the tax code and ... under federal, state and local regulatory law."[164] Woodson also supports contracting with neighborhood organizations to provide basic services to localities. Among his ideas for redesigning the welfare system are making some welfare payments available to employers in the form of vouchers, which they could then use to hire welfare recipients, and allowing recipients of unemployment compensation and other transfer payments to receive benefits in a lump sum in order to invest in a small business or acquire education or job training. As these proposals suggest, Woodson does not oppose government financial assistance to the poor, provided that it is temporary. He does argue, however, that to the maximum extent possible, the spending of the money, whether for welfare or housing programs, should be controlled by its intended low-income beneficiaries.

Race-Neutral Social Programs

Shelby Steele and sociologist William Julius Wilson, among others, argue that existing preferential policies should be replaced by social programs available to people of all races. Citing the need for the "educational and economic development of disadvantaged people, regardless of race," Steele calls for "better elementary and secondary schools, job training, safer neighborhoods, better financial assistance for college, and so on."[165]

---

[162]Woodson, Robert L. "Empowering Poor Neighborhoods." In Perkins, Joseph, ed. *A Conservative Agenda for Black Americans*. Washington, The Heritage Foundation, 1987. p. 53.

[163]Woodson, Robert L. *Private Sector Alternatives to the Welfare State: A New Agenda for Black Americans*. Dallas, National Center for Policy Analysis, Nov. 1987. p. 42.

[164]He describes these districts as "depressed areas where there is an abundance of vacant and unused property and a large, unemployed work force available." Ibid., p. 41.

[165]Steele, *The Content of Our Character*, p. 124.

Wilson's proposed program, as outlined in a 1990 *American Prospect* article, focuses on employment. It consists of "[f]ull employment policies, job skills training, comprehensive health care legislation, educational reforms in the public schools, child care legislation, and crime and drug abuse prevention programs."[166] Although Wilson does not offer details of his program in the article, he has written about full employment policies in earlier work. In his book *The Declining Significance of Race*, Wilson argued that affirmative action was not designed to address the core economic problems of the poor, namely "barriers to desirable jobs that are the result of the use of increasing automation, the relocation of industries, the segmentation of the labor market, and the shift from goods-producing to service-producing industries."[167] Citing the pressing need to deal with such problems, Wilson expressed support for the Humphrey-Hawkins bill, legislation introduced in Congress in the mid-1970s to achieve full employment. He described the version of the bill introduced in the 95th Congress (H.R. 50, S. 50), which was also called the Full Employment and Balanced Growth Act, as follows:

> [T]he Humphrey-Hawkins Bill ... was designed to make the achievement of full employment in the United States a major economic priority. Specifically, this bill established a goal of no more than 4 percent overall unemployment and 3 percent adult unemployment by 1983. The bill also required that the president of the United States spell out programs and policies to affect these goals, and it stipulated that top priority should be given to the stimulation of job growth in the private sector.[168]

The 95th Congress passed the Humphrey-Hawkins bill, but in modified form.[169] Although Wilson described the final version as "watered down," he did consider it "a step in the right direction," in that it "does at least formalize some major federal economic priorities and establish a *framework* for systematic and long-term planning."[170]

Despite general similarities in their approaches, Wilson does not agree with Steele that race-neutral policies should be restricted to the disadvantaged. Rather, in what he describes as "the best political strategy for those committed to racial justice," he would offer these programs "to help all groups, regardless

---

[166]Wilson, William Julius. "Race-Neutral Policies and the Democratic Coalition." *The American Prospect,* no. 1, spring 1990. p. 79.

[167]Wilson, William Julius. *The Declining Significance of Race,* Second Edition. Chicago, University of Chicago Press, 1980. p. 179.

[168]Ibid., p. 180-181.

[169]P.L. 95-523, Oct. 27, 1978, 92 Stat. 1887

[170]Wilson, *The Declining Significance of Race,* p. 181.

of race or economic class."[171] According to Wilson, a policy initiative to improve the quality of the workforce would greatly benefit minorities. At the same time, he argues, such an effort would also benefit nonminorities, and in view of widespread concern about the consequences of having an inadequately prepared workforce, should gain broad public support. As part of this general universal approach, however, Wilson would target certain initiatives, such as programs to combat poverty, exclusively at poor neighborhoods.

V. FUTURE OF AFFIRMATIVE ACTION

There has been much speculation in recent years about the future of affirmative action, prompted, in part, by the changing ideological composition of the Supreme Court. As noted in a recent piece in the *Legal Times,* the Court "has picked up four new justices in four years while losing its three strongest proponents of affirmative action."[172] Paul Starr, for one, has written of the "prospect of a sharp curtailment of affirmative action, or even its end as we have known it," in light of Clarence Thomas's confirmation to the Court.[173] Cases currently before the Supreme Court, or expected to reach the Court in the near future, raise a variety of issues related to affirmative action.[174]

---

[171] Wilson, "Race-Neutral Policies and the Democratic Coalition," p. 79.

[172] Taylor, Stuart, Jr. "Affirmative Action and Ambivalence." *Legal Times,* v. 17, Oct. 17, 1994. p. 25.

[173] Starr, "Civil Reconstruction," p. 7.

[174] See, for example, Biskupic, Joan. "Race is Primary Issue in Pair of Court Cases." *The Washington Post,* Oct. 3, 1994. p. A8; Gladwell, Malcolm. "Testing the Limits of Affirmative Action." *The Washington Post,* Sept. 25, 1994. p. A4.

Challenges to affirmative action, however, are not likely to be limited to the court system. In California, an effort is underway to amend the State constitution to restrict affirmative action. Supporters hope to put the California Civil Rights Initiative before voters in 1996. A draft version of the initiative states, in part:

> Neither the State of California nor any of its political subdivisions or agents shall use race, sex, color, ethnicity or national origin as a criterion for either discriminating against, or granting preferential treatment to, any individual or group in the operation of the State's system of public employment, public education or public contracting.[175]

In the opinion of columnist George Will, "[t]he continent-wide reverberations of this debate [over the California initiative] could lead to a similar amendment to the U.S. Constitution, mandating colorblind public policy."[176]

The Clinton Administration and Affirmative Action

The Clinton Administration has expressed some support for affirmative action. According to Labor Secretary Robert Reich, the Office of Federal Contract Compliance Programs has been "reactivated" and is enforcing

---

[175]Quoted in Kopp, Quentin L., and Bill Leonard. "Take the Initiative on Reverse Discrimination." *Wall Street Journal,* June 6, 1994. p. A12.

[176]Will, George F. "Progressive Retreat." *The Washington Post,* Nov. 3, 1994. p. A23.

affirmative action requirements on Government contractors in accordance with E.O. 11246. At a May 1994 meeting with staff members of the Joint Center for Political and Economic Studies, Secretary Reich reported that the deputy assistant secretary for OFCCP "has got a very clear message from me that affirmative action will be necessary for firms to be in full compliance with the Executive Order."[177] The Clinton Administration has also been supportive of traditional affirmative action efforts in higher education. Reversing the position of the Bush Administration, it has endorsed the awarding of minority scholarships by colleges and universities. Under the Clinton policy, colleges may offer minority scholarships, including those based on race, in order to help remedy past discrimination or to promote campus diversity.[178] A recent Federal appeals court ruling, however, has called this policy into question.[179]

In another reversal of a Bush Administration stance, the Clinton Justice Department recently withdrew support of a white high school teacher who had charged a New Jersey school board with racial discrimination. The white teacher claimed that the school board had acted illegally in 1989 when it fired her, rather than a black teacher, pursuant to an affirmative action policy to promote faculty diversity. (Both teachers were considered to be equal in seniority and qualifications.) In 1992, the Justice Department filed a suit on the white teacher's behalf. A Federal district judge ruled in favor of the white teacher in September 1993, and the case was subsequently appealed. Switching sides in the case, the Clinton Justice Department filed a brief in September 1994 in support of the school board. Deval Patrick, assistant attorney general for civil rights, explained the Justice Department's new position, as follows:

> In such narrow circumstances [where both individuals are equal in seniority and qualifications], an affirmative action plan should have the discretion, for reasons of faculty diversity.[180]

---

[177]Quoted in Joint Center for Political and Economic Studies Political TrendLetter. *Focus*, v. 22, July 1994. p. 3.

[178]See Mulholland, David. "Clinton Reverses Bush's Proposal on Scholarships." *Wall Street Journal*, Feb. 18, 1994. p. B6A. Final policy guidance can be found in: U.S. Dept of Education. "Nondiscrimination in Federally Assisted Programs; Title VI of the Civil Rights Act of 1964." *Federal Register*, v. 59, Feb. 23, 1994. p. 8756.

[179]In October 1994, the U.S. Court of Appeals for the Fourth Circuit ruled that a race-based scholarship program at the University of Maryland was unconstitutional. (*Podberesky* v. *Kirwan*, CA 4, No. 93-2527)

[180]Quoted in O'Brien, Tim. "Behind Justice's Flip-Flop in the N.J. Bias Suit." *Legal Times*, Sept. 19, 1994. p. 16.

Commenting on the case, Attorney General Janet Reno spoke in more general terms: "Diversity should be a factor that employers can consider in developing voluntary affirmative-action plans."[181]

President Clinton has emphasized diversity in making executive appointments. During the 1992 campaign, he pledged that, if elected, his administration would "look like America." As President, he has appointed record percentages of women and members of minority groups.[182]

As evidenced by these actions, the Clinton Administration's view of permissible affirmative action is clearly broader than that of its predecessor. Yet, like President Bush, President Clinton and administration officials have said that their definition of affirmative action does not include hiring quotas. During the 1992 presidential campaign, for example, candidate Clinton was quoted as saying, "I'm not trying to scrap affirmative action, even though I don't believe in quotas."[183] Assistant Attorney General Patrick stated during his March 1994 Senate confirmation hearing that he believed numerical racial quotas would be unlawful. Instead, he indicated support for flexible affirmative action programs.[184] President Clinton has publicly condemned the use of quotas in making executive appointments. After his election, he accused women's groups of being "bean counters" and of "playing quota games and math games," in response to their various demands that he appoint a minimum number of women to the Cabinet.[185]

Following the 1992 election, Evan J. Kemp, who served as EEOC chairman during the Bush Administration, warned of the potential difficulties facing the President-elect on civil rights issues:

---

[181]Quoted in Ibid., p. 2.

[182]See Kamen, Al. "A Government of the Eastern Elite, Still." *The Washington Post,* Sept. 3, 1993. p. A23; Riche, Martha Farnsworth. "The Bean Count Is In!" *The Washington Post,* Jan. 23, 1994. p. C2. Also see U.S. Library of Congress. Congressional Research Service. *Women Appointed to Full-Time Civilian Positions by President Clinton in 1993.* Report No. 94-272 GOV, by Rogelio Garcia. March 16, 1994. Washington, 1994.

[183]Quoted in Roberts, Steven V. "Civil Rights After Guinier." *U.S. News & World Report,* v. 114, June 14, 1993. p. 45.

[184]See "Civil Rights Nominee Testifies." *The Washington Post,* March 11, 1994. p. A23.

[185]Quoted in Marcus, Ruth. "Clinton Berates Critics in Women's Groups." *The Washington Post,* Dec. 22, 1992. p. A1, A12; also see Locin, Mitchell. "Clinton Finishes Cabinet of Diversity." *Chicago Tribune,* Dec. 25, 1992. sec. 1, p. 5.

> President-elect Clinton's promotion of diversity and opposition to group entitlements must be reconciled, and I can tell you from experience that this is nearly an impossible job.[186]

In general, President Clinton seems to prefer race-neutral approaches, over race-based affirmative action strategies, for promoting equal opportunity. During the 1992 presidential campaign, candidate Clinton and his running mate Senator Albert Gore published *Putting People First: How We Can All Change America*, in which they offered proposals to address a host of public policy issues. In a review of the book, political scientist Andrew Hacker commented:

> For at least a generation, black Americans have been seen as requiring separate treatment because of their continued exclusion from larger society. In a sense, the Clinton proposals seek to replace separate treatment with equal treatment based on need.[187]

In December 1993, at the end of President Clinton's first year in office, journalist Juan Williams noted the President's support for a "redefinition of the civil rights agenda," in a *Washington Post* opinion piece. Citing as sources "high-ranking people in his administration, both black and white," Williams wrote:

> Instead of race-specific solutions, he [President Clinton] sees answers in policies that promote general economic growth, improve schools, and address hunger, disease and homelessness as color-blind issues for the American family.[188]

In language that would likewise seem to apply to the alternative strategy advocated by William Julius Wilson, Williams further described "Clinton's idea of addressing racial issues with an emphasis on helping groups—such as indigent children and people lacking health insurance—without regard to color."[189]

Some observers do not agree that President Clinton opposes quotas and prefers race-neutral remedies over race-specific measures. In an August 1994 opinion piece critical of the Clinton Administration's decision to switch sides in the New Jersey affirmative action case, discussed above, Clint Bolick wrote:

---

[186]Quoted in Moore, W. John. "On the March Again?" *National Journal*, v. 24, Dec. 12, 1992. p. 2828.

[187]Hacker, Andrew. "The Blacks and Clinton." *The New York Review of Books*, v. 40, Jan. 28, 1993. p. 15.

[188]Williams, Juan. "Reaganite on Civil Rights?" *The Washington Post*, Dec. 26, 1993. p. C1.

[189]Ibid., p. C4.

> Despite his highly publicized disparagement of "bean-counting," Mr. Clinton has embraced race-based scholarships, minority set-asides and racially gerrymandered voting districts. And he has tapped for virtually all civil rights positions alumni of advocacy groups that persistently support quotas, set-asides and busing.[190]

While not abandoning affirmative action, some civil rights leaders appear to be open to President Clinton's broad social-policy approach to promoting equal opportunity. Former National Urban League President John E. Jacob and others have emphasized the need for renewed self-help efforts within the black community and have called upon the Clinton Administration for support in areas such as business development and job creation.[191] At present, however, the ability of the Administration to provide substantial budgetary support is doubtful, particularly in light of the Republican congressional victories in the November 1994 elections.

The 104th Congress and Affirmative Action

Speculating on the post-1994-election prospects for civil rights policy, a *Legal Times* article stated:

> [M]uch depends on the inclinations of the key [congressional] committee and subcommittee chairmen, who can send legislation forward to the floor or bottle it up.[192]

Comments by Republican Senator Orrin Hatch, chairman of the Senate Judiciary Committee, suggest that the new Congress may impact civil rights policy more through oversight of Clinton Administration policies than through legislation. Senator Hatch has said he intends to study the Justice Department's civil rights policies. He has also said:

---

[190]Bolick, Clint. "Coronation of a Quota King at Justice," *The Wall Street Journal,* Aug. 31, 1994. p. A13.

[191]See, for example, "Urban League Asks Support for Self-Help." *The Washington Post,* Jan. 21, 1994. p. A3.

[192]Groner, Jonathan. "Shifting Right on Rights Policy." *Legal Times,* v. 17, Nov. 14, 1994. p. 10.

> ... I don't want to have this country, in the case of civil rights, move towards quotas. And some of the positions they've [Justice Department officials] taken will move us right in that direction—in fact, will establish and institute quotas.[193]

Clint Bolick and others, however, see an opportunity for the congressional Republicans to advance a new civil rights agenda. Bolick supports passage of "a comprehensive law to prohibit racial preferences in federal programs." In place of preferences, he favors "a 'program of empowerment' for minorities."[194]

The Contract With America, which sets forth the House Republican legislative priorities, does not mention affirmative action. It remains to be seen what actions, if any, the 104th Congress will take in this area.

---

[193]"Hatch's Agenda for Senate Judiciary." *Legal Times,* v. 17, Nov. 21, 1994. p. 14.

[194]Groner, "Shifting Right on Rights Policy," p. 10. Bolick's empowerment approach is discussed in chapter four.

CHAPTER 6A

Government-Imposed Preferential Policies — More Harm Than Good?

Brian W. Jones, President
Center for New Black Leadership

The Center is a new, non-profit think-tank here in Washington that seeks to encourage and promulgate solutions to social and economic problems in the black community that are consistent with the black community's long-held commitments to individual initiative and personal responsibility.

I maintain that government-imposed preferential policies based upon race and gender, whether in the employment or education context, presently do a great deal more harm than good. While thirty years ago such policies may have been an important tool for breaking down the systemic barriers to black entry into the economic mainstream, they have today, I think, reached the point of diminishing returns.

President Lyndon Johnson, speaking at Howard University in 1965, justified his Executive Order 11246, which we have heard discussed here this afternoon, by analogizing African-Americans to a "hobbled" runner in a race. In order to compete effectively in the race for economic and civic reward, he said, blacks needed to be given something of a head start.

At the time of President Johnson's pronouncement, the use of black skin as a proxy for social disadvantage was perhaps justifiable. Blacks were just emerging from the Jim Crow era in much of America and were not represented in any appreciable numbers in the economic or social mainstream. There was, so to speak, a relatively insignificant pool of prepared black talent from which the mainstream economy could draw. In 1965, approximately 15 percent of black families in America were considered middle class. Today, however, nearly half of all black families are middle class. Race today is no longer a sufficient proxy for social disadvantage.

Indeed, as the size of the black middle class expands, the pool of those best positioned to benefit from racial preferences becomes further removed from any manifest disadvantage. Hence, the lion's share of preference accrues to middle and upper class women and minorities. In short, the modern beneficiaries of racial preferences tend to be individuals likely possessing the requisite advantages to effectively compete without the taint of preference.

Conversely, the cost of preference policies can be measured in terms of: 1) the social discord created between preferred and nonpreferred groups, and among the preferred groups; 2) the opportunity cost of mismatched minority talent and capital; and 3) the economic cost to employers of complying with affirmative action mandates.

Furthermore, the costs associated with these divisive policies will likely only escalate over time, while the programs themselves will become ever more resistant to eradication. The inexorable trend of reference policies in America, as everywhere else in the world where they have been tried, is to ceaselessly elevate new groups to preferred status.[1] Indeed, while modern racial preference policies in America were originally intended to provide remediation to blacks disadvantaged by the legacy of slavery and Jim Crow laws, we are quickly approaching the day when nearly 70 percent of Americans will be members of "protected groups" eligible for government preferment.

Of course, the effect, if not the purpose, of this expanding pool of preference is to maintain the political viability of the program. Sadly, however, that trend is creating what one of my Center's directors, Shelby Steele, refers to as a "culture of preference." A culture in which rights accrue not to individuals, but rather to groups—groups which, incidentally, are not always easily defined. The inevitable consequence of this culture of preference is that groups must inevitably emphasize their differences and exalt their victimization to compete for preferred status. Thus, over the long-run, members of preferred groups are not substantially benefited and the larger society suffers the consequences of the social division created by competing groups. To stanch that inexorable tide, Congress, in my view, needs ultimately to eliminate government-sanctioned preference programs root and branch.

This, of course, is not to say that Congress should not have a positive civil rights agenda. Without question, it must. But that agenda must truly emphasize equality of opportunity, rather than equality of results. Over the past thirty years, the Congress, to its moral credit, has taken a valiant stand against invidious discrimination in America. It has erected an array of remedies for its victims.

In that vein, a positive civil rights agenda for the Congress should focus on four spheres of public activity: 1) stiffer enforcement of existing laws proscribing discrimination against individuals; 2) broader advertising and outreach efforts to ensure minority access to government employment and contracting opportunities; 3) encouraging efforts to improve the early education of disadvantaged individuals to ensure their preparedness to meet uniformly high standards for higher education, employment and contracting; and 4) encouraging industry and entrepreneurship within minority communities by

---

[1] See Thomas Sowell, *Compassion Versus Guilt and Other Essays* (New York: William Morrow 1987), p. 197.

reducing tax and regulatory burdens that retard economic development and hinder efforts at self-sufficiency.

With that agenda, Congress can rightly acknowledge that discrimination remains an obstacle to advancement in our society. However, it can also begin to forge a consensus in this country that the problems of our society are complex and are often more fundamental than preference policies admit. Only by encouraging individuals to empower themselves to improve their lives will we begin to see the kind of economic and civic progress we all agree is necessary to a strong and moral American future.

Genesis of Preferences

The Federal Government's experiment with race and gender preferences began some thirty years ago with President Johnson's execution of Executive Order 11246, which requires private firms working on Federal projects to "take affirmative action to ensure that applicants are employed... without regard to their race, creed, color or national origin." In his Howard University address, Johnson stated clearly that the order was intended to achieve, "not just legal equity but human ability, not just equality as a right and a theory but equality as a fact and *equality as a result*." (Emphasis added.) Therein lies the essential flaw of preference policies. They are designed in pursuit of the illusory goal of achieving equal results in the marketplace. But human talent and inclination have never been distributed in proportion to group representation in society. As Justice Thomas said in his important concurring opinion in this week's *Adarand Constructors v. Pena* decision, "[g]overnment cannot make us equal; it can only recognize, respect, and protect us as equal before the law."

Contrary to that notion, the Nixon Administration, with its implementation of the Philadelphia [contract set-aside] Plan, sought to impose equality of result in the procurement of Federal contracts. Under that Plan, the element of intent was essentially removed from the notion of illegal discrimination in contracting, just as the U.S. Supreme Court in *Griggs v. Duke Power Co.*, 401 U.S. 424 (1971), had removed it in the employment context. *Griggs* had held invalid employment practices, however neutral in intent, that caused a disparate impact upon a group protected under the Civic Rights Act of 1964.

From then on, discrimination would be discerned by racial imbalance in the workplace. The Office of Federal Contract Compliance Programs (OFCCP) then began requiring contractors to take "affirmative action" to achieve proportional representation of underrepresented groups in their subcontracts and workforces; and the Equal Employment Opportunity Commission began using demographic disparities in the workplace to discern discrimination in employment.

However, presuming "underrepresentation" to be the consequence of discrimination is wrong in two respects. First, the presumption ignores the fact that the talents and inclinations of individuals are not proportionately distributed. That 60 percent of dry cleaning establishments in New York City are owned by Korean-Americans does not suggest discrimination in the marketplace. It rather underscores the talents, industry and inclinations of a great many Korean immigrants.

Second, the presumption of discrimination where representation is disproportionate leads policymakers and judges to impose group remedies like set-asides and "goals" that are often tantamount to quotas. The objective is to achieve proportional representation, even if that necessitates modifying the standard of competition for preferred groups in order to include "enough" members of a given group in the overall pool. That determination to define down deficiencies in performance by establishing separate standards in order to demonstrate "good faith" in pursuit of affirmative action "goals" ignores the hard work of confronting real deficiencies of academic and economic preparedness in some segments of minority communities—particularly the African-American community.

Indeed, Alfred Blumrosen, the first enforcement chief of the Equal Employment Opportunity Commission, was unusually candid in conceding the expedient motive of presuming discrimination from "underrepresentation." In his book, *Black Employment and the Law,* Blumrosen wrote:

If discrimination is narrowly defined, for example, by requiring an evil intent to injure minorities, then it will be difficult to find that it exists. If it does not exist, then the plight of racial and ethnic minorities must be attributable to some more generalized failures in society, in the fields of basic education, housing, family relations, and the like. *The search for efforts to improve the condition of minorities must then focus in these general and difficult areas, and the answers can come only gradually as basic institutions, attitudes, customs, and practices are changed.* We thus would have before us generations of time before the effects of subjugation of minorities are dissipated. (Emphasis added.)

In other words, holding blacks to the same objective standards as others would, in the short run, yield a disproportionately low representation in the marketplace. However, dealing with the "more generalized failures in society" that contribute to the underrepresentation would require too much time and social energy. Therefore, the government should endeavor to circumvent "the more generalized failures" by in effect requiring rough proportionality of representation in employment by whatever means practicable. Needless to say, rough proportionately could only be achieved through artificial, preferential means. Means that tragically abdicate any responsibility to confront the "more generalized failures" contributing to low performance.

Moreover, enforced proportionality necessarily discriminates against groups whose success exceeds their proportion of the population. For example, earlier in this century, Ivy League universities sought to impose quotas on the number of Jews permitted to enroll in order to maintain rough proportionality of representation. I trust we all agree on the immorality of that policy. Under the present affirmative action regime, however, the University of California was confronted some years ago by the Department of Education for discriminating against Asian-American student in admissions. And this year a group of Chinese-American parents is suing the San Francisco public school district, claiming that an affirmative action program at the premier magnet high school in town, requires Chinese students to score much higher on an admissions test than students of any other ethnic groups. In fact, each ethnic group applying to the school effectively has a separate score that its members must achieve to be admitted to the high school. This to maintain ethnic proportionality and to prevent Asian-American students from achieving too much success in the admissions process.

Enforced proportionality also has the frequent affect of mismatching talent and capital with the wrong opportunities. Much is often said about the cosmetic victory of achieving "diversity" at the front end of the hiring and admissions process. However, a glimpse at the back end often belies any claim of "victory." The University of California boasts about the diversity of its entering classes with nary a word about the fact that over 40 percent of its black students fail to graduate, as opposed to about 10 to 15 percent of whites and Asians. Indeed, statistics suggest that up to 70 percent of black college students at some universities fail to graduate.[2] While the statistics are tragic, the unwillingness to confront the reasons for them is shameful. By admitting black students with lower objective indicators than other students, universities concerned about their diversity numbers are placing some students in an environment where success is unlikely. Most individuals would be better off in settings more commensurate with their objective indicators.

The same is true of capital in the commercial context. By encouraging, through the use of set-asides and other preferences, poorly capitalized firms to enter markets in which they could not otherwise effectively compete, the government is imposing an inefficiency on the market. The same businessperson who is poorly capitalized for government contracting, may in fact be adequately capitalized in another segment of the economy. By directing that capital away from its most efficient use in the marketplace to a market where minorities are "underrepresented," we often in the long-run deprive that businessperson of the most efficient utilization of his or her economic potential.

Theories of Preference

Despite their significant social and economic cost, race and gender preferences in America are today justified essentially on two grounds: 1) the

---

[2] See e.g. Thomas Sowell, *Preferential Policies: An International Perspective* (New York: William Morrow 1991), at pp. 107-112.

remediation of disadvantage caused by past discrimination; and 2) the desire to promote diversity.

A. Remediation of Disadvantage

Remediation of disadvantage was in fact the original moral claim of the proponents of affirmative action. President Johnson's "hobbled runner" metaphor was an expression of that claim. However, that justification today contains insuperable laws. First, preferential policies today tend to benefit the least disadvantaged among and within preferred groups. Middle class white women are now the primary beneficiaries of preferences, largely due to their relatively high level of education and cultural advantage. And even within ethnic minority groups it is the middle class that is best positioned to profit from preference. Despite their well-intended genesis, preferential policies have evolved into a classic middle-class entitlement, almost wholly divorced from any manifest disadvantage of their beneficiaries.

Many defenders of preference maintain that an individualized showing of disadvantage is irrelevant; that the mainstream economy, "the system", is rigged hopelessly in favor of white men. However, the economic and educational success of many non-white immigrants today, as well as the black community's once proud history of overcoming the worst obstacles, militates against the argument that members of preferred groups can only succeed with the tug of government preferment. For example, the ethnic group with the highest rate of entrepreneurship in America today is Korean-Americans (28 percent of Korean-American men own their own business; 20 percent of Korean-American women do).[3] Forty percent of students at the University of California are Asian-America, a number representing the largest single ethnic group at the university, and one far exceeding the Asian-American population of California.[4]

Of course, this is not to suggest that discrimination no longer presents an obstacle to advancement for many minority individuals. It does. Rather, I mean only to rebut the notion that the playing field is hopelessly dominated by white men.[5] To be sure, white men continue to represent a disproportionate share of decision and policy makers in society, however, Asian-Americans, for example, are poised to begin a rapid assent up the ladder of economic and social

---

[3] Heather MacDonald, *Why Korean Americans Succeed*, City Journal, Spring 1995, at 14.

[4] Peter Applebome, *Gains in Diversity Face Attack in California*, N.Y. Times, June 4, 1995, at 1, col. 2.

[5] Indeed, see John Sibley Butler, *Entrepreneurship and Self-Help Among Black Americans* (New York: SUNY Press 1991), for a discussion of the significant economic development of black communities during the apex of the Jim Crow era, an era without preferential policies or government cooperation of virtually any kind. For example, between 1929 and 1932—despite Jim Crow and the Great Depression—black Americans owned some 26,000 retail establishments in America with total net sales in excess of $100 million. Id. at p. 148.

status. That success is attributable not to preferential policies, but to a cultural emphasis on strong families, education, diligence and thrift.[6]

B. Diversity

The second justification for preferential policies is the notion of diversity. By diversifying the ranks of our employees, the theory goes, we will breed transracial familiarity and, consequently, harmoniously dynamic workplaces. Morever, by bringing diverse faces into the shop, we can mitigate against the ostensibly natural tendency to hire and promote people who look like ourselves.

The anecdotal evidence suggests that both of these theories have been woefully inaccurate. Race relations in contexts where preference is writ large—college campuses and municipal employment, for example—have often become toxic as a result of increasing racial antagonism. Litigation over racial preferments in the workplace is escalating, suggesting that personal resentment caused by the policies is growing as well. Colleges, too, are experiencing growing self-segregation among students, rather than an increasing unity.

In the workplace, what Shelby Steele has called the "stab of racial doubt" has infected both preferred and non-preferred groups in such a manner as to impact minority advancement on the job.[7] Having hired members of protected groups based often on a separate, perhaps lower, standard than nonprotected employees, it stands to reason that an employer may be marginally more hesitant to advance protected employees. This stigma attaching to minorities—one which presumes their lesser qualification—is often unfair. But it is not wholly unreasonable in a system that demands that minorities compete under a different—often lower—standard than non-minorities. The clear implication of these policies is that minorities simply cannot compete without "special" help from the government. Thus, the proverbial "glass ceiling" that is said to preclude protected minorities from reaching the professional pinnacle, may in part be a product of the multiple objective standards inherent in preferential policies. Preferential policies thus appear to exacerbate racial resentment and discrimination more effectively than they ameliorate them.

Toward a Constructive Civil Rights Policy

The instituionalization of separate standards of performance for minorities who would otherwise fail to meet the prevailing standard in adequate numbers is what Shelby Steele has described as American society's attempt to buy racial absolution on the cheap. In contrast, the real work of helping

---

[6] See generally MacDonald, supra.
[7] Shelby Steele, *The Content of Our Character* (New York: St. Martin's Press 1990), p. 120.

disadvantaged people meet the highest standard of competition is not cheap in terms of either money or a community's sweat equity.

A truly constructive civil rights policy in America should focus on constructive efforts to confront the real underlying problems of performance in some of America's most distressed communities. Perhaps it is true that if preference policies are abandoned in education, hiring, and contracting, nonAsian minority representation in those spheres would be diminished. But the appropriate response to the diminution should not be to blindly fault discrimination and then to erect group remedies in the form of enforced proportionality and set-asides, in an illusory effort to confront an extraneous enemy. Rather, the diminished representation of some minorities absent preferential policies suggests a much deeper problem of individual performance. A truly affirmative civil rights policy must concern itself with the hard work of improving the performance of disadvantaged individuals.

A 1981 study prepared for this committee suggested that the costs to the Fortune 500 of complying with OFCCP regulations was about $1 billion. A Forbes magazine study estimated that cost in 1993 to be nearly $3 billion.[8] That figure suggests a tragic opportunity cost. The energy and resources expended on implementing preference policies would be much better spent on an earnest effort to improve the early education of truly disadvantaged individuals by supporting families and community institutions like churches and schools; by injecting an element of competition into our failing urban school systems; and, most importantly, by setting the same high standards for kids of all races and genders.

Of course, Congress must still acknowledge the regrettable fact that discrimination persists in America. To that end, reform existing civil rights laws to restore the element of intent to illegal discrimination. That done, Congress can then proceed to significantly strengthen the penalties for discrimination. The deterrent impact of making proven discrimination costly cannot be underestimated. Congress should also ensure that Federal contract and employment opportunities are advertised widely, through outreach programs directed at "underrepresented" communities.

Regulatory barriers to minority entrepreneurship should also be confronted by Congress. Regulations like the Davis-Bacon Act, OSHA, minimum wage laws and certain trade-licensing requirements often present insurmountable barriers to minority entrepreneurs, who are more likely than others to be undercapitalized. I urge this committee to hold hearings, similar to those held by a House Small Business subcommittee last week, which would examine the impact on minority entrepreneurship of a number of Federal and State regulations.

Such a constructive civil rights policy would do much to encourage us all to confront the very real problems that exist in many minority communities today.

---

8 Peter Brimelow and Leslie Spencer, *When Quotas Replace Merit, Everybody Suffers*, Forbes, February 15, 1993, at 80.

Preferential policies, on the other hand, despite all their good intentions, only divert precious energy and private resources from the fundamental problems facing us as Americans.

As the world marketplace moves into a new, competitive information age, we can ill-afford to say to some individuals that their skin color or chromosomes entitle them to opt-out of the highest standards of competition. We owe our children more than that. We owe America's future more than that.

Conclusion

The social costs of racial and gender preferences in America is today prohibitive. The ceaseless emphasis on group difference and victimhood which is demanded by the existing structure is corrosive of social relations in the workplace and the larger society. Moreover, the significant economic costs associated with maintaining the present system represent a tragic opportunity cost: by requiring an adaptation of standards to fit performance, rather than the converse, we simply allow problems of performance to fester and deteriorate. The Congress should remove itself from the burgeoning business of racial and gender preferences. Absent a truly constructive civil rights approach, one that encourages individual achievement of uniformly high standards, we allow the middle class of America to play the fiddle of preference while truly disadvantaged communities burn.

CHAPTER 7

Minority and Small Disadvantaged Business Contracting: Legal and Constitutional Developments

Charles V. Dale

INTRODUCTION

Minority small business development and contracting policies of government at the federal, state, and local level continue to stir legal controversy in the wake of the U.S. Supreme Court's 1995 ruling in *Adarand Constructors v. Pena.*[1] That case for the first time applied the constitutional rigors of "strict scrutiny," an established judicial standard for reviewing state and local affirmative action measures, to race-conscious decisionmaking by the federal government. Thus, to pass constitutional muster, the Department of Transportation (DOT) had to show that a federal program to "compensate" contractors on federal highway projects for the added costs of doing business with "disadvantaged" minority subcontractors furthered a "compelling governmental interest" and was "narrowly tailored" to that end. By a narrow 5 to 4 margin, the U.S. Supreme Court vacated a contrary appeals court ruling and remanded the case for reconsideration in light of these principles.

The standard for judicial review of affirmative action prior to *Adarand* distinguished between racial preferences mandated by Congress and those implemented by the states or localities. In *Croson v. City of Richmond,*[2] which voided a 30% local government set-aside for minority contractors, the Court announced that state or local affirmative action measures were to be strictly scrutinized for a compelling governmental objective and had to be "narrowly tailored." This meant, in practice, that local officials had to demonstrate "specific" and "deliberate" past discrimination in public contracting--usually in the form of "disparity studies" charting minority underutilization as contractors and other anecdotal, direct or indirect evidence of minority exclusion--and a degree of remedial precision that not infrequently led to judicial invalidation of race-conscious remedies. A tradition of deference for Congress' role as "co-equal" enforcer of constitutional equal protection, however, had twice led the Court to affirm racial preferences in federal legislation to promote minority group participation in federal procurement and broadcast licensing proceedings. *Fullilove v. Klutznick*[3] and *Metro Broadcasting Inc. v. F.C.C.*[4] appeared to

---

1 115 S. Ct. 2097 (1995).

2 488 U.S. 469 (1989).

3 448 U.S. 448 (1980).

4 497 U.S. 547 (1990).

permit Congress wider latitude in the formulation of race-conscious remedies based upon historical and nationwide data relative to past minority exclusion or for other important governmental purposes.

On June 2, 1997, the U.S. District Court in Colorado issued its decision on remand from *Adarand* in which it determined how strict scrutiny was to be applied to federal affirmative action measures.[5] Judge Kane determined that while the governmental interest in "reducing discriminatory barriers in federal contracting" was indeed a "compelling" one, the "almost exclusive" emphasis on race and ethnicity in the program as administered was not "narrowly tailored." The Colorado ruling was the first of several cases pending in district courts around the nation to decide the constitutionality of the racial "presumption" used by virtually every major federal agency to allocate the benefits of federal contracts under various programs designed to increase participation by "socially and economically disadvantaged" small businesses (DBEs).

The latest action in *Adarand* is in general accord with other federal decisions invalidating state and local governmental programs to promote minority contracting--in Richmond, San Francisco, San Diego, Dade County, Fla., Atlanta, New Orleans, Columbus, Ohio, Louisiana and Michigan, among others--and new challenges continue to be filed.[6] Joining this judicial chorus, the U.S. Ninth Circuit Court of Appeals recently gave its constitutional imprimatur to efforts of California voters to curtail racial preferences in state employment, education, and contracting activities when it reversed Judge Henderson's order enjoining implementation of Proposition 209 as a violation of minority rights.[7] The Clinton Administration continued its response to *Adarand* on May 8, 1997 by publishing a new Justice Department policy and proposed revisions to the federal procurement regulations.

A BRIEF HISTORY OF FEDERAL STATUTORY MINORITY CONTRACTING PROGRAMS

Present day set-aside programs authorizing preferential treatment in the award of government contracts to "socially and economically disadvantaged" small businesses originated in § 8(a) of the Small Business Act of 1958. Initially, the Small Business Administration (SBA) utilized its § 8(a) authority to obtain contracts from federal agencies and subcontract them on a noncompetitive basis to firms agreeing to locate in or near ghetto areas and provide jobs for the unemployed and underemployed. The § 8(a) contracts awarded under this program were not restricted to minority-owned firms and were offered to all small firms willing to hire and train the unemployed and

---

5 *Adarand Constructors Inc. v. Pena*, 1997 WL 295363 (D.Colo.).

6 *Affirmative Action in Md. Draws Legal Challenges*, Wash. Post B1, B4 (June 5, 1997).

7 *Coalition for Economic Equity v. Wilson*, 110 F.3d 1431 (9th Cir. 1997).

underemployed in five metropolitan areas, as long as the firms met the program's other criteria.[8] As the result of a series of executive orders by President Nixon, the focus of the § 8 (a) program shifted from job-creation in low-income areas to minority small business development through increased federal contracting with firms owned and controlled by socially and economically disadvantaged persons.[9] With these executive orders, the executive branch was directed to promote minority business enterprise and many agencies looked to SBA's § 8(a) authority to accomplish this purpose.

The administrative decision to convert § 8(a) into a minority development program acquired a statutory basis in 1978 with the passage of P.L. 95-507, which broadened the range of assistance that the government--SBA, in particular--could provide to minority businesses. Section 8 (a), or the "Minority Small Business and Capital Ownership Development" program, authorizes SBA to enter into all kinds of construction, supply, and service contracts with other federal departments and agencies. The SBA acts as a prime contractor and then "subcontracts" the performance of these contracts to small business concerns owned and controlled by "socially and economically disadvantaged" individuals, Indian Tribes or Hawaiian Native Organizations.[10]

Applicants for § 8(a) certification must demonstrate "socially disadvantaged" status or that they "have been subjected to racial or ethnic prejudice or cultural bias because of their identities as members of groups without regard to their individual qualities."[11] The Small Business Administration "presumes," absent contrary evidence, that small businesses owned and operated by members of certain groups--including Blacks, Hispanics, Native Americans, and Asian Pacific Americans--are socially disadvantaged.[12] Any individual not a member of one of these groups must "establish his/her individual social disadvantage on the basis of clear and convincing evidence" in order to qualify for § 8(a) certification. The § 8(a) applicant must, in addition, show that "economic disadvantage" has diminished its capital and credit opportunities, thereby limiting its ability to

---

[8] *Minority Contracting: Joint Hearing Before the Senate Comm. on Small Business and the House Subcomm. on Minority Enterprise and General Oversight of the Comm. on Small Business*, 95th Cong., 2d Sess. 37 (1978).

[9] E.O. 11652, 3 C.F.R. § 616 (1971), *reprinted in* 15 U.S.C. § 631 authorized the Office of Minority Business Enterprise created by preceding order, E.O. 11458, to provide financial assistance to public or private organizations that provided management or technical assistance to MBEs. It also empowered the Secretary of Commerce to coordinate and review all federal activities to assist in minority business development.

[10] 15 U.S.C. § 637(a).

[11] 15 U.S.C. § 637(a)(5).

[12] 13 CFR § 124.105(b).

compete with other firms in the open market.[13] Accordingly, nonminority applicants seeking to establish social and economical disadvantage must satisfy specified regulatory criteria.[14]

The "Minority Small Business Subcontracting Program" authorized by § 8(d) of the Small Business Act codified the presumption of disadvantaged status for minority group members that applied by SBA regulation under the § 8(a) program.[15] Prime contractors on major federal contracts are obliged by § 8(d) to maximize minority participation and to negotiate a "subcontracting plan" with the procuring agency which includes "percentage goals" for utilization of small socially and economically disadvantaged firms. To implement this policy, a clause required for inclusion in each such prime contract states that "[t]he contractors shall presume that socially and economically disadvantaged individuals include Black Americans, Hispanic Americans, Native Americans, Asian Pacific Americans, and other minorities, or any other individual found to be disadvantaged by the Administration pursuant to § 8(a). . ." All federal agencies with procurement powers were required by P.L. 95-507 to establish annual percentage goals for the award of procurement contracts and subcontracts to small disadvantaged businesses.

A decade later, Congress enacted the Business Opportunity Development Reform Act of 1988,[16] directing the President to set annual, government-wide procurement goals of at least 20% for small businesses and 5% for disadvantaged businesses, as defined by the SBA. Simultaneously, federal agencies were required to continue to adopt their own goals, compatible with the government-wide goals, in an effort to create "maximum practicable opportunity" for small disadvantaged businesses to sell their goods and services to the government. The goals may be waived where not practicable due to unavailability of DBEs

---

[13] The statute, 15 U.S.C. § 637(a)(6)(A), defines economic disadvantage in terms

> socially disadvantaged individuals whose ability to compete in the free enterprise system has been impaired due to diminished capital and credit opportunities as compared to others who are not socially disadvantaged, and such diminished opportunities have precluded or are likely to preclude such individuals from successfully competing in the open market.

[14] 15 U.S.C. § 637(d). Criteria set forth in the regulations permit an administrative determination of socially disadvantaged status to be predicated on "clear and convincing evidence" that an applicant has "personally suffered" disadvantage of a "chronic and substantial" nature as the result of any of a variety of causes, including "long term residence in an environment isolated from the mainstream of American society," with a negative impact "on his or her entry into the business world."13 C.F.R. § 124.105(c).

[15] 15 U.S.C. § 637(d). *See also* 13 CFR § 124.106.

[16] P.L. 100-656, § 502, 102 Stat. 3887, codified at 15 U.S.C. § 644(g)(1).

in the relevant area and other factors.[17] While the statutory definition of DBE includes a racial component, in terms of presumptive eligibility, it is not restricted to racial minorities but also includes persons subjected to "ethnic prejudice or cultural bias."[18] It also excludes businesses owned or controlled by persons who, regardless of race, are "not truly socially and/or economically disadvantaged."[19] Federal Acquisition Act amendments adopted in 1994 amended the 5% minority procurement goal, and the minority subcontracting requirements in § 8(d), to specifically include "small business concerns owned and controlled by women" in addition to "socially and economically disadvantaged individuals."[20]

Additionally, statutory "set-asides" and other forms of preference for "socially and economically disadvantaged" firms and individuals, following the Small Business Act or other minority group definition, have frequently been added to specific grant or contract authorization programs. For example, Congress early on established goals for participation of small disadvantaged businesses in procurement for the Department of Defense, NASA, and the Coast Guard. It also enacted the Surface Transportation Assistance Act of 1982, the Surface Transportation and Uniform Relocation Assistance Act of 1987, and the Intermodal Surface Transportation Efficiency Act of 1991, each of which contained a minority or disadvantaged business participation goal. Similar provisions were included in the Airport and Airway Improvement Act of 1982 in regard to procurements for airport development and concessions.[21] Finally, in 1994, Congress enacted the Federal Acquisition Streamlining Act, permitting federal agency heads to adopt restricted competition and a 10% "price evaluation preference" in favor of "socially and economically disadvantaged individuals" to achieve government-wide and agency contracting goal requirements.[22]

BACKGROUND PROCEEDINGS IN *ADARAND*

The statutory predicate for the affirmative action program in *Adarand* was the Small Business Act and § 106(c) of the Surface Transportation and Uniform Relocation Assistance Act of 1987 (STURRA). As noted, § 8(d) of the Small

---

[17] *See e.g.* 49 C.F.R. §§ 23.64(e), 23.65 (setting forth waiver criteria for the Department of Transportation.

[18] 15 U.S.C. § 637(a)(5).

[19] *See* 49 C.F.R. Pt. 23, Subpt. D, App. C.

[20] P.L. 103-355, 108 Stat. 3243, 3374, § 7106 (1994).

[21] *See generally "Compilation and Overview of Federal Laws and Regulations Establishing Affirmative Action Goals or Other Preference Based on Race, Gender, or Ethnicity,"* CRS Memorandum, February 17, 1995 (Dale), *reprinted at* 141 *Cong. Rec.* S 3929 (daily ed. 3-15-95).

[22] Pub. L. 103-355, 108 Stat. 3242, § 7104 (1994).

Business Act requires prime contractors to maximize opportunities for participation in the performance of federal contracts by "small business concerns owned and controlled by socially and economically disadvantaged persons [DBEs]." In addition, § 502 of the Act establishes an annual 5% government-wide participation goal for DBEs in federal contracting activities and requires specific goals for businesses owned by minorities and other disadvantaged businesses.[23] To implement this policy, a subcontracting clause must be included in all covered prime contracts stating that "[t]he contractors shall presume that socially and economically disadvantaged individuals include Black Americans, Hispanic Americans, Native Americans, Asian Pacific Americans, and other minorities, or any other individual found to be disadvantaged by the Administration pursuant to § 8(a). . ."

Firms applying for § 8(a) certification must show "socially disadvantaged" status or that they "have been subjected to racial or ethnic prejudice or cultural bias because of their identities as members of groups without regard to individual qualities."[24] SBA's § 8(a) regulations track the minority subcontracting clause by "presuming," absent contrary evidence, that Black, Hispanic, Asian Pacific, Subcontinent Asian, and Native Americans, as well as "members of other groups designated from time to time by SBA," are "socially disadvantaged."[25] Any individual not a member of one of these groups must "establish his/her individual social disadvantage on the basis of clear and convincing evidence." In addition, any § 8(a) applicant, minority or nonminority, must show that "economic disadvantage" has diminished its credit and capital opportunities in the competitive market. Accordingly, while disadvantaged status under the SBA includes a racial component, in terms of presumptive eligibility, it is not restricted to racial minorities, but also includes persons subjected to "ethnic prejudice or cultural bias."[26] It also excludes businesses owned or controlled by persons who, regardless of race, are "not truly socially and/or economically disadvantaged."[27] The Small Business Act definition of DBE also applies to contracts, like that in the *Adarand* case, financed by

---

[23] 15 U.S.C. § 644(g)(1). That law establishes a government-wide goal of at least five percent participation by "socially and economically disadvantaged individuals" in all federal procurements as measured by the total value of all prime contract and subcontract awards. The overall annual goal for the government is set by the President with individual goals determined jointly by the head of each federal agency and the Office of Federal Procurement Policy so as to provide the "maximum practicable opportunity" for DBEs "to participate in the performance of contracts let by such agency."

[24] 15 U.S.C. § 637(a)(5).

[25] 13 C.F.R. § 124.105(c).

[26] 15 U.S.C. § 637(a)(5).

[27] *See* 49 C.F.R. Pt. 23, Subpt. D, App. C.

STURRA--a 1987 DOT appropriations measure which included a 10% disadvantaged business set-aside.[28]

In *Adarand*, the Federal Highway Lands Program, a component of the Federal Highway Administration within DOT, had developed a "race-conscious subcontracting compensation clause (SCC)" program. The SCC did not allocate or set-aside a specific percentage of subcontract awards for DBEs or require a commitment on the part of prime contractors to subcontract with minority firms. Rather, "incentive payments" varying from 1.5% to 2% of the contract amount were paid to prime contractors whose subcontracts with one or more qualified DBEs exceeded 10% of total contract value. The SCC program was challenged by *Adarand*, a white-owned construction firm whose low bid on a subcontract for highway guard rails was rejected in favor of a higher bidding DBE. Both the federal trial court and the Tenth Circuit upheld the program by applying "lenient" judicial review--"resembling intermediate scrutiny"--rather than strict scrutiny under *Croson*, and required no detailed showing of past discrimination as remedial justification for congressionally-mandated affirmative action. Because the program was not limited to racial minorities, and nondisadvantaged minority group members were ineligible to participate, the appeals court concluded, the program was "narrowly tailored." The 10% threshold was deemed "an optional goal, not a set-aside" since it was "entirely at the discretion of the prime contractor" whether to accept or forego the monetary DBE subcontracting incentives.

THE U.S. SUPREME COURT DECISION IN *ADARAND*

Justice O'Connor, author of the majority opinion, was joined by the Chief Justice and Justices Scalia, Thomas and Kennedy in reversing the appeals court decision. The majority rejected the equal protection approach that applied "intermediate scrutiny" or some other relaxed standard of review to racial line-drawing by the Congress for remedial or other "benign" legislative purpose. "Strict scrutiny" of all racial classifications by the government, at whatever level, was required to determine whether benign or invidious motives inspired the legislative action and because the guarantee of equal protection secured by the 5th and 14th Amendments is a "personal" right extending to the "individual" and "not groups." Strict scrutiny of federal race conscious affirmative action was dictated by "three general propositions" that the majority deduced from the constitutional precedents culminating in *Croson*: judicial "skepticism" regarding all disparate governmental treatment based on race or ethnicity; "consistency," without regard to the race of those "burdened or benefitted" by the classification; and "congruence" between equal protection and due process analysis. Consequently, because the "race-based rebuttable presumption" in the DOT program was an "explicit" racial classification, Justice O'Connor determined, "it must be analyzed by a reviewing court under strict scrutiny," and to survive, must be "narrowly tailored" to serve a "compelling governmental interest."

---

[28] P.L. 100-17 § 106(c).

Adarand directly negated prior judicial holdings that Congress has substantially greater latitude than the states or localities in crafting affirmative action measures for racial or ethnic minorities. *Metro Broadcasting* was expressly overruled, and *Fullilove* adjudged "no longer controlling," insofar as those decisions exhibited greater tolerance for race-conscious lawmaking by Congress. The Court refrained, however, from invalidating or deciding the ultimate constitutional fate of the minority subcontracting incentive program in *Adarand*. Rather, "because our decision today alters the playing field in some important respects," Justice O'Connor remanded the case to the lower courts for application of the principles announced by the majority. In a caveat to her opinion, Justice O'Connor made an important observation in which she sought to "dispel the notion," advanced by Justice Marshall's concurrence in *Fullilove*, that "strict scrutiny is 'strict in theory, but fatal in fact.'"[29] The role of Congress as architect of remedies for past societal discrimination is also obliquely acknowledged. "The unhappy persistence of both the practice and the lingering effects of racial discrimination against minorities in this country is an unfortunate reality, and the government is not disqualified from acting in response to it."[30] Thus, a majority of the Justices--all but Justices Scalia and Thomas--may accept some forms of racial preference in at least some circumstances. No further guidance was provided, however, as to the scope of remedial authority remaining in congressional hands, or the conditions for its exercise.

Two members of the majority, Justices Scalia and Thomas, wrote separately to espouse a far more restrictive view that would foreclose all governmental classifications by race or ethnicity. Justice Scalia declared that "government can never have a 'compelling interest' in discriminating on the basis of race in order to 'make up' for past racial discrimination in the opposite direction." Justice Thomas was of the view that the "racial paternalism" of affirmative action was more injurious than beneficial to minorities. "In my mind, government-sponsored racial discrimination based on benign prejudice is just as noxious as discrimination inspired by malicious prejudice. In each instance, it is racial discrimination, plain and simple."

Justices Stevens, Souter, Ginsburg, and Breyer dissented. Justice Stevens, a member of the majority striking down the minority set-aside in *Croson*, chided the majority for ignoring distinctions between invidious discrimination and governmental efforts to "foster equality in society" through racial preferences. "There is no moral or constitutional equivalence between a policy that is designed to perpetuate a caste system and one that seeks to eradicate racial subordination," he declared. Justices Souter and Ginsburg, in separate dissents, shared a belief that federal affirmative action programs remain viable under the majority's analysis. Justice Souter anticipated "some interpretive forks in the road before the significance of strict scrutiny for congressional remedial statutes becomes entirely clear." Despite this, Justices Ginsburg and Breyer felt "[t]he

---

29 115 S. Ct. at 2117.

30 *Id.*

divisions in this difficult case should not obscure the Court's recognition of the persistence of racial inequality and a majority's acknowledgement of Congress' authority to act affirmatively, not only to end discrimination, but also to counteract discrimination's lingering effects."

In *Adarand*, therefore, the Supreme Court did not condemn all federal affirmative action efforts, and even the task of assaying the constitutionality of the specific program before it was remanded to the courts below. Justice O'Connor's order generally echoed *Croson* by asking the lower courts to determine whether the governmental interest served by the federal program is "compelling," whether the program is "narrowly tailored," limited in duration, and whether "any consideration of race-neutral means to increase minority business participation" had preceded adoption of race-conscious remedies. By requiring "strict scrutiny" of racial or ethnic preferences imposed by Act of Congress, however, the ruling implies that both the legislative justification for such programs and the means chosen for their execution will henceforth be subject to closer judicial examination. In its remand order, Justice O'Connor stressed the need to clarify the precise operation of the complex federal statutes and regulations relating to social and economic disadvantage and the race-based presumption under the Small Business Act. The majority sought technical clarification of the regulatory scheme in relation to operation of the presumption and, in particular, whether "individualized showings" of economic disadvantage were required by various SBA and DOT regulations. The answer to questions such as these may reveal whether the "rebuttable" presumptions are irrebuttable in fact, or may be a subterfuge for rigid racial "quotas." By way of parallel, one flaw in the Richmond program voided by *Croson* was the absence of a "waiver" for situations where "the particular MBE seeking a racial preference has [not] suffered from the effects of past discrimination by the city or prime contractors."[31]

THE U.S. DISTRICT COURT INVALIDATES THE DOT PROGRAM

On June 2, 1997, the Colorado federal district court issued its memorandum decision and order on remand in the *Adarand* case.[32] As a threshold matter, the District Judge Kane considered whether the concept of congruence enunciated by Justice O'Connor for the *Adarand* majority required the federal government to make the same particularized showing of past discrimination as demanded of states and localities to support adoption of minority contracting programs or whether Congress, as national legislature, had broader authority to enact remedies for nationwide discrimination. Opting for the latter position, Judge Kane determined that "Congress' constitutionally imposed role as... guardian against racial discrimination" under § 5 of the Fourteenth Amendment distinguished federal authority from that of the states and localities. Consequently, findings of nationwide discrimination derived from congressional

---

31 488 U.S. at 508.

32 *Supra* n. 2.

hearings and statements of individual federal lawmakers were entitled to greater weight than the "conclusory statements" of state or local legislators rejected by *Croson*. "Congress," in other words, "may recognize a nationwide evil, and act accordingly, provided the chosen remedy is narrowly tailored so as to preclude the application of a race-conscious measure where it is not warranted."

The government's brief catalogued congressional hearings over a nearly two decade period depicting the social and economic obstacles faced by small and disadvantaged entrepreneurs, mainly minorities, in business formation and competition for government contracts. In addition, "disparity studies" conducted after *Croson* in most of the nation's major cities comparing minority-owned business utilization with availability had disclosed "a serious pattern of discrimination across all regions. . .and across a wide range of industries." This record satisfied Judge Kane that Congress had a "strong basis in evidence" for concluding that official complicity with private discrimination in the construction industry contributed to discriminatory barriers in federal contracting, a situation the government had a "compelling" interest in remedying.

The "narrow tailoring" aspect of the Judge Kane's decision entailed a fairly technical analysis of the SCC program in actual operation. The rejected white contractor in *Adarand* contended that by linking the race-based presumptions mandated by the SBA programs statutes and regulations with financial "bonus" incentives of the SCC, the program caused prime contractors to discriminate against lower-bidding non-DBE subcontractors. The government countered that the SCC payment was "compensation" designed only to reimburse prime contractors for additional sums they may have to expend as a result of hiring DBE's, an objective directly relevant to the program's remedial purpose. Judge Kane ruled in favor of the nonminority contractor. The record revealed no increased costs to this prime contractor associated with this particular DBE subcontract. The payment thus appeared to the court a "gratuity" for a prime contractor whose choice of a subcontractor was based "only on race" and could not "be said to be narrowly tailored to the government's interest of eliminating discriminatory barriers."

Second, although revised since, the application forms used by the state to grant DBE certification in 1985 when the case arose required minimal information from the applicant as to financial condition and property ownership, centering instead "almost exclusively" on minority status. "Indeed," observed the district judge, "under these standards, the Sultan of Brunei would qualify." For this reason, the racial presumption governing the SCC program was found to be both "overinclusive"--in that its benefits were available to all named minority group members--and "underinclusive"--because it excluded members of other minority groups or caucasians who may share similar disadvantages. "This supports the conclusion that the presumptions of disadvantage set out in federal statutes and regulations are not narrowly tailored to those who have suffered the effects of prior discrimination in that they allow implementation in such a way as to permit an absolute preference to certain business entities based solely on their race."

Also indicative of governmental failure to narrowly tailor the program were inconsistencies between the statutes and regulations, noted in Justice O'Connor's opinion, as to the definition of disadvantaged individual and, in particular, the scope of presumption in relation to economic disadvantage and racial minorities. Whereas the SBA's § 8(a) regulations, for example, presumed social disadvantage only and required individualized inquiry into each participant's economic disadvantage, DOT regulations under related transportation funding measures presumed racial minorities were both socially and economically disadvantaged.[33] While conceding that the SCC program was "more flexible" than the "rigid racial quota" in *Croson*, or the 10% set-aside approved by *Fullilove*, Judge Kane in effect found it tainted by the government-wide 5% goals and transportation set-asides which it implemented.

> Thus, although the SCC's contain no quotas, they are used as one of the methods to attain the percentage goals in the SBA, STURAA and ISTEA, and are thus inextricably linked with these goals. Insofar as the percentage goals are a foundation for the use of the SCCs, rooted in the same race-based presumptions contained in the SCCs, I find the statutory sections containing those goals insufficiently narrowly tailored for the same reasons as I stated in making that determination regarding the SCCs themselves.[34]

For these reasons, the SCC program did not survive strict scrutiny; summary judgment was granted for Adarand Constructors, Inc. and against the federal government. The SBA's 5% government-wide goal, the transportation set-aides of STURAA and ISTEA, and SCC program "as applied to highway construction in the State of Colorado" was declared unconstitutional and enjoined.

Although limited in scope to operation of the SCC program and underlying federal statutes "as applied" to the specific circumstances before the court, Judge Kane's decision may have broader legal ramifications. Both the supporting rational for the order, and sweeping *dicta* from his opinion, suggest that federal

---

33 According to Judge Kane:

> The inconsistencies between these statutes and regulation and the resultant uncertainty as to who may or may not participate in the race-based SCC program preclude a finding of narrow tailoring. As discussed in relation to the different forms which have been used in the certifying process, without a well-defined set of consistent definitions, the SCC program cannot provide the 'reasonable assurance that the application of racial or ethnic criteria will be limited to accomplishing the remedial objectives of Congress and that misapplications of the program will be promptly and adequately remedied administratively." slip op at p. 64 (citing *Fullilove*).

34 Slip opinion at p. 68.

agency consideration of race in the distribution of contracts or other federal benefits--by way of a racial presumption of "social and economic disadvantage" or other explicit preference--may be in substantial constitutional jeopardy. After conceding, on one hand, that Congress is empowered to determine and legislate the national elimination of discriminatory barriers to specific groups, the opinion appears to largely foreclose the exercise of that legislative authority by race-conscious means. In this regard, Judge Kane's stated view that "it [is] difficult to envisage a race-based classification that is narrowly tailored" stands in contrast to Justice O'Connor observation in *Adarand* that strict scrutiny is not "fatal in fact."

Two aspects of the district court's analysis of the "narrow tailoring" requirement could prove most unsettling for federal small disadvantaged business programs in their present form. First, the "optional" or voluntary nature of the SCC program was not enough to save it, notwithstanding the fact that prime contractors were free to accept bid proposals from any subcontractor, regardless of race or ethnicity. The government's failure to prevail on this issue may cast a shadow over other federal minority contracting efforts--e.g. the § 8(a) set-aside, bid or evaluation preferences, and the like--which, under Judge Kane's reasoning, may be viewed as imposing a "choice based only on race" at least as "mandatory" and "absolute" as the incentive payment to prime contractors in *Adarand*, if not more so. Similarly, the fact that the SCC program did not expressly incorporate any "goals, quotas, or set-asides" was not sufficient to divorce it, in the district court's view, from the percentage goal requirements imposed by statutes the program was designed to implement. Those statutory provisions--the 5% minimum disadvantaged small business goal in § 8(d) of the SBA and the parallel 10% requirement in STURAA and ISTEA--were deemed invalid for lack of narrow tailoring. The district court ruling could place in question much of the federal government's current effort to advance minority small business participation in the procurement process by race-conscious means.

RECENT EXECUTIVE AND LEGISLATIVE ACTIONS ON MINORITY PROCUREMENT

Regulatory revisions put forward by the Clinton Administration seek to achieve "narrow tailoring" required of federal minority contracting programs by *Adarand*. An initial focus of the Administration's post-*Adarand* review was a DOD program, known as the "rule of two," developed as a means to attain the 5% goal for DBEs in 10 U.S.C. § 2323. Section 2323 authority--permitting "less than full and open competit[ion]" in DOD procurements provided that the cost of using set-asides or affirmative action measures is not more than 10% above fair market price--was extended to all agencies of the federal government by the Federal Acquisition Streamlining Act in 1994 (FASA).[35] Under the rule of two,

---

[35] Pub. L. 103-355, § 7102, 108 Stat. 3243 (1994). FASA states that in order to achieve goals for DBE participation in procurement negotiated with the SBA, an "agency may enter into contracts using--(A) less than full and open competition by restricting the

whenever a DOD contract officer could identify two or more qualified SDBs to bid on a project within that cost range, the officer was required to set the contract aside for bidding exclusively by SDBs. Due to *Adarand*, use of the rule of two was suspended and FASA rulemaking delayed.

On May 23, 1996, the Justice Department proposed a structure for reform of affirmative action in federal procurement which would set stricter certification and eligibility requirements for minority contractors claiming "socially and economically disadvantaged" status under the § 8(a) and other federal affirmative action programs.[36] The plan would suspend for two years set-aside programs in which only minority firms may bid on contracts. Statistical "benchmarks" developed by the Commerce Department, and adjusted every five years, would provide the basis for estimating expected DBE participation as federal contractors, in the absence of discrimination, for nearly 80 different industries. Where minority participation in an industry falls below the benchmark, bid and evaluation credits or incentives would be authorized for economically disadvantaged firms and prime contractors who commit to subcontract with such firms. Conversely, when DBE participation exceeds an industry benchmark, the credit would be lowered or suspended in that industry for the following year. The new system would be monitored by the Commerce Department, using data already collected to evaluate the percentage of federal contracting dollars awarded to minority-owned businesses, and would rely more heavily on "outreach and technical assistance" to avoid potential constitutional pitfalls.

The Justice Department's response to comments on its proposal, together with proposed amendments to the Federal Acquisition Regulation (FAR) to implement it, were published on May 8, 1997. Three procurement mechanisms would interact with benchmark limits pursuant to the FAR regulation proposed jointly by the Departments of Defense, General Services Administration, and National Aeronautics and Space Administration. A "price evaluation adjustment" not to exceed fair market value by more than 10 %, as authorized by current law, would be available to DBEs bidding on competitive procurements. Second, an "evaluation" credit would apply to bids by nonminority prime contractors participating in joint ventures, teaming arrangements, or subcontracts, with DBE firms. Finally, contracting officers may employ "monetary incentives" to increase subcontracting opportunities for DBEs in negotiated procurements. The comment period for the FAR amendment is 60 days, with a final regulation to follow.

---

competition for such awards to small business concerns owned and controlled by socially and economically disadvantaged individuals described in subsection (d)(3)(c) of section 8 of the Small Business Act (15 U.S.C. 637); and (B) a price evaluation preference not in excess of 10 percent when evaluating an offer received from such a small business concern as the result of an unrestricted solicitation."

[36] 61 *Fed Reg.* 26042, Notices, Department of Justice, Proposed Reforms to Affirmative Action in Federal Procurement, Part IV (May 23, 1996).

The SBA definition of social and economic disadvantage would remain largely intact under the Administration proposal. Members of designated minority groups seeking to participate in DBE and § 8(d) programs would continue to fall within the statutorily mandated presumption of social and economic disadvantage. Such applicants, however, would be required to state their group identification and meet certification criteria for economic disadvantage, according to SBA standards, subject to third party challenge under existing administrative mechanisms. Individuals who do not fall within the statutory presumption may qualify for DBE status by proving that the individuals who own and control the firm are socially and economically disadvantaged. Under current SBA § 8(a) certification policies, persons who are not members of presumed groups must prove social and economic disadvantage by "clear and convincing evidence". The latest DOJ proposal would ease the burden on nonminority applicants by adopting a "preponderance of evidence" rule.

On January 17, 1997, Representative Canady introduced the "Civil Rights Act of 1997," a proposal to abolish most racial, ethnic, and gender preferences in federal law. Senators McConnell and Hatch are lead sponsors of a companion measure in the Senate. H.R. 1909 proposes a broad-based prohibition against discrimination and preferential treatment in the administration of federal contracting, employment, and "any other federally conducted program or activity." Although primarily concerned with "numerical" preferences for "any person or group" predicated on considerations of "race, color, national origin, or sex"--including "a quota, set-aside, numerical goal, timetable, or other numerical objective"--the bill is not limited to such measures. Rather, "an advantage of any kind" in the administration of any program or activity carried out by a federal department or agency, or any officer or employee thereof, would be forbidden by the bill. There are certain exceptions, however. First, there is a basic exemption for federal efforts to expand the "applicant pool" of women and minorities in employment or to "encourage" their participation as federal contractors or subcontractors. Such affirmative recruitment efforts are permitted so long as no preference in selection is involved. In addition, there are specific exemptions for federal actions to aid educational institutions recognized by law as "historically black colleges and universities;" for federal actions authorized by law or treaty in relation to Indian Tribes; or for sex-based classifications where "sex is a bona fide occupational qualification;" or in matters respecting the Armed Forces or the immigration and nationality laws.

CHAPTER 8

Northern Ireland: Fair Employment and the MacBride Principles

Karen Donfried

INTRODUCTION

Successive U.S. Administrations and the U.S. Congress have seen economic development as key to fostering peace in Northern Ireland. Support for the paramilitaries (Catholic and Protestant terrorist groups) is strongest in the communities suffering the highest level of unemployment and economic deprivation; thus, many see the creation of jobs and economic opportunity as on par with working out a political solution to the conflict in Northern Ireland. All major social and economic indicators show that Roman Catholics in Northern Ireland, representing roughly 42% of the population, are more disadvantaged than Protestants, comprising 56% of the population. The most persistent area of inequality has been unemployment. The British government sees inward investment and the creation of employment opportunities, linked to its fair employment legislation, as the best antidotes to Catholic unemployment. Others believe implementation of the MacBride Principles, relating to equal opportunity and affirmative action, would provide an important remedy.[1]

FAIR EMPLOYMENT

The issue of fair employment has many facets, including the incidence of unemployment, and the composition of the work force in both the public and private sectors. High unemployment has been a long-standing grievance of the Catholic community in Northern Ireland. The differential in unemployment rates has marginally declined since 1971, but Catholics still experience rates of unemployment roughly twice as high as Protestants.[2] Among women, Catholics in 1991 were 1.8 times as likely as Protestants to be unemployed. Among men, Catholics in 1991 were 2.2 times as likely as Protestants to be unemployed. The unemployment rate of Northern Irish Catholic males (28.4%)in 1991 was over twice that of Protestant males (12.7%) and Catholics are more likely than Protestants to experience long-term unemployment.

---

[1] For background on issues related to Northern Ireland, see U.S. Library of Congress, CRS, *Northern Ireland: The Peace Process*, by Karen Donfried, CRS Issue Brief 94025, updated regularly.

[2] The figures used in this section date from 1991, because the most up-to-date, comprehensive, and reliable data base is the 1991 Census of Population for Northern Ireland.

Turning to the composition of the work force, the issue of fair participation continues to be sensitive one for Catholics. On the one hand, gains have been made in achieving greater balance in the work force. On the other hand, Catholics continue to be underrepresented in specific, important areas. In comparison with Catholic men, the 1991 Census of Population for Northern Ireland showed that Protestant men were overrepresented in security, managerial, administrative, and skilled engineering occupations. Catholic men were overrepresented in skilled construction trades and manual categories.

In late March 1996, the Fair Employment Commission (FEC), which monitors the composition of the work force in Northern Ireland, released its annual report for 1995. The report shows that the Catholic share of the work force increased by 2.7% to 37.6%.[3] The Catholic proportion of the economically active population is around 40%, and has been increasing for at least the past 15 years, which means that the target for fair participation of Catholics in the work force is not fixed, but is rather growing over time.[4] In commenting on the monitoring report for 1995, the FEC's chairman, Bob Cooper, expressed particular satisfaction with the increase in Catholic representation in professional, administrative and managerial posts, with Catholics representing 39.6% of people in professional occupations.

In Northern Ireland, the public sector employs nearly 40% of the work force. The significant contraction in Northern Ireland's industrial base over the past 25 years has contributed to the public sector's domination of the local economy. At the end of 1995, Catholics comprised 42.6% of public sector employees, excluding security-related occupations.

In the security-related occupations, which include the army, police force, fire service, prison guards and security guards, Protestant men made up 64.3% of the work force in 1991 and Catholic men, 35.7%. In the case of the police force, the Royal Ulster Constabulary (RUC), the imbalance is particularly dramatic: Protestant men comprised 94.7% of the force in 1991; Catholic men, 5.4%.[5] Catholics have not joined the force for many deep-seated reasons. For one, Catholic nationalists (who favor a united Ireland) harbor reservations about

---

[3] Martina Purdy, "More Catholics getting jobs," *Belfast Telegraph*, March 28, 1996.

[4] R.J. Cormack, A.M. Gallagher, and R.D. Osborne, "Fair Enough?," Belfast: Fair Employment Commission for Northern Ireland, June 1993; A.M. Gallagher, R.D. Osborne, and R.J. Cormack, "Fair Shares? Employment, Unemployment and Economic Status," Fair Employment Commission for Northern Ireland, reprinted March 1995. The Department of Employment has stated that the employment differential results from a complex mix of factors, not just discrimination; other factors include "the mismatch between areas where a Catholic population is concentrated and available job opportunities; differences in skills and qualifications between the two communities...," (Rachel Noeman, "N. Ireland Catholics still suffer jobs inequality," Reuters, Oct. 18, 1995).

[5] Gallagher, Osborne, and Cormack, "Fair Shares?," table 3.4, p. 30.

joining a police force with a unionist ethos -- the very name of the force is anathema to them. For another, the IRA is reportedly known to target Catholic members of the force and their families. However, in a recruitment campaign for the RUC following the August 1994 IRA cease-fire, the number of applications from Catholics jumped to 21.5%.[6]

Finally, concerning balance in the public sector's work force, there is a serious underrepresentation of Catholics in the senior ranks of the public service, and in the technical and scientific sections of government employment.

In the private sector, the primary area of Catholic underrepresentation is in large companies, but 40% of their recruits are now Catholic, according to the Fair Employment Commission. In U.S.-owned firms operating in Northern Ireland, Catholics account for nearly 44% of employment.[7]

For Catholics in Northern Ireland, while progress is evident, fair participation has not been achieved. One study concluded that

> the two most striking differentials between Protestant and Catholic profiles are the substantially higher experience of Catholic unemployment and the domination of Protestants in security occupations. As government seeks to assess the impact of its fair employment policies, there is some evidence that significant change in the labor market is starting to occur. On the other hand, the stubborn nature and scale of the unemployment differential will be an important factor shaping the consideration of fair employment and other policy options.[8]

LEGISLATION

The British government, through the Fair Employment Act of 1989 (Northern Ireland), considerably strengthened legislation originally passed in 1976, giving Northern Ireland the toughest anti-discrimination legislation in Europe. The 1989 Act established a Fair Employment Commission to work toward achieving equality of opportunity in employment in Northern Ireland between persons of different religious beliefs and to eliminate unlawful religious and political discrimination in employment. It also established the Fair Employment Tribunal which hears individual cases of alleged religious and political discrimination. Among its provisions, the 1989 Act stipulated that

---

[6] Noeman, "N. Ireland Catholics,"; William Montalbano, "Police Walk a Fine Line in Belfast," *Los Angeles Times*, March 22, 1996, pp. A1, A3; Adrian Guelke, "Policing in Northern Ireland," in Brigid Hadfield, ed., *Northern Ireland: Politics and the Constitution*, Buckingham: Open University Press, 1992, pp. 94-109.

[7] Northern Ireland Information Service, Belfast, November 1995.

[8] "Fair Shares," pp. 10, 84.

employers must take affirmative action by adopting practices to encourage the fair participation of both religious communities and by modifying or abandoning practices that restrict or discourage fair participation. Further, while direct discrimination had been outlawed in 1976, the 1989 act also outlaws indirect discrimination; specifically, job selection requirements or conditions which have a disparate or adverse impact on one group, even if applied equally, were made illegal. Under the Act, all private sector employers with over ten employees must register with the Commission; all public authority employers, regardless of size, are registered. Employers must then submit annual returns on the religious composition of their work force. They must review their recruitment, training and promotion practices once every three years, at the least, and take corrective action if these are shown to be either directly or indirectly discriminatory. Failure to comply with these obligations constitutes a criminal offense. The Commission publishes detailed monitoring information on all registered firms with over 25 employees.

EMPLOYMENT EQUALITY REVIEW

In November 1994, the Secretary of State for Northern Ireland, Sir Patrick Mayhew, invited the Standing Advisory Commission on Human Rights (SACHR) to undertake a comprehensive review of fair employment legislation and relevant government policies. SACHR is a statutory body which provides the British government with independent advice on matters affecting human rights and discrimination in Northern Ireland. In reviewing employment equality, SACHR will judge the effectiveness of the legislation and other government initiatives, and will present detailed recommendations to Secretary of State Mayhew in a report scheduled to be completed in the fall of 1996. SACHR has tried to conduct the review in "as open, accessible and objective a manner as possible"; public participation has been encouraged, and the Commission has received submissions from a wide range of sources.

THE MACBRIDE PRINCIPLES

The MacBride Principles are a set of nine equal opportunity/affirmative action principles, intended to promote employment options for members of underrepresented religious groups in Northern Ireland. The Principles were announced simultaneously in the United States and Northern Ireland in November 1984. Since early 1985, U.S. companies with plants in Northern Ireland have been under pressure to adopt them.

Fashioned loosely after the Sullivan Principles, aimed against the system of apartheid in South Africa, the MacBride Principles were named after Sean MacBride, who died in 1988 after a distinguished career as Irish politician, jurist, diplomat, co-founder of Amnesty International, and Nobel Prize winner. Among other provisions, the Principles call for provocative religious or political emblems to be banned from the workplace; for all job openings to be publicly advertised with special recruitment efforts to attract applicants from underrepresented groups; and for adequate security at the workplace. The Principles were essentially drafted by the Office of the Comptroller of New York City; the Washington-based Irish National Caucus also played a large role in their creation.[9]

The MacBride Principles for Northern Ireland

[signed by Sean MacBride, Dr. John Robb, Inez McCormack, and Father Brian Brady]

In light of decreasing employment opportunities in Northern Ireland and on a global scale, and in order to guarantee equal access to regional employment the undersigned propose the following equal opportunity/affirmative action principles:

1. Increasing the representation of individuals from under-represented religious groups in the workforce including managerial, supervisory, administrative, clerical and technical jobs.
2. Adequate security for the protection of minority employees both at the workplace and while travelling to and from work.
3. The banning of provocative religious or political emblems from the workplace.
4. All job openings should be publicly advertised and special recruitment efforts should be made to attract applicants from under-represented religious groups.
5. Layoff, recall, and termination procedures should not in practice favour particular religious groupings.
6. The abolition of job reservations, apprenticeship restrictions, and differential employment criteria, which discriminate on the basis of religion or ethnic origin.
7. The development of training programs that will prepare substantial numbers of current minority employees for skilled jobs, including the expansion of existing programs and the creation of new programs to train, upgrade, and improve the skills of minority employees.
8. The establishment of procedures to assess, identify, and actively recruit minority employees with potential for further advancement.
9. The appointment of a senior management staff member to oversee the company's affirmative action efforts and the setting up of timetables to carry out affirmative action principles.

---

[9] See U.S. Congress, House of Representatives, Committee on International Relations, Hearing, U.S. Economic Role in the Peace Process in Northern Ireland, March 15, 1995, Washington: Government Printing Office, 1995.

THE MACBRIDE CAMPAIGN

Supporters of the MacBride Principles have launched a two-pronged campaign. First, they would like to have legislation providing for adherence with the MacBride Principles enacted in the United States at the Federal, State and city level. Sixteen States (Connecticut, Florida, Illinois, Maine, Massachusetts, Michigan, Minnesota, Missouri, Nebraska, New Hampshire, New Jersey, New York, Pennsylvania, Rhode Island, Texas, and Vermont)[10] and over 30 cities have adopted legislation on the MacBride Principles. Originally, the focus of State legislation was on requiring that State funds (in general, pension funds) not be invested in U.S. firms operating in Northern Ireland unless those firms had adopted the MacBride Principles. More recently, the emphasis has turned to laws making a firm's implementation of the MacBride Principles a condition of State or local contract eligibility. The State of New York and several cities, including New York, Chicago, and Cleveland, have passed such contract compliance legislation.

Up to this point, no U.S. company operating in Northern Ireland has adopted the MacBride Principles. Instead, about 25 U.S. companies have come to an agreement with the New York City Comptroller's office, whereby they will "make lawful efforts to implement the fair employment standards embodied in the MacBride Principles."[11] Roughly 50 U.S. companies employ over 9,000 people (roughly 9% of the total manufacturing work force) in Northern Ireland. Supporters of the MacBride Campaign believe that their efforts were instrumental in bringing about British passage of the Fair Employment (Northern Ireland) Act of 1989.

REACTION TO THE MACBRIDE PRINCIPLES AND CAMPAIGN

The U.K. government believes that the Principles in themselves are "largely unobjectionable." However, it argues they do not make good law because they are too vague and that the much more detailed fair employment legislation has driven through important change in the workplace. British officials maintain that the MacBride campaign represents a "hassle" factor which has in certain instances harmed employment opportunities by driving away foreign investment critical to creating new jobs. They claim two examples: (1) a major U.S. engineering company, TRW Inc., sold its Northern Irish subsidiary in 1988 due

---

[10] The British government does not consider Texas to have adopted MacBride legislation; others, such as the Investor Responsibility Research Center in Washington, DC and the Office of the Comptroller of the State of New York, do.

[11] For more details, see Heidi Welsh, "A Guide to U.S. Laws and Legislation In Support of the MacBride Principles," Washington: Investor Responsibility Research Center (IRRC), Jan. 1992; Alan Hevesi, "The MacBride Principles and fair employment practices in Northern Ireland," New York: Office of the Comptroller, Dec. 1994, in House Committee on International Relations, Hearing, U.S. Economic Role in the Peace Process in Northern Ireland, Mar. 15, 1995, pp. 159-81.

to pressure from the MacBride campaign, and (2) another, unidentified company decided against an equity investment in Northern Ireland based on the MacBride issue.[12] Others dispute these claims, arguing that evidence of decreased U.S. investment is lacking and emphasizing that in the 10 years of the campaign, net U.S. investment in Northern Ireland has increased significantly.[13]

The unionist parties in Northern Ireland, which are determined to have Northern Ireland remain part of the United Kingdom, strongly oppose both the MacBride Principles and the campaign. The Social Democratic and Labour Party, which represents the majority of the Catholic population and supports a united Ireland, has a more nuanced position, in that it does not oppose the MacBride Principles *per se*, but is anxious that the campaign for their implementation in no way discourage investment in Northern Ireland. Sinn Fein, the political wing of the Provisional Irish Republican Army, is the only Northern Ireland party that unequivocally supports both the principles and the campaign.

The Irish government sees nothing objectionable in the MacBride Principles and shares the main objectives of the Principles, namely the elimination of discrimination in employment. However, the Irish government believes that the primary focus of anti-discrimination measures must be on strong and enforceable legislation within Northern Ireland. Under the Anglo-Irish Agreement (which gives the Irish government the right to put forward views and proposals on matters relating to Northern Ireland), the Irish government has maintained an ongoing dialogue with the British government on matters relating to fair employment in Northern Ireland.

As a presidential candidate, Bill Clinton endorsed the MacBride Principles and reportedly even denied that their implementation would deter investment. As President, however, his Administration has taken a more nuanced stance. In testifying on behalf of the Clinton Administration before the House International Relations Committee on March 15, 1995, former Assistant Secretary of State for European Affairs Richard Holbrooke described the Administration's position on the MacBride Principles:

> The principles themselves are highly commendable and we support them fully. To put them into specific legislation could have an inhibiting effect on the goal we seek. And, therefore, while supporting the principles, we have reserved a strong and formal

---

[12] Northern Ireland: The MacBride Principles Campaign, Northern Ireland Brief, U.K. Government, Jan. 1993; Northern Ireland: Key Facts, Figures, Themes, June 1993, pp. 49-50.

[13] Statement of the Honorable Alan G. Hevesi, Comptroller, City of New York, in House of Representatives, Committee on International Relations, Hearing, U.S. Economic Role in the Peace Process in Northern Ireland, March 15, 1995, p. 44; see also Kenneth A. Bertsch, The MacBride Principles and U.S. Companies in Northern Ireland 1991, Washington, DC: IRRC, 1991, pp. 71, 74.

> position because we do not want to create problems for the very investment that could lead to an improvement of the standard of living of the Catholic portion of Northern Ireland.[14]

The Administration offered no evidence of disinvestment that had resulted from the MacBride Campaign, but, in a written response to questions from the House International Relations Committee, the State Department maintained that the "question that should be asked is how many U.S. companies who might otherwise have invested in Northern Ireland as a base for European operations may have been influenced by MacBride legislation to choose another European location. We have no figures on this possible loss of investment."[15]

THE MACBRIDE PRINCIPLES AND THE INTERNATIONAL FUND FOR IRELAND

The International Fund for Ireland (IFI) is the conduit through which the United States provides assistance to Northern Ireland and the Republic of Ireland. It was created in September 1986 by the British and Irish governments, based on objectives stated in the Anglo-Irish Agreement of 1985; other donors include the European Union, Canada, New Zealand, and Australia. The Fund supports economic and social development projects in the areas most affected by the civil unrest in the North, with roughly 75% of the Fund's resources spent in Northern Ireland and the remainder in border areas of the Republic. Of the money allocated for Northern Ireland, roughly 70% is spent in the most disadvantaged areas. Many of the Fund's projects are focussed on areas suffering from high unemployment, outward migration of young people, lack of facilities, and little private sector investment. The IFI provides seed funding to stimulate private and public sector investment in those areas. The Fund also seeks to "encourage contact, dialogue and reconciliation between nationalists and unionists throughout Ireland." The IFI has assisted roughly 3,100 projects in the areas of tourism, urban development, agriculture and rural development, technology, business and community development. As of September 1994, IFI investment was responsible for the creation of 16,645 direct jobs, together with an additional 7,142 indirect and construction jobs.

The Anglo-Irish Agreement Support Act of September 19, 1986 (P.L. 99-415) authorized U.S. contributions to the Fund. The United States is a major donor, and has requested that its contribution be used primarily to stimulate private sector investment and job creation. On July 11, 1995, the House of Representatives passed the foreign aid appropriations bill (H.R. 1868), which designated $19.6 million for the IFI for FY 1996 and thus rejected the Administration's request for an increase to $29.6 million. The Senate bill, passed on September 21, included no IFI funding. House and Senate conferees decided in late October to appropriate up to $19.6 million for the IFI as

---

[14] HIRC Hearing, U.S. Economic Role, p. 28.

[15] HIRC Hearing, U.S. Economic Role, p. 96, see also pp. 94-5.

proposed by the House. The conferees "strongly" encouraged the IFI "to take every step possible to ensure that all recipients of Fund support are promoting equality of opportunity and non-discrimination in employment." The foreign aid appropriations bill for FY1996 was enacted into law on February 12, 1996 (P.L. 104-107).

House and Senate conferees considering the American Overseas Interests Act (H.R. 1561 -- which authorizes appropriations for foreign assistance programs, including the IFI) decided on March 7, 1996 to authorize $19.6 million for the IFI for FY 1996 and 1997. According to the conference report (104-478), filed on March 8, recipients of U.S. contributions to the Fund, for the first time, need to "employ practices consistent with the principles of economic justice." This condition had been included in the foreign aid authorization bill which the House had passed on June 8, 1995. The principles of economic justice relate to fair employment and are based on the MacBride Principles. They read as follows:

1. Increasing the representation of individuals from underrepresented religious groups in the workforce, including managerial, supervisory administrative, clerical, and technical jobs,
2. Providing adequate security for the protection of minority employees at the workplace,
3. Banning provocative sectarian or political emblems from the workplace,
4. Providing that all job openings be advertised publicly and providing that special recruitment efforts be made to attract applicants from underrepresented religious groups,
5. Providing that layoff, recall, and termination procedures do not favor a particular religious group.
6. Abolishing job reservations, apprenticeship restrictions, and differential employment criteria which discriminate on the basis of religion,
7. Providing for the development of training programs that will prepare substantial numbers of minority employees for skilled jobs, including the expansion of existing programs and the creation of new programs to train, upgrade, and improve the skills of minority employees,
8. Establishing procedures to assess, identify, and actively recruit minority employees with the potential for further advancement, and
9. Providing for the appointment of a senior management staff member to be responsible for the employment efforts of the entity and, within a reasonable period of time, the implementation of the principles described above.

The bill also states that U.S. IFI funds should be directed to areas with higher than average unemployment rates. The House agreed to the conference report on March 12, 1996; the Senate on March 28. President Clinton vetoed the bill on April 12 because of unrelated controversial provisions; an override vote is expected during the week of April 22, but, according to various reports, Congress is unlikely to succeed in overriding the presidential veto.

FAIR EMPLOYMENT: PERSPECTIVE OF THE CHURCHES

In January 1994, officials of Ireland's four largest churches issued "A Call for Fair Employment and Investment in Northern Ireland." It has been described as a significant step forward in developing common ground across religious lines. The statement calls for new economic investment and enforcement of workplace anti-discrimination legislation in Northern Ireland. A particular appeal is made for increased investment by U.S. companies, because "new jobs, fairly distributed,...are a source of cooperation between communities." One element of the call concerns the importance of constructive American involvement and notes that the MacBride Principles "should not be used to discourage investment or encourage disinvestment." The British, Irish, and U.S. governments endorsed the call; in the United States, groups including the AFL-CIO and the Ancient Order of Hibernians in America welcomed it.

LEGISLATION

H.R. 244 (Engel)
Requires certain entities receiving United States funds from the International Fund for Ireland to comply with the MacBride Principles. Introduced January 4, 1995.

H.R. 470 (Gilman)
Provides for adherence with the MacBride Principles by U.S. persons doing business in Northern Ireland. Introduced January 11, 1995.

H.R. 1561 (Gilman)/Conference Report 104-478
Authorizes appropriations for foreign assistance programs, including $19,600,000 for FY1996 and FY1997 for the IFI. Conditions receipt of U.S. funds from IFI on compliance with "principles of economic justice." Conference Report filed March 8, 1996; agreed to by House on March 12, by Senate on March 28; vetoed by President Clinton on April 12.

S. 424 (D'Amato)
Provides for adherence with MacBride Principles by U.S. persons doing business in Northern Ireland. Introduced February 15, 1995.

CONGRESSIONAL HEARINGS, REPORTS, AND DOCUMENTS

U.S. Congress. House of Representatives. Committee on International Relations. Hearing, U.S. Economic Role in the Peace Process in Northern Ireland. March 15, 1995. Washington: Government Printing Office, 1995.

U.S. Congress. House of Representatives. Committee on International Relations. Report 104-128, American Overseas Interests Act of 1995. May 19, 1995. Washington: Government Printing Office, 1995.

CHAPTER 9

Minority and Women-Owned Business Programs of the Federal Government

Mark Eddy

It is a long-standing policy of the federal government to support the development of small disadvantaged businesses (SDBs) owned by minorities and women. SDBs are statutorily defined as small businesses that are owned and controlled by socially and economically disadvantaged individuals who have been subjected to racial or ethnic prejudice or cultural bias and who have limited capital and credit opportunities. Black Americans, Hispanic Americans, Native Americans and Asian Americans are presumed to be socially disadvantaged by the Small Business Act, as amended. Certain others who do not belong to these racial or ethnic groups (such as *non*minority women) can individually establish disadvantaged status for purposes of some federal programs. In other programs, all women are defined as socially disadvantaged and are eligible for participation.

This report is intended as an overview of the major federal programs now in existence and to indicate where interested persons can turn to obtain further information about specific programs.

BACKGROUND

Since the late 1960s, it has been the policy of the federal government to assist small businesses owned by minorities to become fully competitive and viable business concerns. In 1979, businesses owned by women were added to this effort. Federal assistance comes in many forms including preferential treatment in obtaining procurement contracts and subcontracts, management and technical assistance, grants for education and training, surety bonding assistance, and loans and loan guarantees.

Federal programs for minority and women-owned businesses are currently under review—by both the Clinton Administration and the U.S. Congress—as a result of the current controversy over the proper role of affirmative action in such areas as employment, education, and contracting. In addition, the recent Supreme Court decision in the case of *Adarand Constructors, Inc.* v. *Peña*, which challenged a federal program that gives cash bonuses to prime contractors for awarding subcontracts to minority-owned businesses, could have far-reaching implications for all race-conscious governmental programs.[1] On July 19, 1995, President Clinton ordered a review of all federal race-based affirmative action programs in light of the *Adarand* decision. Any program that does not meet the constitutional standard of strict scrutiny as set forth in *Adarand* "must be

[1] *Adarand Constructors, Inc.* v. *Peña*, No. 93-1841 (June 12, 1995). For a legal analysis see: U.S. Library of Congress. Congressional Research Service. *The Supreme Court Decision in* Adarand Constructors Inc. *v.* Peña*: Federal Contracting and Disadvantaged Business Enterprises*. Report No. 95-137 A, by Charles V. Dale. Washington, 1996.

reformed or eliminated."[2] New regulations in response to *Adarand* have been proposed.[3] At the present time, however, the complex web of federal statutes and regulations designed to promote small businesses owned by minorities and women remains largely intact.[4]

This effort finds antecedents in long-established government policies and programs, including contract set-asides, designed to assist small businesses in general. Both the Small Business Act[5] and the Small Business Administration (SBA) it created stand as key elements of the federal government's attempts to enhance the role of *small* businesses in the American economy. The earliest statutory basis for federal aid to *economically disadvantaged* entrepreneurs appeared in the 1967 amendments to the Economic Opportunity Act of 1964, which, in part, directed the SBA to assist small businesses owned by low-income individuals.[6]

During the 1967-69 period of urban unrest, the Small Business Act's theretofore unutilized section 8(a), which authorized the SBA to let federal procurement contracts to *small* businesses, was administratively reformulated to funnel federal procurement contracts to *minority-owned* small businesses.[7] Begun by the Johnson Administration, the section 8(a) program received further impetus during the Presidential campaign of 1968 when candidate Richard Nixon advanced the concept of "black capitalism." The promotion of business ownership opportunities for blacks was widely seen as a desirable way to alleviate the problem of the "hard-core unemployed." With bipartisan support,

---

[2]U.S. President, 1993- (Clinton). Memorandum on Affirmative Action, July 19, 1995. *Weekly Compilation of Presidential Documents*, v. 31, July 24, 1995. p. 1264-65.

[3]U.S. Dept. of Justice, "Response to Comments to Department of Justice Proposed Reforms to Affirmative Action in Federal Procurement," *Federal Register*, vol. 62, no. 90, May 9, 1997, pp. 25648-25653; and U.S. Dept. of Defense, General Service Administration, and National Aeronautics and Space Administration, "Federal Acquisition Regulation; Reform of Affirmative Action in Federal Procurement," *ibid*, pp. 25786-25795.

[4]The 104th Congress did repeal a Federal Communications Commission statute designed to encourage minority ownership of radio and television stations by granting a capital gains tax break for majority-owned broadcast companies that sell broadcast or cable facilities to minority buyers (Public Law 104-7; April 11, 1995; 109 Stat. 93). Other bills in the 104th Congress to restrict or eliminate minority business programs were introduced but not enacted. For recent developments in the 105th Congress, see: U.S. Library of Congress. Congressional Research Service. *Affirmative Action: Recent Congressional and Presidential Activity*. Report No. 97-527 GOV, by Andorra Bruno. Washington, 1997.

[5]Public Law 85-536; July 15, 1958; 15 U.S.C. 631 *et seq*.

[6]Public Law 90-222, § 106 (a), repealed in 1974 by Public Law 93-386, which established the position of Administrator for Minority Small Business within the SBA.

[7]SBA's administrative decision to turn section 8(a) into a minority business program eventually gained statutory basis with the passage in 1978 of Public Law 95-507, which is discussed below beginning on page 7.

the 8(a) program grew rapidly and in recent years has accounted for some 40% of the total value of contract awards to minority-owned firms.

The first law to establish a specific percentage goal for procurement from minority-owned businesses was the Public Works Employment Act of 1977 (P.L. 95-28; 91 Stat. 117). Implemented by the Economic Development Administration within the Department of Commerce, it required that at least 10% of the total dollar value of federal grants for local public works projects be expended through minority business enterprises. Statutes that contain additional percentage goals for individual programs or agencies have followed, as described below.

Over the years, the racial emphasis of this effort has broadened somewhat, from *minority* entrepreneurs to entrepreneurs who are "socially and economically disadvantaged." In 1978, for example, Public Law 95-507 (92 Stat. 1757) explicitly recognized that it is possible for *non*minorities to be disadvantaged. This trend has caused the long-standing term "minority business enterprise" or MBE to be supplemented, and in some cases replaced, by the newer terms "small disadvantaged business" or SDB, and "disadvantaged business enterprise" or DBE.[8] More recently, the U.S. Commission on Minority Business Development has recommended adoption of the term "historically underutilized businesses" or HUBs. The latter acronym has not yet received widespread acceptance, however, and is not used in this report.

DEFINITION OF SMALL DISADVANTAGED BUSINESS

The definitions in federal law of small disadvantaged businesses and women-owned businesses are not uniform. For example, in some statutes women are included within the definition of socially disadvantaged individuals, but in others they are not. Some statutes do not define the terms at all.[9] Section 8(d) of the Small Business Act (15 U.S.C. 637(d)) does, however, contain a comprehensive definition of socially and economically disadvantaged small businesses that applies to SBA programs and that is incorporated by reference into many other statutes.

Section 8(d) defines a small disadvantaged business as a small business concern that is at least 51% owned by a citizen or citizens of the United States who are socially and economically disadvantaged; or, in the case of a publicly

---

[8]The usage of these terms is by no means consistent between programs; women-owned business enterprises (WBEs), for example, are sometimes included in the definition of SDB or DBE and sometimes not (as noted herein in the discussion of the individual programs or statutes).

[9]Section 7107 of the Federal Acquisition Streamlining Act of 1994 (Public Law 103-355; 108 Stat. 3376; 41 U.S.C. 405 note) requires the Office of Federal Procurement Policy (OFPP) to create an interagency panel to review this situation and recommend uniform definitions for SDBs and WBEs and to develop recommendations for a uniform procedure for Federal certification of SDBs and WBEs. See OFPP's request for comments in the *Federal Register*, v. 60, Jan. 4, 1995, p. 456.

owned business, at least 51% of the stock is owned by socially and economically disadvantaged citizens. The daily management and operation of the business concern must also be controlled by an owner or owners who are socially and economically disadvantaged.

Socially disadvantaged individuals are defined by section 8(d) as persons who have been subjected to racial or ethnic prejudice or cultural bias because of their identity as a member of a group, without regard to their individual qualities. As the law specifically states, the social disadvantage of such individuals must stem from circumstances beyond their control. Black Americans, Hispanic Americans, Native Americans and Asian Americans are presumed by statute to be socially disadvantaged, absent evidence to the contrary.

Economically disadvantaged individuals are defined by section 8(d) as socially disadvantaged individuals whose ability to compete in the free enterprise system has been impaired due to diminished capital and credit opportunities, as compared to others in the same or similar line of business and competitive market area who are not socially disadvantaged. (Small businesses owned and managed by economically disadvantaged Indian tribes or Native Hawaiian organizations also fit the definition of small disadvantaged business.)

In order to qualify as *small*, a disadvantaged business must meet the size standard established by regulation for the firm's primary Standard Industrial Classification (SIC) Code. The size standards, which are based upon either the firm's maximum number of employees or its amount of annual receipts, can be consulted in the *Code of Federal Regulations* at 13 CFR Part 121.

WOMEN-OWNED BUSINESS ENTERPRISES

Federal efforts to directly support women business owners began in 1979 with the issuance by President Carter of Executive Order 12138 (44 FR 29637), designed to discourage discrimination against women entrepreneurs and to create programs responsive to their special needs, including assistance in federal procurement. As a result, an Office of Women's Business Ownership was established within the Small Business Administration. This office negotiates annually with each federal agency a percentage goal for the awarding of federal prime procurement contracts to women-owned business enterprises (WBEs). This effort has resulted in federal prime contracts and subcontracts worth at least $5.5 billion going to WBEs in FY1996, amounting to 2.8% of total federal contract dollars awarded in that year, up from $5.3 billion and 2.6% in FY1995.[10]

The federal promotion of WBEs was given statutory authority with the enactment of the Women's Business Ownership Act of 1988 (P.L. 100-533; 102

[10] U.S. Small Business Administration. Office of Government Contracting. Unpublished data. June 1997.

Stat. 2689). This law defined a WBE as a small business that is at least 51% owned, managed and operated by one or more women. It established a new loan guarantee program administered by SBA to guarantee commercial bank loans of up to $50,000 to small firms (not just women-owned firms), created a National Women's Business Council to monitor the progress of federal, state and local governments in assisting WBEs, and authorized grants to private organizations to provide management and technical assistance to WBEs.

Annual procurement goals for WBEs continued to be negotiated between federal agencies and the SBA under the authority of Executive Order 12138 until enactment of the Federal Acquisition Streamlining Act of 1994 (P.L. 103-355; 108 Stat. 3374). This law, known by its acronym "FASA," amended Section 15 of the Small Business Act (15 U.S.C. 644) to establish a 5% annual goal for WBE participation in federal prime contracts and subcontracts. FASA also amended Section 8(d) of the Small Business Act (15 U.S.C. 637(d)) to give WBEs equal standing with small and small disadvantaged businesses in the subcontracting plans of federal prime contractors. Final rules to implement these provisions, contained in Section 7106 of FASA, were published in the *Federal Register* on September 18, 1995 (60 FR 48258).

Further measures to strengthen the federal government's promotion of WBEs were contained in the Small Business Administration Reauthorization and Amendments Act of 1994 (P.L. 103-403; 108 Stat. 4175). This law codified the SBA's Office of Women's Business Ownership, established an Interagency Committee on Women's Business Enterprise to recommend policies to promote the development of WBEs, and restructured the National Women's Business Council as a private advisory panel to the Interagency Committee, the SBA, and Congress. The committee and council held their first meetings simultaneously at the White House in February 1995.

FEDERAL ASSISTANCE FOR STARTING A SMALL BUSINESS

There are no federal programs specifically designed to help disadvantaged individuals obtain start-up capital for new business ventures. The Small Business Administration does offer several forms of financial assistance to a limited number of small business entrepreneurs with sound business plans who are unable to borrow on reasonable terms from conventional lenders. This assistance most often takes the form of loan guarantees under the section 7(a) program, by which the SBA guarantees to pay part of any loss sustained by a bank or other financial institution in the event of default. In general, however, the SBA should be considered a lender of last resort, after other possible sources have been exhausted.

The SBA also helps finance MBEs through its assistance to privately owned Specialized Small Business Investment Companies (SSBICs), also known as

Minority Enterprise Small Business Investment Companies or MESBICS.[11] Located throughout the United States, SSBICs provide equity capital, long-term loans and management assistance to SDBs for expansion, modernization and operating expenses as well as venture capital for start-up costs and research and development expenses. SSBIC assistance to MBEs often takes the form of equity-type investments by which the SSBICs share in the future growth and profits of the firms.

The SSBIC program was strengthened in 1989 by the passage of Public Law 101-162 (103 Stat. 1025; 15 U.S.C. 683), which amended the Small Business Investment Act of 1958 to allow SSBICs to sell their debentures, guaranteed by the SBA, to the private sector, just as the regular Small Business Investment Companies were already permitted to do. This change was designed to enlarge the pool of capital resources available to minority-owned firms. There are some 85 SSBICs in operation at the present time. Information on them can be obtained from the National Association of Investment Companies, 1111 14th Street, N.W., Washington, DC, 20005.

Nonminority women entrepreneurs (as well as minority entrepreneurs) can seek similar assistance from the network of approximately 200 Small Business Investment Companies (SBICs). Created by the Small Business Investment Act of 1958 (P.L. 85-699; 72 Stat. 689), the SBICs, like their specialized counterparts, are private firms that raise funds to provide venture capital for small businesses by selling securities guaranteed by the SBA. Information on them can be obtained from the National Association of Small Business Investment Companies, 666 11th St., N.W., Washington, DC, 20001.

Some federal agencies, such as the Department of Energy and the Farmers Home Administration in the Department of Agriculture, have programs to promote specific kinds of small business creation and development, for which eligible minorities or women can apply. These programs can be identified in the *Catalog of Federal Domestic Assistance* published by the Office of Management and Budget and the General Services Administration. It can be consulted at many libraries and is available by subscription from the Superintendent of Documents, Government Printing Office, Washington, DC 20402.

THE MINORITY BUSINESS DEVELOPMENT AGENCY

Established in 1969 as a result of the issuance by President Nixon of Executive Order 11458 (34 FR 4937),[12] the Office of Minority Business

---

[11]Created in 1969 as a result of Executive Order 11458 (34 FR 4937), and given statutory authority with the passage of the Small Business Investment Act Amendments of 1972 (P.L. 92-595;86 Stat. 1314), SSBICs are also called "Section 301(d) SBICs."

[12]MBDA also operates under the authority of two subsequent Executive Orders: E.O. 11625 (36 FR 19967) issued by President Nixon in 1971, and E.O. 12432 (48 FR 32551) issued by President Reagan in 1983.

Enterprise became in 1979 the Minority Business Development Agency (MBDA). Located in the Department of Commerce, MBDA is the only federal agency charged exclusively with promoting the creation and growth of minority-owned businesses in the United States. MBDA helps federal, state and local government agencies as well as major corporations to increase their purchases from minority-owned firms.

MBDA also provides funding for a network of some 89 Minority Business Development Centers (MBDCs) and 8 Indian Business Development Centers (IBDCs) located throughout the country. These centers provide management and technical assistance to minority entrepreneurs to help them start, expand and manage their businesses. The MBDCs and IBDCs are not sources of capital; they do not make grants or provide loans or loan guarantees. They do, however, offer assistance in identifying possible sources of capital and in preparing financial and bonding proposals for submission to financial institutions or government agencies.

Persons who qualify for assistance from MBDA include blacks, Hispanics, Native Americans, Asian Americans, Eskimos and Aleuts. *Non*minority women are eligible on an individual basis if they are found to be socially or economically disadvantaged, but are not eligible as a group for MBDA assistance. Unlike most other federal programs for disadvantaged businesses, size standards do not apply; MBDA serves minority-owned firms of any size.

Further information about MBDA and its network of MBDCs and IBDCs is available from MBDA regional offices in Atlanta, Chicago, Dallas, New York and San Francisco, and from district offices in Boston, Los Angeles, Miami and Philadelphia.

MBE CONTRACTING AND SUBCONTRACTING GOALS

The enactment in 1978 of Public Law 95-507 (92 Stat. 1757) required all federal agencies to set percentage goals for the awarding of procurement contracts to small minority-owned businesses. These goals are established annually by consultations between each federal agency and the SBA. The same law also amended section 8(d) of the Small Business Act to require prime contractors with federal contracts that exceed $1,000,000 for the construction of any public facility, or $500,000 in the case of all other contracts, to establish percentage goals for the utilization of MBEs as *sub*contractors whenever subcontracting opportunities are present. In FY1996, $15.9 billion of federal procurement funds were expended through MBEs. This sum amounted to almost 8.1% of total federal procurement, compared to 8.0% ($16.2 billion) in FY1995 and 7.1% ($14.0 billion) in FY1994.[13]

---

[13]U.S. Small Business Administration. Office of Government Contracting. Unpublished data. June 1997. (According to the SBA, *total* federal procurement amounted to $197.5 billion in FY1996, $202.3 billion in FY1995, and $196.4 billion in FY1994.)

Public Law 95-507, which can be considered the keystone of the federal SDB edifice, also amended the Small Business Act (15 U.S.C. 644(k)) to require that each federal agency with procurement powers create an Office of Small and Disadvantaged Business Utilization (OSDBU). These offices are responsible for each agency's contracting and development programs for small, disadvantaged and women-owned businesses, and are responsible for coordinating these programs with the SBA. This means, in effect, that virtually every federal agency has procurement programs for MBEs and WBEs. Minority and women entrepreneurs wanting to do business with a specific federal agency should contact the OSDBU of that agency for information on contracting and subcontracting opportunities.

The procedure established by Public Law 95-507 for determining annual MBE procurement goals was changed and strengthened in 1988 by a provision of Public Law 100-656 (102 Stat. 3881; 15 U.S.C. 644(g)-(h)) requiring the President to establish a government-wide procurement goal for SDBs at not less than 5% of the total value of all prime contracts. (The goal for *all* small businesses, including those that are minority-owned, is set at 20%.)[14] The 5% SDB goal went into effect at the beginning of FY1990 and has probably helped to further expand the share of federal contracting and subcontracting dollars going to MBEs despite declining federal procurement budgets.

This government-wide affirmative-action effort for minority-owned businesses was further strengthened by the Federal Acquisition Streamlining Act of 1994 (Sec. 7102; 108 Stat. 3367), which reiterated the 5% SDB goal and extended to civilian agencies two devices previously authorized for use by the Department of Defense in its SDB program. First, when at least two capable SDBs are expected to bid on a contract, that contract can be set aside for exclusive bidding by SDBs. Second, in the case of unrestricted competitions, SDBs can receive a price evaluation preference of up to 10%. (This is achieved by increasing the offers of all non-SDBs by the determined percentage. The winning bid, however, cannot exceed fair market price.) Proposed regulations to implement this new provision of federal procurement law were published in the *Federal Register* on January 6, 1995 (60 FR 2302).[15] Other procurement reforms contained in FASA—such as simplifying acquisition processes for contracts under $100,000 and reserving contracts between $2,500 and $100,000 for exclusive bidding by small businesses—should enlarge contracting opportunities for all small businesses, including minority and women-owned firms.

---

[14]The final policy letter to heads of departments and agencies on implementing small business and SDB goals and on reporting their results to the SBA was published in the *Federal Register* on March 20, 1991 (56 FR 11798). It requires that the five percent SDB goal be applied separately to prime contracts and subcontracts.

[15]Final rules to implement Section 7102 have been held up pending completion of the review of Federal race-based affirmative action programs ordered by the President's directive of July 19, 1995, in response to the Supreme Court's decision in *Adarand Constructors Inc.* v. *Peña*.

Statistics on federal procurement activities, including purchases from MBEs and WBEs, are published quarterly by the federal Procurement Data Center, an agency of the General Services Administration.[16]

SBA's SECTION 8(a) PROGRAM

Named for the section of the Small Business Act from which it derives its authority,[17] the 8(a) program enables the Small Business Administration to enter into contracts with other federal agencies for their procurement needs. The SBA then subcontracts the actual performance of the work to the limited number of economically and socially disadvantaged firms certified by the SBA for participation in the program. During FY1996, a total of 6,115 businesses participated in the 8(a) program. These firms were awarded federal procurement contracts worth about $5.3 billion. The five largest areas of contracting activity were engineering services, computer services, general contractors, physical and biological research, and facility support management services.[18] All federal departments and major independent agencies participate in the 8(a) program.

For purposes of program enrollment, African Americans, Hispanic Americans, Native Americans, and Asian Americans are presumed to be socially disadvantaged. Others, such as women or disabled persons who do not belong to the presumptively disadvantaged minority groups, can individually establish social disadvantage by clear and convincing evidence of personal, chronic and substantial disadvantage stemming from color, national origin, sex, physical handicap, long-term residence in an environment isolated from the mainstream of American society, or other similar circumstance; there are, however, few such persons in the 8(a) program.

Economic disadvantage is established, in part, by the personal net worth of the owners and managers claiming disadvantage. Individuals whose personal net worth exceeds $250,000 (excluding their ownership interests in the firm and the equity in their primary places of residence) will not be considered economically disadvantaged for purposes of 8(a) program entry.

Revised by the Business Opportunity Development Reform Act of 1988 (P.L. 100-656; 102 Stat. 3853), the 8(a) program's new regulations were published in the *Federal Register* on August 21, 1989 (54 FR 34692) and can be consulted in

---

[16]Further information regarding the Federal Procurement Data System reports or capabilities can be obtained from the Federal Procurement Data Center, U.S. General Services Administration, 7th and D Streets, S.W., Room 5652, Washington, DC 20407.

[17]Section 8(a) of The Small Business Act, Public Law 85-536, as amended, can be consulted at 15 U.S.C. 637(a).

[18]U.S. Small Business Administration. Office of Minority Enterprise Development. *A Report to the U.S. Congress on Minority Small Business and Capital Ownership Development for Fiscal Year 1996.* Undated. p. 3.

the *Code of Federal Regulations* at 13 CFR Part 124. Section 8(a) manufacturing contracts over $5 million and other contracts over $3 million must now be awarded on the basis of competition between eligible 8(a) firms. The regulations governing this new requirement were published in the *Federal Register* on October 31, 1989 (54 FR 46004) and appear in the *Code of Federal Regulations* at 48 CFR Parts 5, 6, 19 and 52.

The 8(a) program is designed as a business development program, and certified SDB firms are required to develop comprehensive business plans with specific business targets, objectives and goals. Program participation is limited to a period of nine years. As companies move through the program, they are required to obtain a progressively larger share of their revenues from non-8(a) sources in order to enhance their chances of survival after graduating from the program.

In order to meet these objectives, section 7(j) of the Small Business Act requires the SBA to provide management and technical assistance to 8(a) firms. Assistance is provided in such areas as loan packaging, financial counseling, accounting and bookkeeping, marketing and management. There are also provisions for surety bonding assistance and for advance payments to help in meeting financial requirements necessary to the performance of a contract.

SDBs can participate in many other SBA programs that are available to small businesses in general. These include a national network of Small Business Development Centers that offer technical and management assistance, a surety bonding program for contractors who are unable to obtain bonding through normal channels, and several business development programs that emphasize improvement of management skills. Small business owners interested in participating in the 8(a) program or other SBA assistance programs should contact their nearest SBA field office.

DEPARTMENT OF TRANSPORTATION'S DBE PROGRAMS

The Surface Transportation and Uniform Relocation Assistance Act of 1987 (STURAA) (P.L. 100-17; 101 Stat. 145) required the Department of Transportation (DOT) to expend not less than 10% of federal highway and transit funds with disadvantaged business enterprises. This requirement was reauthorized by the Intermodal Surface Transportation Efficiency Act of 1991 (P.L. 102-240; 105 Stat. 1919). STURAA was one of the first pieces of federal legislation to include women in the definition of socially disadvantaged individuals. Prior to its passage, DOT maintained separate programs and goals for MBEs and WBEs.

Federal transportation funds are distributed by DOT through state departments of transportation and state and local mass transit agencies. These agencies are required to adopt specific annual goals for DBE participation in their highway and transit contracts. The state and local transportation agencies are also responsible for establishing certification procedures for their DBE programs, although all section 8(a) firms are automatically certified. Information on highway and transit contracting opportunities for DBEs can be obtained from state highway departments and state and local transit agencies.

Amendments in 1987 and 1992 to the Airport and Airway Improvement Act of 1982 (49 U.S.C. App. §2204) require DOT to expend not less than 10% of federal airport improvement funds with DBEs. Also, an airport must ensure, to the maximum extent practicable, that at least 10% of concession contracts go to DBEs. This law requires DOT to establish uniform criteria to be used by state governments and airport agencies in certifying whether firms qualify as DBEs and, like STURAA, includes women in the definition of disadvantaged individuals.

DBEs seeking to compete in transportation contracting opportunities can experience difficulties in obtaining capital and meeting bonding requirements. Two programs conducted by DOT's Minority Business Resource Center in Washington are designed to assist DBEs in these areas. Short term working capital at prime interest rates can be obtained through the Short Term Lending Program, and payment and performance bonds can be issued through the Bonding Assistance Program. To be eligible for these assistance programs, certified DBEs must have been awarded a transportation-related contract.

DEPARTMENT OF DEFENSE'S SDB PROGRAM

Section 1207 of the National Defense Authorization Act of 1987 (P.L. 99-661; 100 Stat. 3973) established a goal, for fiscal years 1987 through 1989, of awarding 5% of the total value of Department of Defense (DOD) procurement contracts to minority firms, historically black colleges and universities, and other minority institutions. Repeatedly reauthorized, this requirement was extended for seven years, through FY2000, by the National Defense Authorization Act for Fiscal Year 1993 (P.L. 102-484; 106 Stat. 2442). This same law also codified the program as section 2323 of Title 10, *U.S. Code*. The recently enacted Federal Acquisition Streamlining Act extended section 2323 to the U.S. Coast Guard and the National Aeronautics and Space Administration. Regulations implementing this program can be found in the *Code of Federal Regulations* at 48 CFR Part 219.

In pursuit of the 5% goal, DOD procurement agencies set aside a portion of their procurement contracts for exclusive bidding by SDBs. (DOD is the largest participant by far in the 8(a) program.) Moreover, SDBs can receive a price evaluation preference of up to 10% when competing against non-SDBs in open solicitations and, unlike with civilian agencies, winning bids with DOD are allowed to exceed fair market price. In addition, major DOD prime contractors are required to submit plans and goals for *sub*contracting with SDB concerns. DOD procurement funds going to SDBs in FY1996, including direct contracts, subcontracts and 8(a) contracts, amounted to $9.7 billion, or 8.9% of total DOD procurement dollars, up from $7.0 billion and 6.0% in FY1992, when the 5% goal was first achieved.[19]

DOD contracting offices throughout the country maintain active programs to identify SDB concerns and place them on mailing lists that are used in the solicitation of proposals and bids. Unlike SBA's section 8(a) program and DOT's DBE program, DOD's section 2323 program has no certification requirements. Nonminority women are not presumed to be disadvantaged for purposes of Section 2323.

To encourage DOD contractors to increase SDB participation in subcontracting, Congress in 1990 created the Mentor-Protege Pilot Program. Mandated by section 831 of the National Defense Authorization Act for Fiscal Year 1991 (P.L. 101-510; 104 Stat. 1607), the program authorizes prime contractors (mentors) to award noncompetitive subcontracts to SDBs (proteges) and to provide loans or make other investments in protege firms. Mentors receive incentives in the form of reimbursements for their assistance to proteges and earn credit towards their SDB subcontracting goals. A voluntary program, mentors are responsible for selecting their proteges, subject to the approval of DOD's Office of Small and Disadvantaged Business Utilization, which oversees the program.

Small Business Specialists are available at each defense procurement agency to assist SDBs in marketing their products and services with DOD. Information and guidance are available on defense procurement procedures, how to be placed on solicitation mailing lists, and how to identify prime contracting and subcontracting opportunities. A list of the locations of Army, Navy, Air Force, Defense Logistics Agency and other DOD procurement and contract administration offices, together with the names of each location's Small Business Specialist, can be found in the DOD publication *Small Business Specialists*, which can be purchased from the Superintendent of Documents, U.S. Government Printing Office, Washington, DC 20402.

Two other DOD publications, *Selling to the Military* and *Guide to the Preparation of Offers for Selling to the Military*, provide background information on DOD procurement procedures, items purchased, the location of military purchasing offices, and how to prepare bids and proposals. Subcontracting opportunities with DOD prime contractors can be identified in the DOD directory *Subcontracting Opportunities with DoD Major Prime Contractors*, which lists the names and addresses of DOD prime contractors, the names and telephone numbers of the firms' small business liaison officers, and the products or services being provided to DOD. These publications are also for sale by the Superintendent of Documents.

---

[19] U.S. Department of Defense. Office of the Secretary of Defense. Office of Small and Disadvantaged Business Utilization. Unpublished Data. (Undated tables provided to CRS via telephone facsimile on June 27, 1997.)

LAWS THAT APPLY TO OTHER DEPARTMENTS AND AGENCIES

Other federal laws that contain provisions designed to assist small disadvantaged businesses and that apply to specific executive departments or independent agencies not discussed above include the following. Some of these statutes, as noted, include women as socially or economically disadvantaged, making firms owned by nonminority women eligible for participation.

Department of Energy

The Energy Policy Act of 1992 (P.L. 102-486; 106 Stat. 3133) requires that not less than 10% of the total combined amounts obligated for contracts and subcontracts by each agency under this Act be expended with small business concerns controlled by socially and economically disadvantaged individuals or women, historically black colleges and universities (HBCUs), or colleges and universities having a student body in which more than 20% of the students are Hispanic Americans or Native Americans.

The National Defense Authorization Act for FY1994 (P.L. 103-160; 107 Stat. 1956) establishes for the Department of Energy (DOE) a 5% goal for contracts and subcontracts with SDBs, HBCUs, and minority institutions in carrying out national security programs for the Department of Defense. This goal applies to procurement funds obligated in each fiscal year from 1994 through 2000.

DOE has recently initiated a pilot mentor-protege program, set to run initially for two years, to help energy-related SDBs and WBEs improve their business and technical capabilities in order to obtain a larger share of DOE prime and subcontracts. Final guidelines for this program were published in the *Federal Register* on June 9, 1995 (60 FR 30529).

Department of State

The Omnibus Diplomatic Security and Anti-Terrorism Act of 1986 (P.L. 99-399; 100 Stat. 865), which authorizes funds for the construction and maintenance of U.S. embassies abroad, requires that not less than 10% of the amount appropriated for diplomatic construction or design projects each fiscal year shall be allocated to the extent practicable for contracts with American minority contractors.

The Foreign Relations Authorization Act, Fiscal Years 1990 and 1991 (P.L. 101-246; 104 Stat. 15), requires the Secretary of State to: establish a pilot program of voluntary set-asides to increase SDB participation in contract, procurement, grant, and research and development activities funded by the Department of State and the United States Information Agency (Sec. 126); allocate not less than 10% of the amount of funds obligated for local guard contracts for Foreign Service buildings abroad for contracts with U.S. MBEs

(Sec. 136)[20]; and make available to U.S. SDBs not less than 10% of the amounts available for U.S. contracts for the broadcasting relay station in Israel (Sec. 301). Nonminority women are not presumed to be socially or economically disadvantaged under this law.

Department of the Treasury

The Competitive Equality Banking Act of 1987 (P.L. 100-86; 101 Stat. 620), designed to recapitalize the Federal Savings and Loan Insurance Corporation, extends the forbearance or capital recovery program to viable and well-managed minority-owned thrift institutions primarily serving minority communities and directs the Treasury Department to expand the use of minority-owned S&Ls for federal deposits.

Agency for International Development

The Foreign Operations, Export Financing, and Related Programs Appropriations Act for FY1995 (P.L. 103-306; 108 Stat. 1646) sets a goal of awarding at least 10% of the dollar value of the Agency for International Development's bilateral assistance contracts to SDB enterprises, minority colleges and universities, and private and voluntary organizations controlled by minorities or women. Known as the "Gray amendment," this provision has been renewed by Congress in every AID appropriations act since its first appearance in 1984. The Gray amendment has always included women in its definition of economically and socially disadvantaged individuals.

Environmental Protection Agency

The Superfund Amendments and Reauthorization Act of 1986 (P.L. 99-499; 100 Stat. 1627) authorizes funds to clean up hazardous waste sites throughout the country. While there is no specific set-aside goal or quota in this legislation, it does require the Environmental Protection Agency (EPA) to submit to Congress an annual report on contracts awarded under this law to minority businesses.

Public Law 101-507 (104 Stat. 1374), EPA's appropriations act for FY1991, provided that at least 8% of federal funding for prime contracts and subcontracts awarded in support of authorized programs, including grants, loans and contracts for wastewater treatment and leaking underground storage tanks grants, be made available to SDBs (including WBEs) and historically black colleges and universities. This provision was repeated in EPA's FY1993 appropriations act (P.L. 102-389; 106 Stat. 1602) and remains in effect (42 U.S.C. 4370d).

The Clean Air Act Amendments of 1990 (P.L. 101-549; 104 Stat. 2708), while specifically prohibiting the use of quotas, provides that the EPA shall, to

---

[20]This provision was amended in 1994 by the Foreign Relations Authorization Act, Fiscal Years 1994 and 1995 (Public Law 103-236; 108 Stat. 401) and is codified at 22 U.S.C. 4864.

the extent practicable, require that not less than 10% of total federal funding for any research relating to the requirements of the amendments be made available to disadvantaged business concerns, historically black colleges and universities, colleges and universities having a student body in which 40% of the students are Hispanic, or minority institutions. This law includes women and disabled Americans within its definition of economically and socially disadvantaged individuals.

Federal Deposit Insurance Corporation

The Financial Institutions Emergency Acquisitions Amendments of 1987 (P.L. 100-86; 101 Stat. 625), requires the Federal Deposit Insurance Corporation, when assisting in the emergency interstate acquisition of a minority-controlled bank, to seek an offer from other minority-controlled banks before proceeding with the bidding priorities otherwise required.

National Aeronautics and Space Agency

NASA currently operates under a requirement that at least 8% of the total value of its prime contracts and subcontracts be made available to SDBs and minority educational institutions. First included in its FY1990 appropriations act (P.L. 101-144; 103 Stat. 863) and codified at 42 U.S.C. 2473b, this 8% goal was restated in subsequent NASA appropriations acts to include women.[21] As noted above, the Federal Acquisition Streamlining Act extended to NASA DOD's authority to set aside procurement contracts for exclusive bidding by SDBs, to grant SDBs a price evaluation preference of up to 10% when competing against non-SDBs in open solicitations, and to grant contracts at above fair market price. NASA has also recently formulated its own mentor-protege program[22] and is taking other steps to enhance the capabilities of SDBs and WBEs to perform as NASA contractors and subcontractors.

PROGRAMS FOR NATIVE AMERICANS

In addition to the Minority Business Development Agency's Indian Business Development Centers described above, other federal programs have been created specifically for Native Americans. The Department of the Interior's Bureau of Indian Affairs (BIA) operates several such programs, authorized by the Indian Financing Act of 1974, as amended (P.L. 93-262; 25 U.S.C. 1451). BIA's Indian Business Development Grant Program, for example, provides equity capital for Indian entrepreneurs to establish and develop profit-making business ventures on federal Indian reservations. Eligibility for this program extends to federally recognized Indian tribes or Alaska Native groups, individual members of such

---

[21]See Departments of Veterans Affairs and Housing and Urban Development, and Independent Agencies Appropriations Acts for 1991 (Public Law 101-507; 104 Stat. 1380) and 1993 (Public Law 102-389; 106 Stat. 1610).

[22]The final rules were published in the *Federal Register* (v. 60) on March 24, 1995, p. 15497.

tribes or groups, and Indian-owned corporations, partnerships or cooperative associations. Businesses must be at least 51% owned and controlled by Native Americans and be located on or near federal Indian reservations.

The BIA also operates a guaranteed loan program for federally recognized Indian tribes, Alaska Native groups or individual members of such tribes or groups who are otherwise unable to obtain credit from private lending institutions. Loans may be guaranteed for any profit-making purpose (usually business, industry or agriculture) that will promote the economic development of a federal Indian reservation. The BIA can also make direct loans, funded from a revolving account, to Indians and Indian entities for economic development purposes in cases where funds are unavailable from other sources on reasonable terms and conditions.

The Indian Self-Determination and Education Assistance Act (P.L. 93-638; 25 U.S.C. 450e(b)) requires that Indian organizations and Indian-owned economic enterprises receive preference in the award of subcontracts and subgrants that flow from BIA contracts and grants for the benefit of Indians.

DOD's Defense Logistics Agency administers a program with the dual purpose of maintaining a strong national security by expanding the defense industrial base and improving the business climate and economic development on federal Indian reservations. In this Procurement Technical Assistance (PTA) Program, DOD shares the cost of establishing and supporting PTA programs that are conducted by tribal organizations and Indian economic enterprises to help business firms located on reservations obtain DOD procurement contracts.

The Indian Health Service of the Department of Health and Human Services, in connection with its maintenance and operation of hospital and health facilities for Indians, is authorized to grant preferences to products of Indian firms by the Buy Indian Act (P.L. 61-313, 25 U.S.C. 47).

ADDITIONAL SOURCES OF INFORMATION

The *Commerce Business Daily* (CBD) is a valuable source of information for identifying opportunities for selling goods and services to the federal government. Published by the Department of Commerce every weekday, it lists proposed procurements of all federal agencies, subcontracting opportunities offered by prime contractors, and other information on federal procurement activities. It is available by subscription from the Superintendent of Documents, U.S. Government Printing Office, Washington, DC 20402. The CBD is also available for inspection at DOD procurement offices, at the field offices of the Small Business Administration, the Department of Commerce and the General Services Administration, and at many local chambers of commerce and public libraries.

Field offices of the Small Business Administration, the General Services Administration and the Department of Commerce as well as the procurement offices of the Department of Defense are equipped to assist SDBs in locating federal civilian and military procurement opportunities. Many local chambers of commerce also have facilities to provide similar guidance and assistance.

Products and services purchased by federal civilian agencies are described in the SBA's publication *U.S. Government Purchasing and Sales Directory*, which is available for purchase by mail from the Superintendent of Documents, P.O. Box 371954, Pittsburgh, PA 15250-7954. Information on the availability and cost of this and other executive agency publications mentioned in this report can be obtained by calling the Government Printing Office in Washington, D.C., at 202-512-1800.

The public laws and regulations cited in this report can be consulted in many larger public and academic libraries.

CHAPTER 9A

Affirmative Action and Women*

Marcia D. Greenberger
Co-President of the National Women's Law Center

The Center is a non-profit organization that has been working since 1972 to advance and protect the legal rights of women across the country. The Center focuses on major policy areas of importance to women and their families, including employment, education, and income security—with particular attention paid to the concerns of low-income women. This hearing is about affirmative action and about Federal contractor requirements. We are pleased to be able to address both issues, and how they intersect.

First, I will say at the outset that the Center strongly supports affirmative action, and I am pleased to have this opportunity to discuss why it is so important to women as well as members of racial and ethnic minorities. Affirmative action programs, in their truest sense, have played a critical role in opening up opportunities for women and minorities to begin to take their rightful place in our society, and these measures are as urgently needed today as ever.

Second, the Executive Order program, which bars Federal contractors from engaging in discrimination and requires them to take positive steps to ensure equal opportunity for minorities and women, has been one of the most important Federal efforts to provide equal opportunity in the workplace. As such, it has consistently received broad, bipartisan support since the issuance of its precursor in 1941, through the adoption of the current Executive Order in 1964 and its expansion during the Nixon Administration to include goals and timetables. It continues to deserve that support today.

A few words about the Supreme Court's decision this week in *Adarand Constructors, Inc. v. Pena* (No. 93-1841, June 12, 1995) may be in order here. The precise impact of *Adarand* on e Federal set-aside programs at issue in the case remains to be determined. But whatever *Adarand's* impact in that context, those programs are clearly distinguishable from the Executive Order program,

---

* Excerpted from testimony before the U.S. Senate hearing of the Committee on Human ?????
(could not read what Frank wrote here)

which prohibits workplace discrimination and imposes no quota or "preference" on anyone. Indeed, the Court has consistently upheld affirmative action in the employment context of the type provided for in the Executive Order program. *See, e.g., Johnson v. Transportation Agency of Santa Clara County*, 480 U.S. 616 (1987). *Adarand* therefore does not call into question the appropriateness of the Executive Order program.

At the Center, the Executive Order program has been a focus of our work on gender equity in employment for over 20 years. We have monitored OFCCP enforcement practices throughout this period; on behalf of numerous organizations we have submitted comments on proposed changes in the regulations that implement the Executive Order, and we have served as counsel in several cases that challenge the government's enforcement practices under the Executive Order or pertain to its provisions. In this connection, over the years we have spoken to many women who have relied on OFCCP to help them get a fair shot at jobs and promotions and equal opportunity and the workplace. Our testimony today is based on this experience.

Because we have worked primarily in the area of sex discrimination, our testimony will be directed mainly toward the impact of the Executive Order program on women. We do want to emphasize, however, that women face discrimination not only because of their gender, but also because of their race and national origin, as well as disability and age. Moreover, it is important to remember that discrimination, whatever its basis, has many common elements and that the urgent need for the Executive Order applies across the board.

At the outset, I want to place in context why the Executive Order program which promises the citizens of our country that their tax dollars will not knowingly be used to support companies who discriminate on the basis of race, sex, or national origin, is needed now as much as ever.

Barriers to Advancement for Women Remain Pervasive

Discrimination against women is deeply rooted in our society, and our history of trying to combat this discrimination is very recent. For the first 150 years of the Republic, American women lacked the most fundamental right of citizenship—the right to vote. Throughout most of our history, laws that barred women from engaging in certain occupations, from the practice of law to bartending, were upheld. Many of the Nation's premier colleges and universities were once completely closed to women. Not long ago, the "want ads" listed openings for women and for men separately, and some employers told women (but not men) with young children they need not apply at all. Sex discrimination in employment has been prohibited by Federal law only since enactment of the Civil Rights Act of 1964, and in education only since the Education Amendments of 1972. The Executive Order was amended to include gender in 1968, an amendment which became effective in 1969.

While much has changed in recent years, women are still second class citizens in many ways. For example:

• According to the March 1995 report of the Glass Ceiling Commission, 95 to 97 percent of the senior managers of Fortune 1000 industrial and Fortune 500 companies are male. In the Fortune 2000 industrial and service companies, only 5 percent of senior managers are women (and virtually all of these are white).[1]

• An earnings gap exists between women and men across a wide spectrum of occupations. In 1991, for example, women physicians earned 53.9 percent of the wages of male physicians, and women in sales occupations earned only 59.5 percent of the wages of men in equivalent positions.[2] In 1993 women still earned, on average, only 71.5 cents for every dollar earned by men.[3]

• While women are over half the adult population[4] and nearly half the workforce in this country,[5] women remain disproportionately clustered in traditionally female jobs with lower pay and fewer benefits.[6] For example, in 1991 one in four working women worked in an administrative support job,[7] and 82 percent of administrative workers in all industries are women.[8]

• While the gender gap in higher education has narrowed, and women now earn roughly half of all bachelor's and masters degrees, they still lag behind in many respects. Women earn only about one-third of doctorate and first professional degrees, and remain underrepresented in many areas not traditionally studied by women. In 1992, women received only about 15.4 percent of undergraduate engineering degrees, 9.6 percent of doctorate degrees in engineering, and less than 22 percent of doctorate degrees in mathematics and the physical sciences.[9]

• Women remain severely underrepresented in most non-traditional professional occupations as well as blue collar trades. For example, women are

---

1 Federal Glass Ceiling Commission [FGCC], *Good for Business: Making Full Use of the Nation's Human Capital*, iii-iv (1995).

2 U.S. Department of Labor, Women's Bureau, *Women Workers: Trends and Issues* 35(1993).

3 National Committee on Pay Equity, "The Wage Gap: 1993," citing U.S. Dept. of Commerce, Census Bureau, "Current Population Reports," Series P-60.

4 U.S. Dept. of Commerce, Census Bureau, *Statistical Abstract of the United States* 13 (1994).

5 Id. at 396. See also, U.S. Dept. of Labor, Women's Bureau, "Working Women Count! at 10 (1994).

6 Employee Benefits Research Institute, Sources of Health and Characteristics of the Uninsured, Analysis of the March 1993 Current Population Survey, Issue Brief No. 145, at 61 (Jan. 1994) (women are heavily concentrated in jobs paying under $20,000 where 82 percent of the uninsured workers are also located).

7 9 to 5, "Profile of Working Women," at 1 (1992-93 edition) (data compiled from United States Bureau of Labor and Census Bureau statistics).

8 Equal Employment Opportunity Commission [EEOC], *Job Patterns for Minorities and Women in Private Industry*, table 1, at 1-36 (1993).

9 U.S. Department of Education, National Center for Education Statistics, "Digest of Education Statistics," table 239 (1994).

only 8.6 percent of all engineers; 3.9 percent of airplane pilots and navigators; less than 1 percent of carpenters; 18.6 percent of architects; and just over 20 percent of doctors and lawyers. Women are over 99.3 percent of dental hygienists, but are only 10.5 percent of dentists.[10]

• 65 percent of the 62 million working women in the United States earn less than $20,000 annually, and 38 percent earn less than $10,000.[11]

• Even where women have moved into occupations and professions in significant numbers, they have not moved *up* to the same degree. Women are 23 percent of lawyers,[12] but only 11 percent of partners in law firms.[13] Women are 48 percent of all journalists, but hold only 6 percent of the top jobs in journalism.[14] Women are 72 percent of elementary school teachers, but only 29 percent of school principals.[15]

• Minority women have lagged particularly far behind in both employment and education. In 1993, for example, Black women earned a median income of $19,816, compared to $22,023 for white women and $31,089 for white men. Hispanic women earned a median income of $16,758.[16] Even in sectors where women have made inroads into management, minority women continue to be underrepresented. In the banking industry, only 2.6 percent of executive, managerial and administrative jobs were held by Black women, and 5 percent by Hispanic women, compared to 37.6 percent by white women. In the hospital industry, Black and Hispanic women each held 4.6 percent of these jobs, while white women held 50.2 percent[17] Minority women also earn fewer college degrees than white women. In 1992, white women made up 42.3 percent of college undergraduates and 48.1 percent of graduate students; minority women were only 13.4 percent of undergraduates and 8.4 percent of graduate students.[18]

• Although white men constitute a minority of both the total work force (47 percent)[19] and of college educated persons (48 percent)[20] , they dominate the top

---

[10] U.S. Dept. of Commerce, supra note 4, at 407-409.

[11] U.S. Bureau of the Census, Current Population Reports, "Money Income of Households, Families and Persons in the United States: 1992," Series P-60, No. 184, Table 31.

[12] U.S. Dept. of Commerce, *supra* note 4, at 407.

[13] Curan and Carson, American Bar Foundation, "The Lawyer Statistical Report" (1994).

[14] "A Long Way To Go," Newsweek, April 24, 1989, at 74.

[15] Commission on Professionals in Science and Technology, *Professional Women and Minorities: A Total Human Resource Data Compendium* 142, Table 5-11, (1994).

[16] Institute for Women's Policy and Research, "The Wage Gap: Women's and Men's Earnings," (1995) (citing unpublished data of the U.S. Bureau of the Census, Current Population Reports).

[17] GFCC, supra note 1, at 79.

[18] U.S. Department of Education, supra note 9, at table 203.

[19] Cheryl Russell & Margaret Ambry, *American Incomes* 155, 158, 163 *citing*, Bureau of the Census Current Population Reports, "Money Income of Households, Families, and Persons in the United States: 1991," Series P-60, No. 180 (in 1991, 133,836,000 people over age 15 worked; 62,477,000 or 47 percent, of these were white men).

[20] U.S. Bureau of the Census, Current Population Reports, "Poverty in the United States:

jobs in virtually every field.[21] Moreover, white males' median weekly earnings in 1993 were 33 percent higher than those of any other group in America.[22] The earnings of non-Hispanic white men were 49 percent higher than those of any other group.[23]

How can these disparities be explained? The evidence is overwhelming that they are the result, in large measure, of discrimination. Sex discrimination, including sexual harassment, continues to be a fact of life in our society. In 1993, 11,908 sex discrimination and sexual harassment charges were filed with the EEOC.[24] That number rose to 14,420 in 1994.[25]

In a 1994 survey by the Labor Department, 61 percent of women surveyed said they had little or no likelihood of advancement; and 14 percent of white women and 26 percent of minority women reported losing a job or promotion because of sex or race.[26] The Glass Ceiling Commission report cites another study finding that 25 percent of the women surveyed felt that "being a woman/sexism" was the biggest obstacle they had to overcome, and 59 percent said they had personally experienced sexual harassment on the job.[27]

The notion that women large behind because they want to—that is, because they would rather work less, or in lower-paying jobs, or not at all—is simplistic and demonstrably wrong. While some women clearly choose to devote themselves to family concerns or to jobs with lower pay for a range of reasons, such choices simply do not explain the disparities. A study cited in the Glass Ceiling Commission report found, for example, that women in senior management worked the same number of hours per week as their male counterparts.[28] Another recent study, reported in the Journal of the American Medical Association, shows that after about 11 years on medical school faculties, 23 percent of men but only 5 percent of women, had achieved the rank of full professor—and the gap persisted when the researchers held constant the numbers of hours worked per week.[29] These women have made the same career

---

1991," Series P-60, No. 181, table 11 (of the 34,025,0000 people aged 25 or older who completed college, 16,578000 or 48 percent, were white males).

21 FGCC, *supra* note 1, at iii-iv. *See also*, EEOC, *supra* note 8 (showing that women managers are severely underrepresented in, among other industries, the mining, construction, banking, hospital and women's clothing industries).

22 U.S. Dept. of Commerce, *supra* note 4 at 429.

23 *Id.* (computed from Bureau of Labor Statistics, "Employment and Earnings," Jan. 1995, at 207).

24 Unpublished computerized data compiled by EEOC field offices.

25 *Id.*

26 U.S. Dept. of Labor, Women's Bureau, *supra* note 5, at 7.

27 FGCC, *supra* note 1, at 148.

28 FGCC, *supra* note 1, at 151.

29 Tesch, et al., "Promotion of Women Physicians in Academic Medicine," Journal of the American Medical Association, April 5, 1995.

choices as men, worked the same hours as men, yet still earn less. Discrimination is clearly still with us.

It is important also to underscore the fallacy of the notion that women's wages are supplementary and merely provide discretionary income. For most women, their wages are a critical component of the family's income. A new study by the Whirlpool Foundation found that for American women between the ages of 18 and 55, employment outside the home is the rule rather than the exception. More than two-thirds of the women surveyed in that age group are employed; six in ten work full time (45 percent) or part-time (15 percent) for employers, and 8 percent are self-employed. A majority of the employed women provide at least half of their household's incomes (18 percent provide all of it; 11 percent provide more than half; and 26 percent provide about half). Even among employed women in married couples, nearly half (48 percent) contribute half or more of their family's income.[30] Thus, programs that expand job opportunities for women are helping these women and their families make ends meet.

Affirmative Action as Part of the Executive Order Program

Affirmative action programs have helped to open doors for women in employment. They include recruitment and outreach efforts to include qualified women in the talent pool when hiring decisions are made; training programs to give all employees a fair chance at promotions; and in some cases the use of flexible goals and timetables (not quotas) as benchmarks by which to measure progress toward eliminating sever underrepresentation of qualified women in specific job categories.

Executive Order 11246 and the Federal contract compliance program establish and implement the proposition that government funds should not support illegal discrimination against women and minorities. The Executive Order achieves its objectives by requiring that a clause be included in government contracts (over the specified size thresholds) in which the contractors assure that they will not discriminate against any employee on the basis of race, color, religion, sex, or national origin.

The Executive Order further requires that businesses and institutions that choose to contract with the Federal Government take positive measures to ensure equal opportunity for minorities and women. It is this requirement that is known as affirmative action, and it requires simply a commitment of good faith efforts by contractors. Its very design is the antithesis of fixed quotas. In fact, the regulations explicitly state: "[g]oals may *not* be rigid and inflexible quotas which must be met." 41 C.F.R. 60-2.12(e) (emphasis added). Nor are Federal contractors subject to sanctions in any way for simple failure to meet goals. The

---

[30] Whirlpool Foundation, "Women: The New Providers," a study prepared by the Families and Work Institute with Louis Harris and Associates, Inc. (May 1995).

touchstone of the program is good faith efforts, an eminently reasonable standard.

Since the inception of the Executive Order program in 1941—when President Roosevelt signed the order that was the precursor to Executive Order 11246—each successive Executive Order has strengthened the purview and substance of the Order. Under President Roosevelt, the coverage of the Order expanded from national defense production[31] to all government contracts entered into by the War and Navy Departments.[32] Subsequent Executive Orders added more effective remedies, such as debarment and termination of government contracts,[33] expanded the Order to add sex to the prohibited categories of discrimination,[34] and introduced the concept of affirmative action as a means of attaining the goal of full and prompt utilization of women and minorities.[35] The program has also been strengthened through regulations, such as those issued by the Nixon Administration which implemented the affirmative action concept through the goals and timetables requirement in effect today.

Each of these successive actions was based on the need for a stronger program demonstrated by past experience. The initial phases of the program disclosed that passive nondiscrimination clauses alone did not ensure equal opportunity for minorities. In 1968, the Comptroller General ruled that the affirmative action obligation under the Executive Order was too vague to fulfill the requirement that minimum contract standards be made clear to prospective bidders.[36] Contractors urged the government to define their obligations under the Order and to establish a standard to measure their compliance with the affirmative action requirement. Such standards, which in fact is all that goals and timetables are, is the way business operates in all other spheres. It was in response to this demonstrated need that the Nixon administration issued the regulations that introduced and defined goals and timetables.

When It Is Enforced, the Program Works

The current record of enforcement of the Executive Order program carries with it great promise. Under Shirley Wilcher's direction, OFCCP has been engaged in full consultation with all of the interested parties—including contractors and advocacy organizations concerned with eliminating

---

[31] E.O. 8802,6 Fed Reg. 3109, 3 C.F.R. 1938-43 Comp. 957 (June 25, 1941).

[32] E.O. 9001, 6 Fed. Reg. 6787, 3 C.F.R. 1938-43 Comp. 1054 (Dec. 27, 1941); E.O. 9346, 8 Fed. Reg. 7183, 3 C.F.R. 1938-43 Comp. 1286 (May 27, 1943).

[33] E.O. 10925, 26 Fed. Reg. 1977, 3 C.F.R. 1959-63 Comp. 448 (Mar. 6, 1961).

[34] E.O. 11375, 32 Fed. Reg. 14303 (1967).

[35] E.O. 10925, supra note 33.

[36] 48 Comp. Gen. 326 (1968).

discrimination. In fact, because of OFCCP's example, there has been increased communication among these disparate parties as well. There is a refreshing and hopeful new tone of collaboration and streamlining—all with the common goal of eliminating discrimination in the workplace in the most efficient and effective way.

Unfortunately, this approach has not always been characteristic of OFCCP. For much of the history of the Executive Order program, enforcement in general, and enforcement of the Order's provisions against sex discrimination in particular, have been lax. Executive Order 11246 was not even applicable to sex discrimination until 1969. In a case brought by the Center on behalf of women in academic and organizations concerned with their advancement, in 1977 a court found that OFCCP had failed for almost a decade to enforce the prohibitions against sex discrimination in institutions of higher education, ignoring hundreds of sex discrimination complaints. The court reaffirmed its finding in 1982, based on problems then current in the agency. *Women's Equity Action League v. Bell*, C.A. No. 74-1720 (D.D.C.). And OFCCP did not apply goals and timetables for women in the construction trades until 1978, in response to the suit, *Women Working in Construction v. Marshall*, in which the Center represented tradeswomen's groups from all over the country. C.A. No. 76-527 (D.D.C. 1978). Over the entire history of the Executive Order program, there have been only 38 enforcement actions that resulted in debarment. During the 1980's, there were only eight.

But even with a problematic enforcement history, the Executive Order program has made a difference. A study by OFCCP in 1983 showed that women and minorities had made greater gains in employment at those establishments contracting with the Federal Government than at non-contractors. Based on a review of more than 77,000 companies with over 20 million employees, the study found minority employment to have increased 20.1 percent and female employment 15.2 percent between 1974 and 1980 for Federal contractors, despite total employment growth of only 3 percent. For non-contracting companies, minority employment increased 12.3 percent and female employment 2.2 percent with an 8.2 percent growth in total employment over the same period. The same study showed that Federal contractors employed women at higher levels and in better paying jobs than other firms.[37]

The Executive Order's affirmative action requirements have changed entire industries. When OFCCP first looked at the coal mining industry in 1973, there were virtually *no* women coal miners. By 1980, 8.7 percent were women.[38] In 1978, OFCCP reviewed the employment practices of the five largest banks in Cleveland. Three years later, the percentage of women officials and managers at these institutions had risen more than 20%.[39]

---

[37] Citizen's Commission on Civil Rights, *Affirmative Action to Open the Doors of Job Opportunity* 123-129 (1984).

[38] *Id.*

[39] *Id.*

Statistics tell a part of the story. Actual case examples are also instructive. One of the most successful enforcement efforts came as a result of an OFCCP administrative complaint against the Chicago-based Harris Bank, filed by Women Employed. After years of conciliation efforts failed, OFCCP brought an enforcement action, in which the Center represented Women Employed. Two separate hearings yielded findings of serious sex and race discrimination in the Bank. Ultimately, in 1989, OFCCP, the Bank and we agreed to a settlement of $14 million in back pay—the largest award ever under the Executive Order—and the Bank revised its affirmative action plan, to include enhanced training programs and career development opportunities. Just a few months ago, in fact, Harris Bank named its first woman vice chairman—who is believed to be the highest-ranking woman among the country's largest banks—and announced that it now has 15 women in positions representing 25 percent of senior vice presidents and above at the bank. Clearly, the Executive Order program has much to be proud of at Harris Bank.

The reason affirmative action programs work is that they are an effective way to neutralize the biases, stereotypes and prejudices that often seep into employment processes, consciously or unconsciously. Supervisors making hiring or promotion decisions, for example, rarely engaged in the purely objective, scientific exercise that is sometimes imagined. They are human beings making judgment calls, and their subjective judgment is inevitably influenced by the natural tendency to be most comfortable with people like themselves. Affirmative action programs force employers to reach out beyond the "old boys network" to which they would naturally gravitate, and to give fair consideration to candidates who are qualified but who don't fit their preconceptions.

Johnson v. Transportation Agency of Santa Clara County, 480 U.S. 616 (1987), illustrates the use of affirmative action in practice. There were no women in the agency's 238 "skilled craft worker" positions, which included road dispatchers. Under its affirmative action plan, the agency set a target for increased employment of women in this category (and others in which they had been underrepresented), and in its effort to meet the goal it took gender into account in deciding to promote a woman, rather than a man with substantially equal qualifications, to road dispatcher. Gender was only one factor among many considered, and the woman who received the promotion was fully qualified for the job.

Without affirmative action, the woman in the *Johnson* case, who became her agency's first woman road dispatcher ever, would have been passed over by men who didn't think a woman could do the job. The three male supervisors who interviewed the candidates—one of whom had previously derided the female candidate as a "skirt-wearing person"—had recommended a man for the position. Had it not been for the agency's affirmative action plan, the woman applicant—who is still today successfully performing her duties as road dispatcher—would in all likelihood have been denied the chance she clearly deserved. It is interesting to note that Justice O'Connor, who wrote the controlling opinion in the *Adarand* case, also upheld the validity of the affirmative action program in the *Johnson* case.

The Executive Order Program Complements Title VII

The Executive Order program is an essential complement to the enforcement of Title VII's prohibition against discrimination in employment. While the EEOC and individual victims of discrimination can bring suit under Title VII once a violation has occurred, the contract compliance program serves to *prevent* discrimination. By developing an affirmative action plan, and measuring its own progress toward meeting its goals, a Federal contractor 15 taking steps to ensure that both blatant and subtle forms of discrimination and prejudice are eradicated. The contract compliance program is thus a critically effective, systemic approach to ending discrimination without case-by-case litigation by individuals or the EEOC.

The contract compliance program also alleviates the burdens that case-by-case litigation imposes. Litigation is a daunting, burdensome and costly undertaking for most people, individual plaintiffs and corporate defendants alike. And the EEOC, as this Committee knows, has limited resources and a huge backlog of cases. By ensuring that Federal contractors have effective non-discrimination and affirmative action measures in place, the contract compliance program reduces the instances of discrimination that need to be addressed.

Affirmative Action Benefits Everyone

Programs that increase opportunities for women and minorities are beneficial to our whole society in numerous ways:

• Affirmity action programs that help women advance in the workplace are helping their families to make ends meet. Most women, like men, work because of economic need; indeed, many women are the sole source of support for their families.[40]

• Affirmative action programs expand the talent pool for businesses to draw on, and many companies report that a diverse workforce has led to enhanced performance and productivity. DuPont Co. set—and exceeded—higher goals than any affirmative action regulations required, and the company reports that it has been rewarded by the development of new ideas and markets.[41]

---

[40] Department of Labor, Women's Bureau, *supra* note 2, at 11. See also *supra* note 30. Replacing the "old boys network" with job postings, outreach and training ensures that all workers–women and minorities, but white males, too—have a fair shot at advancing in the workplace.

[41] Jonathan Glater & Martha Hamilton, "Affirmative Action's Corporate Converts,"

• Diverse in our colleges and universities improves the learning process for everyone: As Justice Powell wrote in the *Bakke* case, "the 'Nation's future depends upon leaders trained through wide exposure' to the ideas and mores of students as diverse as the Nation of many peoples."[42]

• Enrollment and scholarship programs that promote diversity in professional schools indirectly serve the public in dramatic ways. For example, it is surely no accident that the advancement of women in fields of medical science has been accompanied by increased attention to women's health issues such as breast cancer and expanded research in those areas.

• Communities benefit from affirmative action in myriad other ways. For example, increased recruitment and training of women police officers, prosecutors, judges and court, personnel has led to an improvement in the handling of domestic violence cases and the treatment of domestic violence like the crime that it is—which benefits women, children and all other members of the family and the community who are affected by violence in the home.

Conclusion

Recruitment, outreach, training and other affirmative action programs have opened doors for women in the workplace, in our Nation's learning institutions, and in other areas of our society. But equal opportunity for women is still a long way off. The tools we have in place to attain that goal, including Executive Order 11246 and the Federal contract compliance program, remain essential. Curtailing or undermining these programs would not only halt the forward progress that women, as well as minorities, have been able to achieve; it would mark a giant leap backward in this Nation's journey toward equal opportunity for all. Thank you.

Washington Post, March 19, 1995 at H1.

[42] *Regents of University of California v. Bakke*, 438 U.S. 265, 313 (1978) (quoting *Kevishian v. Board of Regents*, 385 U.S. 589, 603 (1967).

CHAPTER 10

Sexual Harassment and Violence Against Women: Developments in Federal Law

Charles V. Dale

INTRODUCTION

Gender-based discrimination, harassment, and violence against women in the home, workplace, and society at large have received increasing legislative and judicial attention in recent years. Legal doctrines condemning the extortion of sexual favors as a condition of employment or job advancement, and other sexually offensive workplace behaviors resulting in a "hostile environment," continue to evolve from judicial decisions under Title VII of the 1964 Civil Rights Act and other federal equal employment opportunity laws. In 1994, Congress broke new legal ground by creating a civil rights cause of action for victims of "crimes of violence motivated by gender." The new law also made it a federal offense to travel interstate with the intent to "injure, harass, or intimidate" a spouse, causing bodily harm to the spouse by a crime of violence.[1]

Sexual harassment has also arisen in other legal contexts. The recent military conviction of a drill sargeant at the Army's Aberdeen training facility for rape and sexual harassment of female recruits, and charges of harassment lodged against that branch's highest ranking Sergeant-Major, have focused the public's attention once more upon sexual harassment in the military. Issues surrounding the legal responsibility of school districts or other educational authorities for sexual harassment within the schools are highlighted by judicial decisions and several recently alleged incidents of sexual abuse or unwanted displays of affection involving public school students.

Earlier this term, the U.S. Supreme Court in *Lanier v. United States* reversed a Sixth Circuit decision which had set-aside the conviction of a state judge in Tennessee under 18 U.S.C. § 242 for harassment and sexual assault perpetrated by the judge upon several female court employees and litigants. Section 242, the criminal equivalent of 42 U.S.C. § 1983, penalizes the willful "deprivation of any rights. . .protected by the Constitution" committed by any person "under color of law." Federal prosecutors claimed that the defendant's acts were committed in his capacity as a judge and that his acts deprived the

---

1 18 U.S.C. § 2261(a)(1).

victims of liberty and bodily integrity protected by the Constitution. The prosecution theory was rejected by the appeals court on the grounds that no right to be free from sexually-motivated physical assault had ever been recognized by a Supreme Court decision involving similar facts. That basis of decision was rejected by a unanimous Supreme Court which remanded the case for additional proceedings. The High Court refrained from deciding the central question, however, of whether it is a federal "constitutional crime" under § 242 for state officials or persons acting under "color of law" to deprive another of "bodily integrity" through acts of forcible sexual assault. Final resolution of that issue must now await further judicial consideration and possible appeals following remand.

FEDERAL EQUAL EMPLOYMENT OPPORTUNITY LAW

Title VII of the 1964 Civil Rights Act does not mention sexual harassment but makes it unlawful for employers with 15 or more employees to discriminate against any applicant or employee "because of. . .sex."[2] Federal law on the subject is, therefore, largely a judicial creation, having evolved over nearly a three-decade period from federal court decisions and guidelines of the Equal Employment Opportunity Commission (EEOC) interpreting Title VII's sex discrimination prohibition.[3] Two forms of sexual harassment are forbidden by current Title VII caselaw and EEOC administrative guidelines. The first, or "*quid pro quo*" harassment, occurs when submission to "unwelcome" sexual advances, propositions, or other conduct of a sexual nature is made an express or implied condition of employment, or where it is used as the basis of employment decisions affecting job status or tangible employment benefits. As its name suggests, this form of harassment involves actual or potential economic loss--*e.g.* termination, transfer, or adverse performance ratings, *etc.*-- as a consequence of the employee's refusal to exchange sexual favors demanded by a supervisor or employer for employment benefits. The second form of actionable harassment consists of unwelcome sexual conduct which is of such severity as to alter a condition of employment by creating an "intimidating, hostile or offensive working environment." The essence of a "hostile environment" claim is a "pattern or practice" of offensive behavior by the

---

[2] 42 U.S.C. § 2000e-2(a)(1).

[3] 42 U.S.C. 2000e *et seq.* Sexual harassment in federally assisted education programs is also prohibited by Title IX of the 1972 Education Amendments, 20 U.S.C. §§ 1681 *et seq.* (*Franklin v. Gwinnet County Public Schools,* 503 U.S. 60 (1992)). While Title VII and Title IX are the primary sources of federal sexual harassment law, relief from such conduct has also been sought, *albeit* less frequently, pursuant to § 1983 of Title 42, the Federal Employees Liability Act, and the Equal Protection and Due Process Clauses of the U.S. Constitution. *E.g. Doe v. Taylor Independent School District,* 975 F.2d 137 (5th Cir. 1992)(holding that s student has a firmly established equal protection and due process right to be free form sexual molestation by a state-employed school teacher).

employer, a supervisor, co-workers, or non-employees so "severe or pervasive" as to interfere with the employee's job performance or create an abusive work environment.

In 1980, the federal agency responsible for enforcing Title VII issued interpretative guidelines prohibiting both *quid pro quo* and hostile environment sexual harassment. The EEOC guidelines focus on sexuality rather than gender--in terms of job detriments resulting from "[u]nwelcome sexual advances, requests for sexual favors, and other verbal or physical behavior of a sexual nature"--and require that a "totality of the circumstances" be considered to determine whether particular conduct constitutes sexual harassment.[4] In addition, judicial developments in hostile environment law were anticipated by elimination of tangible economic loss as a factor and by providing that unwelcome sexual conduct violates Title VII whenever it "has the purpose or effect of unreasonably interfering with an individual's work performance or creating an intimidating, hostile, or offensive working environment." According to the EEOC guidelines, an employer is liable for both forms of sexual harassment when perpetrated by supervisors.[5] The employer, however, is liable for harassment perpetrated by coworker or nonemployees only if the employer knew or should have known of the harassment and failed to "take immediate and appropriate corrective action."[6] They also recommend that employers take preventive measures to eliminate sexual harassment[7] and state that employers may be liable to those denied employment opportunities or benefits given to another employee because of submission to sexual advances.[8]

On March 19, 1990, the EEOC issued "Policy Guidance on Sexual Harassment" to elaborate on certain legal principles set forth in its interpretative guidelines from a decade before.[9] First, the later document reasserts the basic distinction between "quid pro quo" and "hostile environment" and states that an employer "will always be held responsible for acts of '*quid pro quo*' harassment" by a supervisor while hostile environment cases require "careful examination" of whether the harassing supervisor was acting in an 'agency capacity'".[10] On the "welcomeness" issue, the policy guide states that "a contemporaneous complaint or protest" by the victim is an "important" but "not a necessary element of the claim." Instead, the Commission will look to all

4 29 C.F.R. §1604.11(a)(1995).

5 *Id.* at § 1604.11(c).

6 *Id.* at § 1604.11(d)-(e) (1995).

7 *Id.* at § 1604.11(f).

8 *Id.* at § 1604.11(g).

9 BNA, FEP Manual 405:6681 *et seq.*

10 *Id.* at 405:6695.

"objective evidence, rather than subjective, uncommunicated feelings" to "determine whether the victim's conduct is consistent, or inconsistent, with her assertion that the sexual conduct is unwelcome."[11] In determining whether a work environment is hostile, several factors are emphasized:

> (1) whether the conduct was verbal or physical or both; (2) how frequently it was repeated; (3) whether the conduct was hostile and patently offensive; (4) whether the alleged harasser was a co-worker or a supervisor; (5) whether others joined in perpetrating the harassment; and (6) whether the harassment was directed at more than one individual.[12]

However, because the alleged misconduct must "substantially interfere" with the victim's job performance, "sexual flirtation or innuendo, even vulgar language that is trivial or merely annoying, would probably not establish a hostile environment."[13] In addition, "the harasser's conduct should be evaluated from the objective standard of a 'reasonable person.'"[14]

QUID PRO QUO HARASSMENT

The earliest judicial challenges involving tangible benefit or *quid pro quo* harassment claims--filed by women who were allegedly fired for resisting sexual advances by their supervisors--were largely unsuccessful. The discriminatory conduct in such cases was deemed to arise from "personal proclivity" of the supervisor rather than "company directed policy which deprived women of employment opportunities." Until the mid-1970's, federal district courts were reluctant either to find a Title VII cause of action or to impose liability on employers who were neither in complicity with, nor with actual knowledge of, *quid pro quo* harassment by their supervisory employees. An historic turning point came when the federal district court in *Williams v. Saxbe*[15] held for the first time that sexual harassment was discriminatory treatment within the meaning of Title VII because "it created an artificial barrier to employment which was placed before one gender and not the other, despite the fact that both genders were similarly situated."[16] Echoing earlier opinions that an employer is not liable for "interpersonal disputes between employees," the court nonetheless refused to dismiss the complaint since "if [the alleged harassment]

---

11 *Id.* at 405:6686.

12 *Id.* at 405:6689.

13 *Id.*

14 *Id.*

15 413 F. Supp. 654 (D.D.C. 1976).

16 *Id.* at 657-58.

was a policy or practice of plaintiff's supervisor, then it was the agency's policy or practice, which is prohibited by Title VII."[17]

Appellate tribunals in several federal circuits soon began to affirm that *quid pro quo* harassment violates Title VII where "gender is a substantial factor in the discrimination," reversing contrary lower court holdings. For example, Judge Spotswood Robinson, writing for the D.C. Circuit in *Barnes v. Costle*[18] disagreed with "the notion that employment conditions summoning sexual relations are somehow exempted from the coverage of Title VII" as implied by the decision below. Finding that it was "enough that gender is a factor contributing to the discrimination in a substantial way," Judge Robinson ruled that differential treatment based upon an employee's rejection of her supervisor's sexual advances violated the statute. Similarly, in *Tomkins v. Public Service Electric & Gas Co.*, the Third Circuit reversed the trial court's denial of Title VII protection to all "sexual harassment and sexually motivated assault," finding that where an employee's "status as a female was a motivating factor in the supervisor's conditioning her continued employment on compliance with his sexual demands," actionable *quid pro quo* harassment had occurred. "[T]o establish a *prima facie* case of *quid pro quo* harassment, a plaintiff must present evidence that she was subject to unwelcome sexual conduct, and that her reaction to that conduct was then used as the basis for decisions affecting the compensation, terms, conditions, or privileges of her employment."[19] And while the loss of a "tangible employment benefit" has most often meant dismissal or demotion, *quid pro quo* claims may also arise from denial of career advantages--job title, duties or assignments--of less immediate economic impact upon the employee. The Seventh Circuit, for example, ruled recently that a tenured professor who was allegedly stripped of her job title and removed from academic committees because she rebuffed the sexual advances of the university provost may have a claim for *quid pro quo* sexual harassment under Title VII.[20]

HOSTILE ENVIRONMENT HARASSMENT AND THE COURTS

The earlier judicial focus on economic detriment or *quid pro quo* harassment--making submission to sexual demands a condition to job benefits--has largely given way to Title VII claims for harassment that creates an

---

17 *Id.* at 660-61.

18 561 F.2d 983 (D.C.Cir. 1977).

19 *Karibian v. Columbia University*, 14 F.3d 773, 777 (2d Cir.), *cert. denied*, 114 S.Ct. 2693 (1994).

20 *Bryson v. Chicago State University*, 1996 U.S. App. Lexis 24652 (7th Cir. 9-18-96).

"intimidating, hostile, or offensive environment." The first federal appellate court to jettison the tangible economic loss requirement and recognize a hostile environment claim of sexual harassment was the D.C. Circuit in *Bundy v. Jackson*.[21] The plaintiff there charged that several supervisors made continual sexual advances and propositions, questioned her about her sexual proclivities, ignored her complaints, criticized her work performance, and attempted to block her bid for promotion. The appeals court ruled that actionable sex discrimination is not limited to gender-based conditions resulting in a tangible job consequence, but occurs whenever sex is a motivating factor in treating an employee in an adverse manner. Despite the plaintiff's failure to prove *quid pro quo* harassment--she was not fired, demoted, or denied a promotion--the court was unwilling to adopt a rule that would permit an employer to lawfully harass an employee "by carefully stopping short of firing the employee or taking any other tangible actions against her in response to her resistance."[22] Another decision important to the judicial development of sexually hostile environment law was *Henson v. Dundee* where the Eleventh Circuit rejected a claim of *quid pro quo* harassment but found that the employee had a right to a trial on the merits to determine whether the misconduct alleged made her job environment hostile.[23]

Meritor Savings Bank v. Vinson[24] ratified the consensus then emerging among the federal circuits by recognizing a Title VII cause of action for sexual harassment. Writing for the Supreme Court in 1986, then-Justice Rehnquist affirmed that a "hostile environment," predicated on "purely psychological aspects of the workplace environment," could give rise to legal liability and that

---

21 641 F.2d 934 (1981).

22 *Id.* at 945.

23 682 F.2d 897 (11th Cir. 1982). In an oft-quoted passage from its opinion, the court stated:

> Sexual harassment which creates a hostile or offensive environment for members of one sex is every bit the arbitrary barrier to sexual equality at the workplace that racial harassment is to racial equality. Surely, a requirement that a man or woman run a gauntlet of sexual abuse in return for the privilege of being allowed to work and make a living can be as demeaning and disconcerting as the harshest of racial epithets. A pattern of sexual harassment inflicted upon an employee because of her sex is a pattern of behavior that inflicts disparate treatment upon a member of one sex with respect to terms, conditions, or privileges of employment. There is no requirement that an employee subjected to such disparate treatment prove in addition that she suffered tangible job detriment. *Id.* at 902

24 477 U.S. 57 (1986).

"tangible loss" of "an economic character" was not an essential element. This holding was qualified by the Court with important reservations drawn from earlier administrative and judicial precedent. First, "not all workplace conduct that can be described as 'harassment' affects a term, condition, or privilege of employment within the meaning of Title VII." For example, the "mere utterance" of an "epithet" engendering "offensive feelings in an employee" would not ordinarily be *per se* actionable, the opinion suggests. Rather, the misconduct "must be sufficiently severe or pervasive to alter the conditions of [the victim's] employment and create an abusive working environment."[25]

Second, while "voluntariness" in the sense of consent is not a defense to a sexual harassment charge,

> [t]he gravamen of any sexual harassment claim is that the alleged sexual advances were 'unwelcome.' . . .The correct inquiry is whether respondent by her conduct indicated that the alleged sexual advances were unwelcome, not whether her actual participation in sexual intercourse was voluntary.[26]

Accordingly, "it does not follow that a complainant's sexually provocative speech or dress is irrelevant as a matter of law in determining whether he or she found particular sexual advances unwelcome. To the contrary, such evidence is obviously relevant."[27]

Finally, turning to the issue of employer liability, the *Vinson* majority held that the court below had "erred in concluding that employers are always automatically liable for sexual harassment by their supervisors."[28] The usual rule in Title VII cases is strict liability, and four Justices, concurring in the

---

25 *Id.* at 62 (quoting *Henson v. Dundee), supra* n. 21 at 904. In *Vinson* the complainant alleged that her supervisor demanded sexual relations over a three-year period, fondled her in front of other employees, followed her into the women's restroom and exposed himself to her, and forcibly raped her several times. She claimed she submitted for fear of jeopardizing her employment. During the period she received several promotions which, it was undisputed, were based on merit alone so that no exchange of job advancement for sexual favors (*quid pro quo* harassment) was alleged or found.

26 *Id.* at 68 (citing 29 C.F.R. § 1604.11(a)(1985)).

27 *Id.* at 69.

28 *Id.* at 72.

judgment, argued that the same rule should apply in the sexual harassment context as well. The majority disagreed, impliedly suggesting that in hostile environment cases no employer, at least none with a formal policy against harassment, should be made liable in the absence of actual or constructive knowledge.[29]

The Supreme Court's failure to clearly define what constitutes a hostile environment in *Meritor Savings* led to frequent conflict in the lower courts. For example, three federal Circuit Courts of Appeals--the Sixth, the Seventh, and the Eleventh--concluded that in a sexual harassment case, a plaintiff must not only prove that the conduct complained of would have offended a reasonable victim and that he or she was actually offended, but also that the plaintiff suffered serious psychological injury as a result of the conduct.[30] On the other hand, three other Circuits, the Third, the Eighth, and the Ninth, held that the Title VII plaintiff need demonstrate only that he or she was actually offended by conduct that would be deemed offensive by a reasonable victim.[31]

Harris v. Forklift Systems, Inc.,[32] revisited and offered some clarification of *Meritor Savings*. The Supreme Court granted certiorari in *Harris* to resolve the conflict among the circuits over whether harassing conduct must produce severe psychological harm to create an actionable hostile environment under Title VII. A company president had subjected a female manager to sexual innuendo, unwanted physical touching, and insults because of her gender. After two years, she left the job. Despite its determination that demeaning sexual comments by the employer had "offended the plaintiff, and would offend the reasonable woman," the trial court ruled against the plaintiff since the conduct alleged was not "so severe as to be expected to seriously affect plaintiff's psychological well-being" or create an "intimidating or abusive" environment. The Sixth Circuit upheld the trial court ruling in a three-paragraph unpublished opinion.

---

29 On the issue of employer liability, *Meritor* states:

> [While] declin[ing] the parties' invitation to issue a definitive rule on employer liability. . .we do agree with the EEOC that Congress wanted courts to look to agency principles for guidance in this area. While such common-law principles may not be transferable in all their particulars to Title VII, Congress' decision to define 'employer' to include any 'agent' of an employer, 42 U.S.C. § 2000e(b), surely evinces an intent to place some limits on the acts of employees for which employers under Title VII are to be held responsible. *Id.* at 72-73.

30 *Rabidue v. Osceola Refining Co.*, 805 F.2d 611 (6th Cir. 1986); *Scott v. Sears Roebuck*, 798 F.2d 210 (7th Cir. 1986); and *Brooms v. Regal Tube*, 830 F.2d 1554 (11th Cir. 1987).

31 *Andrews v. City of Philadelphia*, 895 F.2d 1469 (3d Cir 1990); *Burns v. McGregor Electronic Industries, Inc.*, 955 F.2d 559 (8th Cir. 1992); and *Ellison v. Brady*, 924 F.2d 872 (9th Cir. 1991).

32 114 S. Ct. 367 (1993).

The Supreme Court reversed, deciding in 1993 that hostile environment sexual harassment need not "seriously affect psychological well-being" of the victim before Title VII is violated. *Meritor Savings*, wrote Justice O'Connor, had adopted a "middle path" between condemning conduct that was "merely offensive" and requiring proof of "tangible psychological injury." Thus, a hostile environment is not created by the "'mere utterance of an . . . epithet which engenders offensive feelings in an employee.'" On the other hand, a victim of sexual harassment need not experience a "nervous breakdown" for the law to come into play. "So long as the environment would reasonably be perceived, and is perceived, as hostile or abusive, there is no need for it also to be psychologically injurious."

Harris also addressed the standard of reasonableness to be applied in judging sexual harassment claims, an issue dividing the lower federal courts then and now. Justice O'Connor opted for a two-part analysis, both components of which must be met for a violation to be found. First, the conduct must create an objectively hostile work environment--"an environment that a reasonable person would find hostile and abusive." Second, the victim must subjectively perceive the environment to be abusive. The "totality of circumstances" surrounding the alleged harassment are to guide judicial inquiry, including "the frequency of the discriminatory conduct; its severity; whether it is physically threatening or humiliating or a mere offensive utterance; and whether it unreasonably interferes with an employee's work performance." Significantly, however, *Harris* did not explicitly resolve a fundamental issue raised by several lower courts regarding the appropriate "gender perspective" to consider in assessing sexual harassment claims.[33]

An increasingly broad range of hostile environment harms--frequently as concerned with lewd comments, inquiries, jokes or displays of pornographic materials in the workplace as with overt sexual aggression--have occupied the federal courts in recent years. *Robinson v. Jackson Shipyards, Inc.*[34] was among the first reported decisions to impose liability for sexual harassment

---

[33] *Compare, e.g. Rabidue v. Osceola Refining Co.*, 805 F.2d 611, 622 (6th Cir. 1986)(holding that barrage of "nudie" pictures and litany of degrading comments were "annoying," but would not be sufficiently offensive to a *reasonable person* so as to interfere with the person's work performance), *cert. denied*, 481 U.S. 1041 (1987) with *Robinson v. Jacksonville Shipyards, Inc.*, 760 F. Supp. 1486, 1524 (M.D. Fla. 1991)(applying *reasonable woman* standard to determine that pervasive pornographic pictures, sexual comments, verbal harassment, abusive graffiti, and unwelcome touching of some of plaintiff's female co-workers created a hostile working environment) and *Spenser v. General Electric Co.*, 697 F. Supp. 204, 218 (E.D. Va.1988)(finding that sexual comments and suggestive behavior of plaintiff's superior, such as sitting on female workers' laps and talking about private parts, would have seriously affected the psychological well-being of reasonable female employee), *aff'd*, 894 F.2d 651 (4th Cir. 1990). *See also Ellison v. Brady*, 924 F.2d 872, 879 (9th Cir. 1991)(adopting reasonable woman standard).

[34] 760 F. Supp. 1486 (M.D.Fla. 1991).

based on the pervasive presence of sexually oriented materials--magazine foldouts or other pictorial depictions--and "sexually demeaning remarks and jokes" by male co-workers without allegations of physical assaults or sexual propositions directed at the plaintiff. Some of the pictures were posted on walls in public view, but included in the category of sexually harassing behavior were incidents where male employees were simply reading the offending magazines in the workplace or carrying them in their back pockets. The district court in *Robinson* rejected the suggestion that sexually oriented pictures or comments standing alone cannot form the basis for Title VII liability, stating that "[e]xcluding some forms of offensive conduct as a matter of law is not consistent with the factually oriented approach" required by Title VII.

Consistent with *Vinson* and *Harris*, however, most courts have limited recovery to cases involving repeated sexual demands or other offensive conduct.[35] Claims involving isolated or intermittent incidents have frequently been dismissed as insufficiently pervasive.[36] For example, the Seventh Circuit recently concluded that while an Illinois state employee "subjectively perceived her work environment to be hostile and abusive" the paucity of sexually oriented comments complained of--three suggestive comments by a co-worker over a three-month period--"were not sufficiently severe that a reasonable person would feel subjected to a hostile working environment."[37] Moreover, except for cases involving touching or extreme verbal behavior, courts are often reluctant to find that sexual derision--or claims against pornography in the workplace--when

---

[35] E.g. *Highlander v. K.F.C. Nat'l Management Co.*, 805 F. 2d 644 (6th Cir. 1986)(holding that one instance of fondling and one verbal proposition were not sufficient to establish "hostile environment"); *E.g. Waltman v. Int'l Paper Co.*, 875 F.2d 468, 475 (5th Cir. 1989)("focus is whether [plaintiff] was subjected to recurring acts of discrimination, not whether a given individual harassed [plaintiff] recurrently."); *King v. Board of Regents*, 898 F.2d 533, 537 (7th Cir. 1990)("although a single act can be enough. . .generally repeated incidents create a stronger claim of hostile environment, with the strength of the claim depending on the number of incidents and the intensity of each incident"). *But cf. Vance v. Southern Tel. & Tel. Co.*, 863 F.2d 1503, 1510 (llth Cir. 1989)("the determination of whether the defendant's conduct is sufficiently 'severe or pervasive' to constitute racial harassment does not turn solely on the number of incidents alleged by plaintiff.").

[36] *Chamberlin v. 101 Realty*, 915 F.2d 777 (lst Cir. 1990)(five mild sexual advances by a supervisor, without more, were insufficient); *Drinkwater v. Union Carbide Corp.*, 904 F.2d 853 (3d Cir. 1990)(a claim must demonstrate a "continuous period of harassment and two comments do not create an atmosphere."); *Baskerville v. Culligan Int'l Co.*, 50 F.3d 428, 431 (7th Cir. 1995)(handful of offensive remarks without any physical touching, without any invitations to go out on a date, and without any exposure to pornographic pictures did not constitute sexual harassment); *Ebert v. Lamar Truck Plaza*, 878 F.2d 338 (10th Cir. 1989)(use of foul language and infrequent touching of employees at 24-hour restaurant was not pervasive or severe and management promptly took corrective action whenever complaints were made).

[37] *McKensie v. Illinois Department of Transportation*, 92 F.3d 473 (7th Cir. 1996).

unaccompanied by sexual demands, is sufficient to create a hostile environment.[38] However, conduct need not be overtly sexual; other hostile conduct directed against the victim because of the victim's sex is also prohibited.[39] Finally, in line with *Vinson*, evidence of a sexual harassment claimant's own provocative behavior or prior workplace conduct has generally been deemed relevant to a judicial determination of whether the defendant's conduct was unwelcome.[40]

Of course, a single incident may be actionable if it is linked to a granting or denial of an employment benefit (*quid pro quo* harassment),[41] or if the incident involves physical touching of the employee in an offensive manner under circumstances that preclude her escape.[42] The EEOC policy statement also states that the agency "will presume that the unwelcome, intentional touching of a charging party's intimate body areas is sufficiently offensive to alter the conditions of her working environment and constitute a violation of Title VII."[43]

---

38 For example, in *Hall v. Gus Construction Co.,* 842 F.2d 1010, 1017 (8th Cir. 1988), having found that defendants' conduct had gone "far beyond that which even the least sensitive of persons is expected to tolerate," the Eight Circuit nonetheless felt compelled to add that "Title VII does not mandate an employment environment worthy of a Victorian salon. Nor do we expect that our holding today will displace all ribaldry on the roadway." *See also Jones v. Flagship Int'l,* 793 F.2d 714 (5th Cir. 1986)(holding that two requests for sexual contact plus one incident of bare-breasted mermaids as table decorations for a company party were insufficiently pervasive to create hostile environment), *cert. denied,* 479 U.S. 1065 (1987); *Katz v. Dole,* 709 F.2d 251, 256 (4th Cir. 1983)("Title VII is not a clean language act, and does not require employers to extirpate all signs of centuries-old prejudice.").

39 *See Andrews v. City of Philadelphia,* 898 F.2d 1469, 1485 (3d Cir. 1990)("The Supreme Court [in *Vinson*] in no way limited this concept to intimidation or ridicule of an explicitly sexual nature."); *Bell v. Crackin Good Bakers, Inc.,* 777 F.2d 1497, 1503 (11th Cir. 1985)(holding that valid claim could be based on "threatening, bellicose, demeaning, hostile, or offensive conduct by a supervisor in the workplace because of the sex of the victim"); *McKinney v. Dole,* 765 F.2d 1129, 1140 (D.C.Cir. 1985)(district court erred in assuming that incident of physical force could not constitute sexual harassment unless "explicitly sexual").

40 *See, e.g., Jones v. Wesco Investments Inc.,* 846 F.2d 1154 n.5 (8th Cir. 1988)("A court must consider any provocative speech or dress of the plaintiff in a sexual harassment case."); *Swentek v. USAIR, Inc.,* 830 F.2d 552, 556 (4th Cir. 1987)(affirming trial judge's determination to permit testimony that the plaintiff was "a foul-mouthed individual who often talked about sex," that the plaintiff had placed a "dildo in her supervisor's mailbox" and once grabbed the genitals of a male co-worker and sexually propositioned him).

41 *Neville v. Taft Broadcasting Co.,* 857 F. Supp. 1461 (W.D.N.Y. 1987).

42 *Barrett v. Omaha National Bank,* 726 F. Supp. 424 (D.Neb. 1983).

43 BNA, FEP Manual at 405:6681.

SAME-SEX HARASSMENT

While the courts and EEOC have interpreted Title VII to protect both men and women against workplace sexual harassment by the opposite sex, it has not been definitely resolved whether the Act's prohibitions apply when the harasser and the victim are of the same sex. The *Meritor* Court found that Congress intended "to strike at the entire spectrum of disparate treatment of men and women" in employment and read Title VII to prohibit discriminatory harassment by a supervisor "because of the subordinate's sex." Although Title VII does not prohibit direct discrimination by an employer based on an employee's sexual orientation[44]--whether homosexual, bisexual, or heterosexual--the EEOC[45] and the District of Columbia,[46] Seventh,[47] Eighth[48] and Ninth Circuits[49] have all indicated in dicta that same-sex harassment may be actionable in some

---

[44] *Ulane v. Eastern Airlines, Inc.*, 742 F.2d 1081 (7th Cir. 1984), *cert. denied*, 471 U.S. 1017 (1985).

[45] The EEOC Compliance Manual states that the respective sexes of the harasser and the victim are irrelevant in determining whether Title VII has been violated:

> The victim does not have to be of the opposite sex from the harasser. Since sexual harassment is a form of sex discrimination, the crucial inquiry is whether the harasser treats a member or members of one sex differently from member of the other sex. The victim and the harasser may be of the same sex where, for instance, the sexual harassment is based on the victim's sex (not on the victim's sexual preference) and the harasser does not treat the employees of the opposite sex the same way.

EEOC Compliance Manual, § 615.2(b)(3). While EEOC interpretations of Title VII are not binding on the courts, they are frequently accorded judicial deference. *See Meritor*, 477 U.S. at 65.

[46] *Barnes v. Costle*, 561 F.2d 983, 990 n. 55 (D.C.Cir. 1977)(acknowleging the possibility of actionable Title VII claim where "a subordinate of either gender" is harassed "by a homosexual superior of the same gender.").

[47] *Baskerville v. Culligan Int'l Co.*, 50 F.3d 428, 430 (7th Cir. 1995)(In a heterosexual harassment action, the court noted parenthetically that "sexual harassment of women by men is the most common kind, but we do not mean to exclude the possibility that sexual harassment of men by women, or men by other men, or women by other women would not be actionable in appropriate cases.").

[48] *Quick v. Donaldson Co.*, 71 FEP Cases 551 (8th Cir. 1996)(evidence that male employees were the sole targets of other heterosexuals who practices "bagging" co-worker testicles could lead to finding that such treatment was based on sex).

[49] *Steiner v. Showboat Operating Co.*, 25 F.3d 1459, 1464 (9th Cir. 1994)(commenting that "we do not rule out the possibility that both men and women. . .have viable claims against [a male supervisor] for sexual harassment"), *cert. denied* 115 S. Ct. 733 (1995).

circumstances. An apparent majority of federal district courts to consider the issue have also allowed such claims where the alleged harassment is "because of" the victim's sex.[50] The rationale is that Title VII bars disparate treatment based on the sex or gender of the employee, without regard to whether the harasser is male or female.

The Fifth Circuit in *Garcia v. Elf Atochem North America*[51] denied a claim of same-sex harassment under Title VII. *Garcia* held without any analysis that "harassment by a male supervisor against a male subordinate does not state a claim under Title VII even though the harassment has sexual overtones. Title VII addresses gender discrimination."[52] For its conclusion, the Fifth Circuit cited and apparently relied on *Goluszek v. Smith* involving claims by a male that he had been harassed by several male co-workers and that the employer failed to remedy the situation after repeated complaints. The *Goluszek* court refused "a wooden application of the verbal formulations created by the courts" to salvage same-sex harassment claims, instead focusing on Title VII's concern for "imbalance" and "abuse" of power in the workplace, and the sense of inferiority and "degradation" that results from attacking the sexuality of a "discrete and vulnerable group." Title VII harassment claims are limited, said the court, to the "exploitation of a powerful position to impose sexual demands or pressures on an unwilling but less powerful person." Because the plaintiff was a male in a "male-dominated" work environment, the harassment in question was not "anti-male" or of a kind which treated males as "inferior." *Garcia* and *Goluszek* have been followed by other courts holding that "same-sex harassment is not actionable under Title VII" because the statute "is aimed at a gender-biased atmosphere; an atmosphere of oppression by a 'dominant' gender."[53]

A distinction was drawn by the Fourth Circuit between same-sex harassment predicated on heterosexual and homosexual conduct. In *McWilliams v. Fairfax County Board of Supervisors*,[54] the appeals court refused to recognize same sex harassment under Title VII where neither party was alleged to be homosexual. The opinion focused on Title VII requirement that the discrimination occur "because of the [victim's] sex." This causation requirement could not be met, in the court's view, where the conduct complained of was between heterosexual males because it was not based on the employee's sex.

---

50 *See Gerd v. United Parcel Service, Inc.*, 1996 U.S. Dist. LEXIS 12180 (D.Colo. 8-19-96) and cases cited therein.

51 28 F.3d 449 (5th Cir. 1994).

52 *Id.* at 451-52 (quoting *Giddens v. Shell Oil Co.*, 12 F.3d 208 (5th Cir. 1993).

53 *Vandevanter v. Wabash Nat'l Corp.*867 F. Supp. 790 (N.D. Ind. 1994). See, also *Hopkins v. Baltimore Gas & Electric Co.*, 871 F. Supp. 822 (D.Md. 1994).

54 72 F.3d 1191 (4th Cir. 1996).

The denial of relief was limited to heterosexual males in hostile environment cases, however, and "does not purport to reach any form of same-sex discrimination claims where either victim or oppressor, or both, are homosexual or bisexual." To the contrary is the Eighth Circuit's recent decision in *Quick v. Donaldson Co.*[55] which reversed a determination by the district court that the alleged harassment involving heterosexual male employees was not gender-based because the underlying motive was personal enmity or hooliganism.

On the opening day of its 1996-97 Term, the U.S. Supreme Court left the lower federal courts adrift over the legal status of same-sex harassment when it denied review in *McWilliams*, [56] and in another case from the Sixth Circuit involving the dismissal of a male-on-male harassment claim because the facts alleged failed to demonstrate actual or constructive knowledge on the part of the employer.[57] The Court also refused the appeal of a third ruling, *Hopkins v. Baltimore Gas and Electric Co.*,[58] where the Fourth Circuit ruled that the same-sex misconduct alleged was not of such severity as to create a hostile work environment under Title VII.

REMEDIES

One major aspect of the 1991 Civil Rights Act[59] of particular importance to sexual harassment claimants was the extension of jury trials and compensatory and punitive damages as remedies for Title VII violations. Previously, Title VII plaintiffs had no right to a jury trial and were entitled only to equitable relief in the form of injunctions against future employer misconduct, reinstatement, and limited backpay for any loss of income resulting from any discharge, denial of promotion, or other adverse employment decision. Consequently, victims of alleged sexual harassment were often compelled to rely on state fair employment practices laws,[60] or traditional common law causes of action for assault, intentional infliction of emotional distress, unlawful

---

55 90 F.3d 1372 (8th Cir. 1996).

56 *McWilliams supra n. 55, cert. denied* No. 95-1983, 65 U.S.L.W. 3240 (S.Ct 10-8-96).

57 *Fleenor v. Hewitt Soap Co.* 81 F.3d 48 (6th Cir.), *cert. denied* No. 96-47, 65 U.S.L.W. 3241 (S.Ct 10-8-96).

58 77 F.3d 745 (4th Cir. 1995), *cert. denied* No. 95-1961, 65 U.S.L.W. 3239 (S.Ct 10-8-96).

59 Pub. L. 102-166, 105 Stat. 1071.

60 *E.g., Wirig v. Kinney Shoe Corp.*, 448 N.W. 2d 526, 51 FEP Cases 885 (Minn. Ct.App. 1989), *aff'd in part and rev'd in part on other grounds*, 461 N.W.2d 374 (Minn. Sup.Ct. 1990).

interference with contract, invasion of privacy, and the like, to obtain complete monetary relief.[61] Section 102 of the 1991 Act[62] altered the focus of federal EEO enforcement from reliance on judicial injunctions, where voluntary conciliation efforts fail, to jury trials, and compensatory and punitive damages, in Title VII actions involving intentional discrimination.

Compensatory damages under the 1991 Act include "future pecuniary losses, emotional pain, suffering, inconvenience, mental anguish, loss of enjoyment of life, and other nonpecuniary losses."[63] The compensatory and punitive damages provided by §102 are "in addition to any relief authorized by Section 706(g)" of the 1964 Civil Rights Act.[64] Therefore, plaintiffs may recover damages in addition to equitable relief, including backpay. Punitive damages may also be recovered against private employers where the plaintiff can demonstrate that the employer acted "with malice or reckless indifference" to the individual's federally protected rights. Punitive damages are not recoverable, however, against a governmental entity.[65] In cases where a plaintiff seeks compensatory or punitive damages, any party may demand a jury trial.[66]

The damages newly available under the Act are limited by dollar amount, however, according to the size of the defendant employer during the twenty or more calendar weeks in the current or preceding calendar year. The sum of compensatory and punitive damages awarded may not exceed: $50,000 in the case of an employer with more than 14 and fewer than 101 employees; $100,000 in the case of an employer with more than 100 and fewer 201 employees; $200,000 in the case of an employer with more than 200 and fewer than 501 employees; and $300,000 in the case of an employer with more than 500 employees.[67] In jury trial cases, the court may not inform the jury of the damage caps set forth in the statute.

---

61 *See e.g. Rojo v. Kliger*, 52 Cal.3d 65, 901 P.2d 373 (Cal. Sup,Ct. 1990); *Baker v. Weyerhauser Co.*, 903 F.2d 1342 (10th Cir. 1990); *Syndex Corp. v. Dean*, 820 S.W.2d 869 (Tex. App. 1991).

62 105 Stat. 1072, 42 U.S.C. § 1981a.

63 42 U.S.C. § 1981a(b)(3).

64 *Id.* at § 1981a(a)(1).

65 *Id.* at § 1981a(b)(1).

66 *Id.* at § 1981a(c).

67 *Id.* at § 1981a(b)(3).

This expansion of Title VII remedies may dramatically affect the level of relief available in cases of intentional sex discrimination, where plaintiffs for the first time have the prospect of federal compensatory and punitive damage recoveries and the right to a jury trial. In particular, the Act now provides a monetary remedy for victims of sexual harassment in employment not tied to lost wages.[68] Since harassment of the hostile environment type often occurs without economic loss to the employee, in terms of pay or otherwise, critics of the prior law charged that the sexual harassment victim was frequently without any effective federal relief. Title VII plaintiffs may now seek monetary compensation for emotional pain and suffering, and other pecuniary and nonpecuniary losses, caused by sexual harassment. Moreover, federal claims may be joined with pendent state-law claims for damages unlimited by the caps in the federal law or an election made between pursuing state and federal remedies.

Legislation was introduced during the 104th Congress in both the House and Senate to remove the damage caps under the 1991 Act.[69] The Equal Remedies Act of 1995, identical to bills first proposed two years earlier, calls for elimination of the compensatory and punitive damage ceiling for plaintiffs charging intentional discrimination under Title VII and the Americans with Disabilities Act, thereby affording the same remedies to those claiming sex, religious, and disability discrimination as race discrimination claimants under the Civil Rights Act of 1866.[70] The legislation had earlier been approved by the Senate Labor and Human Resources Committee, but failed to reach the Senate floor. No House action occurred on the measure in either the 103d or 104th Congress.

---

68 Substantial damage awards in sexual harassment cases brought under state law have recently been reported. For example, in *Stockett v. Tolin*, 791 F. Supp. 1536 (S.D.Fla. 1992), a sexually harassed film-studio employee was held entitled not only to front pay and back pay but also to $ 250,000 in damages for a variety of torts and a $ 1 million punitive damage award against the dominant owner of the studio. A jury award of $ 315,000 in damages and attorneys fees was obtained by a sexual harassment plaintiff asserting a claim of assault and intentional infliction of emotional distress in *Syndex Corp. v. Dean*, 820 S.W.2d 869 (Tex.App. 1991). Of course, the amount of such awards under federal law would be subject to the caps currently imposed by the 1991 Act.

69 H.R. 96, 104th Cong., 1st Sess. (1995) ; S. 296, 104th Cong., 1st Sess. (1995).

70 42 U.S.C. § 1981.

LIABILITY OF EMPLOYERS AND SUPERVISORS FOR MONETARY DAMAGES

The addition of monetary damages to the arsenal of Title VII remedies has rekindled inquiry into an employer's liability for harassment perpetrated by its supervisors and nonsupervisory employees, and of the personal liability of individual harassers. The lower courts have uniformly declared employers vicariously liable for *quid pro quo* sexual harassment committed by supervisors.[71] By definition, only those with actual authority to hire, promote, discharge or affect the terms and conditions of employment can engage in *quid pro quo* harassment and are held to act as agents of the employer, regardless of their motivations. *Quid pro quo* harassment is viewed no differently than other forms of discrimination prohibited by Title VII, for which employers have routinely been held vicariously liable. Because Title VII defines employer to include "any agent" of the employer, the statute is understood to have incorporated the principle of *respondeat superior*, in effect holding "employers liable for the discriminatory [acts of] . . . supervisory employees whether or not the employer knew, should have known, or approved of the supervisor's actions."[72] However, the suggestion in *Meritor Savings Bank* that courts look to agency law in developing liability rules for hostile work environment cases has resulted in a rejection of vicarious liability by most circuit courts confronting hostile work environment claims.

Most courts before and after *Meritor* have made an employer liable for a hostile environment only if it knew or should have known about the harassment and failed to take prompt remedial action to end it. They reason that, unlike *quid pro quo* cases, in which a supervisor exerts actual authority to affect the terms, conditions, or privileges of a subordinate's employment, the supervisor is cloaked with no actual or apparent authority to create a hostile environment. In other words, the employer is directly liable for its own wrongdoing in not stopping harassment of which it was or should have been aware but is not automatically or "strictly" liable for supervisory misconduct.[73] A minority view, however, recognizes vicarious liability when the harasser is a supervisor[74] and creates a hostile environment through threats and intimidation.[75] Similarly, an employer without actual or constructive knowledge is generally not liable for co-worker harassment since the discriminatory conduct is not within the scope

---

[71] See *Horn v. Duke Homes*, 755 F.2d 599, 604 (7th Cir. 1985)(noting that all circuits reaching the issue have held employers strictly liable for *quid pro quo* harassment).

[72] *Meritor Savings*, 477 U.S. at 70-71.

[73] *Lipsett v. University of Puerto Rico*, 864 F.2d 881, 901 (lst Cir. 1988); Bouton v. BMW of North America, Inc., 29 F.3d 103 (3d Cir. 1994); *Waltman v. International Paper co.*, 875 F.2d 468 (5th Cir. 1989); *Juarez v. Ameritech Mobile Communications, Inc.*, 957 F.2d 317 (7th Cir. 1992); *Burns v. McGregor Elec. Indus.*, 995 F.2d 559 (8th Cir. 1992); *Ellison v. Brady*, 924 F.2d 872 (9th Cir. 1991).

[74] *Kaufman v. Allied Signal, Inc.*, 970 F.2d 178 (6th Cir.), *cert. denied*, 113 S.Ct. 831 (1992).

[75] *E.g.Karibian v. Columbia University*, 14 F.3d 773, 780 (2d Cir. 1994)(actions of a "supervisor at a sufficiently high level in the hierarchy would necessariy be imputed to the company").

of employment and the employer usually has conferred no authority, real or apparent, to facilitate the harassment.[76]

Similar divisions exist, again because "agent[s]" are included within the Title VII definition of "employer," as to the personal liability of individual supervisors and co-workers for hostile environment harassment or other discriminatory conduct. A majority of federal circuit courts to address the question--the Second,[77] Fifth,[78] Seventh,[79] Ninth,[80] Tenth[81] and Eleventh[82] and District of Columbia[83]--have interpreted agents in the statutory definition as merely incorporating *respondeat superior* and refused to impose personal liability on agents. These courts also note the incongruity of imposing personal liability on individuals while capping compensatory and punitive damages based on employer size, as the statute does, and exempting small businesses that employ less than 15 persons from Title VII altogether. Of the Courts of Appeals, only the Fourth Circuit[84] has extended Title VII liability to supervisors in both their personal capacity where the supervisor exercised significant control over the plaintiff's hiring, firing, or conditions of employment. The First Circuit, the Third Circuit, the Sixth Circuit, and the Eight Circuit have yet to decide the issue, leading to contradictory results among the district courts in those jurisdiction.[85]

Several recent federal circuit court rulings strongly suggest that the most effective defensive strategy for employers to avoid liability for a hostile work environment may be a proactive approach. As noted, even where the conduct of a supervisor or co-workers creates a hostile environment, the courts will

---

76 *See e.g. Baker v. Weyerhauser Co.*, 903 F.2d 1342 (10th Cir. 1990); *Steele v. Offshore Shipbuilding, Inc.*, 867 F.2d 1311 (11th Cir. 1989); *Swentek v. USAir, Inc.*, 830 F.2d 552 (4th Cir. 1987).

77 *Tomka v. Seiler Corp.*, 66 F.3d 1295 (2d Cir. 1995).

78 *Grant v. Loan Star Co.*, 21 F.3d 649 (5th Cir.), *cert. denied*, 115 S. Ct. 574 (1994).

79 *EEOC v. AIC Sec. Investigations, Ltd.*, 55 F.3d 1276 (7th Cir. 1995).

80 *Miller v. Maxwell's Int'l Inc.*, 991 F.2d 583 (9th Cir. 1993), *cert. denied*, 114 S. Ct. 1049 (1994).

81 *Haynes v. Williams*, 88 F.3d 989 (10th Cir. 1996).

82 *Busby v. City of Orlando*, 931 F.2d 764 (11th Cir. 1991).

83 *Gary v. Long*, 59 F.3d 1391 (D.C. Cir. 1995), *cert. denied*, 116 S.Ct. 569 (1995).

84 *See Paroline v. Unisys Corp.*, 879 F.2d 100 (4th Cir. 1989), *rev'd in part, aff'd in relevant part*, 900 F.2d 27 (4th Cir. 1990 (*en banc*).

85 *See Hernandez v. Wangen*, 1996 U.S. Dist. LEXIS 11533 (D.P.R. 8-1-96) and cases listed therein.

generally not hold the employer responsible unless he or she knew or should have known of the situation and failed to take prompt corrective action and disciple the alleged harasser. Thus, in *McKenzie v. Illinois Department of Transportation*,[86] the "prompt and remedial action" taken by the state employer in barring further workplace contacts between the allegedly harassing co-worker and the complainant was held to prevent recovery on a hostile environment claim. Conversely, a federal jury recently awarded $2 million to a former Wal-Mart clerk who claimed that the retailer fostered a hostile work environment by ignoring her reports of sexual harassment by a fellow employee who attacked and threatened her. The compensatory damages, which included recovery for extensive treatment for post-traumatic stress suffered by the employee after the attack, will be reduced to $300,000 in conformity with the "cap" imposed by the 1991 Civil Rights Act.[87]

In addition, the courts are generally reluctant to impose Title VII liability on employers who act "prophylactically" to stem harassing conditions before they begin. This is illustrated by *Gary v. Long*[88] where the D.C. Circuit dismissed a hostile environment lawsuit against the Washington Metropolitan Area Transit Authority (WMATA) as the result of repeated verbal and physical harassment, and eventual rape, of a female employee by a supervisor. Claims of *quid pro quo* harassment were rejected due to lack of economic detriment. Moreover, WMATA escaped liability on the hostile environment claim because it had an "active and firm" policy against the sexual harassment which it publicized through staff notices, seminars, and EEO counselors, and because it maintained detailed grievance procedures for reporting acts of discrimination. Perhaps the most practical lesson for employers is to formulate and communicate to employees a specific policy forbidding workplace harassment; to establish procedures for reporting incidents of harassment that bypass the immediate supervisor of the victim if he or she is the alleged harasser; to immediately investigate all alleged incidents and order prompt corrective action (including make-whole relief for the victim) when warranted; and to appropriately discipline the harasser.

---

[86] 92 F.3d 473 (7th Cir. 1996).

[87] *Holmes v. Wal-Mart Stores Inc.*, F. Supp. (M.D.Fla. 1996). *See also Varner v. National Supermarkets Inc.*, F.3d (8th Cir. 1996)(Supermarket chain liable for compensatory damages of $30,000 to female employee harassed by co-worker because supervisor took no corrective action and company policy dictated referral of complaints to human resources department, "in effect requir[ing]. . .supervisor to remain silent notwithstanding his knowledge of the incidents.").

[88] 59 F. 3d 1391 (D.C. Cir 1995).

SEXUAL HARASSMENT IN THE SCHOOLS

Issues surrounding the legal responsibility of school districts or other educational authorities for sexual harassment within the schools are highlighted by recent media reports of disciplinary proceedings against students for alleged sexual abuse or unwanted displays of affection directed at their peers. On October 7, 1996, the U.S. Supreme Court denied review of an appeal from *Rowinsky v. Bryan Independent School District*[89] where the Fifth Circuit refused to award damages or injunctive relief against a local school district under Title IX of the 1972 Education Act Amendments for an alleged hostile environment resulting from the misconduct of students. In *Rowinsky*, male students "physically and verbally abused" two eighth grade daughters of the petitioner by "swatting" and "grabbing" them by various private body parts. Despite repeated complaints by the girls to their bus driver, and by the parents to numerous school and district officials, no investigation or corrective action was taken. In denying relief, the Fifth Circuit disapproved of incorporating the hostile environment concept from Title VII into a peer harassment Title IX case. It pointed to the lack of an agency relationship between the school and the harasser and to its view that there is no "power relationship" between the harasser and the victim, so that "[u]nwanted sexual advances of fellow students do not carry the same coercive effect or abuse of power as those made by a teacher, employer, or co-worker."[90] The Court's refusal to hear the *Rowinsky* case may exacerbate differences of opinion that have emerged to date from lower federal court rulings on the issue of school district liability for student-to-student or so-called "peer" sexual harassment.

Title IX provides that "[no] person in the United States shall, on the basis of sex, be excluded from participation in, be denied the benefits of, or be subjected to discrimination under any education program or activity receiving Federal financial assistance."[91] Under the statute, student victims of any form of sex discrimination, including sexual harassment, may file a written complaint with the Office of Civil Rights (OCR)[92] for administrative determination and possible imposition of sanctions--including termination of federal funding--upon the offending educational institution. OCR interprets Title IX as imposing liability on a recipient educational institution if the institution knew, or should have known, that a student was being subjected to hostile environment sexual harassment by other students and fails to take appropriate corrective action. OCR had applied this interpretation in the course of its enforcement activities on numerous occasions since at least 1989, as confirmed on August 14, 1996 when it issued a Title IX policy guidance regarding peer sexual harassment.

89 80 F.3d 1006 (5th Cir. 1996), *cert. denied* No. 96-4, (10-9-96).

90 80 F.3d at 1015 n. 11.

91 20 U.S.C. § 1681 (a).

92 34 C.F.R. § 100.7(d)(1)(1995).

Title IX also provides student victims with an avenue of judicial relief. In *Cannon v. University of Chicago,*[93] the Supreme Court ruled that an implied right of action exists under Title IX for student victims of sex discrimination who need not exhaust their administrative remedies before filing suit. However, the availability of monetary damages under Title IX remained uncertain until *Franklin v. Gwinnett County Public Schools.*[94] In *Franklin*, a female high school student brought an action for damages under Title IX against her school district alleging that she had been subjected to sexual harassment and abuse by a teacher. The Supreme Court held that damages were available to the sexual harassment victim if she could prove that the school district had intentionally violated Title IX. Since *Franklin*, there has been general agreement among the courts that Title IX prohibits both *quid pro quo* and hostile environment teacher-student harassment and that schools may be held liable on the basis of agency principles applied in the Title VII context, discussed above. There is less judicial consensus, however, regarding legal standards for holding an educational institution liable for a sexually hostile educational environment created by student misconduct of which the institution was or should have been aware.

First, the federal circuit courts disagree as to the obligation on school officials to take prompt and appropriate corrective action to halt student-to-student or "peer" hostile environment harassment. In the first appellate ruling on point, *Davis v. Monroe County Board of Education*,[95] the Eleventh Circuit concluded that peer harassment in an educational setting may be compared to co-worker harassment and applied Title VII principles to hold a school district potentially liable for its failure to respond adequately to a student-created hostile environment of which it knew or should have known. Several other courts of appeals appear to have aligned themselves with the Eleventh Circuit by assuming, without directly deciding, that Title IX, like Title VII, requires schools to take prompt corrective action in response to known hostile environment harassment by students or other third parties.[96] In apparent conflict with these courts is *Rowinsky* decision which the Supreme Court refused to hear this Term. The Fifth Circuit there held that a school is not liable for mere inattention to peer sexual harassment claims unless it treated male and female harassment victims differently. Rejecting the Title VII standard based

---

93 441 U.S. 677 (1979).

94 112 S. Ct. 1028 (1992).

95 74 F.3d 1186 (11th Cir. 1996).

96 *Murray v. New York Univ. College of Dentistry*, 57 F.3d 243, 248-50 (2d Cir. 1995)(discussing Title VII standards in analyzing Title IX sexual harassment claim); *Brown v. Hot, Sexy and Safer Products, Inc.*, 68 F.3d 525, 540 (1st Cir. 1995)(applying Title VII principles to Title IX hostile environment sexual harassment claim), *cert. denied* 116 S. Ct. 1044 (1996); and *Clyde K. v. Puyallup School Dist.*, 35 F.3d 1396, 1402 (9th Cir. 1994)("school officials might reasonably be concerned about liability for failing to remedy peer sexual harassment that exposes female students to a hostile educational environment).

on actual or constructive knowledge, the *Rowinsky* court concluded that there must be an act of discrimination by the school itself--beyond condoning the sexual harassment by students--in order to sustain a school's liability for peer sexual harassment. Thus, the court dismissed the eighth grade students' claims that their school's persistent failure to curtail other students repeated sexual assaults, touching and harassment violated Title IX.

Another judicial fault line divides the circuits as regards the nature of proof required to show "intentional discrimination," justifying Title IX monetary damage awards under *Franklin*. One approach is that taken by the Eleventh Circuit in *Davis*[97] which appears to infer motive or intent sufficient to establish damages liability from a school's failure to respond to student complaints of hostile environment harassment. A stricter intent standard was imposed by *Rowinsky*, however, in effect requiring a plaintiff to prove subjective discriminatory motive on the part of educational officials in order to obtain damages for a failed institutional response to charges of peer sexual harassment.[98]

VIOLENCE AGAINST WOMEN ACT

The Violence Against Women Act (VAWA) was enacted by Congress in 1994 "to protect the civil rights of victims of gender-motivated violence." It creates a private cause of action under federal law against persons who perpetrate "crime[s] of violence motivated by gender."[99] Specific "crimes of violence" triggering statutory coverage include "State or Federal offenses" that would constitute "a felony against the person. . .or a felony against the property," as recognized by federal law,[100] and which pose "a serious risk of physical injury to another," whether or not the misconduct alleged ever resulted in actual charges or a prior criminal action. To be actionable under VAWA, however, the complainant has to show that the offense was "motivated by gender," i.e., that the predicate crime was committed "because of gender or on the basis of gender,"[101] and was at least partially due to "an animus based on the victim's gender." In other words, no cause of action will lie for injury resulting from mere "random" acts of violence, regardless of the gender of the victim, where it is not proven that the perpetrator was gender-motivated.[102]

97 74 F.3d at 793. *See also Murray supra* n. 94, 57 F.3d at 248-49.

98 80 F.3d at 1016.

99 42 U.S.C. § 13981.

100 18 U.S.C. § 16. In effect, the bill incorporates the existing federal criminal code definition of "crime of violence" as predicate for a civil rights violation under VAWA.

101 *Id.* at § 13981(e)(1).

102 Under evidentiary standards prescribed by § 13981(e)(1), the complainant must prove gender motivation "by a preponderance of the evidence."

The enforcement mechanism provided for this new right to be free of gender-related violent crime is a private civil action in federal (or state) court. The prevailing plaintiff in a judicial action may obtain compensatory and punitive damages, injunctive relief, and "such other relief as the court deems appropriate." While predicated upon conduct that is made criminal by other federal and state law provisions, the statute does not require a prior criminal complaint, prosecution, or conviction to establish the elements of a cause of action. No federal administrative scheme is authorized for VAWA enforcement,[103] nor are additional criminal penalties provided, but parallel civil and criminal proceedings for conduct which constitutes a VAWA offense are not precluded.

VAWA may to some extent overlap and provide supplemental protection to Title VII for women victimized by gender-motivated violence and harassment in the workplace. Title VII applies only to employment but even there excludes the large segment of the national workforce employed by companies and firms with fewer than 15 employees. A condition precedent to a Title VII judicial action is that the complaining employee or applicant first resort to the EEOC administrative process for voluntary negotiation and conciliation of the matter between the parties. Moreover, while the 1991 amendments added provisions for jury trials and compensatory and punitive damage awards in Title VII actions, such relief is limited by monetary "caps" that find no parallel in later law. The element of "violence," however, is not a requisite of the offense under either the Title VII or Title IX.

The new law's statement of purpose anchors the civil rights remedy for gender-motivated violent crime to the "affirmative" power of Congress under the Commerce Clause of the U.S. Constitution and § 5 of the Fourteenth Amendment. Congressional power to prohibit or remedy equal protection or due process violations has historically been limited by judicial construction of the Fourteenth Amendment to "state action" or private conduct actively supported by the state or its agents. The scope of Congress' authority to regulate purely private conduct pursuant to its §5 enforcement powers is constitutionally unsettled, as is the corollary question of the status of purely private action for purposes of application of equal protection and due process safeguards.[104] Consequently, the Commerce Clause is frequently invoked to support civil rights laws like VAWA that protect persons against discriminatory conduct by private persons unaided by the state. However, judicial developments following from the Supreme Court' 1995 decision in *United States v. Lopez*[105] have raised new questions concerning the scope of Congress' authority to regulate non-economic activities "affecting commerce" by imposition of federal criminal penalties.

---

103 This is in contrast to the voluntary negotiation and conciliation procedures of the Equal Employment Opportunity Commission which must be pursued before filing a federal lawsuit seeking relief from sexual harassment in the workplace under Title VII of the 1964 Civil Rights Act. 42 U.S.C. §§ 2000e *et seq.*

104 *See e.g. U.S. v. Guest*, 383 U.S. 745 (1966); *U.S. v. Price*, 383 U.S. 787 (1966).

105 115 S.Ct. 1624 (1995).

In the *Lopez* case, the Supreme Court invalidated, as exceeding Congress' commerce powers, the Gun-Free School Zones Act of 1990[106], which made a federal offense of possessing a firearm within 1,000 feet of a school. As traditionally applied, the Commerce Clause permits Congress to regulate "use of the channels" and "instrumentalities" of interstate commerce, as well as activities that "substantially affect" its flow. Despite the absence of congressional findings, the Government in *Lopez* claimed that the statute regulated an activity which substantially impacted interstate commerce because possession of firearms in a school zone may result in an increase in violent crime. Criminal violence, in turn, affects the national economy by increasing insurance costs, reducing the willingness of persons to travel to areas of the country perceived as unsafe, and by diminishing productivity due to impaired student learning environments. The Supreme Court concluded, however, that the regulated activity--firearm possession within a school zone--was beyond Congress' constitutional reach since it had "nothing to do with 'commerce' or any sort of economic enterprise, however broadly one might define those terms."[107] The Court rejected the Government's "cost of crime" argument as an overexpansive theory which would permit Congress to "regulate not only all violent crime, but all activities that might lead to violent crime, regardless of how tenuously they relate to interstate commerce."[108] Were this argument successful, the Court reasoned, "it is difficult to perceive any limitation on federal power, even in areas such as criminal law enforcement or education where States historically have been sovereign."[109]

Two federal district courts have reached opposite conclusions regarding the constitutionality of VAWA's civil rights provision based on *Lopez*. In *Doe v. Doe*,[110] the plaintiff alleged a pattern of "systematic and continuous" physical and emotional abuse at the hands of her spouse over a seventeen year period resulting in severe emotional distress, trauma, and depression. The defendant spouse moved to dismiss, claiming that Congress lacked authority under either the Commerce Clause or the Fourteenth Amendment to enact the WAVA remedy for gender-based violence. The federal district court rejected the motion, however, finding support for Congress' judgment that violence against women was a "national problem with substantial impact on interstate commerce." A "rational basis" for the legislation was found in "statistical, medical, and

---

106 18 U.S.C. § 922(a)(1)(A).

107 *Id.* at 1631.

108 *Id.* at 1632.

109 *Id.* at 1632.

110 929 F. Supp. 608 (D.Conn. 1996).

economic data before the Congress" that was lacking in *Lopez*. The Senate Report, for example, indicated that 50% of rape victims leave the work force involuntarily and that "fear of gender-based crimes restricts movement, reduces employment opportunities, increases health expenditures, and reduces consumer spending, all of which affect interstate commerce and the national economy."[111] Moreover, VAWA was found to "complement" rather than encroach upon state procedures because it remedied "deficiencies" in existing state and federal legal protections against gender-based violence while preserving traditional state tort remedies. The federal safeguards were further justified, said the *Doe* Court, given the special harm, community unrest, and likelihood of retaliation, provoked by bias-inspired crime.

Conversely, the VAWA claim of a female student at a state university who had allegedly been raped by two male students was rejected in *Brzonkala v. Virginia Polytechnic and State University*.[112] The district judge there ruled that the "totality of circumstances"--including vulgar statements made by the defendants concerning the assaults and the "gang rape" aspect of the case--was sufficient to establish the required "gender animus." Since the law was concerned with neither the channels of interstate commerce, nor commodities moving therein, however, the court applied *Lopez* to analyze the conduct prohibited by the statute in terms of its "substantial effect" on commerce.
Such effects were found lacking by *Brzonkala*. First, like the *Lopez* statute, VAWA regulated "non-economic intrastate activity" and there was no requirement that an interstate connection be shown in each individual case. The congressional findings and legislative history relied upon by the *Doe* court were insufficient to supply the missing nexus since "[s]howing that something affects the national economy does not suffice to show that it has a substantial effect on interstate commerce." The court noted that family law issues and most criminal issues "affect the national economy substantially" and have "some effect" on interstate commerce, but to equate the two and "extend Congress' power to these issues would unreasonably tip the balance away from the states."

As noted, Congress is also granted specific power to enforce civil rights remedies pursuant to §5 of the Fourteenth Amendment. Under § 5 Congress has power independent of the courts to identify equal protection and due process violations and to prescribe remedies for constitutional wrongs. The scope of this legislative authority remains undetermined, however, insofar as congressional regulation of private conduct that is unsupported by state action is concerned. The district court in *Brzonkala* read the Supreme Court rulings in *Morgan* and *Guest supra* to preclude extension of Congress' § 5 power to gender-based violent crime not attributable to the state or its agents. Since the remedy

---

111 S.Rep. 138, 103d Cong., lst Sess. 54 (1993).

112 1996 U.S. Lexis 10766 (W.D.Va. 7-26-96).

prescribed by VAWA runs against the private individual who commits a criminal act, rather than the state criminal justice system, it could not be justified as a remedy for state inaction or inadequate action in prosecuting gender-based violent crime.

> While remedying the state criminal system's deficiencies is a legitimate Fourteenth Amendment concern, VAWA does not address this concern, because VAWA provides no remedy for the deficiencies. It does not provide a remedy to the victim for the denial of the victim's equal protection rights by either undoing or stopping the specific equal protection violation or by compensating the victim for the violation, nor does it provide a remedy against the equal protection violator.

In short, because VAWA provides a remedy against private persons who commit gender-based violence, but does nothing to address deficiencies in state criminal processes regarding prosecution for rape or other violent crimes against women, it was not a proper exercise of Congress' § 5 authority, according to the *Brzonkala* court.

To date, no federal appellate tribunal has addressed the legal and constitutional issues raised by the VAWA civil action provisions. Such appeals may be anticipated, however, and a ruling by the Supreme Court this term in the *Lanier* case may provide additional guidance.

UNITED STATES V. LANIER

On March 31, 1997, the U.S. Supreme Court vacated a ruling by the Sixth Circuit U.S. Court of Appeals which had reversed the conviction of David Lanier, a Tennessee Chancery Court judge, for willful deprivation of federal constitutional "rights, privileges, or immunities" under color of law in violation of 18 U.S.C. § 242. The charges against Lanier stem from allegations that he raped, assaulted, or harassed eight women in his chambers who either worked for the judge, worked with him, or had cases pending before his court. The "right, privilege or immunity" allegedly violated was identified as a Fourteenth Amendment due process guarantee of "bodily integrity"--specifically, the right to be free of sexual assault by a state official. After a trial, Lanier was convicted on two felony and five misdemeanor counts of violating § 242 and was sentenced to a total of 25 years in prison. A panel of the Court of Appeals for the Sixth Circuit affirmed the conviction and sentence, but the full court overturned the decision and granted rehearing *en banc*.[113]

Invoking established rules of construction for criminal statutes, and the Supreme Court ruling in *Screws v. United States*,[114] the *en banc* majority set-aside the conviction on the grounds that existing § 242 precedents failed to adequately notify the public that simple or sexual assault crimes invaded a constitutional right or liberty protected by the statute. To avoid unconstitutional vagueness, a plurality of the *Screws* Court had construed the statute to require proof of "specific intent" to deprive the victim of a right "made

---

[113] 43 F.3d 1033 (6th Cir. 1995).

[114] 325 U.S. 91 (1945).

specific either by the express terms of the Constitution. . .or by decisions interpreting them." The federal government had argued that a due process right to be free of unwarranted assault recognized by lower court decisions in other contexts provided adequate notice of criminal conduct to be punished. But due to the statute's "abstract" nature, and discrepancies among the circuits and federal district courts in their recognition of "new" constitutional rights, Chief Judge Merritt felt that "[o]nly a Supreme Court decision with nationwide application can make specific a right that can result in § 242 liability" and only when the right had been made to apply in "a factual situation fundamentally similar to the one at bar." The *en banc* court conceded the "outrageous" nature of Judge Lanier's conduct, but found that since the Supreme Court had not so ruled in a "fundamentally similar" situation, the supposed right to be free of sexual assault could not form the basis for a federal prosecution.

Writing for a unanimous Supreme Court, Justice Souter faulted the Sixth Circuit for applying too restrictive a standard and for concluding that § 242 could never incorporate "newly-created constitutional rights." The "fair warning" requirement in *Screws* was not a "categorical rule" excluding from the universe of §242 safeguards any right not specifically identified by prior Supreme Court decisional law. To interpret the statute so restrictively, said the Court, was "unsound," contradicting both the legislative and judicial history of the criminal civil rights provisions and decisional law governing the corollary "clearly established" qualified immunity standard applied by the courts to determine civil liability of state officials under 42 U.S.C. 1983. The "touchstone" for imposing § 242 criminal liability is whether the statute, either standing alone or as construed by the courts at all levels, "made it reasonably clear at the relevant time that the defendant's conduct was criminal." According to Justice Souter, "general statements of the law" could provide "fair and clear warning" and may apply "with obvious clarity," in at least some situations, even though the particular conduct in question had not previously been held unlawful in precisely the same circumstances.

The Supreme Court's disposition of *Lanier* avoided decision of the main substantive issue in the case--that is, the constitutional status of the right to be free from sexual harassment and abuse at the hands of state officials. Other aspects of the ruling, however, and its contemporary legal background may suggest the probable legal outcome of the case on remand. First, in a concluding footnote, the Court rejected "as plainly without merit" several arguments--including the unavailability of § 242 to enforce due process rights--made by Judge Lanier and relied upon by the Sixth Circuit to reach its earlier decision. This will presumably complicate the task of defending Judge Lanier's position on remand. In his background discussion of the case, Justice Souter also quotes with seeming approval from the trial judge's instruction to the jury that the Fourteenth Amendment protection of bodily integrity includes "the right to be free from certain sexually motivated physical assaults and coerced sexual battery. This instruction appears to conform to the weight of existing lower federal court precedent, including a Sixth Circuit decision since *Lanier*,[115] making it difficult for the appeals court to reiterate its earlier finding that Judge Lanier did not have "fair warning" that his conduct violated constitutional rights.[116] In addition, Congress has enacted legislation based on the assumption that § 242 punishes sexual assaults. [117] Finally, the U.S. Justice Department brief in *Lanier* notes that it prosecutes 30 cases per year under § 242, many based on a due process right to bodily integrity. Since 1981, the Civil Rights Division of DOJ has prosecuted at least 29 § 242 cases involving sexual assault by public officials, most involving a woman who was sexually assaulted by a jailor, police officer, or border patrol agent. However, three other cases besides *Lanier* involved sexual assault by state judges--two resulting in guilty pleas, the third in acquittal.

In sum, *Lanier* questioned the fundamental nature of "constitutional crimes" prohibited by § 242, a statute notable for its definitional vagueness and described by the court of appeals as "perhaps the most abstractly worded statute among the more than 700 crimes in the federal criminal code." Since the federal "rights, privileges, or immunities" whose official invasion may be the predicate for a § 242 prosecution are not plainly spelled out by statute, its scope has traditionally been determined by the courts according to contemporary constitutional understanding of those terms. Justice Souter, in his opinion, appears largely unmoved by respondent's argument that to permit a § 242 prosecution of Judge Lanier would encroach upon the traditional police powers of the state and impermissibly "federalize," by judicial decree, state offenses like rape and sexual assault into a federal "common law" of crime. Nonetheless, as noted earlier, solicitude for federalism and our dual system of government was a factor limiting Congress' commerce power to enact the Gun-Free School Zones Act in *Lopez* and could inform judicial review of the corollary issue posed by *Lanier*. To what extent, if any, such objections may influence renewed judicial consideration of the case can only be speculated. At this point, however, *Lanier* appears to expand the general availability of § 242 as a safeguard against official deprivation of federal constitutional rights and, in addition, may constitutionally buttress the civil remedy for gender-motivated violence in VAWA, at least as applied to acts of violence by governmental agents or others acting under color of law.

---

[115] *Doe v. Claiborne County*, 1996 WL 734583 (12-26-96).

[116] *See, e.g. Doe v. Taylor Independent School District*, 15 F.3d 443, 451 (5th Cir.), *cert. denied*, 115 S. Ct. 70 (1994)(teacher's sexual abuse of a student "deprived [the student] of a liberty interest recognized under the substantive due process component of the Fourteenth Amendment"); *Dang Vang v. Vang Xiong X. Toyed*, 944 F.2d 476, 479 (9th Cir. 1991)(plaintiff's constitutional right were violated in a § 1983 case when she was raped by a state welfare official); and *Stoneking v. Bradford Area School District*, 882 F.2d 720, 727 (3d Cir. 1989), *cert. denied*, 493 U.S. 1044 (1990)("the constitutional right. . .to freedom from invasion of. . .personal security through sexual abuse, was well established" by the early 1980's).

[117] In the Violent Crime Control and Law Enforcement Act of 1994, Congress required enhanced punishment for several crimes in aggravated circumstances, including sexual violence. That enhancement provision applied to violations of § 242. *See* P.L. 103-322 § 320103(b)(3), 108 Stat. 2109.

CHAPTER 11

Sexual Harassment Policy: Rules Applicable to Congressional Offices

Leslie W. Gladstone

Summary

Policy on sexual harassment in congressional offices is governed by P.L. 104-1, the Congressional Accountability Act of 1995 (CAA) that applies 11 civil rights and labor laws[1] to the legislative branch of the federal government. One of the statutes applied, Title VII of the Civil Rights Act of 1964, has been interpreted by the Supreme Court to forbid sexual harassment.[2] Procedures for implementing the laws made applicable by the Act have been drawn up by the Office of Compliance, an independent office within the legislative branch that was established under the CAA to inform individuals of their rights under the applied statutes.

Sexual Harassment Protections Under the Congressional Accountability Act

For some years, federal statutes, as interpreted by the courts and executive agencies, have protected most workers in the public and private sectors from sexual harassment, but congressional workers have been granted equivalent protection only since 1995. Partly in response to public pressure for lawmakers to apply to themselves the same employment statutes they have enacted for other employers, Congress extended certain civil rights and labor laws to its own employees under the Congressional Accountability Act. Included was the law relating to sexual harassment, Title VII of the 1964 Civil Rights Act.[3]

---

[1]Coverage is also applied under the Fair Labor Standards Act of 1938; title I the Americans With Disabilities act of 1990; the Age Discrimination in Employment Act of 1967; the Family and Medical Leave Act of 1993; the Occupational Safety and Health Act of 1970; Chapter 71 (relating to federal service labor-management relations) of title 5, U.S.C.; the Employee Polygraph Protection Act of 1988; the Worker Readjustment and Retraining Notification Act; the Rehabilitation Act of 1973; and Chapter 43 (relating to veterans' employment and reemployment) of title 38, U.S.C.

[2]*Williams v. Saxbe*, 413 F. Supp. 654 (D.D.C., 1976).

[3]42 U.S.C. §2000e *et seq.*

Sexual harassment in the employment context was ruled in 1976 to be discrimination based on sex, a violation of Title VII of the 1964 Civil Rights Act, a designation affirmed in 1986 by the Supreme Court.[4] The Civil Rights Act as originally passed covered only private employers with more than 15 employees. In 1972, it was amended to include government employees, including federal employees in the competitive service. Since congressional employees are not in the competitive service, they were not covered by this amendment.

Coverage of congressional employees under the CAA was drafted to parallel coverage of private sector employees. Section 201 of the CAA extends the rights and protections under §703 of Title VII of the Civil Rights Act of 1964, which bar discrimination based on race, color, religion, sex, or national origin. The Office of Compliance has established procedural rules[5] for processing allegations of violations under Title VII. In adjudicating claims it will refer to precedents and guidelines that have been established by the Equal Employment Opportunity Commission (EEOC) for settling Title VII claims in the private sector. Procedures outlined include counseling, mediation, election of a proceeding, filing a complaint, appointment of a hearing officer, resolution or dismissal of a complaint, and filing of a civil action. Section 416(c) of the CAA requires that all proceedings and deliberations, as well as any records, are to be confidential.

The remedies for intentional violation of the Civil Rights Act are those specified under §706(g) of the Civil Rights Act[6] and include reinstatement or hiring, with or without back pay, or any other equitable relief a hearing officer or court deems appropriate. Appropriate compensatory damages may be awarded, as well. The rights extended under Title VII became effective January 23, 1996.

Under guidelines[7] issued in 1980 by the EEOC, sexual harassment is described as:

> ... unwelcome sexual advances, requests for sexual favors, and other verbal or physical conduct of a sexual nature ... when (1) submission to such conduct is made either explicitly or implicitly a term or condition of an individual's employment, (2) submission to or rejection of such conduct by an individual is used as the basis for employment decisions affecting such an individual, or (3) such conduct has the purpose or effect of unreasonably interfering with an individual's work performance or creating an intimidating, hostile, or offensive working environment.

---

[4] *Meritor Savings Bank, FSB v. Vinson,* 477 U.S. 57 (1986).

[5] *The Congressional Accountability Act of 1995: Procedural Rules.* Office of Compliance, January 1996.

[6] 42 U.S.C. 2000e-5(g).

[7] *Guidelines on Discrimination Because of Sex*, 29 CFR 1604.11(a). In 1988, following the Supreme Court ruling in *Meritor Savings Bank, FSB v. Vinson*, the EEOC also issued a guidance memorandum setting out standards for evaluating charges of sexual harassment. *Daily Labor Review*. October 18, 1988. p. E-1.

History of Congressional Employee Protection Against Discrimination

Beginning in the mid-1970s, legislative action to protect congressional employees from employment discrimination took the form of policy statements amending the rules of the House and Senate. Rule XLIII, clause 9, of the Rules of the House of Representatives, effective January 14, 1975, provided that:

> A Member, officer, or employee of the House of Representatives shall not discharge or refuse to hire any individual, or otherwise discriminate against any individual with respect to compensation, terms, conditions, or privileges of employment because of such individual's race, color, religion, sex, age, or national origin.

Rule XLII of the Standing Rules of the Senate, "Employment Practices," adopted September 8, 1976, provided that:

> No Member, officer, or employee of the Senate shall, with respect to employment by the Senate or any office thereof—(a) fail or refuse to hire an individual; (b) discharge an individual; or (c) otherwise discriminate against an individual with respect to promotion, compensation, or terms, conditions, or privileges of employment on the basis of such individual's race, color, religion, sex, national origin, age, or state of physical handicap.

The House went on record again regarding employment discrimination on October 3, 1988, when it adopted H.Res. 558, made permanent on January 3, 1991, as new House rule LI,[10] which provided that:

> Personnel actions affecting employment positions in the House of Representatives shall be made free from discrimination based on race, color, national origin, religion, sex (including marital or parental status), handicap, or age, but may take into consideration domicile or political affiliation of such individual. [Section 2(a)]

An enforcement mechanism introduced under H.Res. 558 established an Office of Fair Employment Practices to receive complaints, provide counseling, mediate
With regard to liability for harassment by supervisors, the EEOC guidelines state that:

> ... an employer ... is responsible for its acts and those of its agents and supervisory employees with respect to sexual harassment regardless of whether the specific acts complained of were authorized or even forbidden by the employer and regardless of whether the employer knew or should have known of their occurrence.[8]

The EEOC guidelines also urge employers to establish an explicit policy against sexual harassment and to make available to employees a mechanism for hearing complaints and investigating and remedying the problem.[9]

---

[8] *Guidelines*, 29 CFR 1604.11(c).

[9] *Ibid.*, 29 CFR 1604.11(f).

[10] *Congressional Record*, Vol. 137, p. H 8.

disputes, conduct hearings, and issue decisions. Final review of decisions was conducted by a panel that included both House Members and employees. Remedies under House rules could include monetary compensation, injunctive relief, costs and attorney fees, and employment reinstatement or promotion.[11]

Section 2 (b) of the Resolution provided that interpretations of the ban on discrimination were to "reflect the principles of current law, as generally applicable to employment." In October 1989, the House Committee on Standards of Official Conduct, in its first decision on a case alleging sexual harassment, found that sexual harassment is discrimination for purposes of House Rule XLIII, clause 9. In a report issued following this decision, the Committee noted that "the House rule was intended to parallel requirements applicable to other employers [and concluded] that this means Equal Employment Opportunity Commission law." [12]

While these modifications of House rules afforded increased protection against discrimination generally, including sexual harassment, employees were limited to seeking redress through "in-house" procedures, and could not proceed further via the judicial system (see footnote #10), already a right of federal employees in the competitive service and most employees in the private sector.

The Senate in 1990 strengthened employee protection against discrimination by an amendment to the Americans With Disabilities Act (ADA),[13] to include coverage of Senate employees under the ADA, as well as under the Civil Rights Act of 1964 (see discussion above) and under two other fair employment statutes, the Age Discrimination in Employment Act of 1967 and the Rehabilitation Act of 1973. Enforcement was vested in the Select Committee on Ethics, which was responsible for the investigation and adjudication of claims. Remedies, "to the extent practicable," were the same as those available under the acts named. The Senate, however, did not issue any public ruling defining the extent to which sexual harassment might be deemed discrimination.

---

[11] The Resolution's sponsors argued that once a statutory remedy was provided, civil action would not be possible because the courts would not accept jurisdiction of discrimination lawsuits by House employees. *Congressional Record*, Vol. 134, p. H 9307-8.

Sponsors were referring to the Supreme Court decision in *Davis v. Passman* in which the Court affirmed the right of a congressional employee, Shirley Davis, to sue her employer, Rep. Otto Passman, for sex discrimination under Due Process Clause of the Fifth Amendment, noting that she had "no effective means other than the judiciary to vindicate these rights." *Davis v. Passman*, 442 U.S.C. 228, 243 (1979). The establishment of an Office of Fair Employment Practices under H.Res. 558 creates the statutory damage remedy for congressional employees that the Court found lacking in the *Davis* case.

[12] U.S. Congress. House. Committee on Standards of Official Conduct. *In the Matter of Jim Bates*. H.Rept. 101-293, 101st Cong., 1st Sess., October 18, 1989. Washington, U.S. Govt. Print. Off., 1989. p. 9-10.

[13] P.L. 101-336, §509(a), 104 Stat. 327.

CHAPTER 12

Congressional Majority-Minority Redistricting

Thomas M. Durbin

I. INTRODUCTION

On June 13, 1996, the Supreme Court in two congressional redistricting decisions involving North Carolina and Texas held that the state congressional redistricting plans were unconstitutional racial gerrymanders violating equal protection. In these cases, the Court revisited the issue of congressional Majority-Minority redistricting and the constitutional parameters that would allow the drafting of race-based congressional districts. The Supreme Court invalidated the North Carolina redistricting plan in *Shaw v. Hunt*[1] and the Texas plan in *Bush v. Vera*[2].

The North Carolina and Texas decisions followed on the heels of the 1995 Supreme Court decision invalidating the Georgia Majority-Minority redistricting plan in *Miller v. Johnson*[3] which left many questions unanswered as to such redistricting. The summary affirmance by the Supreme Court in June 1995 in the California Majority-Minority decision, *DeWitt v. Wilson,*[4] gave some indication as to what the Supreme Court may allow constitutionally in this area of congressional redistricting.

These cases and similar cases are discussed *infra* (listed alphabetically by state) under the appropriate state.

II. BACKGROUND

In the 1990's, the Supreme Court once again entered the so-called "political thicket"[5] of reapportionment and redistricting to determine whether groups of

---

1 See, *Shaw v. Hunt, (Shaw II)* 64 U.S.L.W. 4437 (June 13, 1996). This case was essentially the 1992 *Shaw v. Reno (Shaw I)* case on remand to the District Court for the Eastern District of North Carolina and then appealed again to the U.S. Supreme Court.

2 See, *Bush v. Vera,* 64 U.S.L.W. 4452 (June 13, 1996). Previously, on June 29, 1995, the Supreme Court noted probable jurisdiction and consolidated related cases. 63 U.S.L.W. 3468, 3494, and 3917 (1995).

3 115 S.Ct. 2475 (1995).

4 63 U.S.L.W. 3917 (1995); see also, *DeWitt v. Wilson*, 856 F.Supp. 1409 (three-judge court, E.D. CA 1994).

5 For many years, the Supreme court refrained from addressing congressional redistricting issues since doing so was viewed by the Court as getting involved in a "political thicket." *Colegrove v. Green,* 328 U.S. 549, 556 (1946).

voters have been discriminated against when some states created Majority-Minority districts to enable certain minorities such as blacks and Hispanics to be elected in certain congressional districts. Congressional and state legislative redistricting are premised on different constitutional provisions. First, congressional redistricting is premised on the following constitutional provisions: (1) Article I, § 2 cls 1 and 3;[6] (2) Article I, § 4[7] and (3) Fourteenth Amendment, § 2.[8] And second, state legislative redistricting is premised on the Equal Protection Clause of the Fourteenth Amendment which provides in pertinent part: "...nor shall any State...deny any person within its jurisdiction the equal protection of the laws." The Supreme Court has construed congressional redistricting differently from state legislative redistricting in that it has imposed a stricter standard of precise mathematical equality on congressional redistricting[9] while allowing a more liberal standard with *de minimis* variations from a strict mathematically equal standard for state legislative redistricting.[10] The question concerning Majority-Minority congressional redistricting is how far will the Supreme Court go in shifting the focus of the constitutionality of redistricting plans from a quantitative standard to a more qualitative one requiring more representation or some form of proportional representation for protected racial, Hispanic, and other minority groups?

Previously, the Supreme Court decisions construing the constitutionality of congressional and state legislative redistricting plans had been gradually evolving from an equality-quantitative standard to also encompass some type of qualitative standard requiring meaningful representation for certain minority

---

6 Article I, § 2, cls. 1 and 3:

Clause 1: "The House of Representatives shall be composed of Members chosen every second Year by the People of the several States, and the Electors in each State shall have the Qualifications requisite for Electors of the most numerous Branch of the State Legislature."

Clause 3: "Representatives and direct taxes shall be apportioned among the several states which may be included within this union according to their respective numbers, which shall be determined by adding to the whole number of free persons, including those bound to service for a term of years, and excluding Indians not taxed, three-fifths of all other persons. The actual enumeration shall be made within three years after the first meeting of the Congress of the United States, and within every subsequent term of ten years in such manner as they shall by law direct." (Underlined portion changed by §2 of the Fourteenth Amendment.)

7 Article I, § 4: "The Times, Places and Manner of holding Elections for Senators and Representatives, shall be prescribed in each State by the Legislature thereof; but the Congress may at any time by Law make or alter such Regulations, except as to the Places of chusing Senators."

8 Fourteenth Amendment, § 2: "Representatives shall be apportioned among the several States according to their respective numbers counting the whole number of persons in each State...."

9 See generally, *Karcher v. Daggett*, 462 U.S. 725, 727, 732-33. (1983).

10 See generally, *Mahan v. Howell*, 410 U.S. 315, 325-30 (1973).

groups such as black and Hispanic groups protected under the Voting Rights Act of 1965, as amended (hereinafter Voting Rights Act or Act).[11] The focus of the Supreme Court and federal courts in the 1960's, 1970's and early 1980's has generally been on the mathematical equality of congressional and state legislative districts. With the Voting Rights Act Amendments of 1982,[12] a shift in focus in redistricting appeared to have occurred from a quantitative focus to some form of qualitative focus requiring more representation of protected minority groups in legislative bodies on the federal, state, and local levels.[13] In the 1990's, the emergence of Majority-Minority redistricting both at the congressional and state legislative district levels has been the dominating concern, and the constitutionality of such redistricting has been the focus of the federal courts in cases in California, Florida, Georgia, Louisiana, North Carolina, and Texas.

III. THE CREATION OF MAJORITY-MINORITY CONGRESSIONAL DISTRICTS

When the states had to redistrict following the 1990 census, certain state legislatures, especially in states covered under the Voting Rights Act and having to preclear their election laws under section 5 with the Justice Department,[14] decided to create Majority-Minority black and Hispanic districts, sometimes at the encouragement and even prodding of the Justice Department. Some state legislatures drafted such districts with irregular district boundary lines that sometimes twisted, convolved, and even reversed directions in an effort to carve out such districts.[15] In the 103d Congress (1993-94), a record number of 39 black Members and 17 Hispanic Members were elected to Congress in 1992.[16] Also, there were 13 new black Members and 6 new Hispanic Members elected to

[11] The Voting Rights Act of 1965, as amended can be found at 42 U.S.C. §§ 1971-1973p.

[12] See The Voting Rights Act Amendments of 1982, Pub. L. 97-205, 96 Stat. 131 (1982).

[13] See, *e.g.*, *Thornburg v. Gingles*, 478 U.S. 30 (1986), focusing on the qualitative standard in a North Carolina state legislative redistricting plan, which established a new test requiring a minority group to prove, under the totality of circumstances, the existence of: (1) a voting majority bloc that usually is able to defeat candidates supported by (2) a politically cohesive and (3) geographically insular minority group. *Id.*, 50-51.

[14] For a listing of the states and other political jurisdictions covered under section 4(b) (42 U.S.C. § 1973b(b)) and required to preclear their election statutes under the Voting Rights Act, see generally 28 C.F.R. Pt. 51 App. (1996).

[15] Majority-minority congressional districts created after the 1990 decennial census which had some of the more irregular shapes were: (1) Alabama 7th District, (2) Florida 3d District, (3) Georgia 11th District, (4) Illinois 4th District, (5) Louisiana 4th District, (6) New York 12th District, and (7) North Carolina 12th District. And see, *Redistricting Update*, CONGRESSIONAL QUARTERLY, Vol. 52, No. 6, April 23, 1994 at p. 940.

[16] *Minorities In Congress*, CONGRESSIONAL QUARTERLY, Vol. 50, Supp. to No. 44, Nov. 7, 1992 at p. 8; see also, Ronald Smothers, *Black District in Georgia Is Ruled Invalid*, N.Y. TIMES, Aug. 13, 1994, at A14.

Congress in 1992, and for the first time since the Reconstruction era, the House delegations from Alabama, Florida, North Carolina, South Carolina, and Virginia included black Members.[17] The elections of these Members were largely the result of the creation of the Majority-Minority districts. Some of these Majority-Minority congressional districts have been challenged in certain states, listed alphabetically below, as being violative of the Equal Protection Clause on the ground that such redistricting plans were constitutionally discriminatory against certain classes of voters.

A. California Majority-Minority Districts--*DeWitt v. Wilson* (Sup. Ct.Doc. No. 94-275)

On June 29, 1995, the Supreme Court in *Dewitt v. Wilson* by summary order affirmed "...questions 1 through 4 presented by the statement as to jurisdiction...."[18] This order essentially affirmed the holding of a three-judge federal district court opinion in *Dewitt v. Wilson*[19] that the Masters' California Majority-Minority redistricting plan which was approved by the California Supreme Court was not a racial gerrymander, but rather a thoughtful and fair example of a plan which applied the traditional redistricting principles, while being conscious of race. This congressional redistricting plan may be the type of plan that becomes the model for future congressional and state legislative Majority-Minority redistricting since the affirmance has indicated approval by the U.S. Supreme Court as apparently being narrowly tailored to meet a compelling state interest while utilizing traditional redistricting principles.[20]

B. Florida Majority-Minority 3rd Congressional District-- *Johnson v. Mortham* (1996 WL 189235 (N.D.Fla.))

A three-judge federal district court in *Johnson v. Mortham*[21] held on April 17, 1996 that Florida's horse-shaped Third Congressional District was an unconstitutional race-based gerrymander and must be redrawn by the Florida Legislature.[22] The three-judge panel, relying on the Supreme Court's 1995 decision in *Miller v. Johnson*,[23] involving Georgia's 11th Congressional District,

---

17 H. Idelson and J. Gruenwald, *Court Considers Question Of Minority Districts*, CONGRESSIONAL QUARTERLY, April 22, 1995 at pp. 1133-34.

18 Supreme Court Summary Disposition, June 29, 1995, 63 U.S.L.W. 3917.

19 856 F.Supp. 1409, 1413-14 (E.D. Ca 1994).

20 *Ibid.* See also, *Wilson v. Eu,* 4 Cal. Rptr. 2d 379, 385-86, 823 P.2d 545, 549-52 (Cal. Sup. Ct. 1992).

21 ___F. Supp.___ ; 1996 WL 189235 (N.D.Fla); see also, J. Gruenwald, *Florida Black-Majority District Is Ruled Unconstitutional,* CONGRESSIONAL QUARTERLY, April 20, 1996, vol. 54, No. 16 at p. 1071.

22 *Id.,* ___ F. Supp. ___ (N.D. Fla, 1996); 1996 WL 189235 at p. 23.

23 515 U.S. ___ (1995); 115 S.Ct. at 2491, 2592-94.

concluded that congressional remaps cannot use race as the predominant factor in crafting congressional district lines; likewise, "...compliance with federal anti-discrimination laws [the Voting Rights Act] cannot justify race-based districting where the challenged district was not reasonably necessary under a constitutional reading and application of those laws."[24]

According to the three-judge panel, Florida's Third Congressional District was a racially gerrymandered district which was not tailored to further a compelling governmental interest and therefore violated the Equal Protection Clause of the Fourteenth Amendment. The Court concluded that the Third District could not survive a constitutional equal protection challenge, and thus the District had to be redrawn for the 1996 congressional elections.[25] The Court retained jurisdiction to enter an order for a redistricting plan in the event the Florida Legislature could not timely draft a new remap.[26] On May 2, 1996, the Legislature struggled to redraft the new Third District by providing for more geographical continuity in uniting blacks in Jacksonville and Orlando by running through nine counties; the newly redrawn Third District would have 41.5 percent black voting age population while the old District had 51 percent black voting age population.[27] The Legislature's new remap will be sent back to the three-judge panel for judicial approval. Certain plaintiffs have again challenged the remap as an unconstitutional racial gerrymander and have appealed the three-judge decision to the United States Supreme Court and requested a stay from that Court.[28] However, at a hearing, on June 2, 1996, the three-judge court indicated that the November general election would likely be conducted under the congressional district map recently redrawn in May 1996 by the Legislature.[29]

---

24 *Id.*, quoting *Miller v. Johnson*, 115 S.Ct. 2491.

25 *Ibid.*

26 *Ibid.* However, if the Florida Legislature were able to draft a timely remap, a federal court may authorize an emergency interim use of the plan for the 1996 congressional elections without first obtaining preclearance under section 5 of the Voting Rights Act; however, the State of Florida would be required to obtain preclearance for the use of such plan for any elections occurring after 1996. See, 28 C.F.R. § 51.18(c).

27 N. Roman, *Redrawn districts leave blacks in doubt,* THE WASHINGTON TIMES, pp. A1, A9, May 6, 1996; see also, J. Gruenwald, *Florida Lawmakers Agree on New Map,* CONGRESSIONAL QUARTERLY, vol. 54, no. 18, p. 1241, May 4, 1996.

28 B. Sheffner, *Florida Legislature Sends New Map Back To Three-Judge Panel,* ROLL CALL, vol. 41 No. 81, May 6, 1996, pp. 11, 16. J. Gruenwald, CONGRESSIONAL QUARTERLY, *Florida Lawmakers Agree on New Map,* at 1241.

29 B. Sheffner, *New Florida 3rd Likely To Stand As Is*, ROLL CALL, June 3, 1996, p. 29.

C. Georgia Majority-Minority 11th Congressional District-- *Miller v. Johnson* (115 S.Ct. 2475 (1995))

In June 1995, the U.S. Supreme Court, in *Miller v. Johnson* by a 5 to 4 decision, held that Georgia's congressional redistricting plan violated the Equal Protection Clause of the Fourteenth Amendment. With Justice Kennedy writing for the majority, the Court clarified the standard set forth in the 1993 in *Shaw v. Reno (Shaw I)* [30], that a plaintiff states a claim under the Equal Protection Clause by showing that a redistricting plan, on its face, has no rational explanation except as an effort to separate voters based on their race.[31]

The Court found that appellants' contention that *Shaw I* requires plaintiffs to show that a district's shape is "so bizarre that it is unexplainable other than on the basis of race," was a misapprehension of the Court's holding in *Shaw I*, as well as of the equal protection precedent upon which *Shaw I* was based.[32] The Court noted that whether a district is bizarrely shaped is relevant to *Shaw I's* equal protection analysis because it may provide persuasive circumstantial evidence that race, and not other principles of redistricting, was the Legislature's primary reason for drawing the district. The Court clarified, however, that bizarreness was not a *necessary* element for demonstrating a violation under the Fourteenth Amendment, nor was it a threshold requirement of proof.[33]

The Court then proceeded to consider the requirements of proof for such an equal protection challenge: plaintiffs must demonstrate, either through circumstantial evidence such as the shape or demographics of a district, or through more direct evidence of legislative intent, that "race was the predominant factor motivating the legislature's decision to place a significant number of voters within or without a particular district."[34] Specifically, a plaintiff must prove "that the legislature subordinated traditional race-neutral districting principles, including but not limited to, compactness, contiguity, respect for political subdivisions or communities defined by actual shared interests, to racial considerations."[35]

Applying the requirements of proof to the 11th congressional district, the Supreme Court held that the lower court's finding, that race was the predominant factor motivating the drawing of the district, was not clearly

---

30 113 S. Ct. 2816 (1993).

31 115 S.Ct. 2475, 2482-83 (June 29, 1995).

32 *Id.* at 2485-86.

33 *Ibid.*

34 *Id.* at 2488.

35 *Ibid.*

erroneous.[36] Taking into account the shape of the district and the relevant racial demographics, the lower court had found that the drawing of narrow land bridges to incorporate outlying populations containing almost 80% of the district's total black population was clearly a deliberate attempt to garner black populations into the district.[37] Acknowledging that this evidence of intent was compelling, the Court determined that it did not need to ascertain whether this evidence alone was sufficient to establish a claim under *Shaw I*. That is, there was considerable *additional* evidence demonstrating that the Georgia Legislature was primarily motivated by an intent to create a third Majority-Minority district in order to comply with the preclearance demands of section 5 of the Voting Rights Act.[38] Therefore, the Court found that the District was subject to strict scrutiny and could only be sustained if it was narrowly tailored to meet a compelling governmental interest.[39]

According to the Court, compliance with section 5 of the Voting Rights Act, as it was being enforced by the Justice Department, was not a compelling governmental interest; that is, the drawing of the 11th congressional district was not reasonably necessary under the Voting Rights Act.[40] The Court found that the Department's policy of requiring states to create Majority-Minority districts whenever possible, i.e. a maximization policy, was an expansion of its statutory authority, exceeding congressional intent for section 5. As the Court recognized in *Beer v. United States*, "the purpose of §5 has always been to insure that no voting-procedure changes would be made that would lead to retrogression in the position of racial minorities with respect to their effective exercise of the electoral franchise."[41] The Court found that the Justice Department's implicit command to the states that they engage in "...presumptively unconstitutional race-based districting brings the Voting Rights Act, once upheld as a proper exercise of Congress' authority under §2 of the Fifteenth Amendment into tension with the Fourteenth Amendment."[42] While the holding in *Miller v. Johnson* applied only to Georgia, it provided the basis and the rationale, as did *Shaw I*, for other cases challenging the constitutionality of such Majority-Minority districts both on the federal and state levels.

On August 14, 1995, the Georgia Legislature met in a special session to redraw the congressional district lines; however, after spending 20 days in

---

36 *Ibid.*

37 *Id.* at 2488-89 (citing *Johnson v. Miller,* 864 F. Supp. 1375-76 (S.D. Ga. 1994)).

38 *Id.* at 2490-91.

39 *Id.* at 2490.

40 *Id.* at 2490-92.

41 *Id.* at 2493 (quoting *Beer v. United States,* 425 U.S. at 141 (1976)).

42 *Id.* at 2493 (citing *South Carolina v. Katzenbach,* 383 U.S. 301, 327, 337 (1966)).

session, the legislators failed to reach a consensus on a new re-map consequently ceded that responsibility in September 1995 to the three-judge court[43] which originally invalidated the Georgia plan. The judges' new re-map included only one majority-black congressional district whereas the 1992 and 1994 congressional redistricting maps had three. The Supreme Court refused to stop the implementation of the new three-judge court remap until the Court could consider a formal appeal of the decision,[44] which would mean that it would be the map used for the 1996 elections.[45]

However, on May 20, 1996, the Supreme Court granted review in this case *sub nom. Abrams v. Johnson* and will take it up in the 1996-97 term.[46] The Court will consider the legal and constitutional issues concerning the decision of the three-judge panel which reduced the number of majority-black congressional districts in Georgia from three to one.[47] This case raises such questions as a federal court's discretion to draft its own redistricting remap to cure constitutional defects after the Legislature deadlocked and failed to act on a new redistricting plan.[48]

D. Louisiana 4th Majority-Minority Congressional District-- *United States v. Hays*

This case began in 1992, when the Louisiana Legislature enacted Act 42 with the intent to increase the number of black congressional representatives to two, out of a total of seven. The 1992 congressional redistricting map provided for two Majority-Minority districts, one of which was the 4th Congressional District, also known as the "Z" district or the "Zorro" district because of its Z-shaped boundary lines. As Louisiana was covered by the preclearance provisions of section 5 of the Voting Rights Act, it determined that it was required to increase its Majority-Minority districts in order to win approval from the Justice Department.

In December 1993, a three-judge federal district court in *Hays v. Louisiana*, held that Louisiana's congressional redistricting plan was an unconstitutional racial gerrymander under the Equal Protection Clause of the Fourteenth

---

[43] K. Sack, *Legislators Letting Court Remap Georgia,* NEW YORK TIMES, Sept. 13, 1995 at A14.

[44] J. Gruenwald, *Several Minority-Majority Districts...Still Face Constitutional Challenges,* CONGRESSIONAL QUARTERLY, February 24, 1996 at p. 456.

[45] See, generally, J. Yang, *Remapping the Politics of the South,* THE WASHINGTON POST, April 16, 1996 at pp. A1, A4.

[46] 64 U.S.L.W. 3773 (May 20, 1996).

[47] *Ibid.* And see, L. Greenhouse, *Justices Take Up Issue of Cut In Black-Majority Districts,* NEW YORK TIMES, May 21, 1996, at p. A20.

[48] *Ibid.*

Amendment and must be redrawn. The Court held that the congressional redistricting plan, specifically its Majority-Minority districts, was not narrowly tailored to serve a compelling governmental interest and violated historically important redistricting principles. Although a state has the right to create a Majority-Minority district, it can only do so without violating the equal protection rights of voters.[49] The plan was found to be unconstitutional in violation of the Equal Protection Clause, and Louisiana was enjoined from holding future congressional elections under the plan.[50] This decision was appealed to the U.S. Supreme Court in 1994.[51]

It wasn't until June 29, 1995 that the Supreme Court had the opportunity in *United States v. Hays* to address the substantial constitutional issues of the Louisiana redistricting plan. But rather than deciding the substance of the issues, the Court decided a procedural issue instead holding that the appellees lacked standing to challenge Louisiana's congressional redistricting plan.[52] Although appellees were residents of the fifth congressional district, the primary focus of the appellees' claim was the fourth congressional district, a Majority-Minority district.

According to the Court, there are three elements of standing that must be proven: (1) the plaintiff must have suffered an injury in fact that is concrete and actual, not imminent; (2) there must be a causal relationship between the injury and the conduct complained of; and (3) it must be likely, not merely speculative, that the injury will be redressed by a favorable decision.[53] The Court noted that voters living in a racially gerrymandered district may suffer the special representational harms that can be caused by racial classifications and could therefore prove to have standing. Voters not living in such a district, on the other hand, did not suffer these harms and ergo, could only show a generalized grievance that was insufficient to prove standing.[54]

The case on remand was amended with new plaintiffs who lived in the 4th congressional district and was brought again before the three-judge panel. On January 5, 1996, the panel again ruled, relying on the recent Supreme Court redistricting decisions, that the Louisiana congressional redistricting plan was unconstitutional because of race-based redistricting. The District Court rejected the remap as unconstitutionally drawn on the basis of race and ordered the State to redistrict and follow new boundaries which would eliminate one of the

---

49 839 F.Supp. 1188, 1190-91 (W.D. La 1993).

50 *Id.*, 1209.

51 62 U.S.L.W. 3670.

52 63 U.S.L.W. 4679-81 (June 29, 1995).

53 *Id.* at 4681 (citing *Lujan v. Defenders of Wildlife,* 504 U.S. 555, 560-61 (1992)).

54 *Id.* at 4682.

two black-majority districts.[55] The three-judge court imposed its own plan that featured one rather than two black-majority districts which was District 2 in the New Orleans area while the District 4 black-majority district was redrawn by the three-judge panel transforming it to a District that was 71.4% white and 27.6% black. Appeals were made to the United States Supreme Court. On June 24, 1996, the Supreme Court dismissed the Louisiana appeals as moot with Justice Stevens dissenting. The Court did not issue a written opinion accompanying the order.[56]

E. North Carolina Majority-Minority 12th Congressional District-- *Shaw v. Reno (Shaw I)*, (113 S.Ct. 2816 (1993)) and *Shaw v. Hunt (Shaw II)*, (Sup. Ct. Doc. No. 94-923 (1996))

Shaw v. Hunt (*Shaw II*), decided by the Supreme on June 13, 1996, was essentially the 1993 *Shaw v. Reno* (*Shaw I*) case on remand. First, it is necessary to examine the original 1993 *Shaw I* decision in which the Court strongly suggested that North Carolina's congressional redistricting plan might have been a product of an unconstitutional racial gerrymandering.[57] The 1993 *Shaw I* [58] decision was the first major Supreme Court case construing the constitutionality of congressional Majority-Minority districts created after the 1990 decennial census. Rather than expand on the analysis and interpretation of section 2 of the Voting Rights Act, the Supreme Court in *Shaw I* appeared to reverse its direction on the issue of Majority-Minority redistricting by calling into question the constitutionality of such districts under the Equal Protection Clause of the Fourteenth Amendment rather than examining their legality under the Act.

As to the irregularly shaped North Carolina 12th Congressional District (known as the "I-85" District), the 1993 Court held: "...that appellants have stated a claim under the Equal Protection Clause by alleging the North Carolina General Assembly adopted a reapportionment scheme so irrational on its face that it can be understood only as an effort to segregate voters into separate voting districts because of their race, and that the separation lacks sufficient justification."[59] According to the Court, classifications based solely on race are

---

55 *Cleo Fields' District Rejected; Court Overturns Race-Based Boundary*, THE TIMES-PICAYUNE, January 6, 1996 at p. A2.

56 64 U.S.L.W. 3848 (June 24, 1996). See also, the Supreme Court Order List, Monday, June 24, 1996, "Appeals--Summary Disposition" at p. 1 concerning (1) *Louisiana v. Hays*, Sup. Ct. Doc. No. 95-1681, (2) *La Legislative Black Caucus v. Hays*, Sup. Ct. Doc. No. 95-1682, (3) *United States v. Hays*, Sup. Ct. Doc. No. 95-1710.

57 113 S.Ct. 2816, 2824-25 (1993).

58 *Id.* at 2832 (1993).

59 *Ibid.*

"...by their very nature odious to a free people whose institutions are founded upon the doctrine of equality."[60]

In *Shaw I* the Court found that state redistricting legislation which expressly makes distinctions among citizens because of their race is subject to strict judicial scrutiny to determine whether such distinctions further a compelling governmental interest. While race consciousness *per se* in redistricting does not lead inevitably to impermissible race discrimination, the redistricting plan itself may reflect other legitimate purposes such as, compactness, contiguity, or the maintenance of the integrity of political subdivisions which have been recognized as legitimate state interests in drafting districts.[61] Furthermore, the North Carolina congressional redistricting plan, especially as to the 12th "I-85" congressional district, was so extremely irregular on its face that it appeared to segregate races for purposes of voting without any consideration of the traditional principles of redistricting and of any compelling state governmental interests.[62]

The three-judge court in the decision on remand from the 1993 *Shaw I* decision [63] held that North Carolina had compelling interests in drafting such redistricting plan since such action was necessary to bring its redistricting scheme into compliance with the Voting Rights Act of 1965. The three-judge panel found that a state necessarily had a compelling interest in engaging in race-based redistricting when such action is necessary to avoid a violation of the Act.[64] An appeal was filed with the U.S. Supreme Court[65] to determine the constitutionality of the redistricting plan.[66]

On June 13, 1996, the Court in a 5-to-4 decision in *Shaw v. Hunt* (*Shaw II)* invalidated the 12th congressional district as a racial gerrymander since race was the dominant and controlling consideration of the State Legislature in crafting such a District.[67] *Shaw II* concluded that the North Carolina plan was indeed a racial gerrymander and violated the Equal Protection Clause because

---

60 Quoting from *Hirabayashi v. United States,* 320 U.S. 81, 100 (1943), *id.*, 2824.

61 *Id.*, 2826.

62 113 S.Ct. 2816, 2823-24 (1993).

63 *Shaw v. Hunt,* 861 F.Supp, 408 (E.D.N.C. 1994)

64 *Id.*, 438-39.

65 An appeal was filed with the U.S. Supreme Court on November 11, 1994. 63 U.S.W.L. 3439.

66 The Supreme Court in June 1995 noted probable jurisdiction and heard oral arguments in December 1995. 63 U.S.L.W. 3917.

67 *Shaw v. Hunt,* 64 U.S.L.W. 4437, 4439 (June 13, 1996).

it was not tailored to serve a compelling state interest.[68] Chief Justice Rehnquist, writing for the majority, found that racial classifications are antithetical to the Fourteenth Amendment whose purpose was to eliminate racial discrimination in the states. Under certain circumstances, the drafting of racial districts would be permissible if a state legislature were pursuing a compelling state interest which would be narrowly tailored to achieve such compelling interest.[69]

The Court identified three compelling state interests that were argued by appellees to sustain District 12 namely: (1) remedying the effects of past and present racial discrimination, (2) complying with the preclearance provisions of section 5[70] of the Act, and (3) complying with section 2[71] of the Act. District 12 was not justified by any of these three interests. First, as to the state interest in remedying the effects of past or present racial discrimination, such interest may in proper cases justify a state's use of racial distinctions, but it must be a compelling interest which would identify the discrimination with some specificity before race-conscious relief can be employed, and it must not be only a generalized assertion of past discrimination.[72]

As to the second compelling governmental interest argument advanced by appellees that the creation of District 12 was constitutionally justified to comply with section 5 of the Act, the Court concluded that creating an additional majority-black district was not required under a correct reading of section 5.[73] In utilizing section 5, the Justice Department's maximization policy to create Majority-Minority districts wherever possible went beyond its authority under the Act, beyond the legislative intent of Congress, and beyond the holdings of the Supreme Court.[74] As to the third compelling state interest argument, the Court found that compliance with section 2 by creating District 12 does not survive strict scrutiny since the creation of District 12 was not narrowly tailored to the asserted end. If a section 2 violation were proven, it would stem from the fact that blacks "...have less opportunity than other members of the electorate to participate in the political process and to elect representatives of their choice" (42 U.S.C. § 1973(b)). To remedy a section 2 violation, the minority group must be geographically compact which District 12 was not. Section 2 does not authorize the creation of a Majority-Minority district in one part of the state to correct a violation in another part since the vote dilution injuries suffered by

---

68 *Id.* at 4438-39.

69 *Id.* at 4440.

70 See generally, 42 U.S.C. § 1973c (section 5).

71 See generally, 42 U.S.C. § 1973 (section 2).

72 64 U.S.L.W. 4440-41.

73 *Id.* at 4441.

74 *Ibid.*

black minorities are not remedied by creating a safe majority-black district somewhere else in the state. The right protected by section 2 is an individual right and not a group right since the right to an undiluted vote does not belong to the minority as a group but to its individual members.[75]

According to the three-judge Court in a ruling on July 30, 1996, North Carolina will not have to change its congressional district lines before the 1996 general election in November since changing boundaries would be too disruptive of the election process.[76]

F. Texas' Majority-Minority Districts--*Bush v. Vera* (Sup. Ct Doc. No. 94-805)[77]

On June 13, 1996 the Supreme Court upheld[78] the three-judge district court's decision[79] rejecting Texas' plan on the ground that the three Majority-Minority districts created by the plan violated the Equal Protection Clause. This was the latest in a series of Supreme Court decisions involving racial gerrymandering constitutional challenges to state congressional redistricting plans after the 1990 decennial census.

The background of this case began in 1991 when the Texas Legislature drafted a redistricting plan which included two black-majority districts, District 30 and District 18, and a new majority-Hispanic district, District 29. The Department of Justice precleared the plan under section 5 of the Voting Rights Act. However, the plan was challenged by certain voters in the District Court for the Southern District of Texas alleging unconstitutional racial gerrymanders in violation of the Equal Protection Clause of the Fourteenth Amendment.[80]

The three-judge district court in 1994 in *Vera v. Richards* struck down as unconstitutional the three Majority-Minority congressional districts which had been drafted to boost minority representation in the Texas congressional delegation.[81] The three-judge panel found that the three congressional districts were so racially gerrymandered that they bore the odious imprint of

---

75 *Id.* at 4442-43.

76 "Election Rulings," USA TODAY, July 31, 1996 at p. 3A.

77 See also, *Lawson v. Vera,* (Sup. Ct. Doc. No. 94-806) 63 U.S. L.W. 3468 on appeal to the U.S. Supreme Court raising similar constitutional questions concerning Texas' congressional redistricting plan as those in *Richards v. Vera* (Sup. Ct. Doc. No. 94-805). And see, *U.S. v. Vera* (Sup Ct. Doc. No. 94-988). On June 29, 1995, the Supreme Court noted probable jurisdiction and consolidated these cases, and oral argument was heard on December 5, 1995. 63 U.S.L.W. 3917.

78 *Bush v. Vera,* 64 U.S.L.W. 4452, 4454.

79 *Vera v. Richards,* 861 F. Supp. 1304 (S.D. Tex. 1994).

80 *Id.* at 4454.

81 *Vera v. Richards,* 861 F. Supp. 1304, 1344-46 (S.D. Tex. 1994).

racial apartheid. The districts were created for the purpose of providing safe seats in Congress for two African-American representatives and an Hispanic representative.[82] Thus, it was concluded that the race-consciousness of the districts combined with the disregard of the traditional redistricting standards resulted in an unconstitutional gerrymandering of the districts and that they were not narrowly tailored to further the State's concern about being in compliance with the Voting Rights Act.[83]

The Texas congressional redistricting plan was appealed to the U.S. Supreme Court, and on June 13, 1996, in a 5-4 decision in *Bush v. Vera,* the Court held that the three districts in question were unconstitutional racial gerrymanders.[84] In affirming the District Court, the Supreme Court found that, under the *Miller v. Johnson* (Georgia) and under the *Shaw I* and *Shaw II* (North Carolina) decisions, the remap was subject to strict scrutiny and that it was not tailored to serve a compelling state interest. The Court found that all three districts in question were bizarrely shaped and far from compact which resulted in racially motivated gerrymanders.[85]

Racial classifications are subject to strict scrutiny because such scrutiny is necessary to determine whether they are benign or whether they misuse race and foster harmful and divisive stereotypes without compelling justification. If the plan had been drawn with race neutral, traditional redistricting standards which would have predominated over racial ones, strict scrutiny of the plan would not have been necessary.[86] After the Court concluded that strict scrutiny was applicable, it then examined whether the racial classifications in the three districts were narrowly tailored to serve compelling state interests.[87] Texas asserted three compelling state interests[88]: (1) the interest in avoiding liability under the "results" test of section 2(b) of the Voting Rights Act,[89] (2) the interest in remedying past and present racial discrimination, and (3) the "non-retrogression" principle of section 5 of the Voting Rights Act.

---

[82] *Id.,* 1345.

[83] *Id.,* 1344.

[84] *Bush v. Vera,* 64 U.S.L.W. 4452, 4454.

[85] *Id.* at 4460.

[86] *Id.* at 4456.

[87] *Id.* at 4459.

[88] *Ibid.*

[89] In 1982, Congress amended the Voting Rights Act of 1965 by providing for a "results" test if there was a violation of the Act. Under 42 U.S.C. § 1973(b) a violation would occur if, "based on the totality of circumstances, it is shown that the political processes leading to nomination of election in the State or political subdivision are not equally open to participation by members of a class of citizens...in that its members have less opportunity than other members of the electorate to participate in the political process and to elect representatives of their choice."

As to the first compelling governmental interest, it was contended that the creation of each of the three Majority-Minority districts was justified by Texas' compelling state interest in complying with the "results" test. The Court rejected this argument by noting that it had been unsuccessfully raised as a defense to charges of racial gerrymandering in previous cases.[90] The Court noted that the districts must be drawn so as not to subordinate traditional redistricting principles to race more than would be reasonably necessary to avoid section 2 liability, but the districts in question failed to meet these requirements.[91] The Court rejected the second compelling governmental interest argument that the districts were necessary to ameliorate the effects of racially polarized voting attributable to past and present racial discrimination by noting that "...such problems will not justify race-based districting unless the State employ[s] sound districting principles...." The third compelling state interest argument of the "non-retrogression" principle of section 5 of the Voting Rights Act was rejected since the State sought to justify not a maintenance but a substantial augmentation of the African-American population percentage, especially as to District 18. According to the Court, "[n]on-retrogression is not a license for the State to do whatever it deems necessary to insure continued electoral success...."[92]

The Court concluded by noting that Fourteenth Amendment jurisprudence is committed to the elimination of "...unnecessary and excessive governmental use and reinforcement of racial stereotypes...." Moreover, "...the Equal Protection Clause prohibits a State from taking any action based on crude, inaccurate racial stereotypes."[93] Thus, the three-judge panel's decision holding the districts to be unconstitutional racial gerrymanders in violation of the Fourteenth Amendment was affirmed.

IV. FUTURE OF MAJORITY-MINORITY CONGRESSIONAL REDISTRICTING

Since the 1990 census, the creation of Majority-Minority congressional districts has been in a state of flux and instability as the Supreme Court decisions in California, Florida, Georgia, Louisiana, North Carolina, and Texas demonstrate. Such flux and instability in the congressional redistricting processes in the states may continue well after the decennial census of the year 2000 without further direction by either the U. S. Congress or the U. S. Supreme Court as to Majority-Minority redistricting. The Congress by new amendments to the Voting Rights Act or by re-enacting the former statutory redistricting standards of compactness, contiguity, and equality, and by setting

---

90 *Bush v. Vera, id.* at 4459-60.

91 *Id.* at 4460.

92 *Id.* at 4461.

93 *Id.* at 4462.

guidelines for the states to follow in the drafting of Majority-Minority districts, could aid the state legislatures--often immersed in partisan considerations--in the drafting of such districts.

The Supreme Court has handed down five decisions since 1993 applying the Equal Protection Clause to the newly created Majority-Minority congressional districts in: *Shaw I* (North Carolina), *Miller* (Georgia), *Hays* (Georgia), *Shaw II* (North Carolina) and *Bush* (Texas). In analyzing the Supreme Court and federal court cases concerning Majority-Minority congressional districts, this is what can be concluded at this time: (1) Majority-Minority districts are valid and constitutional as long as they are properly drafted by the states to serve compelling state governmental interests by adhering to the traditional principles of redistricting such as compactness, contiguity, equality, and maintaining the integrity of local political subdivisions and communities of interest and (2) the legislature's intent in drafting a redistricting plan must not be to racially and ethnically gerrymander districts in violation of the Fourteenth Amendment's Equal Protection Clause by creating irregularly shaped race or ethnic based districts while ignoring the traditional redistricting principles.

Many of the Majority-Minority districts created in 1990's may still be salvageable constitutionally in other parts of the states where the black and Hispanic populations are the most concentrated by drafting compact, contiguous, and equal minority-dominated districts there. As to the issue of maximizing the number of Majority-Minority congressional districts in a state whenever possible,[94] this practice may now be questionable in light of the 1996 three-judge court holding in the Florida case in *Johnson v. Mortham* which rejected the maximization policy of the Department of Justice to create under Section 2 of the Voting Rights Act as many minority districts as possible. Also, the Supreme Court in 1994 found that Section 2 of the Voting Rights Act does not require the maximizing of minority-dominated districts in a state legislative redistricting plan.[95] In the 1995 *Miller* decision[96] and the 1996 *Shaw II* decision, the Court rejected the Justice Department's expansive interpretation of the Voting rights Act by requiring a maximization policy in creating Majority-

---

[94] 1996 WL 189235 at p. 17, fn. 50; *cf. Thornburg v. Gingles*, 478 U.S. at 94 (O'Connor, J., concurring) It was not the intention of Congress in the Voting Rights Act to provide minority voters with the "maximum feasible minority voting strength."

[95] The June 30, 1994 Supreme Court decision in *Johnson v. De Grandy*, 114 S.Ct. 2647 (1994), involving Florida's state legislative redistricting plan did not add impetus to the creation of more majority-minority congressional districts since the Court held that the states were under no obligation to maximize the number of minority-dominated districts and that Section 2 of the Voting Rights Act does not require the states to maximize the number of such districts. As the *De Grandy* Court noted that: "[T]here is no violation of § 2...where in spite of continuing discrimination and racial bloc voting, minorities form effective voting majorities in a number of House districts roughly proportional to their respective shares in the voting-age population." 114 S.Ct. at 2651. While the *De Grandy* case applies to state legislative redistricting, its holdings pose serious implications for maximizing majority-minority congressional districts under Section 2 of the Voting Rights Act.

[96] *Miller v. Johnson,* 115 S. Ct at 2493 (1995).

Minority congressional districts wherever possible. The maximization policy was insupportable and went beyond what Congress intended under section 5 of the Act and what the Supreme Court has upheld.[97]

Many questions still remain unanswered in this area of redistricting as to how to proceed in drafting constitutional Majority-Minority districts. However, some answers may be found in the California congressional redistricting plan, which created a number of Majority-Minority districts, while applying traditional redistricting standards, which the Supreme Court affirmed in a June 29, 1995 summary order in *Dewitt v. Wilson.*[98] The Supreme Court, however, will soon revisit the Majority-Minority redistricting issue.

---

[97] *Shaw v. Hunt,* at 64 U.S.L.W. 4441.

[98] 63 U.S.L.W. 3917; and see generally 856 F.Supp. 1409, 1413-14 (E.D. Ca 1994); see also, *Wilson v. Eu,* 4 Cal. Rptr. 2d 379, 385-86, 823 P.2d 545, 549-51 (Ca Sup. Ct. 1992).

CHAPTER 13

Race and Ethnicity: Possible Revision of OMB'S Classifications

Jennifer D. Williams

INTRODUCTION

The Office of Information and Regulatory Affairs in the Office of Management and Budget (OMB) is reviewing, for possible revision, the standards for classifying race and ethnicity that are set forth in OMB's Statistical Policy Directive Number 15.

Directive 15: OMB's Standards for Classifying Race and Ethnicity

Race

White. A person with "origins in any of the original peoples of Europe, North Africa, or the Middle East."

Black. A person with "origins in any of the black racial groups of Africa."

American Indian or Alaskan Native. A person who has "origins in any of the original peoples of North America, and who maintains cultural identification through tribal affiliation or community recognition."

Asian or Pacific Islander. A person with "origins in any of the original peoples of the Far East, Southeast Asia, the Indian subcontinent, or the Pacific Islands. This area includes, for example, China, India, Japan, Korea, the Philippine Islands, and Samoa."

Ethnicity

Hispanic. "A person of Mexican, Puerto Rican, Cuban, Central or South American, or other Spanish culture or origin, regardless of race."

The categories now contained in Directive 15 initially were adopted in 1977[1] to meet a perceived need for standardized terms for collecting and

---

[1] On May 12, 1977, the Director of the Office of Management and Budget issued these categories to the heads of federal executive departments and establishments. (Wallman, Katherine K. and John Hodgdon. Race and Ethnic Standards for Federal Statistics and Administrative Reporting. *Statistical Reporter*, no. 77-10, July 1977. p. 450-454.) Directive 15, containing the identical categories, was issued a year later. (Office of Management and Budget. Directive No. 15. Race and Ethnic Standards for Federal Statistics and Administrative Reporting. *Federal Register*, v. 43, May 4, 1978. p. 19269-19270.)

reporting racial and ethnic data throughout the federal government. The directive has civil rights enforcement and regulatory program applications, as well as statistical uses. Instances in which the standardized terms are called for include: enforcement of the Civil Rights Act, the Equal Credit Opportunity Act, the Fair Housing Act, and the Voting Rights Act; review of state redistricting plans; development and evaluation of federal affirmative action plans; assessment of affirmative action and discrimination in private sector employment; enforcement of public school desegregation plans; assistance to minority business development programs; oversight of the availability of home loans to minorities under the Home Mortgage Disclosure Act; and compilation of demographic data, such as population, education, and labor force data, vital records, and health statistics.[2]

Although Directive 15 never has been revised, it has undergone increased scrutiny. (See Appendix 1 for a chronology of the directive.) OMB considered revising the standards in 1988,[3] but left them unmodified when the proposed revision encountered opposition. In 1993 hearings, the (former) House Subcommittee on Census, Statistics, and Postal Personnel reviewed how the federal government measures race and ethnicity, especially in the decennial census.[4] In 1994, the National Academy of Sciences' Committee on National Statistics held a workshop for discussion of the issues surrounding Directive 15.[5] Also in 1994, OMB announced the formation of an Interagency Committee for the Review of the Racial and Ethnic Standards (hereafter called the "Interagency Committee"). In response to *Federal Register* notices, OMB has received numerous comments, in letters and at hearings, from the public and from federal agencies concerning a possible revision of Directive 15.[6]

---

[2] Office of Management and Budget. Advance Notice of Proposed Review and Possible Revision of OMB's Statistical Policy Directive No. 15, Race and Ethnic Standards for Federal Statistics and Administrative Reporting; and Announcement of Public Hearings on Directive No. 15. *Federal Register*, v. 59, June 9, 1994. p. 29833.

[3] Office of Management and Budget. Guidelines for Federal Statistical Activities. *Federal Register*, v. 53, Jan. 20, 1988. p. 1552.

[4] U.S. Congress. House. Committee on Post Office and Civil Service. Subcommittee on Census, Statistics, and Postal Personnel. *Review of Federal Measurements of Race and Ethnicity*. Hearing, 103rd Cong., 1st Sess., April 14, June 30, July 29, and Nov. 3, 1993. Washington, U.S. Govt. Print. Off., 1994.

[5] National Academy of Sciences. Committee on National Statistics. *Spotlight on Heterogeneity: The Federal Standards for Racial and Ethnic Classification. Summary of a Workshop*. Washington, National Academy Press, 1996.

[6] Office of Management and Budget. Interim Notice of Review and Possible Revision of OMB's Statistical Policy Directive No. 15, Race and Ethnic Standards for Federal Statistics and Administrative Reporting: Summary and Analysis of Public Comments and Brief Discussion of Research Agenda. *Federal Register*, v. 60, Aug. 28, 1995. p. 44675. (Hereafter cited as OMB, Interim Notice of Review of Race and Ethnic Standards.)

The latest reexamination of the directive comes at a time when some of its applications—such as for affirmative action—are being called into question, and Congress is considering whether the federal role in various programs should devolve to the states. Simultaneously, large-scale immigration and more interracial marriages[7] may be making the standards less adequate to describe the increasingly diverse U.S. population. The 1990 decennial census counted about 4.0 million children of interracial couples (or couples made up of Hispanics and non-Hispanics).[8] Some of these couples maintain that their children cannot be classified correctly or fairly under the standards. The current categories also perplex or affront enough respondents to make misreporting and nonreporting a problem.

Nevertheless, any revision of Directive 15 would be controversial because, as OMB has pointed out, public consensus about classifying race and ethnicity does not exist. Some persons think of these terms with reference to national origin or ancestry; others think of physical or cultural attributes. Over time, a group may change its preferred designation. Some persons favor a category that will maximize their group's size and thus, presumably, its political influence. The members of some relatively small groups want them designated separately, despite the practical constraints against doing so.[9]

Moreover, according to OMB, changes in Directive 15 would affect many thousands of state and local agencies, school districts, businesses, and other entities required to report racial and ethnic data to the federal government. With revised standards, these entities would incur substantial costs from having to update their administrative records. In addition, new standards—particularly if they contained more detailed categories—would mean increased data collection and processing costs.[10]

OMB tentatively plans to complete its review of Directive 15 by mid-1997, in time for the Bureau of the Census to incorporate any revised racial or ethnic categories into the 2000 census questionnaire.

GUIDING PRINCIPLES FOR THE REVIEW OF DIRECTIVE 15

The Office of Management and Budget, through the Interagency Committee, has formulated a set of principles to guide the reexamination, and any revision, of Directive 15. As OMB pointed out, the principles may reflect certain "competing goals" for the standards (the necessity to balance statistical

---

[7] U.S. Dept. of Commerce. Bureau of the Census. *Marital Status and Living Arrangements: March 1994. Current Population Reports*. P20-484. Washington, U.S. Govt. Print. Off., 1996. p. viii.

[8] OMB, Interim Notice of Review of Race and Ethnic Standards, p. 44685.

[9] Ibid., p. 44680.

[10] Ibid.

concerns, data needs, and social matters). Following is a summary of the principles.[11]

- The categories in the directive should not be considered primarily biological or genetic. Race and ethnicity are based not only on ancestry, but also on sociocultural characteristics.

- The categories should be considered a minimum set. More categories should be permitted if they do not exceed a manageable number and can be aggregated to the minimum categories.

- Insofar as practical, self-identification is preferable to observer identification of race and ethnicity.

- The standards should be clear, should have broad public acceptance, and should not burden respondents unduly.

- The categories should yield compatible, nonduplicated data that can be exchanged among federal agencies. Primary consideration should be given to aggregated data for statistical analyses and administration and assessment of programs. The standards are not intended to be used to establish eligibility for participation in programs.

- The standards should meet at least federal government requirements, but also should take into account the data needs of subnational governments and the larger society.

- Any revision of the current categories should be based on sound research, including evaluations of how changes might affect the usefulness and historical comparability of racial and ethnic data. Public and private costs to implement a revision should be considered.

- Any revision should provide a bridge between the old and new categories, to permit the statistical adjustment of historical data series for comparative purposes. Agencies should be given time to phase in new categories and should not be required to update historical records.

- Any revision should be the result of interagency collaboration and should be applicable throughout the federal statistical system. Revised standards must be usable with the decennial census, current surveys, and administrative records, including those that rely on observer identification.

---

[11] Ibid., p. 44691-44692.

ISSUES RAISED BY THE PUBLIC AND BY FEDERAL AGENCIES

In a discussion summarized below, OMB has presented the comments it received from the public and from federal agencies concerning Directive 15. Some research findings are summarized as well.[12]

Whether Any Standards Are Necessary

Some members of the public objected to any collection of racial and ethnic data. This practice, according to its critics, is unnecessary, unscientific, disquieting (given a perceived potential for misuse of the data to persecute specific groups), and divisive. Other persons contended that the government should collect data only on ethnicity or ancestry, not on race.

Most persons, however, favored the continued gathering of racial and ethnic data. Moreover, federal statutes and regulations require this collection. To end it would necessitate the amendment or repeal of certain statutes, such as the Civil Rights Act and the Voting Rights Act. Federal agencies also reported that uniform racial and ethnic categories facilitate data exchange among agencies and among states.

Whether Directive 15 Should Be Revised

Persons who supported a revision held that, because of sociodemographic changes in the U.S. population, racial and ethnic identification are shifting continually. In their opinion, Directive 15 should be revised now and reexamined periodically to ensure that it remains up to date.

Federal agencies that use Directive 15 for civil rights enforcement and regulatory programs generally opposed a revision. In their view, the standards provide the benefit of practical guidelines for identifying minorities who historically have experienced discrimination. However, agencies that analyze social and economic trends tended to want more detail than Directive 15 gives.

As OMB noted, a two-part directive might meet contrasting agency needs. One part would consist of the classifications first issued in 1977. The other part would present more detailed categories, which, to avoid creating unrelated data sets, would have to be capable of being combined to equal the 1977 categories.

How Better to Classify Hispanics

How to improve the classification of Hispanics is problematic in several respects. On the one hand, many Hispanics evidently are confused when asked to separate race from ethnicity. In the 1990 census, 43% of Hispanics listed themselves in the "other race" category, and reinterviews with a sample of census respondents showed inconsistent reporting of race by many Hispanics. On the other hand, persons who favored separating race and Hispanic ethnicity

---

[12] Ibid., p. 44676-44680.

noted that Hispanics are a multiracial group and wanted a way to distinguish, for example, Asian from American Indian Hispanics. Some non-Hispanics questioned why Hispanics are the only ethnic group specifically mentioned in Directive 15. The few federal agencies that commented on Hispanic identification were divided about the advisability of separating race from ethnicity.

Self-Identification vs. Observer Identification

Much public criticism of Directive 15 stemmed from the opinion that the standards inaccurately categorize too many persons. Interracial persons especially objected to the current limited choices for their classification.

A related issue is whether individuals should identify themselves or be identified by observers. Self-identification is preferred for federal censuses, surveys, and vital records. In contrast, federal agencies responsible for civil rights enforcement favor observer identification. Their rationale is that discrimination is based, not on self-perceptions, but on others' (observers') perceptions of race and ethnicity. These agencies opposed changes—including a "multiracial" category and classification of geographic origins or ethnicities, such as "Arab" or "Cape Verdean"—that would complicate observer identification.

One technical matter is that the federal government increasingly matches administrative records with survey data for trend analysis. Insofar as the two types of data record race and ethnicity by different means, the same individual might be classified inconsistently, making matching difficult.

It should be noted that American Indian groups registered another sort of concern about self-identification. Their special case pertains to programs and funding based on their legal, not racial, status. OMB explained this point as follows:

> The federal trust responsibility to provide various educational, health, and housing services extends only to federally recognized American Indian and Alaskan Native tribes and their members and descendants of members. More people self-identify as being of American Indian or Alaskan Native race or descent than are enrolled in tribes or can prove descendance, which tribal governments feel deprives their people of benefits rightfully belonging to them.[13]

Whether to Consider a Group's Size and Geographic Distribution

Some groups who sought separate categorization in revised standards are small and narrowly distributed in the United States and its insular areas. Examples are Arabs, Cape Verdeans, Louisiana (French) Creoles, Native Hawaiians, and Pacific Islanders. Collecting reliable data in national sample surveys becomes more difficult and expensive as the size of the group decreases.

---

[13] Ibid., p. 44684.

SUGGESTED CHANGES IN DIRECTIVE 15

The Office of Management and Budget has noted the impossibility of accommodating all the public's requests for racial and ethnic classifications. The result would be an excessively long list and contradictory categories. What categories, then, should revised standards include? Below are the current classifications, with the major changes the public has suggested for them, and some of OMB's points for and against each option. In addition, proposals for classifying interracial persons are discussed.[14]

White

OMB received requests to categorize white ethnic groups by their ancestors' geographic origins (German, Irish, Scottish, etc.). While this change would accommodate those whites who identify more closely with ancestry than with race, the option also presents several disadvantages. Listing origins would lengthen forms, add to the tedium of telephone interviews, and complicate data analysis; observers could not determine ancestry; and whites might not know their forebears' origins.

"Whites" currently include persons of Arab or Middle Eastern origin or descent, some of whom asked to be classified separately. A separate category for Arabs (an ethnic group) might improve the quality of the data on them and would allow them to be considered similarly to Hispanics (another ethnic group). However, the public disagreed about the definitions of "Arab" and "Middle Eastern"—although "Middle Eastern" generally is understood to be the broader term—and about the name of the new category. Consensus was lacking about Arabs' geographic origins and whether "Middle Easterners" include Pakistanis and Asian Indians.

Black

Some persons asked OMB to identify black ethnic groups by ancestral geographic origins (African, Brazilian, Haitian, Jamaican, etc.). Among the positive aspects of this option are that it would preserve historical continuity of data on blacks and would generate useful research data. The disadvantages are the same as for listing whites' ancestral origins.

Another suggestion was to substitute "African American" for "black." An advantage of "African American" is its fairly wide usage, but the term has several drawbacks as well. It is not favored by some blacks with long U.S. family histories; it would exclude African immigrants who are not American citizens; it could confuse whites or Asians of African birth; blacks of Brazilian or Caribbean birth tend not to identify with the term; and it could affect historical comparability of the data.

---

[14] Ibid., p. 44680-44690.

American Indian or Alaskan Native

The term "American Indian" confused some 1990 census respondents. Certain Asian Indians, for example, misreported their children as "American Indians." One proposal would rename "American Indian or Alaskan Native" as "Native American," a term many American Indians find unacceptable and other Americans might use erroneously to indicate their U.S. birth. Another designation, "Aboriginal Population," is technically accurate; it offends some persons, however, and could increase misreporting because it is not widely understood.

Asian or Pacific Islander

OMB received requests to make "Asians" and "Pacific Islanders" separate categories. (Examples of Pacific Islanders are American Samoans, Carolinians, Chamorros, and Native Hawaiians.) Points in favor of this option are that Asians and Pacific Islanders are ethnically and culturally distinct, and that the categories could be aggregated to ensure historical continuity of the data. A disadvantage would be the need for an additional category.

Another suggestion was that OMB identify Asians by nationality groups (Chinese, Japanese, Korean, Vietnamese, etc.). This option would recognize the diversity of the Asian population, would have research applications, and was used successfully in the 1990 census. Points against listing nationality groups are longer forms, more difficult observer identification, and more tedious telephone interviews.

Proposals for Classifying Interracial Persons

Some persons suggested a broader "Native American" category than the one previously mentioned. The new category would include the indigenous populations of American Samoa, Guam, the Hawaiian Islands, and the Northern Marianas, as well as indigenous Americans whose identity derives from tribal affiliation or community recognition (American Indians, Alaskan Indians, Eskimos, and Aleuts). Although many Native Hawaiians and some Asians preferred this option, most American Indian tribal governments opposed it. The latter organizations expressed concern about the effects of a combined category on the quality of American Indian data for programs and funding. Further, OMB noted that the category would be too heterogeneous to yield meaningful research data.

Directive 15 instructs anyone who does not belong solely in one category to choose the category most compatible with the person's recognition in his or her community. Some interracial persons commented to OMB that this instruction denies their existence or their full heritage and requires them to choose between their parents. Alternatively, interracial persons are offered (in limited instances, such as the decennial census) an "other" category, which they reported finding objectionable. Some interracial couples commented that they do not know how to classify their children under the current standards. Failure to address these problems may increase nonresponses or erroneous responses by interracial persons. As OMB has pointed out, however, federal statutes assume that a person can identify with a single current category, and most persons are able to comply.

For persons who cannot comply, various options are being considered. They include: a single "multiracial" category; a "multiracial" category with subcategories for specific races; an open-ended question on race; an "other" category added to Directive 15; retention of the current categories, with an instruction that respondents should "mark all that apply" to them; and a focus on ancestry instead of race or ethnicity. All options except the single "multiracial" category would allow multiple responses and would yield potentially valuable research data. Every option would disrupt historical continuity of the data, would increase the chances for inconsistent identification of the same person, would make observer identification harder or impossible, and might complicate civil rights enforcement. Other favorable and unfavorable points about the options are noted briefly below.

A single "multiracial" category would add only one space per form, would be relatively easy to incorporate into telephone surveys, and might benefit the few states that already include this category in their administrative records. Most subnational government records, though, do not provide for multiracial identification. Without such an addition, subnational and federal records would not match. Moreover, respondents would need precise instructions about whether to consider only their parents' races or those of previous generations. A "multiracial" classification that did not include subcategories for specific races would be too heterogeneous for research or for civil rights enforcement and regulatory programs. Nevertheless, the inclusion of subcategories—like the use of an open-ended question on race, the adoption of an "other" category, or the option to "mark all [current categories] that apply"—would involve the expense of a new system to classify and tabulate myriad responses.

An open-ended question on race might please more respondents because they could classify themselves without restrictions. However, the foreign born and persons not proficient in English might have difficulty answering an open-ended question, as they had with the ancestry question in the 1990 census.[15]

---

[15] Item 13 on the 1990 census questionnaire asked, "What is this person's ancestry or ethnic origin?" Immediately after the question, sample responses were listed: "For example: German, Italian, Afro-American, Croatian, Cape Verdean, Dominican, Ecuadoran, Haitian, Cajun, French Canadian, Jamaican, Korean, Lebanese, Mexican, Nigerian, Irish, Polish, Slovak, Taiwanese, Thai, Ukrainian, etc." The instructions that accompanied the questionnaire stated, for guidance in completing item 13, "Ancestry refers to the person's ethnic origin or descent, 'roots,' or heritage. Ancestry also may refer to the country of birth of the person or the person's parents or ancestors before their arrival in the United States." Item 13 appeared only on the long-form census questionnaire, which was sent to a sample (about 17%) of U.S. households. In contrast, the short-form questionnaire was designed to gather data on "race" (item 4) and (continued...)

The addition of an "other" category would provide flexibility, but, as previously noted, "other" has proved offensive to some minority group members.

Allowing respondents to select all the current categories that apply to them would not add any categories to forms. However, preserving even limited historical continuity of the data would require complex allocations of persons.

The last option would avoid the concepts of race or ethnicity. Instead, respondents would select, from a list, their ancestors' geographic origins. While geography might be less ambiguous than race or ethnicity, this option has several drawbacks: respondents might not know their ancestors' origins; a given individual might list multiple origins, increasing the likelihood of his or her inconsistent identification on different forms; and many persons of U.S. birth might choose "North American" (a choice that would be correct only for American Indians and Alaskan Natives).

Hispanic

Some public comments to OMB recommended the collection of data for Hispanic subgroups (Mexicans, Puerto Ricans, Cubans, and other Hispanics), as is done already in, for example, the decennial census. An advantage of this option is that it would describe a diverse population more thoroughly; a disadvantage is that it would make visual identification harder.

Other comments revealed considerable confusion about whether the term "Hispanic" encompasses Spaniards, Portuguese, Brazilians, and certain American Indians who trace their lineage partly to Latin American Indian tribes. Some persons suggested replacing "Hispanic" with "Latino" or "Latin." To other persons, however, "Latino" or "Latin" includes Italians, French, and Romanians, as well as Spaniards and Portuguese. Americans of Mexican origin or descent registered disagreement about their preferred designation; some of them, for example, wished to be called "Chicanos," but others considered this term demeaning.

The public comments also showed a lack of consensus about whether to list Hispanics in a combined race and ethnicity classification or to separate race from Hispanic ethnicity.

---

[15](...continued)
"Spanish/Hispanic origin" (item 7) from all households.

While every decennial census from 1790 onward has collected information about "race" or "color," the 1980 census was the first to ask for self-identification of ancestry. The ancestry item replaced questions from the 1970 and earlier censuses about the respondent's and his or her parents' countries of birth. Answers to these questions were used to derive numbers of first- and second-generation Americans. (U.S. Dept. of Commerce. Bureau of the Census. *1990 Census of Population and Housing. Guide. Part A. Text.* 1990 CPH-R-1A. Washington, U.S. Govt. Print. Off., 1992. p. 11, 13.)

PUBLIC COMMENTS VS. CPS SUPPLEMENT RESULTS

The public comments to OMB came from a self-selected, nonscientific sample of the U.S. population. In contrast, the respondents to a May 1995 Current Population Survey (CPS) supplement that was designed to test possible changes in Directive 15 were scientifically chosen to be representative of the U.S. civilian noninstitutionalized population. The CPS supplement, commissioned by the Bureau of Labor Statistics (BLS) at the request of the Interagency Committee, examined the effects of separating race from ethnicity in Directive 15 and of adding a "multiracial" category.[16] The major survey findings are summarized below.

- Respondents were more likely to identify themselves as "Hispanic" when this choice was presented separately from race than when it was included as a racial category. Yet more than 60% of Hispanic respondents expressed preference for making "Hispanic" a racial category.

- Just over 1.5% of respondents identified themselves as "multiracial."

- Neither the availability of the "multiracial" option nor the inclusion of "Hispanic" as a racial category affected the percentages of respondents who reported themselves to be "black" or "Asian or Pacific Islander."

- However, the "multiracial" option did lower the percentage of persons in the "American Indian, Eskimo, or Aleut" category (which can be aggregated to "American Indian or Alaskan Native"). This finding suggests that the category may not provide a reliable way to classify the persons it is intended to classify.

- Respondents were asked how they wanted to be designated. More than half of Hispanics (57.9%) expressed preference for "Hispanic," while another 11.7% favored "Latino," and about the same fraction

---

[16] U.S. Dept. of Labor. Bureau of Labor Statistics. *A CPS Supplement for Testing Methods of Collecting Racial and Ethnic Information: May 1995*. Press Release, USDL 95-428, Oct. 1995.

The Current Population Survey (CPS), conducted monthly by the Census Bureau for the Bureau of Labor Statistics, collects household labor force data. In May 1995, the sample consisted of approximately 60,000 households, but currently is about 49,000.

A CPS supplement is a set of questions asked after the regular survey. For the May 1995 CPS supplement, the households were split into four panels (groups) of about 15,000 each.

> chose "of Spanish origin." Whites overwhelmingly (61.7%) favored "white"; about 16.5% preferred "Caucasian"; only 2.4% chose "European American." The three terms most preferred by blacks were "black" (44.2%), "African American" (28.1%), and "Afro-American" (12.1%). Half of American Indians selected "American Indian," but more than a third (37.4%) favored "Native American." Of multiracial persons, 28.4% preferred "multiracial." Almost the same proportion reported "no preference," and 16% favored "mixed race."

A difference between the public comments and the findings from the CPS supplement is that the comments indicated greater support for revised standards. Two factors may have contributed to this divergence. First, members of the public (especially, but not only, those affiliated with racial and ethnic advocacy groups) who took the initiative to answer OMB's requests for comments might have been less satisfied with the classificatory status quo than was the population at random. Some persons who wrote or gave testimony to OMB might have been expressing—by means far less structured than a survey—their deep concerns about the existing racial and ethnic categories. Second, an undetermined number of survey respondents simply might have been endorsing the categories most familiar to them from nearly 20 years' use. When the respondents were asked what they wanted to be called, majorities of whites, American Indians, and Hispanics, and a plurality of blacks, chose their current designations; and about as many multiracial persons said they had no preferred designation as expressed preference for "multiracial."

FURTHER RESEARCH ON DIRECTIVE 15

The Interagency Committee's Research Working Group, which is co-chaired by the Census Bureau and BLS, reviewed the responses to OMB's June 9, 1994 *Federal Register* notice and pointed out several possible changes in the standards that need further study.[17] These areas include: classifying multiracial persons; combining race and Hispanic ethnicity; combining the concepts of race, ethnicity, and ancestry; renaming the current categories; and adding categories. The May 1995 CPS supplement, discussed above, constituted part of the recommended research. In addition, the Census Bureau's preparations for the 2000 census include two major research projects on some alternatives for collecting racial and ethnic data. The National Content Test was conducted in March 1996. The Race and Ethnic Targeted Test is scheduled for June 1996.[18] When the test results become available, they should contribute to the evaluation of certain options being considered to revise Directive 15.

---

[17] OMB, Interim Notice of Review of Race and Ethnic Standards, p. 44690.

[18] Ibid., p. 44690-44691.

APPENDIX 1. A CHRONOLOGY OF DIRECTIVE 15

May 12, 1977 After consulting with federal agencies and testing a draft set of racial and ethnic categories, the Office of Management and Budget (OMB) circulated for use by all federal agencies the categories now included in Directive 15.[1]

May 4, 1978 OMB issued Directive 15, which contains the same categories as those adopted in 1977. The directive presents the standards for collecting and reporting racial and ethnic data for statistical purposes, as well as for civil rights enforcement and regulatory programs.[2]

Jan. 20, 1988 OMB published a *Federal Register* notice soliciting public comments on a proposed revision of Directive 15 that would have added an "other" racial category and required self-identification of race and ethnicity.[3] The responses showed support for this proposal from certain multiracial and multiethnic groups, but opposition from some large corporations and federal entities (such as the Civil Rights Division of the Department of Justice, the Department of Health and Human Services, the Equal Employment Opportunity Commission, and the Office of Personnel Management). Opponents cited among their arguments cost and loss of historical comparability of racial and ethnic data. Further, some members of minority groups objected to "other" as a demeaning term. These individuals also expressed concern that the proposal might create dissention within their groups and produce lower official counts of minorities. The standards thus were left unchanged.

Apr. 14, June 30, July 29, and Nov. 3, 1993
The (former) House Subcommittee on Census, Statistics, and Postal Personnel held hearings on how the federal government measures race and ethnicity, particularly in the decennial census.[4] The subcommittee heard testimony principally from racial and ethnic advocacy groups and federal agencies, as well as from Congress and universities.

---

[1] Wallman, Katherine K. and John Hodgdon. Race and Ethnic Standards for Federal Statistics and Administrative Reporting. *Statistical Reporter*, no. 77-10, July 1977. p. 450-454.

[2] Office of Management and Budget. Directive No. 15. Race and Ethnic Standards for Federal Statistics and Administrative Reporting. *Federal Register*, v. 43, May 4, 1978. p. 19269-19270.

[3] Office of Management and Budget. Guidelines for Federal Statistical Activities. *Federal Register*, v. 53, Jan. 20, 1988. p. 1552.

[4] U.S. Congress. House. Committee on Post Office and Civil Service. Subcommittee on Census, Statistics, and Postal Personnel. *Review of Federal Measurements of Race and Ethnicity*. Hearing, 103rd Cong., 1st Sess., April 14, June 30, July 29, and Nov. 3, 1993. Washington, U.S. Govt. Print. Off., 1994.

Feb. 17 and 18, 1994

At the request of OMB, the National Academy of Sciences' Committee on National Statistics sponsored a workshop for discussion of the issues involved in a review of Directive 15.[5] The workshop participants came largely from federal agencies, but also from Congress, universities, research organizations, racial and ethnic advocacy groups, the private sector, and one county public school system.

June 9, 1994 OMB published a *Federal Register* notice of its proposed review and possible revision of Directive 15.[6] The notice solicited public comments and announced the formation of the Interagency Committee for the Review of the Racial and Ethnic Standards. OMB received almost 800 letters in response to the June 9 notice and heard testimony from 94 witnesses at hearings in Boston, Denver, San Francisco, and Honolulu.

Aug. 28, 1995 OMB published a *Federal Register* notice discussing the issues raised by the public, by federal agencies, and by research on Directive 15.[7] The notice set an agenda for further research and invited public comments on the principles that may guide OMB's final decision about the standards for classifying race and ethnicity.

Oct. 26, 1995 The Bureau of Labor Statistics (BLS) released the results of a May 1995 Current Population Survey (CPS) supplement, commissioned by BLS at the request of the Interagency Committee for the Review of the Racial and Ethnic Standards, to examine the effects of separating race from ethnicity in Directive 15 and of adding a "multiracial" category.[8]

---

[5] National Academy of Sciences. Committee on National Statistics. *Spotlight on Heterogeneity: The Federal Standards for Racial and Ethnic Classification. Summary of a Workshop.* Washington, National Academy Press, 1996.

[6] Office of Management and Budget. Advance Notice of Proposed Review and Possible Revision of OMB's Statistical Policy Directive No. 15, Race and Ethnic Standards for Federal Statistics and Administrative Reporting; and Announcement of Public Hearings on Directive No. 15. *Federal Register*, v. 59, June 9, 1994. p. 29831-29835.

[7] Office of Management and Budget. Interim Notice of Review and Possible Revision of OMB's Statistical Policy Directive No. 15, Race and Ethnic Standards for Federal Statistics and Administrative Reporting: Summary and Analysis of Public Comments and Brief Discussion of Research Agenda. *Federal Register*, v. 60, Aug. 28, 1995. p. 44674-44693.

[8] U.S. Dept. of Labor. Bureau of Labor Statistics. *A CPS Supplement for Testing Methods of Collecting Racial and Ethnic Information: May 1995.* Press Release, USDL 95-428, Oct. 1995.

CHAPTER 14

The Age Discrimination in Employment Act (ADEA): Overview and Current Legal Developments

Kimberly D. Jones

BACKGROUND

The Age Discrimination in Employment Act (ADEA)[1] of 1967, as amended, seeks to address the longstanding problem of age discrimination in the workplace.[2] The ADEA, which prevents employment discrimination against persons over the age of 40, was enacted "to promote employment of older persons based on their ability rather than age; to prohibit arbitrary age discrimination in employment; [and] to help employers and workers find ways of meeting problems arising from the impact of age on employment."[3] The ADEA makes it unlawful for an employer "to fail or refuse to hire or to discharge any individual or otherwise discriminate against any individual with respect to his compensation, terms, conditions, or privileges of employment, because of such individual's age."[4] It applies, not only in hiring, discharge and promotion, but also prohibits discrimination in employee benefit plans such as health coverage and pensions. In addition to employers, the ADEA also applies to labor organizations and employment agencies.

Age discrimination in employment is a growing issue as the average American can expect to live until almost 80 years of age.[5] By 2004, the entire

---

1 29 U.S.C.A. §§ 621-634 (West 1985 & Supp. 1996).

2 Employees seeking a remedy for age discrimination in employment also have the option of a constitutional claim. The Equal Protection Clause states in part, "[n]o state shall . . . deny to any person within its jurisdiction the equal protection of the laws." U.S. Const. amend. XIV, § 1. Before an equal protection argument could be made, the plaintiffs would have to show state action. In *Gregory v. Ashcroft*, 501 U.S. 452 (1991), the U.S. Supreme Court considered a Fourteenth Amendment Equal Protection Clause challenge to a state mandatory retirement law. In *Ashcroft*, the plaintiffs were Missouri state judges required to retire at the age of 70 by state law. The Court reviewed the judges' claim under the rational basis test, noting that "age is not a suspect classification under the Equal Protection Clause" and the plaintiffs did not "have a fundamental interest in serving as judges." *Ashcroft*, 501 U.S. at 470. Ultimately, the Court held that the voters of Missouri had a legitimate and rational basis for requiring retirement of their state judges to ensure the competency and efficacy of their judiciary.

3 29 U.S.C.A. § 621. 4 29 U.S.C.A. § 623.

5 Steven D. Kaye, Mary Lord, Pamela Sherrid, *Stop Working? Not boomers: The Me Generation May Not Know It Yet, But Many Will Need a Paycheck into their 70s*, U.S. News & World Report, June 12, 1995.

baby boomer generation, or those born between 1946 and 1964, will be covered by the ADEA.[6] Currently, baby boomers make up 45 percent, or 60 million of 134 million workers in the American labor force.[7] Approximately, 17,000 age discrimination complaints were filed annually between 1991 and 1995.[8]

The issue of age discrimination has concerned Congress for several years. Prior to the ADEA, section 715 of the Civil Rights Act of 1964, required the Secretary of Labor to study the issue of age discrimination in employment.[9] The resulting report surmised that a clear-cut federal policy was needed to address age discrimination. President Lyndon B. Johnson suggested the Age Discrimination in Employment Act in his Older Americans message delivered in early 1967.

After passage, the ADEA went through a series of amendments to strengthen and expand its coverage of older employees. Originally, the ADEA only covered employees between the ages of 40 and 65. Eventually the upper age limit was extended to age 70, and then eliminated altogether. In 1978, as part of the Reorganization Plan No. 1, enforcement authority of the ADEA was transferred from the Department of Labor to the Equal Employment Opportunity Commission (EEOC).[10]

CURRENT ADEA PROVISIONS

The ADEA prevents employers,[11] employment agencies[12] and labor organizations[13] from discriminating because of age in the hiring, termination, placement, representation or any other manner against employees 40 years of age and older. It also prevents retaliation against employees for filing or participating in an ADEA claim.[14]

---

[6] Kirstin Downey Grimsley, *Next for Boomers: Battles Against Age Bias?*, Wash. Post. Feb. 9, 1997, at H1.

[7] *Id.*

[8] *Id.*

[9] Pub. L. No. 88-352, 78 Stat. 241, 265 (1964).

[10] Reorg. Plan No. 1 of 1978, 92 Stat. 3781 (1978). *See also* 29 U.S.C.A. § 626(a).

[11] 29 U.S.C.A. § 623(a).

[12] 29 U.S.C.A. § 623(b).

[13] 29 U.S.C.A. § 623(c).

[14] 29 U.S.C.A. § 623(d). The U.S. Supreme Court, in *Robinson v. Shell Oil Co.*, 519 U.S. ___, 117 S. Ct. 843 (1997), extended the protection from retaliation provided to employees who file or participate in discrimination suits. The lower court had held that (continued...)

The ADEA also prohibits age-biased advertisements.[15] According to the EEOC's regulations, want ads that contain phrases such as, "age 25 to 35," "young", "college student", "recent college graduate","boy", "girl," or similar terms are prohibited under the Act, unless an exception applies.[16] Even phrases that favor some members of the class, but discriminate against others is prohibited, *e.g.*, "age 40 to 50", "age over 65", "retired person", or "supplement your pension."[17] On the other hand, the request for the age or date of birth of an applicant on an employment application or use of the phrase "state age" on a want ad is not necessarily a violation of the Act.[18] It is not per se a violation because there may be legitimate reasons for requesting the age or date of birth of an applicant. But the EEOC will "closely [scrutinize the application] to assure that the request is for a permissible purpose and not for purposes proscribed by the Act."[19]

WHO IS COVERED UNDER THE ADEA

The ADEA covers employees[20] forty years and older.[21] However, the ADEA does not prohibit the compulsory retirement of a bona fide executive or high policymaker who has reached age 65 and is entitled to a nonforfeitable

---

[14](...continued)
such protection applied only to current employees, not past employees. The Court refused to so limit the interpretation of "employee," concluding that "employee" as defined in Title VII also applies to former employees. Since the ADEA is closely modeled after Title VII of the Civil Rights Act, it will apply to those former employees who filed ADEA claims.

[15] 29 U.S.C.A. § 623(e).

[16] 29 C.F.R. § 1625.4 (1996).

[17] 29 C.F.R. § 1625.4(a).

[18] 29 C.F.R. § 1625.4(b), 1625.5.

[19] 29 C.F.R. § 1625.5.

[20] According to 29 U.S.C.A. § 630(f), an "employee" is defined as "an individual employed by any employer . . ." Excluded from the definition of employee are state elected officials or an appointee of such person. However, state employees covered by civil service laws, are considered employees, as well as American citizens working for American employers abroad. Section 633a of the ADEA extends its application to Federal Government employees. The Congressional Accountability Act of 1995, 2 U.S.C.A. § 1301-1438 (West 1985 & Supp. 1997), extended the rights and protections of the ADEA to Congressional employees. In *Gregory v. Ashcroft*, 501 U.S. 452 (1991), the Court upheld a Missouri statute that required mandatory retirement of judges at age 70. The majority found, after an analysis of the definition of an employee and its exclusions, that state judges fall within the exception to the ADEA regarding "appointee on the policymaking level." *Id.* at 467.

[21] 29 U.S.C.A. § 631(a).

annual retirement benefit of at least $44,000.[22] The Age Discrimination in Employment Amendments of 1996 reinstated the exemption for certain bona fide hiring and retirement plans applicable to state and local firefighters and law enforcement officers.[23] The ADEA Amendments of 1996 also require the Secretary of Health and Human Services to develop tests to gauge the ability of firefighters and law enforcement officials to accomplish their jobs.[24]

An employer under the ADEA is a "person engaged in an industry affecting commerce who has twenty or more employees for each working day in each of twenty or more calendar weeks in the current or preceding calendar year."[25] It is unlawful for an employer "to fail or refuse to hire or to discharge any individual or otherwise discriminate against any individual with respect to his compensation, terms, conditions, or privileges of employment, because of such individual's age."[26] The term "employer" includes agents, states, their political subdivisions and accompanying agents, but excludes the United States or any corporation wholly owned by the United States Government.[27] However, the ADEA does cover employees in certain military departments, executive agencies, the United States Postal Service, the Postal Rate Commission, certain District of Columbia employees, Federal Government legislative and judicial employees in competitive service and employees in the Library of Congress. Congressional

---

[22] 29 U.S.C.A. § 631(c)(1).

[23] Omnibus Consolidated Appropriations Act of 1997, Pub. L. No. 104-208, 110 Stat. 3009 (1996). The ADEA Amendments of 1996 state that an employer is not in violation of the Act "if the individual was discharged after the date described in such section, and the individual has attained

(A) the age of hiring or retirement, respectively, in effect under applicable State or local law on March 3, 1993; or

(B)(i) if the individual was not hired, the age of hiring in effect on the date of such failure or refusal to hire under applicable State or local law enacted after the date of enactment of the Age Discrimination in Employment Amendments of 1996; or

(ii) if applicable State or local law was enacted after the date of enactment of the Age Discrimination in Employment Amendments of 1996 and the individual was discharged, the higher of

(I) the age of retirement in effect on the date of such discharge under such law; and

(II) age 55;"

[24] *Id.*

[25] 29 U.S.C.A. § 630(b). An "industry affecting commerce" is defined as "any activity, business, or industry in commerce or in which a labor dispute would hinder or obstruct commerce or the free flow of commerce and includes any activity or industry 'affecting commerce' within the meaning of the Labor-Management Reporting and Disclosure Act of 1959."

[26] 29 U.S.C.A. § 623. [27] 29 U.S.C.A. § 630.

employees of the House and Senate are covered by the ADEA pursuant to the Congressional Accountability Act of 1995.[28]

A labor organization is covered by the ADEA if it is "engaged in an industry affecting commerce, and any agent of such an organization, and includes any organization of any kind, any agency, or employee representation committee, group, association, or plan . . . dealing with employers concerning grievances, labor disputes, wages, rates of pay, hours, or other terms or conditions of employment."[29] The ADEA defines a labor organization engaged in an industry affecting commerce as one that has a hiring hall or is a certified employee representative, or if not certified, holds itself out as the employee's bargaining representative.[30]

An employment agency and its agent are subject to the ADEA if they "regularly undertake with or without compensation" the procurement of employees for an employer, other than an agency of the United States.[31]

FILING AN ADEA CLAIM

The Equal Employment Opportunity Commission (EEOC) is responsible for enforcing the provisions of the ADEA.[32] The Act requires the EEOC, after receiving a charge of unlawful discrimination, to seek compliance with the Act through methods such as conciliation, conference, or persuasion before instituting legal proceedings.[33] A claimant under the ADEA may bring a civil action in state or federal court and seek a jury trial, unless the EEOC brings suit on behalf of the aggrieved, in which case his right to bring suit yields to the EEOC.[34]

---

[28] Certain federal employees are covered under Section 633a and Congressional employees are covered under the Congressional Accountability Act of 1995. 2 U.S.C.A. §1301.

[29] 29 U.S.C.A. § 630(d).

[30] 29 U.S.C.A. § 630(e).

[31] 29 U.S.C.A. § 630.

[32] 29 U.S.C.A. § 626(a). The Department of Labor was originally responsible for enforcement of the ADEA. The authority was transferred to the EEOC in 1978 pursuant to Reorg. Plan No. 1 of 1978, 92 Stat. 3781 (1978).

[33] 29 U.S.C.A. § 626(b).

[34] *Lehman v. Nakshian*, 453 U.S. 156 (1981). The Court held that ADEA did not grant the right to a jury trial to an employee suing the Federal Government.

No civil action may be filed until 60 days after "a charge alleging unlawful discrimination has been filed with the [EEOC]."[35] The timeline for filing an ADEA charge varies depending on where the alleged violation occurred. Generally, a grievant must file a complaint with the EEOC within 180 days of the alleged discriminatory act. However, if the state where the alleged unlawful practice took place has an age discrimination law and a corresponding enforcement agency, then the time by which a grievant must file with the EEOC is extended to within 300 days of the alleged unlawful practice.[36] A charge must be filed with the EEOC within 30 days upon notification that the state agency has terminated its proceedings.[37] The sixty-day deferral period for filing a civil suit also applies to charges filed with a state agency, unless the state agency proceedings are earlier terminated. Due to the 60 day deferral period, a complainant must file with the corresponding state or local agency within 240 days of the alleged discriminatory act to ensure that the charge will be filed with the EEOC within the 300-day limit.[38]

In non-deferral states, or states without a corresponding enforcement agency, the grievant must file a claim with the EEOC within 180 days of the alleged unlawful practice. No civil action may be filed until 60 days after filing a charge with the EEOC.[39] However, if the EEOC terminates or dismisses the charge, even within the 60 day period, then the grievant may file a civil action within 90 days of receipt of termination.

When bringing a civil case, there are two types of discrimination claims, disparate treatment and disparate impact. Disparate treatment occurs when an employer intentionally discriminates against an employee or enacts a policy with the intent to treat or affect the employee differently from others because of the

---

35 29 U.S.C.A. § 626(d).

36 29 U.S.C.A. § 626(d).

37 29 U.S.C.A. § 633(b). The U.S. Supreme Court, in *Oscar Mayer & Co. v. Evans*, 441 U.S. 750 (1979), held that the ADEA requirement of pursuing a remedy under state law is mandatory, not optional. However, the Court also held that this provision is satisfied by filing with the applicable state agency and that exhaustion of state remedies is not needed before filing a complaint with the EEOC.

38 *Mohasco Corp. v. Silver*, 447 U.S. 807 (1980). A complaint filed with a state or local agency after 240 days may still be timely if the state or local agency terminates its proceedings before 300 days.

39 29 U.S.C.A. § 626(d). The statute of limitations for civil actions is two years from the date the cause of action accrued, or, in the case of willful violations, three years from the date the cause accrued. 29 U.S.C.A. § 255 (West 1985 & Supp. 1996). However, the statute of limitations is tolled when the EEOC is seeking to resolve claims through conciliation and conference. However, the statute of limitations will not be tolled beyond one year. 29 U.S.C.A. § 626(e)(2).

employee's age.[40] Disparate impact occurs when the employer's acts or policies are facially neutral, but have an adverse impact on a class of employees and are not justified as job related and consistent with business necessity. According to the Court in *Hazen Paper Co. v Biggins*, the ADEA explicitly allows disparate treatment claims, but the Court has yet to decide whether an employee may recover under the disparate impact theory.[41] This has resulted in confusion for litigants, and courts alike, as some federal courts of appeals allow disparate impact claims, while others do not.[42]

Since the ADEA was modeled after Title VII, courts look to Title VII decisions for guidance on adjudicating ADEA claims. However, the unique protections of the ADEA have not always fit neatly into the Title VII framework. In cases where the plaintiff is alleging disparate treatment and there is no direct evidence of discrimination, courts refer to the Title VII burden of proof framework established by the U.S. Supreme Court in *McDonnell Douglas v. Green*,[43] and *Texas Dept. of Community Affairs v. Burdine*.[44] The burden

---

40 In proving disparate treatment based on age the plaintiff can show that age was a motivating factor in the employer's decision. The plaintiff does not have to show that it was the only factor. *Kralman v. Illinois Dept. of Veteran's Affairs*, 23 F.3d 150 (7th Cir. 1994), *cert. denied*, 115 S. Ct. 359, 130 L.Ed.2d 313 (1994).

41 507 U.S. 604 (1993). The majority states: "[t]he disparate treatment theory is of course available under the ADEA, as the language of that statute makes clear. . . . By contrast, we have never decided whether a disparate impact theory of liability is available under the ADEA." *Id.* at 609-610. The facts of *Biggins* reflect a growing concern among older workers who are close to the vesting of their pensions. The plaintiff, Walter Biggins, was fired weeks before he was scheduled to vest under his employer's pension plan. The plan allowed vesting after ten years of service. Although the Court held that firing an employee to prevent vesting is actionable under the Employees Retirement Income Security Act (ERISA), 29 U.S.C.A. § 1001 *et seq.* (West 1985 & Supp. 1996), such firing "would not constitute discriminatory treatment on the basis of age." *Id.* at 612. However, the Court did not dismiss the possibility of pension status being used as a proxy for age. The Court was not faced with a situation where vesting was based on age rather than length of service. If vesting were based on an employee's age, then firing an employee to avoid vesting could possibly result in liability under both the ADEA and ERISA. *Id.* at 613.

42 The Courts of Appeals for the Eighth Circuit and the D.C. Circuit have allowed disparate impact claims. *Smith v. City of Des Moines, Iowa*, 99 F.3d 1466 (8th Cir. 1996); *Koger v. Reno*, 98 F.3d 631 (D.C. Cir. 1996). However, the Third, Seventh and Tenth Circuit Courts of Appeals have not. *DiBiase v. Smith Kline Beecham Corp.*, 48 F.3d 719 (3d Cir. 1995), *cert. denied*, 116 S. Ct. 306 (1995); *Gehring v. Case Corp.*, 43 F.3d 340 (7th Cir. 1994), *cert. denied*, *Gehring v. J.I. Case Corp.*, 115 S. Ct. 2612 (1995); *Furr v. Seagate Tech.*, 82 F.3d 980 (10th Cir. 1996), *cert. denied*, *Doan v. Seagate Tech.*, 117 S. Ct. 684 (1997). *See also* Frances A. McMorris, *Age-Bias Suits May Become Harder to Prove*, Wall St.J., Feb. 20, 1997, at B1.

43 411 U.S. 792 (1973).

44 450 U.S. 248 (1981).

of proof requires the plaintiff to establish a prima facie case. Once the plaintiff, by a preponderance of the evidence, proves a prima facie case then the burden of production shifts to the employer, "to articulate some legitimate, nondiscriminatory reason for the employee's rejection."[45] If the employer rebuts the employee's prima facie case, the employee may still prevail if he can show that the employer's defense is merely a pretext and that the employer's behavior was actually motivated by discrimination.[46] While the burden of production shifts to the employer to rebut the employee's prima facie case, the burden of persuasion remains on the plaintiff at all times.[47]

The confusion occurs when defining what constitutes a prima facie case under the ADEA. According to *McDonnell Douglas* (a Title VII case), a prima facie case is made when the plaintiff shows: "(1) that he belongs to a racial minority;
(2) that he applied and was qualified for a job for which the employer was seeking applicants; (3) that, despite his qualifications, he was rejected; and
(4) that, after his rejection, the position remained open and the employer continued to seek applicants from persons of complainant's qualifications."[48]

The Supreme Court has attempted to clarify the prima facie case applicable to the ADEA in its decisions in *Trans World Airlines, Inc. v. Thurston*,[49] and *O'Connor v. Consolidated Coin Caterers Corp.*[50] In *Thurston*, the Court held that the prima facie elements of *McDonnell Douglas* are inapplicable where the plaintiff produces evidence of direct discrimination.[51] In *Thurston*, the Court

45 *McDonnell Douglas*, 411 U.S. at 802.

46 *St. Mary's Honor Center v. Hicks*, 509 U.S. 502 (1993). In *Hicks*, the Supreme Court revisited the burden of proof scheme established by *McDonnell Douglas* and *Burdine*. Justice Scalia, writing for the majority, held that it is not enough for the plaintiff to show that the employer's proffered reason was false. The plaintiff must show that the employer's proffered reason is both false and that the employer's actions were motivated by discrimination.

47 *Burdine*, 450 U.S. at 255-256.

48 *McDonnell Douglas*, 411 U.S. at 802.

49 469 U.S. 400 (1985).

50 116 S. Ct. 1307 (1996).

51 The Court agreed with the court of appeals stating:

TWA contends that the respondents failed to make out a prima facie case of age discrimination under *McDonnell Douglas v. Green*, 411 U.S. 792 (1973), because at the time they were retired, no flight engineer vacancies existed. This argument fails, for the *McDonnell Douglas* test is inapplicable where the plaintiff presents direct evidence of discrimination. . . . The shifting burdens of proof set forth in *McDonnell*

(continued...)

upon finding direct evidence of discrimination, then considered the employer's defenses. While not explicitly stated in *Thurston*, it appears that even after evidence of direct discrimination, the burden of production shifts to the employer to articulate a legitimate reason for the discriminatory behavior. If the employer succeeds, the employee still has an opportunity to prove the employer's proffered reason is merely a pretext for discrimination. Again, the burden of persuasion remains at all times on the plaintiff.

In *Consolidated Coin*, the Court held that a prima facie case is not made out by simply showing that an employee was replaced by someone outside of the class. The plaintiff must show that he was replaced because of his age.[52] The Court evaluated whether the prima facie elements evinced by the Fourth Circuit Court of Appeals were required to establish a prima facie case. The Fourth Circuit held that a prima facie case is established under the ADEA when the plaintiff shows that: "(1) he was in the age group protected by the ADEA; (2) he was discharged or demoted; (3) at the time of his discharge or demotion, he was performing his job at a level that met his employer's legitimate expectations; and (4) following his discharge or demotion, he was replaced by someone of comparable qualifications outside of the protected class."[53] The Court held that the fourth prong, replacement by someone outside of the class, is not the only manner in which a plaintiff can show a prima facie case under the ADEA.[54] A violation can be shown even if the person was replaced by someone within the protected class. For example, replacing a 76 year old with a 45 year old may be a violation of the ADEA, if the person was replaced because of her age.

EMPLOYER DEFENSES TO THE ADEA

The ADEA provides several defenses for employers. The available defenses strike a balance between the ability of employers to conduct their business and the interest of the government in eliminating age discrimination in employment.

---

[51](...continued)
Douglas are designed to assure that the 'plaintiff [has] his day in court despite the unavailability of direct evidence'. *Id.* at 121 (quoting *Loeb v. Textron, Inc.*, 600 F.2d 1003 (1st Cir. 1979)).

[52] *O'Connor v. Consolidated Coin Caterers Corp.*, 116 S. Ct. 1307 (1996).

[53] 116 S. Ct. 1307, 1309 (1996).

[54] Justice Scalia, writing for the majority states:

As the very name 'prima facie case' suggests, there must be at least a logical connection between each element of the prima facie case and the illegal discrimination for which it establishes a 'legally mandatory' rebuttable presumption. . . . The element of replacement by someone under 40 fails this requirement. The discrimination prohibited by the ADEA is discrimination 'because of [an] individual's age.'" *Consolidated Coin*, 116 S. Ct. at 1310 (quoting *Texas Dept. of Community Affairs v. Burdine*, 450 U.S. 248, 254, n.7 (1981)).

The ADEA is not violated if the action taken against an employee is due to a "bona fide occupational qualification [BFOQ] reasonably necessary to the normal operation of the particular business."[55] According to the Court in *Thurston*, in order to be considered a valid BFOQ "the age-based discrimination must relate to a 'particular business.'"[56] The particular business referred to "is the job from which the protected individual is excluded."[57] In *Johnson v. Mayor of City Council of Baltimore*, the Court held that Baltimore's reliance on the Federal Government's mandatory retirement provision for Federal firefighters was not a BFOQ which Baltimore could rely on to require mandatory retirement of city firefighters under the age of 70.[58] The Court in *Western Air Lines, Inc., v. Criswell*, upheld a jury instruction given by the Fifth Circuit Court of Appeals regarding the BFOQ defense.[59]

> The court recognized that the ADEA requires that age qualifications be something more than 'convenient' or 'reasonable'; they must be 'reasonably necessary . . . to the particular business,' and this is only so when the employer is compelled to rely on age as a proxy for the safety-related job qualifications validated in the first inquiry. This showing could be made in two ways. The employer could establish that it 'had reasonable cause to believe, that is, factual basis for believing, that all or substantially all [persons over the age qualifications] would be unable to perform safely and efficiently the duties of the job involved.'
>
> Alternatively, the employer could establish that age was a legitimate proxy for the safety-related job qualifications by proving that it is 'impossible or highly impractical' to deal with the older employees on an individualized basis. 'One method by which the employer can carry this burden is to establish that some members of the discriminated-against class possess a trait precluding safe and efficient job performance that cannot be ascertained by means other than knowledge of the applicant's membership in the class.'[60]

The Older Americans Act Amendments provided an exemption to employers where compliance with the ADEA with regard to an employee based in a foreign

---

[55] 29 U.S.C.A. § 623(f)(1). According to the Supreme Court in *Western Air Lines Inc. v. Criswell*, 472 U.S. 400 (1984), the BFOQ must be more than "convenient" or "reasonable", but must be "'reasonably necessary . . . to the particular business.'". *Id.* at 414. The employer could prove a BFOQ defense of an age-based qualification due to safety concerns based on either of two ways. First the employer could show that it had factual basis for believing that persons over a certain age would be unable to perform the job safely. In the alternative, the employer could show that "age was a legitimate proxy for the safety-related job qualifications by proving that it is 'impossible or highly impractical' to deal with the older employees on an individualized basis." *Id.*

[56] *Thurston*, 469 U.S. at 122.

[57] *Id.*

[58] 472 U.S. 353 (1984).

[59] *Id.* at 414.

[60] *Id.* at 414-15.(quoting *Weeks v. Southern Bell Telephone & Telegraph Co.*, 408 F.2d 228 (5th Cir. 1969)).

country would violate the laws of that country.[61] The ADEA does not apply where the company is not controlled by an American employer.[62] The Act provides courts with a four prong analysis to determine whether a company is under an American employer's control. The determination is based on the interrelation of operations, common management, centralized control of labor relations and common ownership or financial control between the employer and the corporation.[63]

The ADEA is also not violated when the action taken is pursuant to a bona fide seniority system or employee benefit plan.[64] The seniority system may not require or permit mandatory retirement of employees because of age.[65] A bona fide employee benefit plan must satisfy the "equal cost equal benefit" principle which provides parity between the amount employers spend on benefits for older and younger workers.[66] If it costs more to provide the same benefit to the protected class, the employer has the option of paying the same amount for benefits of the protected class as it does for employees outside of the protected class. This is so, even if it results in workers in the protected class receiving fewer benefits. However, employers may not pay less for benefits of members of the protected class than they pay for younger employees.

Another exemption to the ADEA is if "the differentiation is based on reasonable factors other than age."[67] Of course, a defense to the ADEA is that the employee was discharged or disciplined for good cause, not age.[68]

---

[61] 29 U.S.C.A. § 623(f)(1).

[62] 29 U.S.C.A. § 623(h)(2).

[63] 29 U.S.C.A. § 623(h)(3)(A)-(D).

[64] 29 U.S.C.A. § 623(f)(2). Bona fide is defined as a system or plan that is not being used to evade the purposes of the Act.

[65] 29 U.S.C.A. § 623(f)(2)(A). The ADEA explicitly allows *voluntary* retirement as an incentive of early retirement plans. 20 U.S.C.A. § 623(f)(2)(B)(ii). The ADEA does exempt from its provisions bona fide executives, high policy-makers and state and local firefighters and law enforcement officers.

[66] 29 U.S.C.A. § 623(f)(2)(B).

[67] 29 U.S.C.A. § 623(f)(1).

[68] 29 U.S.C.A. § 623(f)(3). In *McKennon v. Nashville Banner Pub. Co.*, 513 U.S. 352 (1995), the Court considered whether after-acquired evidence of employee misconduct would bar an ADEA claim. The Court, held that after-acquired evidence, which if discovered would have led to the employee's discharge, does not bar an ADEA claim, but may reduce the amount of damages.

An employee may waive his rights under the ADEA, if such waiver was knowing and voluntary.[69] A knowing and voluntary waiver is defined in the act by a consideration of factors.[70] A waiver given in settlement of a charge filed with the EEOC or in a civil action is not considered knowing and voluntary unless the general requirements for a waiver are met and the individual has a reasonable opportunity to consider the settlement.[71] The person asserting validity of the waiver has the burden of proving that the waiver was knowing and voluntary. The waiver provision is inapplicable to the EEOC, and an employer may not interfere with an employee's participation with the EEOC in investigating or pursuing a claim of alleged unlawful practices.

A related issue is the effect of arbitration clauses on ADEA claims. The Court held in *Gilmer v. Interstate/Johnson Lane Corp.*,[72] that the ADEA does not preclude enforcement of a compulsory arbitration clause. The plaintiff in *Gilmer*, signed a registration application with the New York Stock Exchange

---

69 29 U.S.C.A. § 626(f).

70 29 U.S.C.A. § 626(f)(1). A waiver is knowing and voluntary if:
(A) the waiver is part of an agreement between the individual and the employer that is written in a manner calculated to be understood by such individual, or by the average individual eligible to participate;
(B) the waiver specifically refers to rights or claims arising under this chapter;
(C) the individual does not waive rights of claims that may arise after the date the waiver is executed;
(D) the individual waives rights or claims only in exchange for consideration in addition to anything of value to which the individual already is entitled;
(E) the individual is advised in writing to consult with an attorney prior to executing the agreement;
(F)(i) the individual is given a period of at least 21 days within which to consider the agreement; or
(ii) if a waiver is requested in connection with an exit incentive or other employment termination program offered to a group or class of employees, the individual is given a period of at least 45 days within which to consider the agreement;
(G) the agreement provides that for a period of at least 7 days following the execution of such agreement, the individual may revoke the agreement, and the agreement shall not become effective or enforceable until the revocation period has expired;
(H) if a waiver is requested in connection with an exit incentive or other employment termination program offered to a group or class of employees, the employer (at the commencement of the period specified in subparagraph (F)) informs the individual in writing in a manner calculated to be understood by the average individual eligible to participate, as to--
(i) any class, unit, or group of individuals covered by such programs, any eligibility factors for such program, and any time limits applicable to such program; and
(ii) the job titles and ages of all individuals eligible or selected for the program, and the ages of all individuals in the same job classification or organizational unit who are not eligible or selected for the program.

71 29 U.S.C.A. § 626(f)(2).

72 500 U.S. 20 (1990).

(NYSE), as required by his employer. The application provided that the plaintiff would agree to arbitrate any claim or dispute that arose between him and Interstate. Gilmer filed an ADEA claim with the EEOC upon being fired at age 62. Interstate filed a motion to compel arbitration based on the application and the Federal Arbitration Act (FAA),[73] which was enacted to change the "longstanding judicial hostility to arbitration . . . ."[74]

The Court of Appeals held that nothing in the language of the ADEA or its legislative history prohibited arbitration of ADEA claims.[75] The U.S. Supreme Court agreed. Since the FAA represents a federal policy favoring arbitration, it is the burden of the person agreeing to arbitrate to show that Congress evinced an intent to prevent arbitration.[76] Initially, the Court did not find that the goal of the ADEA was hindered by allowing arbitration of ADEA claims.[77] In a prior decision the Court held "by agreeing to arbitrate a statutory claim, a party does not forgo the substantive rights afforded by the statute; it only submits to their resolution in an arbitral, rather than a judicial, forum."[78] Nor would compulsory arbitration interfere with the duty of the EEOC to enforce the provision.[79] The Act's emphasis on informal methods of dispute resolution, such as conciliation and persuasion, weighed in favor of arbitration, instead of against it.[80] In addition, the Court found the arbitration procedures of the NYSE were more than adequate to safeguard the employee's rights under the ADEA. NYSE's arbitration procedures addressed concerns of bias,[81] discovery procedures,[82] the type of relief granted,[83] and unequal bargaining power.[84]

---

73 9 U.S.C.A. § 1 *et seq.* (West 1970 & Supp. 1997).

74 According to Justice White, writing for the majority, the FAA was enacted to "reverse the longstanding judicial hostility to arbitration agreements that had existed at English common law and had been adopted by American courts." *Id.* at 24.

75 *Id.* at 24.

76 *Id.* at 26.

77 *Id.* at 26-28.

78 *Mitsubishi Motors Corp. v. Soler Chrysler-Plymouth, Inc.*, 473 U.S. 614, 628 (1987).

79 *Id.* at 28-29.

80 *Id.* at 29.

81 *Id.* at 30.

82 *Id.* at 31.

83 *Id.* at 32.

84 *Id.* at 32-33.

Justice White, writing for the majority, found that Gilmer's reliance on the Court's decision in *Alexander v. Gardner-Denver Co.*,[85] was misplaced. *Gardner-Denver* held that a plaintiff's civil action under Title VII is not precluded by an arbitration decision handed down pursuant to a collective-bargaining agreement.[86] The cases were found to be distinguishable since *Gardner-Denver* did not deal with enforceability of an agreement to arbitrate statutory claims; occurred under a collective bargaining agreement to resolve contractual rights; and was not covered by the Federal Arbitration Act.[87] Ultimately, the Court found that Gilmer failed to meet his burden of showing an intent by Congress to preclude arbitration of ADEA claims.

REMEDIES

The remedies available under the ADEA are adapted from the Fair Labor Standards Act.[88] The prevailing plaintiff may be entitled to "employment, reinstatement, promotion, and the payment of wages lost and an additional amount as liquidated damages."[89] The wages received are considered unpaid minimum wages or unpaid overtime compensation.[90] A wilful violation of the Act gives rise to liquidated damages. According to the Court in *Trans World Air Lines v. Thurston*, "a violation of the Act [would be] 'willful' if the employer knew or showed reckless disregard for the matter of whether its conduct was prohibited by the ADEA."[91] The plaintiff, upon proving his claim of age discrimination, is entitled to reasonable attorney's fees and costs.[92]

---

[85] 415 U.S. 36 (1974).

[86] *Gardner-Denver*, 415 U.S. at 59-60.

[87] *Gilmer*, 500 U.S. at 35.

[88] Section 626(b) states: "The provisions of this chapter shall be enforced in accordance with the powers, remedies, and procedures provided in sections 211(b), 216 (except for subsection (a) thereof), and 217 of this title, and subsection (c) of this section."

[89] 29 U.S.C.A. § 216(b).

[90] 29 U.S.C.A. § 626(b).

[91] 469 U.S. 111, 126 (1985).

[92] 29 U.S.C.A. § 216(b).

APPENDIX

AMENDMENTS TO THE ADEA

1974 AMENDMENT

Prior to 1974 an "employer" was covered if he had twenty-five or more employees.[93] The 1974 amendments reduced the number of required employees from twenty-five to twenty, thereby expanding the coverage of the ADEA. The Act was also amended to apply to Federal, state and local government employees, but excluded state elected officials and their personal staff and appointees.[94] Funding for the Act was increased from three million to five million dollars.

1978 AMENDMENT

In 1978, Congress extended coverage of the ADEA by increasing the upper-age limit of the protected class of non-federal employees from 65 to 70 years of age, and eliminating the upper age limit for federal employees. Congress also commissioned the Secretary of Labor to conduct a study of the effect of the increase of the upper age limit with an eye toward eliminating the upper age limit for non-federal employees.

In regard to involuntary retirement, the 1978 Amendments prohibited use of a bona fide seniority system or employee benefit plan to require involuntary retirement due to age.[95] This amendment clarified the ADEA's application to employee benefit plans that pre-dated the ADEA.[96] However high ranking executives, policy makers and employees under an unlimited tenure contract at

---

[93] Fair Labor Standards Amendments of 1974, Pub. L. No. 93-259, §28, 88 Stat. 55, 78 (1974).

[94] The Supreme Court in *EEOC v. Wyoming*, 460 U.S. 226 (1983), declared constitutional the extension of the ADEA to state and local government employees as a valid use of Congress' authority under the Commerce Clause.

[95] This change to the ADEA was in response to the Supreme Court decision in *United Air Lines v. McMann*, 434 U.S. 192 (1977).

[96] The Fifth Circuit Court of Appeals in *Brennan v. Taft Broadcasting Co.*, 500 F.2d 212 (5th Cir. 1974), upheld mandatory retirement under an employee benefit plan that pre-dated the ADEA. The Fourth Circuit of the Court of Appeals in *McMann v. United Air Lines, Inc.*, 542 F.2d 217 (4th Cir. 1976) held that mandatory retirement compelled by an employee benefit plan constituted a 'subterfuge' to evade the provisions of the ADEA. The U.S. Supreme Court in *United Air Lines, Inc., v. McMann*, 434 U.S. 192 (1977), overturned the Fourth Circuit's decision. Congress responded with the Age Discrimination in Employment Act Amendments of 1978, legislatively overturning the Supreme Court's decision.

an institution of higher education, between the ages of 65 and 70, were exempt from this provision.[97]

The 1978 Amendments also sought to strengthen the enforcement procedures of the ADEA. First, the right to a jury trial was codified into the ADEA.[98] Second, the Amendments detailed the time line for filing an ADEA claim. An allegation of violation of the ADEA should be filed with the Secretary within 180 days of the alleged unlawful practice. An individual may file suit under the ADEA 60 days after filing a charge with the Secretary of Labor. If the alleged unlawful practice occurred in a state having a prohibition against age discrimination in employment, and a corresponding enforcement agency, then the grievant must file with the Secretary within 300 days from the alleged unlawful practice or within 30 days after receipt of notice of termination of proceedings under State law. The Secretary, upon receipt of a charge of an unlawful practice, is responsible for seeking an elimination of the alleged practice through informal methods of conciliation. An informal resolution must not exceed one year.

1982 AMENDMENT

The 1982 Amendments entitled employees between the ages of 65 and 69 to coverage under any group health plan also offered to employees under age 65.[99]

1984 AMENDMENTS

The Deficit Reduction Act of 1984 amended the ADEA to entitle spouses of employees ages 65 through 69 to coverage under group health benefits similar to spouses of employees under age 65.[100] The Older Americans Act Amendments extended coverage of the ADEA to U.S. citizens working abroad for American companies.[101] However, employers are exempted from complying

---

97 High ranking executives and policy makers were defined as someone who held such a position the immediately proceeding two years and was entitled to certain forms of annual employees benefits totaling, at least, $27,000.

98 29 U.S.C.A. § 626(c)(2) (West 1985). The Supreme Court in *Lorillard v. Pons*, 434 U.S. 575 (1977), considered whether "there is a right to a jury trial in private civil actions for lost wages under the [ADEA]." *Id.* at 576. The Court held that, although not explicitly stated in the Act, a right to a jury trial was available based on the statutory scheme of the ADEA.

99 Tax Equity and Fiscal Responsibility Act of 1982, Pub. L. No. 97-248, Title I, § 116(a), 96 Stat. 353 (1982).

100 Deficit Reduction Act of 1984, Pub. L. No. 98-369, Title III, § 2301(b), 98 Stat. 1063 (1984).

101 Older Americans Act Amendments, Pub. L. No. 98-459, Title VIII, § 802(a), 98 Stat. 1792 (1984).

with the ADEA, if to do so, would violate the laws of the country where the employee is working.[102] Whether the employer of a U.S. citizen working abroad is liable under the ADEA is based on the determination of whether the U.S. employer controls the corporation. Factors to determine control include: "interrelation of operations, common management, centralized control of labor relations, and common ownership or financial control."[103]

1986 AMENDMENTS

The Age Discrimination in Employment Amendments of 1986 eliminated the upper age limit for non-federal employees, hereby covering most employees age 40 or older.[104] Elimination of the upper age limit was motivated by the fact that the population most affected by the limitation was the most vulnerable group, poor workers. Concern over the cost of retirement has caused workers to stay in the workforce beyond retirement.

On the other hand, the ADEA did not apply to the hiring, discharge or mandatory retirement of a firefighter or law enforcement officer pursuant to state law or a bona fide hiring or retirement plan. This exemption expired on December 31, 1993, but was reinstated by the Age Discrimination in Employment Amendments of 1996.[105] The 1986 Amendments required a joint study by the Secretary of Labor and the Equal Employment Opportunity Commission (EEOC) on the effectiveness of physical and mental fitness tests for firefighters and law enforcement officers. The EEOC would use the results of the study to create guidelines for the use of physical and mental fitness tests in determining the ability of firefighters and law enforcement officers to perform their jobs.

The 1986 Amendments also allowed for the mandatory retirement of tenured employees at institutions of higher education who have reached 70 years of age until December 31, 1993. At that time this exemption expired, and tenured faculty are now protected under the ADEA. A study was also commissioned to examine the effects of eliminating mandatory retirement for tenured employees.

---

[102] The ADEA does not apply where the employer is a foreign person not controlled by an American employer.

[103] 29 U.S.C.A. § 623(h)(3)(A)-(D).

[104] Age Discrimination in Employment Amendments of 1986, Pub. L. No. 99-592, 100 Stat. 3342 (1986). The upper age limit was actually removed months earlier by the Budget Reconciliation Act, Pub. L. No. 99-272, Title IX, § 9201(b), 100 Stat. 171 (1986). The Older Americans Pension Benefits subtitle, included in the Budget Reconciliation Act Public Law 99-509 section 9201, prohibited age discrimination in employee pension benefit plans.

[105] Omnibus Consolidated Appropriations Act of 1997, Pub. L. No. 104-208, 110 Stat. 3009 (1996).

1988 AMENDMENTS

The Age Discrimination Claims Assistance Act of 1988 extended the statute of limitations for claims the EEOC failed to process before the statute of limitations expired.[106] Another extension was granted two years later with the Age Discrimination Claims Assistance Act of 1990.[107]

1990 AMENDMENTS

The Older Workers Protection Act sought to clarify the ADEA's application to employee benefit plans. The Act overturned the U.S. Supreme Court decision, *Public Employees Retirement System of Ohio v. Betts*,[108] which held that bona fide employee benefit plans which were not a subterfuge for discrimination were permissible under the ADEA. One of the concerns surrounding the enactment of the ADEA was the cost to employers of providing employee benefits to older workers. The "equal benefit or equal cost" principle allowed employers to proportionally reduce the amount of money spent on an older worker's employee benefits, so that the amount spent on the older worker is equivalent to the amount spent on a younger worker. This principle did not allow employers to reduce or deny benefits because of age, but did allow employers to deduct for any increased costs that would make insuring or providing benefits to older workers more expensive. It was believed that to not account for increased costs would prevent employers from hiring older workers. This is permissible under the ADEA even if such a reduction reduces the amount of benefits an older worker receives. The Older Workers Protection Act restored the use of the "equal benefit or equal cost" principle after it had been invalidated by the Supreme Court in *Betts*. In addition, the 1990 Amendment established criteria for waiving any rights of claims under the ADEA.

---

106 29 U.S.C. § 626 (1994). *See also* Pub. L. No. 100-283, 102 Stat. 78 (1988).

107 29 U.S.C. § 626 (1994). *See also* Pub. L. 101-504, 104 Stat. 1298 (1990).

108 492 U.S. 158 (1989).

1995 AMENDMENT

The Congressional Accountability Act of 1995 extended the rights and protections of the ADEA, and several other civil rights laws, to congressional employees.[109]

1996 AMENDMENTS

The Age Discrimination in Employment Amendments of 1996 reinstated the exemption for state and local firefighters and law enforcement officers created by the 1986 Amendments.[110] The exemption created by the 1986 Amendments had expired on December 31, 1993. The 1996 Amendments also reinstated the requirement that the Secretary of Health and Human Services identify or create tests that would assess the ability of firefighters and law enforcement officials to perform their tasks.

---

[109] 2 U.S.C.A. § 1301. "Employees" as defined under the Congressional Accountability Act include employees of the:

(A) House of Representatives
(B) Senate
(C) Capitol Guide Service
(D) Capitol Police
(E) Congressional Budget Office
(F) Office of the Architect of the Capitol
(G) Office of the Attending Physician
(H) Office of Compliance; or
(I) Office of Technology Assessment

[110] Federal law enforcement officers and federal firefighters are covered under different provisions. Section 3307 of Title 5 allows heads of agencies to establish its own minimum and maximum age limits for original appointments of federal law enforcement officers and firefighters. 5 U.S.C.A. § 3307 (West 1996). Section 8425 gives the mandatory retirement ages of federal firefighters and law enforcement officers. 5 U.S.C.A. § 8425 (West 1996).

CHAPTER 15

The Americans with Disabilities Act (ADA): An Overview of Major Provisions and Issues

Nancy Lee Jones

BACKGROUND

The Americans with Disabilities Act, ADA, P.L. 101-336, has often been described as the most sweeping nondiscrimination legislation since the Civil Rights Act of 1964. It provides broad nondiscrimination protection for individuals with disabilities in employment, public services, public accommodation and services operated by private entities, transportation, and telecommunications. As stated in the Act, its purpose is "to provide a clear and comprehensive national mandate for the elimination of discrimination against individuals with disabilities."[1] Enacted on July 26, 1990, the majority of the ADA's provisions took effect 1992. Although the ADA is still in the early developing years for civil rights jurisprudence, several major issues have surfaced. These include questions concerning what constitutes a disability, and what is a "reasonable accommodation." This report will briefly examine the major provisions of the ADA and selected issues that have arisen under the Act.

Prior to this examination, it would be helpful to note the historical antecedents of the ADA. An existing federal statutory provision, section 504 of the Rehabilitation Act of 1973, 29 U.S.C. § 794, prohibits discrimination against an otherwise qualified individual with a disability, solely on the basis of the disability, in any program or activity that receives federal financial assistance, the executive agencies or the U.S. Postal Service.[2] Many of the concepts used in the ADA originated in section 504 and its interpretations; however, there is one major difference: while section 504's prohibition against discrimination is tied to the receipt of federal financial assistance, the ADA also covers entities not receiving such funds. The ADA contains a specific provision stating that except as otherwise provided in the Act, nothing in the Act shall be construed to apply a lesser standard than the standards applied under title V of the Rehabilitation Act (which includes section 504) or the regulations issued by federal agencies pursuant to such title.[3]

---

[1] 42 U.S.C. § 12101(b)(1).

[2] 29 U.S.C. § 794.

[3] 42 U.S.C. § 12201(a).

DEFINITION OF DISABILITY

The definitions in the ADA, particularly the definition of "disability", are the starting point for an analysis of rights provided by the law. The term "disability", with respect to an individual, is defined as "(A) a physical or mental impairment that substantially limits one or more of the major life activities of such individual; (B) a record of such an impairment; or (C) being regarded as having such an impairment."[4] This definition, which has been the subject of numerous cases brought under the ADA, is drawn from the definitional section applicable to section 504.[5]

The definition of "disability" was further elaborated in title V of the ADA. Section 510 provides that the term "individual with a disability" in the ADA does not include an individual who is currently engaging in the illegal use of drugs when the covered entity acts on the basis of such use.[6] An individual who has been rehabilitated would be covered. However, the conference report language clarifies that the provision does not permit individuals to invoke coverage simply by showing they are participating in a drug rehabilitation program; they must refrain from using drugs.[7] The conference report also indicates that the limitation in coverage is not intended to be narrowly construed to only persons who use drugs "on the day of, or within a matter of weeks before, the action in question."[8] The definitional section of the Rehabilitation Act that applies to section 504 was also amended to create uniformity with this definition.

Section 508 provides that an individual shall not be considered to have a disability solely because that individual is a transvestite.[9] Section 511 similarly provides that homosexuality and bisexuality are not disabilities under the Act and that the term disability does not include transvestism, transsexualism, pedophilia, exhibitionism, voyeurism, gender identity disorders not resulting from physical impairments, or other sexual behavior disorders, compulsive gambling, kleptomania, or pyromania, or psychoactive substance use disorders resulting from current illegal use of drugs.[10]

---

[4] 42 U.S.C. § 12102(2).

[5] 29 U.S.C. § 706(8).

[6] 42 U.S.C. § 12210.

[7] H.Conf.Rep.No. 101-596, 101st Cong., 2d Sess. 64; 1990 U.S.Code Cong. & Admin. News 573.

[8] *Id.*

[9] 42 U.S.C. § 12208.

[10] 42 U.S.C. § 12211.

The issues involving the definition of "disability" have been among the most controversial under the ADA. The Equal Employment Opportunity Commission (EEOC) issued detailed guidance on the definition on March 15, 1995. The EEOC found that the following conditions would not constitute impairments: environmental, cultural, and economic disadvantages; age; pregnancy; common personality traits; and normal deviations in height, weight and strength. However, certain aspects of these conditions could give rise to an impairment. For example, complications arising from pregnancy or conditions associated with age, such as hearing loss, could be considered to be disabilities. The guidance also included the EEOC's interpretation of the third prong of the definition -- "regarded as having a disability." This category was seen by EEOC as including individuals who are subjected to discrimination on the basis of genetic information relating to illness, disease or other disorders.[11]

Cases brought concerning the definition of "disability" under the ADA have included questions on obesity,[12] cancer,[13] HIV infection,[14] and infertility.[15] In addition, a recent case found that, contrary to EEOC guidance, a disability that can be controlled by medication was not to be considered a disability under

---

[11] *EEOC Compliance Manual*, Section 902; *BNA's Americans with Disabilities Act Manual* 70:1131. The issue of coverage of genetic disorders has been widely discussed. See Jones, "Genetic Information: Discrimination and Privacy Issues," CRS Rep. No. 96-808 A.

[12] The EEOC's ADA regulations state that absent unusual circumstances, "obesity is not considered a disabling impairment." 29 C.F.R. § 1630.2(j)(Appendix). However, several cases have found situations where obesity might be covered. See, e.g., *Cook v. Rhode Island*, 10 F.3d 17 (1st Cir. 1993), and *EEOC v. Texas Bus Lines*, 923 F.Supp. 878 (S.D. Tex. 1996).

[13] In most cases, an individual with cancer would most likely be covered by the ADA, since the cancer would probably limit a major life activity. But the fifth circuit court of appeals held that a woman who received radiation treatments for breast cancer was not covered, since she missed very few days of work and was therefore not limited in a major life activity. *Ellison v. Software Spectrum, Inc.*, 85 F.3d 187 (5th Cir. 1996).

[14] The majority of cases have following the lead of the EEOC, which has found that HIV infection is "inherently substantially limiting." [29 C.F.R. § 1630.2(j)(Appendix)]. However, see *Ennis v. National Association of Business and Educational Radio*, 53 F.3d 55 (4th Cir. 1995), where the court found that a child who was HIV-infected but asymptomatic did not have a disability for ADA purposes.

[15] A recent court of appeals case found that infertility is not a disability because the ability to reproduce is not a major life activity. *Krauel v. Iowa Methodist Medical Center, 95 F.3d 674* (8th Cir. 1996). However, cases at the district court level are split. See, e.g., *Pacourck v. Inland Steel Co.*, 916 F.Supp. 797 (N.D. Ill 1996), where the court found that reproduction was a major life activity; *Krauel v. Iowa Methodist Medical Center*, 915 F.Supp. 102 (S.D. Iowa 1995), *aff'd*, 95 F.3d 674 (8th Cir. 1996), where the court found that reproduction is a "lifestyle choice" and not a major life activity.

the ADA.[16] Although a detailed analysis of these cases is beyond the scope of this report, two general observations may be made. First, any argument that attempts to make a blanket determination that all individuals with a particular disability are covered is viewed with suspicion by the courts and will often fail. Second, the interpretation of the ADA is still evolving. The courts are not in agreement on a number of these questions, and they do not always agree with the interpretation advanced by the EEOC.

EMPLOYMENT

General Requirements

Title I of the ADA provides that no covered entity shall discriminate against a qualified individual with a disability because of the disability in regard to job application procedures, the hiring, advancement, or discharge of employees, employee compensation, job training, and other terms, conditions, and privileges of employment.[17] The term employer is defined as a person engaged in an industry affecting commerce who has 15 or more employees.[18] Therefore, the employment section of the ADA, unlike the section on public accommodations, which will be discussed subsequently, is limited in scope to employers with 15 or more employees. This parallels the coverage provided in the Civil Rights Act of 1964.

The term "employee" with respect to employment in a foreign country includes an individual who is a citizen of the United States; however, it is not unlawful for a covered entity to take action that constitutes discrimination with respect to an employee in a workplace in a foreign country if compliance would cause the covered entity to violate the law of the foreign country.[19]

If the issue raised under the ADA is employment related, and the threshold issues of meeting the definition of an individual with a disability and involving an employer employing over fifteen individuals are met, the next step is to determine whether the individual is a qualified individual with a disability who, with or without reasonable accommodation, can perform the essential functions of the job.

Title I defines a "qualified individual with a disability". Such an individual is "an individual with a disability who, with or without reasonable accommodation, can perform the essential functions of the employment positions

---

[16] *Murphy v. United Parcel Service,* 1996 U.S.Dist LEXIS 17619 (D.Kan. 1996).

[17] 42 U.S.C. § 12112(a).

[18] 42 U.S.C. § 12111(5).

[19] P.L. 102-166 added this provision.

that such person holds or desires."[20] The ADA incorporates many of the concepts set forth in the regulations promulgated pursuant to section 504, including the requirement to provide reasonable accommodation unless such accommodation would pose an undue hardship on the operation of the business.[21]

"Reasonable accommodation" is defined in the ADA as including making existing facilities readily accessible to and usable by individuals with disabilities, and job restructuring, part-time or modified work schedules, reassignment to a vacant position, acquisition or modification of equipment or devices, adjustment of examinations or training materials or policies, provision of qualified readers or interpreters or other similar accommodations.[22] "Undue hardship" is defined as "an action requiring significant difficulty or expense."[23]

The concepts of reasonable accommodation and undue hardship were discussed by the seventh circuit in *Vande Zande v. State of Wisconsin Department of Administration.*[24] In *Vande Zande* the court found that the cost of the accommodation cannot be disproportionate to the benefit. "Even if an employer is so large or wealthy--or, like the principal defendant in this case, is a state, which can raise taxes in order to finance any accommodations that it must make to disabled employees--that it may not be able to plead 'undue hardship', it would not be required to expend enormous sums in order to bring about a trivial improvement in the life of a disabled employee."[25]

---

[20] 42 U.S.C. § 12111(8). The EEOC has stated that a function may be essential because (1) the position exists to perform the duty, (2) there are a limited number of employees available who could perform the function, or (3) the function is highly specialized. 29 C.F.R. § 1630(n)(2). A number of issues have been litigated concerning essential functions. For example, most courts have found that regular attendance is an essential function of most jobs. See, e.g., *Carr v. Reno,* 23 F.3d 525 (D.C. Cir. 1994).

[21] See 45 C.F.R. Part 84.

[22] 42 U.S.C. § 12111(9).

[23] 42 U.S.C. § 12111(10). The definition also provides various factors to be considered in determining whether an action would create an undue hardship. These include the nature and cost of the accommodation, the overall financial resources of the facility, the overall financial resources of the covered entity, and the type of operation or operations of the covered entity.

[24] 44 F.3d 538 (7th Cir. 1995).

[25] *Id.* at 542-543. See also *Schmidt v. Methodist Hospital of Indiana,* 89 F.3d 342 (7th Cir. 1996), where the court found that reasonable accommodation does not require an employer to provided everything an employee requests.

Another issue that has arisen is the interplay between rights under the ADA for reasonable accommodation and collective bargaining agreements. In a recent seventh circuit court of appeals decision, the court found that "the ADA does not require disabled individuals to be accommodated by sacrificing the collectively bargained, bona fide seniority rights of other employees."[26] This decision was contrary to arguments which had been advanced by the EEOC. The EEOC had argued that although the EEOC does not require displacement of another employee to accommodate an individual with a disability, employers and unions have a responsibility to negotiate in good faith a variance from the collective bargaining agreement.

Employment Inquiries Relating to Disability

Before an offer of employment is made, an employer may not ask a disability related question or require a medical examination.[27] The EEOC in its guidance on this issue stated that the rationale for this exclusion was to isolate an employer's consideration of an applicant's non-medical qualifications from any consideration of the applicant's medical condition.[28] However, once an offer is made disability related questions and medical examinations are permitted as long as all individuals who have been offered a job in that category are asked the same questions and given the same examinations.[29]

Defenses to a Charge of Discrimination

The ADA specifically lists some defenses to a charge of discrimination, including (1) that the alleged application of qualification standards has been shown to be job related and consistent with business necessity and such performance cannot be accomplished by reasonable accommodation, (2) the term "qualification standards" can include a requirement that an individual shall not pose a direct threat to the health or safety of other individuals in the workplace,[30] and (3) religious entities may give a preference in employment to individuals of a particular religion to perform work connected with carrying on the entities' activities.[31] In addition, religious entities may require that all applicants and employees conform to the religious tenets of the organization. The Secretary of Health and Human Services has, pursuant to a statutory

---

[26] *Eckles v. Consolidated Rail Corporation,* 94 F.3d 1041, 1051 (7th Cir. 1996).

[27] 42 U.S.C. § 12112.

[28] EEOC, "ADA Enforcement Guidance: Preemployment Disability-Related Questions and Medical Examinations," Oct. 10, 1995.

[29] *Id.*

[30] The EEOC in its regulations states that the following factors should be considered when determining whether an individual poses a direct threat: the duration of the risk, the nature and severity of the potential harm, the likelihood that the potential harm will occur and the imminence of the potential harm. 29 C.F.R. § 1630.2(r).

[31] 42 U.S.C. § 12113.

requirement, listed infectious and communicable diseases transmitted through the handling of food and if the risk cannot be eliminated by reasonable accommodation, a covered entity may refuse to assign or continue to assign an individual with such a disease to a job involving food handling.

Drug Addicts and Alcoholics

A controversial issue that arose during the enactment of the ADA regarding employment concerned the application of the Act to drug addicts and alcoholics. The ADA provides that, with regard to employment, *current* illegal drug users are not considered to be qualified individuals with disabilities. However, former drug users and alcoholics would be covered by the Act if they are able to perform the essential functions of the job. In the appendix to its regulations, EEOC further notes that "an employer, such as a law enforcement agency, may also be able to impose a qualification standard that excludes individuals with a history of illegal use of drugs if it can show that the standard is job-related and consistent with business necessity."[32] Title I also provides that a covered entity may prohibit the illegal use of drugs and the use of alcohol at the workplace.[33]

Remedies

The remedies and procedures set forth in sections 705, 706, 707, 709, and 710 of the Civil Rights Act of 1964,[34] are incorporated by reference. This provides for certain administrative enforcement as well as allowing for individual suits. The Civil Rights Act of 1991, P.L. 102-166, expanded the remedies of injunctive relief and back pay.[35] A plaintiff who was the subject of unlawful intentional discrimination (as opposed to an employment practice that is discriminatory because of its disparate impact) may recover compensatory and punitive damages. In order to receive punitive damages, the plaintiff must show that there was a discriminatory practice engaged in with malice or with reckless indifference to the rights of the aggrieved individual. The amount that can be awarded in punitive and compensatory damages is capped, with the amounts varying from $50,000 to $300,000 depending upon the size of the business. Similarly, there is also a "good faith" exception to the award of damages with regard to reasonable accommodation.

---

[32] 29 C.F.R. Appendix §1630.3.

[33] 42 U.S.C. § 12114(c); 29 C.F.R. § 1630.16(b)(4).

[34] 42 U.S.C. §§ 2000e-4, 2000e-5, 2000e-6, 2000e-7.

[35] For a detailed discussion of this Act see "The Civil Rights Act of 1991: A Legal History and Analysis," CRS Rep. 92-85A (Jan. 10, 1992).

PUBLIC SERVICES

Title II of the ADA provides that no qualified individual with a disability shall be excluded from participation in or be denied the benefits of the services, programs, or activities of a public entity or be subjected to discrimination by any such entity.[36] "Public entity" is defined as state and local governments, any department or other instrumentality of a state or local government, and certain transportation authorities. The ADA does not apply to the executive branch of the Federal Government; the executive branch is covered by section 504 of the Rehabilitation Act of 1973.[37]

The Department of Justice regulations for title II contain a specific section on program accessibility. Each service, program, or activity conducted by a public entity, when viewed in its entirety, must be readily accessible to and usable by individuals with disabilities. However, a public entity is not required to make each of its existing facilities accessible.[38] Program accessibility is limited in certain situations involving historic preservation. In addition, in meeting the program accessibility requirement, a public entity is not required to take any action that would result in a fundamental alteration in the nature of its service, program, or activity or in undue financial and administrative burdens.[39]

Although title II has not been the subject of as much litigation as title I, several issues have been raised. For example, a Hawaii regulation requiring the quarantine of all dogs, including guide dogs for visually impaired individuals, was found to violate title II.[40] Cases have also arisen concerning the extent to which title II requires state examiners to modify their exam procedures for individuals with disabilities;[41] when curb ramps are required;[42] the

---

[36] 42 U.S.C. §§ 12131-12133.

[37] 29 U.S.C. § 794.

[38] 28 C.F.R. §35.150.

[39] *Id.*

[40] *Crowder v. Kitagawa,* 81 F.3d 1480, 1484 (9th Cir. 1996). The court stated: "Although Hawaii's quarantine requirement applies equally to all persons entering the state with a dog, its enforcement burdens visually-impaired persons in a manner different and greater than it burdens others. Because of the unique dependence upon guide dogs among many of the visually-impaired, Hawaii's quarantine effectively denies these persons...meaningful access to state services, programs, and activities while such services, programs, and activities remain open and easily accessible by others."

[41] This has most commonly arisen concerning bar exams. See *D'Amico v. New York State Board of Law Examiners,* 813 F.Supp. 217 (W.D.N.Y. 1993), where the court ordered that a visually impaired individual be allowed to take the bar exam over a four day, rather than a two day, time period.

application of title II to a city ordinance allowing open burning;[43] the application of title II to prisons;[44] and discrimination among individuals with disabilities.[45]

This title also provides specific requirements for public transportation by intercity and commuter rail and for public transportation other than by aircraft or certain rail operations.[46] All new vehicles purchased or leased by a public entity that operates a fixed route system must be accessible, and good faith efforts must be demonstrated with regard to the purchase or lease of accessible used vehicles. Retrofitting of existing buses is not required. Paratransit services must be provided by a public entity that operates a fixed route service, other than one providing solely commuter bus service.[47] Rail systems must have at least one car per train that is accessible to individuals with disabilities.[48]

The enforcement remedies of section 505 of the Rehabilitation Act of 1973, 29 U.S.C. § 794a, are incorporated by reference.[49] These remedies are similar to those of title VI of the Civil Rights Act of 1964, and include damages and injunctive relief. The Attorney General has promulgated regulations relating to subpart A of the title,[50] and the Secretary of Transportation has issued regulations regarding transportation.[51]

---

[42] In *Kinney v. Yerusalim,* 812 F.Supp. 547 (E.D. Pa. 1993), *aff'd* 9 F.3d 1067 (3d Cir. 1993), *cert. den.* 114 S.Ct. 1545 (1994), the court found that street repair projects must include curb ramps for individuals with disabilities. See also 28 C.F.R. § 35.151(e)(1), where the Department of Justice detailed the requirements for curb ramps.

[43] *Heather K. v. City of Mallard, Iowa, 1996 WL 683587* (N.D.Iowa).

[44] There is currently a split concerning whether the ADA applies to state prisons. A California district court has held that state prisons are covered. *Armstrong v. Wilson,* 942 F.Supp. 1252 (N.D. Calif. 1996). On the other hand, the fourth circuit has held that the ADA does not apply to prisons. *Torcasio v. Murray,* 57 F.3d 1340 (4th Cir. 1995).

[45] In *Helen L. v. DiDario,* 46 F.3d 325 (3d Cir. 1995), *cert. denied,* 116 S.Ct. 64 (1995), the court found that title II would cover discrimination among individuals with disabilities.

[46] 42 U.S.C. §§ 12141-12165.

[47] 42 U.S.C. § 12143.

[48] 42 U.S.C. § 12162.

[49] 42 U.S.C. § 12133.

[50] 28 C.F.R. Part 35.

[51] 49 C.F.R. Parts 27, 37, 38.

PUBLIC ACCOMMODATIONS

Title III provides that no individual shall be discriminated against on the basis of disability in the full and equal enjoyment of the goods, services, facilities, privileges, advantages, or accommodations of any place of public accommodation by any person who owns, leases (or leases to), or operates a place of public accommodation.[52] Entities that are covered by the term "public accommodation" are listed, and include, among others, hotels, restaurants, theaters, auditoriums, laundromats, museums, parks, zoos, private schools, day care centers, professional offices of health care providers, and gymnasiums.[53] Religious institutions or entities controlled by religious institutions are not included on the list.

There are some limitations on the nondiscrimination requirements, and a failure to remove architectural barriers is not a violation unless such a removal is "readily achievable."[54] "Readily achievable" is defined as meaning "easily accomplishable and able to be carried out without much difficulty or expense."[55] The nondiscrimination mandate also does not require that an entity permit an individual to participate in or benefit from the services of a public accommodation where such an individual poses a direct threat to the health or safety of others. Similarly, reasonable modifications in practices, policies or procedures are required unless they would fundamentally alter the nature of the goods, services, facilities, or privileges or they would result in an undue burden.[56] An undue burden is defined as an action involving "significant difficulty or expense."[57]

Title III contains a specific exemption for religious entities.[58] This applies when an entity is controlled by a religious entity. For example, a preschool that is run by a religious entity would not be covered under the ADA; however, a preschool, that is not run by a religious entity but that rents space from the religious entity, would be covered by title III.

One of the issues that has arisen under title III is whether a place of public accommodation is limited to actual physical structures. The First Circuit Court of Appeals has held that public accommodations are not so limited, reasoning

---

[52] 42 U.S.C. § 12182.

[53] 42 U.S.C. § 12181.

[54] 42 U.S.C. § 12182(b)(2)(A)(iv).

[55] 42 U.S.C. § 12181.

[56] 42 U.S.C. § 12182(b)(2)(A).

[57] 28 C.F.R. § 36.104.

[58] 42 U.S.C. § 12187.

that "to exclude this broad category of businesses from the reach of Title II and limit the application of Title III to physical structures which persons must enter to obtain goods and services would run afoul of the purposes of the ADA."[59] A related issue is whether franchisors are subject to title III. In *Nef v. American Dairy Queen Corp.*, the Fifth Circuit Court of Appeals found that a franchisor with limited control over the store a franchisee runs is not covered under title III of the ADA.[60]

Title III also contains provisions relating to the prohibition of discrimination in public transportation services provided by private entities. Purchases of over-the-road buses are to be made in accordance with regulations issued by the Secretary of Transportation.[61]

The remedies and procedures of title II of the Civil Rights Act of 1964 are incorporated in title III of the ADA. Title II of the Civil Rights Act has generally been interpreted to include injunctive relief, not damages. In addition, state and local governments can apply to the Attorney General to certify that state or local building codes meet or exceed the minimum accessibility requirements of the ADA. The Attorney General may bring pattern or practice suits with a maximum civil penalty of $50,000 for the first violation and $100,000 for a violation in a subsequent case. The monetary damages sought by the Attorney General do not include punitive damages. Courts may also consider an entity's "good faith" efforts in considering the amount of the civil penalty. Factors to be considered in determining good faith include whether an entity could have reasonably anticipated the need for an appropriate type of auxiliary aid to accommodate the unique needs of a particular individual with a disability. Regulations relating to public accommodations have been promulgated by the Department of Justice[62] and regulations relating to the transportation provisions of title III have been promulgated by the Department of Transportation.[63]

---

[59] *Carparts Distribution Center, Inc. v. Automotive Wholesaler's Association of New England, Inc.*, 37 F.3d 12 (1st Cir. 1994).

[60] 58 F.3d 1063 (5th Cir. 1995).

[61] This section was amended by P.L. 104-59 to provide that accessibility requirements for private over-the-road buses must be met by small providers within three years after the issuance of final regulations and with respect to other providers, within two years after the issuance of such regulations.

[62] 28 C.F.R. Part 36.

[63] 49 C.F.R. Parts 27, 37, 38.

TELECOMMUNICATIONS

Title IV of the ADA amends title II of the Communications Act of 1934[64] by adding a section providing that the Federal Communications Commission shall ensure that interstate and intrastate telecommunications relay services are available, to the extent possible and in the most efficient manner, to hearing-impaired and speech-impaired individuals. Any television public service announcement that is produced or funded in whole or part by any agency or instrumentality of the federal government shall include closed captioning of the verbal content of the announcement. The FCC is given enforcement authority with certain exceptions.[65]

MISCELLANEOUS PROVISIONS IN TITLE V

Title V contains an amalgam of provisions, several of which generated considerable controversy during ADA debate. Section 501 concerns the relationship of the ADA to other statutes and bodies of law. Subpart (a) states that "except as otherwise provided in this Act, nothing in the Act shall be construed to apply a lesser standard than the standards applied under title V of the Rehabilitation Act ... or the regulations issued by Federal agencies pursuant to such title." Subpart (b) provides that nothing in the Act shall be construed to invalidate or limit the remedies, rights and procedures of any federal, state or local law that provides greater or equal protection. Nothing in the Act is to be construed to preclude the prohibition of or restrictions on smoking. Subpart (d) provides that the Act does not require an individual with a disability to accept an accommodation which that individual chooses not to accept.[66]

Subpart (c) of section 501 limits the application of the Act with respect to the coverage of insurance; however, the subsection may not be used as a subterfuge to evade the purposes of titles I and III. The exact parameters of insurance coverage under the ADA are somewhat uncertain. As the EEOC has stated: "The interplay between the nondiscrimination principles of the ADA and employer provide health insurance, which is predicated on the ability to make health-related distinctions, is both unique and complex."[67] In a case that may

---

[64] 47 U.S.C. §§201 *et seq.*

[65] 47 U.S.C. §225.

[66] 29 U.S.C. §§790 *et seq.*

[67] EEOC: Interim Policy Guidance on ADA and Health Insurance, June 8, 1993. This guidance deals solely with the ADA implications of disability-based health insurance plan distinctions and states that "Insurance distinctions that are not based on disability, and that are applied equally to all insured employees, do not discriminate on the basis of disability and so do not violate the ADA." An example given of this permitted distinction was differences between the levels of coverage for physical and mental conditions.

have wide impact, the Eighth Circuit Court of Appeals issued a preliminary injunction compelling the plaintiff's employer to pay for chemotherapy that required an autologous bone marrow transplant. The plaintiff was diagnosed with an aggressive form of breast cancer and her oncologist recommended entry into a clinical trial program that randomly assigns half of its participants to high dose chemotherapy that necessitates a autologous bone marrow transplant. Because of the possibility that the plaintiff might have the more expensive bone marrow treatment, the employer's health plan refused to precertify the placement noting that the policy covered high dose chemotherapy only for certain types of cancer, not breast cancer. The court concluded that, "if the evidence shows that a given treatment is non-experimental -- that is, if it is widespread, safe, and a significant improvement on traditional therapies -- and the plan provides the treatment for other conditions directly comparable to the one at issue, the denial of treatment violates the ADA."[68]

Another significant decision involving insurance coverage found that the plaintiff was entitled to have an opportunity to show that the distinction between mental and physical disabilities in long-term disability coverage is not justified by sound actuarial principles. Also of note with regard to this decision is that it was brought not under title I but under title III. The court found that "the statutory language of the Disabilities Act is sufficiently broad to prohibit discrimination in the contents of insurance products, not just physical access to insurance company offices."[69]

Section 502 abrogates the Eleventh Amendment state immunity from suit. Section 503 prohibits retaliation and coercion against an individual who has opposed an act or practice made unlawful by the ADA. Section 504 requires the Architectural and Transportation Barriers Compliance Board (ATBCB) to issue guidelines regarding accessibility. Section 505 provides for attorneys' fees in "any action or administrative proceeding" under the Act. Section 506 provides for technical assistance to help entities covered by the Act in understanding their responsibilities. Section 507 provides for a study by the National Council

---

[68] *Henderson v. Bodine Aluminum, Inc.*, 70 F.3d 958 (8th Cir. 1995).

[69] *Ouida Sue Parker v. Metropolitan Life Insurance Co.,* 99 F.3d 181, 182 (6th Cir. 1996).

on Disability regarding wilderness designations and wilderness land management practices and "reaffirms" that nothing in the Wilderness Act is to be construed as prohibiting the use of a wheelchair in a wilderness area by an individual whose disability requires the use of a wheelchair. Section 513 provides that "where appropriate and to the extent authorized by law, the use of alternative means of dispute resolution ... is encouraged...."[70] Section 514 provides for severability of any provision of the Act that is found to be unconstitutional.

The coverage of Congress was a major controversy during the House-Senate conference on the ADA. Although the original language of the ADA did provide for some coverage for the congressional branch, Congress expanded upon this in the Congressional Accountability Act, P.L. 104-1. The major area of expansion was the incorporation of remedies that were analogous to those in the ADA applicable to the private sector.[71]

---

[70] 42 U.S.C. §12212.

[71] For a more detailed discussion of the application of the ADA to Congress see "Congressional Accountability Act of 1995," CRS Rep. No. 95-557A (1995). Congress recently applied the employment and public accommodation provisions of the ADA to the Executive Office of the President. P.L. 104-331 (October 26, 1996).

CHAPTER 16

Wage Mobility, Growth, and Inequality in the United States, 1979 - 1989

Gerald Mayer

Studies of income examine three basic issues: the level of income, the distribution of income, and mobility (i.e., changes in the ranking of individuals or families in the distribution of income). The results of these studies often differ, depending on the definition of income, the data series used, and the time period studied.

For most Americans, wages represent the largest source of money income. Individual weekly or annual wages are a function of hourly wages and the number of hours worked. Since individuals do not work the same number of hours in a week or year, differences in individual hourly wages reflect differences in the return to labor. This study examines the level and distribution of hourly real wages in 1979 and again in 1989.[1] These years are chosen because they are comparable years in the business cycle.

Most studies of wages use time-series data (i.e., data collected from periodic surveys of different samples of individuals drawn from the same general population). However, with time-series data it is generally not possible to measure changes in the ranking of individuals within the distribution of wages. This study uses longitudinal data (i.e., data collected from periodic surveys of the same sample of individuals) to measure the amount of wage mobility from 1979 to 1989.

Finally, this study examines the relative positions of individuals by gender, years of education, and race within the overall distribution of wages. The study also examines how the relative status of these social and demographic groups changed from 1979 to 1989.

Policy Issues

This study examines several economic issues that have implications for public policy. The level and distribution of real wages are issues that concern most, if not all, policymakers. Thus, the findings from this study should interest policymakers who believe that the government has a limited role in promoting real wage growth as well as policymakers who believe that the government can

---

[1] Real wages are actual, or nominal, wages adjusted for inflation. In this report, hourly wages in 1979 are stated in 1989 dollars. Hourly 1979 wages were multiplied by the ratio of the CPI-U-X1 for 1989 and the CPI-U-X1 for 1979. Appendix A explains why the CPI-U-X1 was used in this report.

play a role in improving living standards. Policymakers who believe that the government can help raise the level of real wages may support a range of polices, including legislation that promotes competition, saving and investment, research and development, and investment in human capital (e.g., education, training, and health care).

Similarly, the findings should interest policymakers who believe that the government should not attempt to influence the distribution of wages. But the findings are also relevant to policymakers who believe that the government should promote competition and to those who believe that, even if most markets are perfectly competitive, the distribution of wages is socially unacceptable.[2] For example, policymakers who support greater competition may support deregulation of certain product or labor markets. Policymakers who support greater wage equality may support legislation that alters the distribution of wage-producing resources (e.g., by increasing aid to education, developing academic standards for elementary and high school education, or improving access to health care). The findings should also be of interest to policymakers who support policies that may directly affect the distribution of aftertax wages (e.g., through progressive taxation, a higher real minimum wage, restrictions on foreign trade, or an expansion of the bargaining strength of unions).

Some of the findings may contribute to an assessment of whether the government should intervene in employer decisions to hire and promote workers. Thus, the findings are relevant to questions about whether the government should help expand employment opportunities for women and minorities in markets that may not be perfectly competitive.[3] The findings are also relevant to those who believe that, even if markets are competitive, the government has a role in correcting past instances of employment discrimination.

The findings of this study relate to each of the above economic issues. On the other hand, the study is a descriptive analysis of before-tax hourly real wages. Thus, it does not attempt to explain the causes of wage mobility or of changes in the level and distribution of real wages. Nor does the study explore all the causes of differences in the relative status of different social and demographic groups within the distribution of hourly wages.[4]

---

[2] According to standard economic theory, perfect competition generally results in the most efficient allocation of resources (i.e., labor, capital, and land). In turn, according to standard economic analysis, an efficient allocation of resources provides the greatest amount of output and consumer satisfaction.

[3] According to the model of perfect competition, when hiring and promoting workers, employers do not distinguish between equally qualified individuals. Equally qualified persons are considered perfect substitutes.

[4] For an overview of explanations of recent changes in real earnings and earnings inequality, see: Levy, Frank, and Richard J. Murnane. U.S. Earnings Levels and Earnings Inequality: A Review of Recent Trends and Proposed Explanations. *Journal of Economic Literature*, v. 30, September 1992. p. 1354-71; and Kodrzycki, Yolanda K. (continued...)

Data and Methods

This section describes the data and methodology used in this study. It also explains some of the shortcomings of the approach used. A more detailed description of the data and methods used is provided in appendix A.

Data

Most analyses of the level and distribution of wages use cross-sectional time-series data (hereafter referred to as time-series data). This study uses longitudinal data. Both kinds of data are generally collected from periodic (e.g., monthly or annual) surveys of households or employers. Time-series data are collected from periodic surveys of different samples of individuals drawn from the same general population. Longitudinal data are collected from periodic surveys of the same sample of individuals.[5]

Both time-series and longitudinal data can be used to compare the level and distribution of hourly wages at different points in time. But with longitudinal data it is also possible to compare the wages of the same individuals at different points in time. Therefore, with longitudinal data it is possible to measure changes in the ranking of individuals from one point in time to another.

This study uses longitudinal data from the Panel Study of Income Dynamics (PSID). The PSID is an annual household survey conducted by the Survey Research Center at the University of Michigan.

Unit of Analysis

This study compares the hourly real wages of a sample of wage and salary workers in 1979 with the hourly real wages of the same workers in 1989. Salaries are converted to hourly wages. The sample consists of prime-age adults: men and women who were between the ages of 25 and 54 in 1979. By analyzing the hourly wages of prime-age adults, young adults who may be in the labor force but attending school and many retired persons are excluded from the analysis. On the other hand, since the individuals in this study aged 10 years from 1979 to 1989, the findings compare the wages of workers who were between the ages of 25 and 54 in 1979 with the wages of workers who were

---

[4](...continued)
Labor Markets and Earnings Inequality: A Status Report. *New England Economic Review*, May/June 1996. p. 11-24.

[5] Technically, data collected from surveys of different samples drawn from the same general population are called pooled cross-sectional time-series data. Longitudinal data are sometimes called panel data, although the term panel survey sometimes refers to surveys where respondents remain in a sample for a fixed period and are then replaced by respondents with similar characteristics.

between the ages of 35 and 64 in 1989. Over time, individual real wages may change for several reasons, including increased work experience. Therefore, unlike a comparison of the wages of workers who were between the ages of 25 and 54 in both 1979 and 1989, the findings from this study are more likely to reflect the effects of increased work experience.[6]

Wages Versus Income

This report focuses on hourly money wages. Hourly wages represent payments for a unit of labor services and, therefore, are a better measure of differences in the return to labor than either weekly or annual wages.

Hourly wages provide different information than a measure of hourly labor income. Hourly wages do not include the value of employer-paid fringe benefits. In addition, hourly wages are not necessarily an indicator of economic well-being. First, not everyone works the same number of hours per week, the same number of weeks per year, or the same number of years in their lifetimes. Second, although wages represent the largest source of money income,[7] many individuals receive income from sources other than work. Third, one worker may support more individuals than another worker who earns the same wages. Finally, some families have more wage earners than other families. Accordingly, the results of an analysis of individual hourly wages will likely differ from a study that uses a different measure of income or a different unit of analysis (e.g., the family or household).

Concepts of Mobility

This study uses two different concepts of mobility: relative mobility and absolute mobility. Measurements of mobility based on these concepts typically yield very different results.

Relative mobility is defined as the extent to which individuals move ahead or fall behind other individuals in the distribution of wages. In studies of relative wage mobility, individuals are ranked according to their income in a base year and again according to their income in a subsequent year. For each year, individuals are often separated into quintiles (i.e., fifths), or some other equal-size groups. Their quintiles in the ending year are then compared to their

---

[6] The findings from this study may differ from the findings using time series data for another reason. To be included in this study, individuals had to report hourly wages in both 1979 and 1989. Thus, the sample used in this study may underrepresent individuals with less stable employment. (Individuals who reported hourly wages did not have to be working at the time of the survey. See appendix A.)

[7] In 1989, wages and salaries accounted for 81.6% of total money income of persons between the ages of 25 and 64. U.S. Department of Commerce. Bureau of the Census. *Money Income of Households, Families, and Persons in the United States: 1988 and 1989*. Series P-60, No. 172. Washington, U.S. Govt. Print. Off., July 1991. p. 180-82.

quintiles in the base year. The results are displayed in tables called transition matrices.

Absolute mobility is defined as movement from one fixed income interval, or wage class, to another. In some studies, the income intervals are defined by the researcher (e.g., less than $10,000, $10,001 to $20,000, etc.). In other studies, the income intervals are derived from the data. Individuals are first ranked according to their wages in a base year. Then, in the subsequent year, individuals are grouped according to the real wage intervals that define the wage intervals for the base year. The distribution of individuals by wage class in the ending year is then compared to the distribution of individuals by wage class in the base year.

Measurements of relative mobility show the extent to which the ranking of individuals changes over time. But the approach does not reveal whether real wages have changed (i.e., whether the wage structure has shifted upward or downward) or whether the distribution of hourly real wages has changed (i.e., whether the shape of the wage structure has changed). Measurements of absolute mobility, on the other hand, capture changes in the ranking of individuals as well as changes in the wage structure.

This study measures the amount of relative and absolute hourly wage mobility between 1979 and 1989, two years that represent comparable points in the business cycle in the United States.[8] The civilian unemployment rate was at a low point in both years and total industry capacity utilization was at a high point in both years.[9]

---

[8] At the time of this study, the most recent year for which final data were available was 1992.

[9] Other studies have used PSID data to examine the amount of relative and absolute family income mobility, where family income includes wages, investment income, and transfer payments. For example, Hungerford used family money income per family member to measure the degree of relative and absolute mobility from 1969 to 1976 and from 1979 to 1986. (Hungerford, Thomas L. U.S. Income Mobility in the Seventies and Eighties. *Review of Income and Wealth*, v. 39, December 1993. p. 404-412.) The civilian unemployment rate was significantly higher in 1986 than in 1979 (7.0% versus 5.8%, respectively). Bureau of Labor Statistics, *Employment and Earnings*, v. 43, October 1996, p. 12.

Cox and Alm used family money income per "active" member of the labor force to measure the amount of relative and absolute mobility in the United States from 1975 to 1991. Active members of the labor force were defined as persons age 16 and over who were either "earning money or seeking to earn money." These persons included individuals who were employed, unemployed, students, or retired. (Cox, W. Michael, and Richard Alm. *By Our Own Bootstraps: Economic Opportunity and the Dynamics of Income Distribution*. Dallas, Federal Reserve Bank of Dallas, 1995. p. 6-10, 12-14.) Depending on the indicator used, 1975 and 1991 may or may not be comparable years in the business cycle. The National Bureau of Economic Research (NBER) dates March 1975 and July 1990 as troughs in the business cycle. (U.S. Department of Commerce. U.S. Business Cycle Expansions and Contractions. *Survey of Current Business*, v. 74,

(continued...)

Findings From Longitudinal Data

This section begins with a description of the findings on relative wage mobility among prime-age adults in the United States from 1979 to 1989. Next, the section compares the distribution of individuals by real wage class in 1979 and 1989. The final section provides a summary of the results and relates the findings to the policy issues described on pages 1 and 2.

Since most studies of wage growth and inequality use time-series data, the findings of this study are compared, where appropriate, to the results from selected studies that use time-series data. A summary of the findings from these selected time-series studies is provided in appendix B.

Wage Mobility

In this study, relative wage mobility is defined as movement from one quintile of the hourly wage distribution in 1979 to a different quintile of the wage distribution in 1989. The findings on wage mobility are shown in tables 1 through 5, beginning on page 27. Table 1 provides a summary of the general results from tables 2 through 5. Table 2 shows the amount of wage mobility among prime-age adults. Tables 3 through 5 show the relative positions of individuals by gender, years of education, and race within the overall distribution of hourly wages. The analysis of the findings in tables 3 through 5 begins with a description of the relative positions of these social and demographic groups in 1979. The analysis then describes how the relative status of these groups changed from 1979 to 1989.[10]

Prime-Age Adults

From 1979 to 1989, there was a significant amount of hourly wage mobility among prime-age adults in the United States. The summary findings from table 1 (row 1) show that 50.4% of all adults were either upwardly (26.3%) or downwardly (24.1%) mobile. The remaining adults (49.7%) were in the same

---

[9](...continued)
October 1994. p. C-51.) However, the civilian unemployment rate was significantly higher in 1991 than in 1975 (8.5% versus 6.8%, respectively). Bureau of Labor Statistics, *Employment and Earnings*, v. 43, October 1996, p. 12.

[10] The findings in this report with respect to wage mobility and the relative movement of individuals within subgroups defined by gender, educational attainment, and race are consistent with the findings from research using data from the March Current Population Survey (CPS). About half of households that are in the CPS sample for a given month in one year are in the CPS sample for the same month in the following year. Gittleman and Joyce matched individuals from consecutive March surveys and were able to construct a series of datasets that tracked the same individuals over two-year periods. The authors studied the period from 1967 to 1991. Gittleman, Maury, and Mary Joyce. Earnings Mobility in the United States, 1967-91. *Monthly Labor Review*, v. 118, September 1995. p. 4-7.

quintiles in both 1979 and 1989.[11] An individual who is upwardly mobile moves ahead of other individuals in the distribution of hourly wages, but the individual may experience either an increase or decrease in hourly real wages. Likewise, an individual who is downwardly mobile may experience either a rise or fall in hourly real wages. (More will be said on this subject below in the discussion of the "Distribution of Individuals by Wage Class.")

Row 7 of table 2 shows the percentage of persons who were in the same quintiles in both 1979 and 1989. These results show that there was more mobility in the middle of the hourly wage distribution than at either the upper or lower ends of the distribution. Two-thirds (66.6%) of individuals who were in the highest quintile in 1979 were still in the highest quintile in 1989, while 63.6% of individuals who were in the lowest quintile in 1979 were still in the lowest quintile in 1989. For individuals in the middle three quintiles, roughly two-fifths (i.e., between 36.9% and 41.1%) were in the same quintiles in 1989 as in 1979.

In part, the finding that there was greater movement in the middle of the hourly wage distribution than at the top or bottom of the distribution reflects the fact that persons at the top or bottom of the distribution can move in only one direction. Persons in the lowest quintile cannot move to a lower quintile, and persons in the highest quintile cannot move to a higher quintile. Also, the hourly wage intervals that define the quintiles in the middle of the wage distribution are narrower than at the top or bottom of the distribution. Therefore, for a person in the middle of the wage distribution, a given absolute change in hourly wages is more likely to result in a movement to another quintile than the same change in hourly wages for someone in the lowest or highest quintile.[12]

Given the amount of wage mobility shown in tables 1 and 2, the degree of hourly wage inequality observed in 1979 and 1989 likely differs from the amount

---

[11] Other research has found that mobility declines with age. (Atkinson et al., *Empirical Studies of Earnings Mobility*, p. 79-80.) Using data on hourly wages from the National Longitudinal Survey for Youth (part of the National Longitudinal Surveys of Labor Market Experience, conducted by the Center for Human Resource Research at Ohio State University), Veum tracked male high school graduates who were between the ages of 16 and 22 in 1979. He found that, by 1989, only 27.4% of the men in the survey were in the same quintile as in 1979. The calculations were based on 454 weighted observations. Veum, Jonathan R. Wage Mobility and Wage Inequality Among Young Workers. *Contemporary Policy Issues*, v. 11, October 1993, p. 31-33, 35.

[12] In this study, the average change in hourly real wages for persons who moved from the third to either the second or fourth quintile was smaller than the average change in hourly real wages for persons who moved from the lowest to the second quintile, but larger than the average change in hourly wages for persons who moved from the highest to the fourth quintile.

of inequality that would be observed using a measure of individual average hourly wages for the entire ten-year period.[13]

Gender

Table 3 shows the relative status of men and women within the overall distribution of hourly wages. Table 3 is derived from the data in table 2. In table 3, the individuals in each cell in table 2 are separated according to gender. Each cell in panel A of table 3 shows the percentage of the total number of men in each cell in table 2, while each cell in panel B shows the percentage of the total number of women in each cell in table 2.[14]

Column 6 of each panel in table 3 shows the percentage of men and women in each quintile in 1979, while row 6 of each panel shows the percentage of men and women in each quintile in 1989. The bottom row of each panel shows the ratio between the percentage of individuals in each quintile in 1989 and the percentage of individuals in each quintile in 1979. For example, 2.10 (row 7, column 1 of panel A) is the ratio of 11.9% (row 6, column 1 of panel A) to 5.6% (row 1, column 6 of panel A).[15]

The data in tables 1 and 3 reveal three important findings. First, table 3 shows that, in 1979 a majority of men were in the upper part of the hourly wage distribution, while a majority of women were in the lower part of the distribution. In 1979, three-fifths (61.1%) of men were in the top two quintiles, compared to 14.4% of women (rows 4 and 5, column 6 of panels A and B). In

---

[13] Two statistical tests (the Gini coefficient and the coefficient of variation) indicate that, when individual hourly wages for 1979 and 1989 are averaged, the distribution of average hourly real wages was more equal than the distribution of hourly real wages for either 1979 or 1989. According to a third statistical test (the variance of the natural log of hourly real wages), the distribution of average hourly wages was slightly less equal than the distribution of hourly wages in 1979, but more equal than the distribution of hourly wages in 1989. These three measures of inequality vary in their sensitivity to changes in different parts of the wage distribution. The Gini coefficient is most sensitive to changes in the middle of the wage distribution, while the variance of the natural log of wages is most sensitive to changes at the lower end of the distribution. A discussion of these measures can be found in: Levy and Murnane, U.S. Earnings Levels and Earnings Inequality: A Review of Recent Trends and Proposed Explanations, p. 1338-39.

[14] Tables 3 through 5 show the relative positions of different social and demographic groups within the overall distribution of hourly wages. With this approach it is possible to determine whether the distribution of wages of certain subgroups became more or less like the distribution of wages among all workers. An alternative approach would be to construct separate transition matrices for each subgroup (i.e., the members of each subgroup would be ranked and divided into quintiles for 1979 and again for 1989). Both the latter approach and the approach used here are used in: Gittleman and Joyce, Earnings Mobility in the United States, 1967-91, p. 5-9.

[15] The ratios in tables 2 through 5 and 7 through 10 were calculated before the percentages were rounded to one decimal place. Therefore, the ratios that appear in the tables may not be the same as the ratios calculated from the rounded percentages.

the same year, 64.4% of women were in the bottom two quintiles, compared to only 19.8% of men (rows 1 and 2, column 6 of panels A and B).

Second, table 1 shows that, from 1979 to 1989, the pattern of mobility for women was the opposite of the pattern of mobility for men. Between 1979 and 1989, there was a similar amount of mobility among men and women: 49.8% of men and 51.1% of women were either upwardly or downwardly mobile (the sum of columns 2 and 3, rows 2 and 3). But table 1 also shows that, from 1979 to 1989, women were more likely to be upwardly than downwardly mobile (35.4% versus 15.7%), while men were more likely to be downwardly than upwardly mobile (31.0% versus 18.8%).[16]

Finally, table 3 shows that despite the relative gains achieved by women during the years from 1979 to 1989, in 1989, a majority of men (53.2%) were still in the top two wage quintiles, while a majority of women (55.9%) were still in the bottom two quintiles (row 6 of panels A and B).[17]

The differences in the relative economic status of men and women in this study persisted despite small differences in educational attainment. In 1989, 32.0% of men and 27.3% of women reported that they had completed 16 or more years of education. In the same year, 34.2% of men and 39.5% of women reported that they had completed 12 years of education only.[18,19]

---

[16] The difference in the percentage of men who were upwardly mobile and the percentage of women who were upwardly mobile was statistically significant. The difference in the percentages of men and women who were downwardly mobile was also statistically significant. In this report, all statistical tests of differences in proportions assume that the subgroup samples are independent. However, the PSID sample used in this study includes some two-earner married couples. In these cases, the chance of one spouse being included in the sample is dependent on the other spouse being included. All statistical tests of significance in this report were made at the .05 significance level. Statistically significant findings indicate that the observed percentages probably reflect actual differences between groups.

[17] Using data on hourly earnings from the PSID survey, Blau and Kahn found that, from 1975 to 1987, women made gains relative to men in the distribution of hourly earnings. (In the PSID survey, earnings include hourly wages plus other sources of labor income, such as overtime pay, bonuses, and that part of business income that is traceable to the business owner's work.) Blau, Francine D, and Lawrence M. Kahn. Rising Wage Inequality and the U.S. Gender Gap. *American Economic Review*, v. 84, May 1994. p. 23-28.

[18] The individuals in this study had slightly higher educational attainment in 1989 than the civilian labor force. In 1989, 28.2% men and 24.3% of women between the ages of 25 and 64 who were in the civilian labor force reported that they had completed four or more years of college, while 36.9% of men and 42.9% of women in this group reported that they had completed 12 years of education. (U.S. Department of Commerce. Bureau of the Census. *Statistical Abstract of the United States: 1991*. Washington, U.S. Govt. Print. Off., 1991. p. 385.)

Education

Table 4 shows the relative status of different educational groups within the overall distribution of hourly wages. The table shows the relative positions of persons who completed 16 or more years of school, 13 to 15 years of school, 12 years of school, and fewer than 12 years of school. The analysis in table 4 is based on the number of years of education completed as of 1989.[20]

Table 4 shows that, in 1979, a person's wage quintile was directly related to his or her years of education.[21,22] For example, 38.4% of individuals with 16 or more years of education were in the highest quintile, but only 6.5% were in the lowest quintile (column 6 of panel A). On the other hand, 9.5% of individuals with no more than a high school education were in the highest quintile, but 24.6% were in the lowest quintile (column 6 of panel C).

Table 1 shows that, from 1979 to 1989, better-educated workers made additional gains relative to less-educated workers. Similar percentages of individuals with 16 or more years of education and individuals with some college were upwardly mobile (30.7% and 31.1%, respectively).[23] But significantly smaller percentages of high school graduates (24.5%) and high school dropouts

---

[19](...continued)

[19] According to data from the March 1996 CPS, 29.3% of working men and 28.0% of working women between the ages of 25 and 64 reported that they were college graduates, while 32.3% of working men and 34.0% of working women in this age group reported that they were high school graduates only. (Calculated by CRS.) The findings from the CPS data are not strictly comparable to the findings from the PSID data used in this study. The CPS data represent individuals who were working at the time of the March 1996 survey, while the PSID data represent individuals who were working at the time of both the 1979 and 1989 surveys. Also, the questions about educational attainment in the two surveys are different.

[20] The reason for choosing years of education completed as of 1989, instead of 1979, was to allow for the effect on wages of additional years of education attained during the period from 1979 to 1989. Individuals with 12 years of education are high school graduates, but some of the individuals with 16 or more years of education may not be college graduates. The questions about educational attainment in the PSID survey are not asked of family heads and spouses each year. Therefore, some of the information on educational attainment in the 1989 survey was carried forward from previous years.

[21] In tables 4 and 5, some cells have few or no individuals. Therefore, comparisons between cells are less reliable than comparisons between quintiles.

[22] Research has found a positive correlation between ability and investment in higher education. Thus, the higher earnings of college-educated persons are probably a reflection of both greater ability and higher educational attainment. Becker, Gary. *Human Capital: A Theoretical and Empirical Analysis, with Special Reference to Education*. 2nd ed. Chicago, University of Chicago Press, 1975. p. 85, 156.

[23] The difference in the percentages of individuals with 16 or more years of education and individuals with some college who were upwardly mobile was not statistically significant.

(12.9%) were upwardly mobile (rows 4 through 7 of table 1).[24] On the other hand, the percentages of individuals who were downwardly mobile were inversely related to years of education.[25] Therefore, persons with 16 or more years of education started the period from 1979 to 1989 from a higher relative position and, during the decade, moved further ahead of less-educated workers.

Race

Table 5 shows the relative status of African-American and white workers within the overall distribution of hourly wages. Because of the differences in the pattern of mobility between men and women described above, table 5 also shows the relative status of white men and women and black men and women within the overall wage distribution.

All Adults. Table 5 shows that, in 1979, the distribution of white adults by quintile was skewed slightly upward. On the other hand, the distribution of black adults was skewed sharply downward. In 1979, 17.3% of white adults were in the lowest wage quintile, while 22.1% were in the highest quintile (column 6 of panel A). By contrast, 39.6% of African-American adults were in the lowest quintile, but only 2.5% were in the highest quintile (column 6 of panel B).

Table 1 shows that, from 1979 to 1989, there was slightly more mobility among white adults than among African-American adults: 51.5% of white adults and 44.0% of black adults were either upwardly or downwardly mobile (the sum of columns 2 and 3, rows 8 and 9). In addition, white adults were more likely than black adults to be upwardly mobile (26.9% versus 21.7%), while similar percentages of white and black adults were downwardly mobile (24.6% and 22.3%).[26] These differences in upward and downward mobility suggest that, on average, between 1979 and 1989, blacks may have lost ground relative to whites. (More will be said on this subject below in the discussion of the "Distribution of Individuals by Wage Class.")

One reason for the difference between African-American and white workers in the distribution of wages is that, in the sample of individuals used in this study, the percentage of white workers with 16 or more years of education in 1989 was more than twice as great as the percentage of black workers with 16

---

[24] The difference in the percentages of individuals with 16 or more years of education and individuals with a high school education and the difference in the percentages of individuals with 16 or more years of education and individuals with less than a high school eduction who were upwardly mobile were statistically significant.

[25] The differences in the percentage of individuals with 16 or more years of education who were downwardly mobile and the percentages of individuals in each of the other educational categories who were downwardly mobile were statistically significant.

[26] The difference in the percentages of black and white adults who were upwardly mobile was statistically significant, while the difference in the percentages of black and white adults who were downwardly mobile was not statistically significant.

or more years of education (31.7% versus 14.3%). On the other hand, the percentage of black workers with less than a high school education in 1989 was more than twice as great as the percentage of white workers with less than a high school education (24.8% versus 11.0%).[27]

Men. As noted in table 3, in both 1979 and 1989, a majority of men in this study were in the top two quintiles of the hourly wage distribution. However, table 5 shows that there were differences in the relative positions of white and black men in the overall distribution of hourly wages. In both 1979 and 1989, white men were more likely to be in the upper part of the wage distribution (column 6 and row 6 of panel C), while black men were more likely to be in the lower part of the distribution (column 6 and row 6 of panel D). In 1989, 55.0% of white men were in the top two quintiles, compared to 30.9% of black men; while 49.7% of black men were in the bottom two quintiles, compared to 25.0% of white men.

Table 3 showed that, from 1979 to 1989, men were more likely to be downwardly than upwardly mobile. Table 1 shows that there were similarities in the general pattern of mobility among black and white men: 18.9% of white men and 17.3% of black men were upwardly mobile, while 31.4% of white men and 31.3% of black men were downwardly mobile (rows 10 and 11, columns 2 and 3).[28]

The similarity in the general pattern of mobility among black and white men disguises some noticeable differences. First, between 1979 and 1989, the percentage of black men in the highest wage quintile rose from 6.1% to 14.5%, while the percentage of white men in the highest quintile fell from 34.4% to 31.1%. Second, while the percentage of black men in the bottom quintile increased from 17.1% to 29.1%, the percentage of white men in the bottom quintile more than doubled from 4.4% to 10.3. These findings suggest that, during the 1980s, some groups of black men made gains relative to white men in the distribution of hourly wages. (More will be said on this subject below in the discussion of the "Distribution of Individuals by Wage Class.")

One reason for the difference between African-American and white men in the distribution of hourly wages is that, in this study sample, the percentage of white men with 16 or more years of education in 1989 was twice as great as the percentage of black men with 16 or more years of education (33.4% versus

---

[27] According to data from the March 1996 CPS, 29.9% of white workers and 18.4% of black workers between the ages of 25 and 64 reported that they were college graduates, while 9.8% of white workers and 13.2% of black workers in this age group reported that they had not graduated from high school. (Calculated by CRS.) Compared to the calculations from the PSID data used in this study, the CPS data suggest that, in recent years, the gap in educational attainment between African-American and white workers has narrowed. See footnote 19 for a description of the differences between the CPS data and the PSID data used in this study.

[28] The differences in the percentages of black and white men who were upwardly and downwardly mobile were not statistically significant.

15.5%). On the other hand, the percentage of black men with less than a high school education in 1989 was twice as great as the percentage of white men with less than a high school education (26.9% versus 12.3%).[29]

Women. Although the relative positions of black and white men in the overall wage distribution differed, this distinction did not exist between black and white women. Table 3 showed that, in both 1979 and 1989, the majority of women were in the bottom two quintiles of the hourly wage distribution. Table 5 shows that, in both 1979 and 1989, a majority of both black women and white women were in the lower part of the overall wage distribution, but that the concentration of black women at the bottom of the wage distribution was greater than the concentration of white women (column 6 and row 6 of panels E and F). For instance, in 1989, 52.5% of white women and 75.2% black women were in the bottom two wage quintiles.

Table 3 showed that, from 1979 to 1989, women were more likely to be upwardly than downwardly mobile. Table 1 shows that both white and black women made gains relative to men, but that white women made greater gains than black women (rows 12 and 13.) White women were more likely than black women to be upwardly mobile (37.4% versus 24.5%). But white women were as likely as black women to be downwardly mobile (15.6% and 16.5%, respectively).[30]

Table 5 shows where the difference in upward mobility between black and white women occurred. In the top two quintiles of the hourly wage distribution, black women gained ground relative to white women, but they lost ground relative to white women in the bottom two quintiles. In the two top quintiles, the percentage of black women more than doubled (from 4.5% to 9.8%), while the percentage of white women increased by two-thirds (from 16.3% to 26.6%). On the other hand, the percentage of white women in the bottom two quintiles fell from 62.8% to 52.5%, while the percentage of black women in the bottom two quintiles remained approximately the same, at 73.5% and 75.2%, respectively. These findings suggest that, on average, black women did not gain ground relative to white women. (More will be said on this subject below in the discussion of the "Distribution of Individuals by Wage Class.")

One reason for the difference between black and white women in the distribution of hourly wages is that, in this study sample, the percentage of white women with 16 or more years of education in 1989 was twice as great as

---

[29] According to data from the March 1996 CPS, 30.7% of working white men and 15.9% of working black men between the ages of 25 and 64 reported that they were college graduates, while 11.5% of working white men and 16.0% of working black men in this age group reported that they had not graduated from high school. (Calculated by CRS.) See footnote 19 for a description of the differences between the CPS data and the PSID data used in this study.

[30] The difference in the percentages of black and white women who were upwardly mobile was statistically significant, but the difference in the percentages of black and white women who were downwardly mobile was not statistically significant.

the percentage of black women with 16 or more years of education (29.5% versus 13.5%). On the other hand, the percentage of black women with less than a high school education in 1989 was more than twice as great as the percentage of white women with less than a high school education (23.4% versus 9.2%).[31]

Distribution of Individuals by Wage Class

The previous section analyzed changes in the ranking of individuals in the distribution of hourly wages from 1979 to 1989. But an analysis of relative mobility does not capture changes in real wages or in the distribution of hourly wages. This section of the report uses the concept of absolute mobility, a broader concept of mobility, to examine changes in the distribution of individuals by wage class from 1979 to 1989.

In the previous section, individuals were ranked according to their hourly wages in 1979 and again according to their hourly wages in 1989. For each year, individuals were divided into quintiles. Their quintiles in 1989 were compared to their quintiles in 1979. That approach shows the extent to which the rankings of individuals changed from 1979 to 1989, but it does not reveal whether there were changes in the level or distribution of hourly real wages.

In this section, individuals are ranked and divided into quintiles according to their hourly real wages in 1979. Then, instead of ranking and grouping individuals into quintiles based on their hourly real wages in 1989, individuals are arranged according to the real wage intervals that define the hourly real wage quintiles in 1979.[32] The distribution of individuals by wage class in 1989 is then compared to the distribution of individuals by wage class in 1979.

The differences between the findings in this section and the findings in the previous section reflect changes in the wage structure from 1979 to 1989. If the wage structure did not change, the wage intervals that define the quintiles for 1989 would be the same as the wage intervals that define the quintiles for 1979. In that case, the findings in this section would be the same as the findings in the previous section, and the measurements of relative and absolute mobility would be the same.

---

[31] According to data from the March 1996 CPS, 29.0% of working white women and 20.7% of working black women between the ages of 25 and 64 reported that they were college graduates, while 7.7% of working white women and 10.8% of working black women in this age group reported that they had not graduated from high school. (Calculated by CRS.) See footnote 19 for a description of the differences between the CPS data and the PSID data used in this study.

[32] The hourly real wage intervals that define the 1979 quintiles (where 1979 hourly wages are stated in 1989 dollars) are: lowest quintile, more than $0.00 but less than or equal to $6.70; second quintile, more than $6.70 but less than or equal to $9.22; third quintile, more than $9.22 but less than or equal to $12.35; fourth quintile, more than $12.35 but less than or equal to $15.92; and highest quintile, more than $15.92.

The findings on the distribution of individuals by wage class are shown in tables 6 through 10, beginning on page 35. Table 6 provides a summary of the general findings from tables 7 through 10. Table 7 shows the change in the distribution of prime-age adults by wage class from 1979 to 1989. Tables 8 through 10 show the relative positions of individuals by gender, years of education, and race within the overall distribution of individuals by wage class and how the relative status of these social and demographic groups changed from 1979 to 1989. Since the wage intervals used in the tables in this section are based on the wage intervals that define the wage quintiles for 1979, the percentages in column 6 in tables 7 through 10 are the same as the percentages in column 6 in tables 2 through 5.

Prime-Age Adults

Many individuals who experienced downward *relative* mobility from 1979 to 1989 nevertheless experienced upward *absolute* mobility. Table 1 showed that, between 1979 and 1989, one-half (50.4%) of individuals were either upwardly or downwardly mobile. The percentage of individuals who moved to a higher quintile was approximately the same as the percentage of individuals who moved to a lower quintile (26.3% versus 24.1%). Table 6 (row 1) shows that, from 1979 to 1989, one-half (52.0%) of the individuals in this study moved to higher or lower wage classes. But more than twice as many individuals moved to higher wage classes than to lower wage classes (36.5% versus 15.5%).

The reason for the difference between the movement of individuals by quintile and the movement of individuals by wage class is that, during the 1980s, the wage structure shifted upward. Among the individuals in this study, both the average and median hourly real wage increased at an annual rate of 1.1%.[33] From 1979 to 1989, the average real wage increased from $11.90 to $13.27, while the median real wage increased from $9.78 to $10.93.[34,35] Therefore, many individuals who lost ground relative to other individuals during the 1980s nevertheless experienced an increase in hourly real wages.[36] This increase in hourly real wages may understate the increase in real compensation.

---

[33] If hourly wages are ranked from highest to lowest, the median wage is the wage in the middle of the distribution; half of all wages are above the median and half of all wages are below the median.

[34] In this report, all calculations of average and median hourly real wages consist of weighted averages and medians. See page 44 for a discussion of PSID sample weights.

[35] In this report, the average hourly wage is higher than the median hourly wage because there are more extreme values at the upper end of the wage distribution than at the lower end.

[36] In table 7, individuals are grouped by real wage intervals. Therefore, other than the observation that 36.5% of individuals moved to higher wage intervals and 15.5% of individuals moved to lower wage intervals, it is not possible to say what percentage of individuals experienced an absolute increase or decrease in hourly real wages.

since fringe benefits increased as a share of total employee compensation during the 10-year period.[37]

The upward shift in the wage structure does not reveal whether there was a change in the distribution of hourly real wages. Three different statistical tests indicate that, between 1979 and 1989, the distribution of hourly wages among individuals in the study sample become more unequal.[38]

The findings of an increase in hourly real wages and an increase in wage inequality are consistent with results from studies using time-series data.

Gender

Table 3 showed that, between 1979 and 1989, the pattern of relative wage mobility for women was the opposite of the pattern of mobility for men: women were more likely to be upwardly than downwardly mobile, while men were more likely to be downwardly than upwardly mobile. Table 6, on the other hand, shows that both sexes made gains in hourly real wages (rows 2 and 3). However, because they gained ground relative to men, more women than men moved into higher wage classes. From 1979 to 1989, almost twice as many women as men moved to higher wage classes (47.7% versus 27.3%), while twice as many men as women moved to lower wages classes (20.0% versus 10.1%).[39]

The relative gains made by women in this study are also reflected in changes in the wage gap between men and women. Between 1979 and 1989, both the average and median hourly real wages of women increased relative to the average and median hourly real wages of men. From 1979 to 1989, the average wage of women increased from 59.9% to 67.8% of the average wage of men. The median wage of women increased from 53.9% to 65.4% of the median wage of men. These findings are consistent with results from time-series studies.

Table 8 reveals an important difference in the pattern of change in the distribution of men and women by wage class.[40] Among women, there was a general movement to higher wage classes (row 7 of panel B). For instance, the

---

[37] Between 1979 and 1989, supplements to wages and salaries increased from 16.5% to 17.6% of total employee compensation. U.S. Department of Commerce. Bureau of Economic Analysis. *Survey of Current Business*, v. 76, January/February 1996. p. 116.

[38] Three statistical tests of equality were performed on the distribution of hourly wages for 1979 and for 1989. Each test showed that the distribution of wages became more unequal during the 10-year period. The three statistical tests were: the Gini coefficient, the variance of the natural log of wages, and the coefficient of variation. See footnote 13 for a brief description of these statistical tests.

[39] The differences in the percentages of men and women who moved to higher and lower wages classes were statistically significant.

[40] In tables 8 and 9, some cells have few or no individuals. Therefore, comparisons between cells are less reliable than comparisons between wage classes.

percentage of women in the lowest wage class fell from 37.3% to 24.2%, while the percentage of women in the highest wage class increased from 5.2% to 13.7% (column 6 and row 6 of panel B). But, among men, there was movement towards both the highest and lowest wage classes (row 7 of panel A). The percentage of men in the highest wage class increased from 32.3% to 39.7%, while the percentage of men in the lowest wage class increased from 5.6% to 9.5% (column 6 and row 6 of panel A).[41]

Research using time-series data has found that, among men, there was a polarization in the distribution of wages and a hollowing out of the middle of the wage distribution during the 1980s. These findings have led some analysts to argue that, among men in the 1980s, there was a decline in "middle class" jobs. The analysis here, using longitudinal data, indicates that, among men, there was a polarization in the distribution of hourly real wages, but, depending on how the middle class is defined, there may or may not have been a hollowing out of the wage distribution. Table 8 shows that the percentage of men in the middle three wage classes decreased from 62.2% to 50.8%, but the percentage of men in the middle wage class remained steady at 19.2%. Thus, if the middle class is defined as individuals in the middle three wage classes, the findings in this study are consistent with the findings from time-series studies that have found a polarization in wages among men and a hollowing out of the middle of the wage distribution. On the other hand, if the middle class is defined as individuals in the middle wage class, the findings in this study are not consistent with findings from time-series studies. (More will be said on the subject of wage polarization in the section on "Race" below.)

One reason for the different findings on wage polarization in this study, compared to the findings from studies using time-series data, is that hourly wages tend to increase with age (i.e., work experience). Studies based on time-series data generally compare the wages of similar cross sections of the population (e.g., persons between the ages of 25 and 64) at different points in time. In this study, the wages of individuals who were between the ages of 25 and 54 in 1979 are compared to the wages of the same individuals who were between the ages of 35 and 64 in 1989. Thus, the sample for 1989 has up to 10 more years of work experience than the sample for 1979 (depending on whether an individual worked continuously from 1979 to 1989). Thus, unlike the findings from time-series studies, the findings from this study are more likely to reflect the effects of increased work experience.[42]

---

[41] Between 1979 and 1987, there was an increase in the average annual hours worked by women, but not by men. (Levy and Murnane, U.S. Earnings Levels and Earnings Inequality: A Review of Recent Trends and Proposed Explanations, p. 1334.) Therefore, an analysis of annual wages could yield results different from an analysis of hourly wages.

[42] Bound and Johnson found that, in 1988, except for women with less than a high school education, the largest increase in the return to experience was between persons with less than 10 years of potential experience and persons with 10-19 years of potential experience. The authors examined the return to experience among persons with 0-9, 10-

(continued...)

Education

Table 1 showed that, between 1979 and 1989, individuals with at least some college were more likely to be upwardly than downwardly mobile, while individuals with a high school education or less were more likely to be downwardly than upwardly mobile. Nevertheless, because of the upward shift in the wage structure, table 6 shows that, at each educational level, more individuals moved to higher wage classes than moved to lower wage classes (rows 4 through 7).

Table 6 suggests that the gains in hourly real wages experienced by better-educated workers were greater than the gains experienced by less-educated workers. Except for persons with less than a high school education, individuals in each educational category experienced similar gains; 39.3% of individuals with 16 or more years of education, 39.5% of individuals with some college, and 37.1% of individuals with a high school education moved to higher wage classes.[43] But the percentage of individuals who moved to lower wage classes was inversely related to educational attainment. Thus, 10.6% of individuals with 16 or more years of education moved to lower wage classes, compared to 20.7% of individuals with less than a high school education.[44]

An analysis of average hourly real wages confirms the findings from table 6. The average hourly wage of individuals with 16 or more years of education increased at an annual rate of 1.8% (from $15.38 to $18.47). The average hourly wage of individuals with some college increased at an annual rate of 1.1% (from $11.61 to $12.90). And the average hourly wage of high school graduates increased at an annual rate of 0.6% (from $10.35 to $11.02). But the average hourly wage of individuals with less than a high school education decreased at an annual rate of 0.7% (from $8.78 to $8.22). Thus, between 1979 and 1989, the wage gap between individuals with 16 or more years of education and each of

---

[42](...continued)
19, 20-29, and 30 or more years of potential experience. (Bound, John, and George Johnson. Changes in the Structure of Wages in the 1980's: An Evaluation of Alternative Explanations. *American Economic Review*, v. 82, June 1992 p. 373.) Potential work experience and is usually calculated as an individual's age minus years of education minus 6 (to account for the age at which most children begin school).

[43] The difference in the percentages of individuals with 16 or more years of education and individuals with some college and the difference in the percentages of individuals with 16 or more years of education and individuals with a high school education who moved to higher wage classes were not statistically significant. But the difference in the percentages of individuals with 16 or more years of education and individuals with less than a high school education who moved to higher wage classes was statistically significant.

[44] The differences in the percentage of individuals with 16 or more years of education who moved to lower wage classes and the percentages of individuals in each of the other educational categories who moved to lower wage classes were statistically significant.

the other educational categories increased.[45] These findings are consistent with the results from time-series studies.

Table 6 indicates that, among individuals with less than a high school education, more individuals moved to higher wage classes than moved to lower wage classes. But an analysis of average hourly wages indicates that the average hourly wage of these individuals declined. Panel D of table 9 reveals the reason for this apparent inconsistency. Among individuals who fell to lower wages classes, two out of five (39.3%) fell more than one wage class. But among individuals who moved to higher wage classes, only one in five (19.4%) rose more than one wage class. Thus, the decline in the average hourly wage among individuals who moved down was greater than the increase in the average hourly wage among individuals who moved up.[46]

Race

All Adults. Table 10 shows the relative distribution of white and African-American workers within the distribution of individuals by wage class. Table 1 showed that white adults were more likely than black adults to be upwardly mobile, but that similar percentages of black and white adults were downwardly mobile. Table 6 shows that, because of rising real wages during the 1980s, similar percentages of white and black workers moved to higher wage classes (36.8% and 34.8%, respectively). Likewise, similar percentages of white and black workers moved to lower wages classes (15.5% and 16.9%, respectively).[47]

The differences in the percentages of black and white workers who moved to higher and lower wage classes were not statistically significant, but the direction of the differences suggests that the wage gap between black and white workers may have widened. The percentage of white workers who moved to higher wage classes was slightly greater than the percentage of black workers who moved to higher wage classes, while the percentage of black workers who moved to lower wage classes was slightly greater than the percentage of white workers who moved to lower wage classes. An analysis of hourly real wages indicates that the average hourly real wage of both white and black workers increased. However, the wage gap between white and black workers also increased. The average hourly wage of white workers increased at an annual rate of 1.1% (from $12.29 to $13.73), while the average hourly wage of black

---

[45] In 1979, the average hourly real wage of college graduates was 32.5% higher than the hourly wage of individuals with some college, 48.6% higher than the hourly wage of high school graduates, and 75.3% higher than the average hourly wage of individuals with less than a high school education. In 1989, these percentages increased to 43.2%, 67.6%, and 124.6%, respectively.

[46] Among individuals who moved to lower wage classes, the average hourly real wage decreased by $5.49 (from $13.83 to $8.34). Among individuals who moved to higher wage classes, the average hourly real wage increased by $3.25 (from $7.85 to $11.10).

[47] The differences in the percentages of black and white adults who moved to higher and lower wage classes were not statistically significant.

workers increased at an annual rate of 0.7% (from $8.79 to $9.46). At the same time, the average hourly wage of black workers decreased from 71.5% to 68.9% of the average wage of white workers.

Men. Table 1 showed that similar percentages of white and black men were upwardly and downwardly mobile. Likewise, table 6 shows that similar percentages of white and black men moved to higher (26.9% and 31.4%) and lower wages classes (19.9% and 23.1%).[48] Table 1 also showed that, among both black and white men, more men were downwardly than upwardly mobile. However, because of rising real wages, table 6 shows that more men of both races moved to higher wages classes than moved to lower wage classes.

An analysis of hourly real wages indicates that, while the average hourly real wage of both white and black men increased, the wage gap between the two groups also increased. The average hourly wage of white men increased at an annual rate of 0.7% (from $14.85 to $15.85), while the average wage of black men increased at an annual rate of 0.4% (from $11.06 to $11.47). At the same time, the average hourly wage of black men decreased from 74.5% to 72.4% of the average wage of white men. The findings from time-series data differ, depending on the dataset used and the sample studied. Some studies have found that, from 1979 to 1989, the wage gap between black and white men decreased, while other studies have found that the gap increased.

One reason for the decline in the percentage of black men in the middle wage class was that black men with 16 or more years of education tended to move out of the middle wage class into the highest wage class, while black men with only a high school education tended to move out of the middle wage class into lower wage classes.[49]

Table 10 reveals a difference in the distribution of white and black men by wage class. Table 7 showed that, among men, there was a movement toward both the highest and lowest wage classes. The percentage of men in the three middle wage classes decreased, but the percentage of men in the middle wage class remained the same. Table 10 shows that this was also the pattern of change among white men (row 7 of panel C). The pattern of change among black men was similar, but not identical, to the pattern of change among white men. Like the pattern among white men, there was a movement among black men toward both the highest and lowest wages classes. But, unlike the pattern among white men, the percentage of black men in the middle wage class declined. These findings are consistent with the results from time-series studies of the 1980s that found that, for all men, there was a polarization in the distribution of wages and a hollowing out of the middle of the wage distribution.

---

[48] The differences in the percentages of black and white men who moved to higher and lower wages classes were not statistically significant.

[49] The increase in the percentage of white men with 16 or more years of education who were in the highest wage class was approximately the same as the increase in the percentage of black men with 16 or more years of education who were in the highest (continued...)

Women. Table 1 showed that more white women than black women were upwardly mobile, but that similar percentages of black and white women were downwardly mobile. Likewise, table 6 shows that significantly more white women than black women moved to higher wage classes (49.8% versus 37.0%), but that similar percentages of black and white women moved to lower wage classes (9.6% and 12.9%).[50]

An analysis of hourly real wages indicates that, while the average hourly real wage of both white and black women increased, the wage gap between the two groups also increased. The average hourly wage of white women increased at an annual rate of 2.0% (from $8.95 to $10.96), while the average hourly wage of black women increased at an annual rate of 1.1% (from $7.32 to $8.17). But the average hourly wage of black women decreased from 81.8% to 74.5% of the average hourly wage of white women. These findings are generally consistent with the findings from time-series studies.

Table 10 reveals a difference in the distribution of white and black women by wage class. Among white women, there was a general movement toward higher wage classes (row 7 of panel E). Among black women, there was a movement to the next-to-lowest wage class and to the top two wage classes (row 7 of panel F). Thus, the percentage of white women in the next-to-lowest wage class decreased, while the percentage of black women in the next-to-lowest wage class increased.

One reason for the increase in the percentage of black women in the next-to-lowest wage class was that black women with 16 or more years of education tended to move out of the lowest wage class to higher wage classes, while some black women with only a high school education moved out of the middle wage class to the next-to-lowest wage class.[51]

---

[49](...continued)
wage class (5.0 and 5.8 percentage points, respectively). But the upward movement of white men was mainly from the next-to-highest wage class, while the upward movement of black men was mainly from the middle wage class. (The percentage of white men with 16 or more years of education who were in the next-to-highest wage class decreased by 3.9 percentage points, while the percentage of black men with 16 or more years of education who were in the middle wage class decreased by 4.0 percentage points.) At the same time, the percentage of black men with only a high school education who were in the middle wage class declined by 8.1 percentage points, with most of these men moving to the two lowest wage classes. (The percentage of black men with only a high school education who were in the two lowest wage classes increased by 10.1 percentage points.) On the other hand, the percentage of white men with only a high school education who were in the middle wage class declined by only 0.6 percentage points.

[50] The difference in the percentages of black and white women who moved to higher wage classes was statistically significant, but the difference in the percentages of black and white women who moved to lower wage classes was not statistically significant.

[51] The upward movement of black women with 16 or more years of education was mainly from the lowest wage class, while the upward movement of white women with 16
(continued...)

Summary

This section summarizes the findings from this study and relates the findings to several economic issues that have policy implications.

Wage Mobility and the Wage Structure

The study found that, from 1979 to 1989, there was a significant amount of wage mobility as well as a noticeable change in the level and distribution of real wages. The study found that:

Half (50.4%) of all workers moved to either higher (26.3%) or lower (24.1%) quintiles in the distribution of hourly wages.

The distribution of hourly wages became more unequal.

There was an increase in average and median hourly real wages.

More than twice as many workers moved to higher wage classes than moved to lower wage classes (36.5% versus 15.5%).

These findings reflect the dynamic nature of labor markets in the United States. During the 1980s, many individuals experienced temporary or permanent changes -- in some cases, large changes -- in hourly real wages. As a result, although wage inequality increased from 1979 to 1989, measuring the distribution of individual average hourly wages over the 10-year decade would likely show a different degree of inequality than the amount of inequality found in either 1979 or 1989. In addition, the findings show that, although many individuals fell behind others in the distribution of hourly wages, many of these individuals nevertheless experienced an increase in hourly real wages.

---

[51](...continued)
or more years of education was mainly from the next-to-lowest and middle wage classes. As a result, the percentage of white women with 16 or more years of education who were in the next-to-lowest wage class decreased (by 4.1 percentage points), but the percentage of black women with 16 or more years of education who were in the next-to-lowest wage class was unchanged. At the same time, the percentage of black women with only a high school education who were in the next-to-lowest wage class increased by 10.6 percentage points, while the percentage of white women with only a high school education who were in the next-to-lowest wage class decreased by 1.4 percentage points. The percentages of both black and white women with only a high school education who were in the lowest wage class decreased. But the percentage of black women with only a high school education who were in the middle wage class decreased (by 3.1 percentage points), while the percentage of white women with only a high school education who were in the middle wage class increased (by 4.4 percentage points).

Gender

This study found that, from 1979 to 1989, women made significant gains relative to men in the distribution of hourly wages. Among men, there was a polarization in the distribution in hourly real wages.

- From 1979 to 1989, the percentage of women in the top two wage quintiles increased from 14.4% to 24.1%, while the percentage of women in the bottom two quintiles decreased from 64.4% to 55.9%.

- The percentage of men in the top two wage quintiles decreased from 61.1% to 53.2%, while the percentage of men in the bottom two quintiles increased from 19.8% to 26.8%. Nevertheless, because of rising real wages, more men moved to higher wage classes than moved to lower wage classes (27.3% versus 20.0%).

- The average hourly real wage of women increased from 59.9% to 67.8% of the average hourly real wage of men.

- The percentage of men in the top and bottom wages classes increased (by 7.4 and 3.9 percentage points, respectively), while the percentage of men in the middle three wage classes declined (from 62.2% to 50.8%).

Although the level of educational attainment among men and women in the study sample was similar, women were underrepresented at the top of the hourly wage distribution at both the beginning and end of the study period. Nevertheless, the findings show that as women gained work experience their wages increased relative to the wages of men. The findings also suggest that employment opportunities for women improved during the 1980s.[52] Whether these findings indicate that women have yet to achieve equal opportunities in employment is uncertain, since equal opportunities may nevertheless result in unequal hourly wages.

The findings suggest that there was also a change in employment opportunities for men. Some men reaped the benefits of increased work experience and other changes that increased their real wages. But, for other men, an increase in work experience did not offset the effect of changes in employment that resulted in stagnant or falling real wages.

---

[52] This report does not explore the causes of the observed changes in hourly real wages from 1979 to 1989. Employment opportunities may change for several reasons, including changes in employer hiring practices, government policies (e.g., with respect to regulation of product markets, trade, taxes, spending, and the minimum wage), union membership, technology, and consumer tastes.

Education

The study found that, from 1979 to 1989, there was an increase in the wage gap between better-educated and less-educated workers.

- From 1979 to 1989, the percentage of persons with 16 or more years of education in the top two wage quintiles increased from 61.4% to 67.8%, while the percentage of persons with no more than a high school degree in the top two quintiles fell from 30.7% to 27.1%.

- Larger percentages of individuals at each educational level moved to higher wage classes than moved to lower wage classes. Among workers with 16 or more years of education, 39.3% moved to higher wage classes, while 10.6% moved to lower wage classes. Among workers with a high school education only, 37.1% moved to higher wage classes, while 17.8% moved to lower wage classes.

- Although more high school dropouts moved to higher wage classes than to lower wage classes, the average hourly real wage of high school dropouts declined.

These findings show the increased importance of education and training in United States labor markets during the 1980s. In 1979, the average hourly real wage of better-educated workers was greater than the average hourly real wage of less-educated workers. From 1979 to 1989, better-educated workers made additional gains relative to less-educated workers. On the other hand, for most workers, the findings show the effects of increased work experience and other changes in raising real wages. Despite the increase in the wage gap between better- and less-educated workers and the decline in average hourly real wages of high school dropouts, more less-educated workers moved to higher wage classes than moved to lower wage classes.

Race

All Adults. The study found that, between 1979 and 1989, some groups of black workers gained ground relative to white workers, while other groups of black workers lost ground. However, the average hourly real wage of black workers declined relative to the average hourly real wage of white workers.

- From 1979 to 1989, the distribution of white workers by wage quintiles was virtually unchanged. On the other hand, the percentage of African-American workers in the top wage quintile increased from 2.5% to 7.1%, while the percentage of black workers in the bottom two quintiles increased from 58.3% to 65.2%.

- Among both white and African-American workers, the percentage of workers who moved to higher wage classes was greater than the percentage of workers who moved to lower wage classes (36.8%

versus 15.5% for white workers, and 34.8% versus 16.9% for black workers).

- The average hourly real wage of black workers decreased from 71.5% to 68.9% of the average hourly real wage of white workers.

Men. The study found that, from 1979 to 1989, black men gained ground relative to white men at the highest and lowest quintiles of the hourly wage distribution. The gap in average hourly real wages between black and white men increased. There was a polarization in the distribution wages among both black and white men.

- From 1979 to 1989, the percentage of black men in the top quintile increased from 6.1% to 14.5%, while the percentage of white men in the top wage quintile fell from 34.4% to 31.1%. In the bottom wage quintile, the percentage of black men increased from 17.1% to 29.1%, while the percentage of white men more than doubled from 4.4% to 10.3%.

- Among both white and African-American men, more workers moved to higher wage classes than moved to lower wage classes (26.9% versus 19.9% for white men, and 31.4% versus 23.1% for black men).

- The average hourly real wage of black men decreased from 74.5% to 72.4% of the average hourly real wage of white men.

- The percentage of white men in the top and bottom wage classes increased by 6.4 and 3.7 percentage points, respectively. The percentage of black men in the top and bottom wage classes increased by 13.6 and 7.3 percentage points, respectively. The percentage of black men in the middle wage class declined (from 22.4% to 14.8%), while the percentage of white men in the middle wage class remained approximately the same (at 18.9% and 19.6%, respectively).

Women. The study found that, from 1979 to 1989, black women gained ground relative to white women at the top of the hourly wage distribution, but lost ground relative to white women at the bottom of the distribution. The gap in average hourly real wages between black and white women increased.

- From 1979 to 1989, the percentage of black women in the top two wage quintiles more than doubled (from 4.5% to 9.8%), while the percentage of white women in the top two quintiles increased by almost two-thirds (from 16.3% to 26.6%). On the other hand, the percentage of white women in the bottom two quintiles fell (from 62.8% to 52.5%), while the percentage of black women in the bottom two quintiles remained approximately the same (at 73.5% to 75.2%, respectively).

- Almost five times as many white women moved to higher wage classes as moved to lower wage classes (49.8% versus 9.6%), while three times as many black women moved to higher wage classes as moved to lower wage classes (37.0% versus 12.9%).

- The average hourly real wage of black women decreased from 81.8% to 74.5% of the average hourly real wage of white women.

These findings show that as some black workers gained work experience, their wages increased relative to the wages of white workers. The findings also suggest that, for some black workers, employment opportunities improved during the 1980s. But, for other black workers, an increase in work experience did not offset the effect of changes in employment that led to stagnant or declining real wages.

To some extent, the different patterns of mobility between African-American and white workers reflect differences in educational attainment. Approximately twice as many white workers as black workers in the study sample had completed 16 or more years of education, while approximately twice as many black workers as white workers had less than a high school degree. (This relationship held among both men and women.) Although educational attainment is only one factor affecting relative wages, the findings from this study reflect the importance of educational opportunities and attainment in today's economy. Thus, to some extent, gains in relative educational attainment by black workers would likely translate into gains in relative wages.[53]

---

[53] In addition to years (i.e., quantity) of schooling, some research has found that wage differentials between whites and African-Americans are influenced by differences in the quality of education. In this case, closing the gap in years of schooling should reduce, but may not eliminate, the gap in wages. Maxwell, Nan L. The Effect on Black-White Wage Differences of Differences in the Quantity and Quality of Education. *Industrial and Labor Relations Review*, v. 47, January 1994. p. 258; Card, David, and Alan B. Krueger. School Quality and Black-White Relative Earnings: A Direct Assessment. *Quarterly Journal of Economics*, v. 107, February 1992. p. 187, 194.

TABLE 1. Summary of Findings on Wage Mobility, 1979-89	No Change in Quintile (1)	Higher Quintile (2)	Lower Quintile (3)	Total (4)
Table 2: Wage Mobility, Prime-Age Adults, 1979-89 (1)	49.7%	26.3%	24.1%	100.0%
Table 3: Wage Mobility, by Gender, 1979-89				
Men (2)	50.3%	18.8%	31.0%	100.0%
Women (3)	48.9%	35.4%	15.7%	100.0%
Table 4: Wage Mobility, by Years of Education, 1979-89				
16 Years or More (4)	51.3%	30.7%	17.9%	100.0%
Between 13 and 15 Years (5)	44.7%	31.1%	24.2%	100.0%
12 Years (6)	48.1%	24.5%	27.4%	100.0%
Fewer than 12 Years (7)	57.7%	12.9%	29.3%	100.0%
Table 5: Wage Mobility, by Race and Gender, 1979-89				
White Adults (8)	48.5%	26.9%	24.6%	100.0%
African-American Adults (9)	56.0%	21.7%	22.3%	100.0%
White Men (10)	49.7%	18.9%	31.4%	100.0%
African-American Men (11)	51.4%	17.3%	31.3%	100.0%
White Women (12)	47.0%	37.4%	15.6%	100.0%
African-American Women (13)	59.0%	24.5%	16.5%	100.0%

Notes: Column 1 is the sum of the diagonal cells in each table (i.e., the cells running from the upper left to the lower right of each table). Column 2 is the sum of the cells above the diagonal in each table. Column 3 is the sum of the cells below the diagonal. Because of rounding, the percentages in tables 2 through 5 may not add to the percentages in table 1. Totals in table 1 may not add because of rounding.

TABLE 2. Percent of Individuals from Each 1979 Quintile in Each 1989 Quintile: Prime-Age Adults

Quintile in 1979	Quintile in 1989					
	Lowest (1)	Second (2)	Third (3)	Fourth (4)	Highest (5)	All (6)
Lowest (1)	12.7%	4.9%	1.5%	0.8%	0.1%	19.9%
Second (2)	3.8%	8.2%	5.5%	1.8%	0.7%	20.0%
Third (3)	1.9%	4.5%	7.4%	5.1%	1.1%	20.0%
Fourth (4)	1.1%	1.9%	4.2%	8.0%	4.8%	19.9%
Highest (5)	0.5%	0.4%	1.4%	4.4%	13.4%	20.1%
All (6)	20.0%	19.9%	20.0%	20.0%	20.0%	100.0%
Percent of Individuals Remaining in the Same Quintile (7)	63.6%	41.1%	36.9%	40.0%	66.6%	

Notes: Prime-age adults are persons who were 25 to 54 years of age in 1979. The percentages in table 2 were calculated by CRS using data from the Panel Study of Income Dynamics (PSID). The percentages are based on 1,741 weighted observations. Totals may not add because of rounding.

TABLE 3. Percent of Individuals from Each 1979 Quintile in Each 1989 Quintile: Prime-Age Adults, by Gender

	Quintile in 1989					
	A. Men					
Quintile in 1979	Lowest (1)	Second (2)	Third (3)	Fourth (4)	Highest (5)	All (6)
Lowest (1)	4.2%	0.6%	0.7%	0.1%	0.0%	5.6%
Second (2)	3.3%	6.3%	3.2%	1.0%	0.3%	14.2%
Third (3)	1.8%	4.2%	7.5%	4.4%	1.3%	19.2%
Fourth (4)	1.6%	3.1%	6.3%	10.7%	7.1%	28.8%
Highest (5)	1.0%	0.7%	2.3%	6.7%	21.6%	32.3%
All (6)	11.9%	14.9%	20.0%	22.9%	30.3%	100.0%
Ratio of 1989 Quintile to 1979 Quintile (7)	2.10	1.05	1.04	0.80	0.94	
	B. Women					
	Lowest (1)	Second (2)	Third (3)	Fourth (4)	Highest (5)	All (6)
Lowest (1)	23.0%	10.1%	2.4%	1.5%	0.2%	37.3%
Second (2)	4.3%	10.5%	8.3%	2.7%	1.2%	27.1%
Third (3)	2.1%	4.8%	7.3%	6.0%	0.9%	21.1%
Fourth (4)	0.4%	0.6%	1.6%	4.7%	1.9%	9.2%
Highest (5)	0.0%	0.0%	0.3%	1.5%	3.4%	5.2%
All (6)	29.9%	26.0%	20.0%	16.5%	7.6%	100.0%
Ratio of 1989 Quintile to 1979 Quintile (7)	0.80	0.96	0.95	1.80	1.45	

Notes: Prime-age adults are persons who were 25 to 54 years of age in 1979. The percentages in table 3 were calculated by CRS using data from the Panel Study of Income Dynamics (PSID). The percentages are based on weighted observations for 897 men and 844 women. Totals may not add because of rounding.

TABLE 4. Percent of Individuals from Each 1979 Quintile in Each 1989 Quintile: Prime-Age Adults, by Level of Education

Quintile in 1979	Quintile in 1989					
	A. 16 or More Years of Education in 1989					
	Lowest (1)	Second (2)	Third (3)	Fourth (4)	Highest (5)	All (6)
Lowest (1)	2.6%	1.0%	1.7%	0.9%	0.3%	6.5%
Second (2)	2.0%	3.4%	4.1%	2.4%	0.9%	12.8%
Third (3)	1.0%	2.7%	6.9%	5.7%	3.1%	19.4%
Fourth (4)	0.2%	0.8%	3.5%	7.8%	10.6%	23.0%
Highest (5)	1.0%	0.3%	1.0%	5.3%	30.8%	38.4%
All (6)	6.8%	8.2%	17.2%	22.1%	45.7%	100.0%
Ratio of 1989 Quintile to 1979 Quintile (7)	1.05	0.64	0.89	0.96	1.19	
	B. Between 13 and 15 Years of Education in 1989					
	Lowest (1)	Second (2)	Third (3)	Fourth (4)	Highest (5)	All (6)
Lowest (1)	10.2%	5.6%	1.4%	0.8%	0.0%	18.0%
Second (2)	2.2%	7.8%	8.2%	3.9%	1.7%	23.9%
Third (3)	2.5%	3.5%	5.6%	5.5%	0.5%	17.7%
Fourth (4)	1.3%	2.4%	5.1%	8.6%	3.5%	20.8%
Highest (5)	0.0%	0.9%	2.0%	4.3%	12.4%	19.7%
All (6)	16.1%	20.3%	22.3%	23.2%	18.1%	100.0%
Ratio of 1989 Quintile to 1979 Quintile (7)	0.90	0.85	1.26	1.11	0.92	continued

See notes at the end of the table.

TABLE 4. Percent of Individuals from Each 1979 Quintile in Each 1989 Quintile: Prime-Age Adults, by Level of Education -- continued

	Quintile in 1989					
	C. 12 Years of Education in 1989					
Quintile in 1979	Lowest (1)	Second (2)	Third (3)	Fourth (4)	Highest (5)	All (6)
Lowest (1)	14.8%	7.7%	1.1%	0.9%	0.0%	24.6%
Second (2)	4.0%	10.4%	6.1%	0.7%	0.2%	21.4%
Third (3)	2.6%	6.8%	8.7%	5.1%	0.2%	23.4%
Fourth (4)	0.8%	3.0%	5.0%	9.8%	2.5%	21.2%
Highest (5)	0.4%	0.3%	1.1%	3.3%	4.3%	9.5%
All (6)	22.7%	28.2%	22.0%	19.8%	7.3%	100.0%
Ratio of 1989 Quintile to 1979 Quintile (7)	0.92	1.32	0.94	0.93	0.77	
	D. Fewer than 12 Years of Education in 1989					
	Lowest (1)	Second (2)	Third (3)	Fourth (4)	Highest (5)	All (6)
Lowest (1)	33.9%	4.9%	2.4%	0.1%	0.0%	41.3%
Second (2)	9.7%	14.0%	2.8%	0.0%	0.0%	26.5%
Third (3)	1.3%	3.5%	7.3%	2.6%	0.0%	14.7%
Fourth (4)	3.5%	0.8%	1.9%	2.6%	0.1%	8.9%
Highest (5)	0.6%	0.1%	2.5%	5.4%	0.0%	8.6%
All (6)	49.0%	23.4%	16.9%	10.6%	0.1%	100.0%
Ratio of 1989 Quintile to 1979 Quintile (7)	1.19	0.88	1.15	1.19	0.01	

Notes: Prime-age adults are persons who were 25 to 54 years of age in 1979. The percentages in table 4 were calculated by CRS using data from the Panel Study of Income Dynamics (PSID). The percentages are based on weighted observations for 417 individuals with 16 or more years of education, 351 individuals with 13 to 15 years of education, 643 individuals with 12 years of education, and 311 individuals with fewer than 12 years of education. Data on education were missing for 19 individuals. Totals may not add because of rounding.

TABLE 5. Percent of Individuals from Each 1979 Quintile in Each 1989 Quintile: Prime-Age Adults, by Race and Gender

	Quintile in 1989					
	A. Whites					
Quintile in 1979	Lowest (1)	Second (2)	Third (3)	Fourth (4)	Highest (5)	All (6)
Lowest (1)	10.3%	4.6%	1.4%	0.9%	0.1%	17.3%
Second (2)	3.7%	8.3%	5.9%	1.7%	0.7%	20.3%
Third (3)	1.5%	4.4%	7.1%	5.6%	1.2%	19.8%
Fourth (4)	1.1%	1.8%	4.4%	8.3%	4.8%	20.4%
Highest (5)	0.6%	0.5%	1.6%	5.0%	14.5%	22.1%
All (6)	17.3%	19.6%	20.4%	21.4%	21.3%	100.0%
Ratio of 1989 Quintile to 1979 Quintile (7)	1.00	0.96	1.03	1.05	0.96	
	B. African-Americans					
	Lowest (1)	Second (2)	Third (3)	Fourth (4)	Highest (5)	All (6)
Lowest (1)	29.4%	7.7%	2.3%	0.2%	0.0%	39.6%
Second (2)	5.0%	8.5%	2.6%	2.0%	0.7%	18.7%
Third (3)	5.2%	5.4%	9.5%	1.7%	0.4%	22.1%
Fourth (4)	0.6%	3.3%	2.1%	6.7%	4.2%	17.0%
Highest (5)	0.0%	0.0%	0.2%	0.4%	1.8%	2.5%
All (6)	40.2%	25.0%	16.8%	11.0%	7.1%	100.0%
Ratio of 1989 Quintile to 1979 Quintile (7)	1.02	1.33	0.76	0.65	2.79	continued

See notes at the end of the table.

TABLE 5. Percent of Individuals from Each 1979 Quintile in Each 1989 Quintile: Prime-Age Adults, by Race and Gender -- continued

	Quintile in 1989					
	C. White Men					
Quintile in 1979	Lowest (1)	Second (2)	Third (3)	Fourth (4)	Highest (5)	All (6)
Lowest (1)	3.1%	0.6%	0.6%	0.2%	0.0%	4.4%
Second (2)	3.2%	6.3%	3.4%	0.8%	0.4%	14.0%
Third (3)	1.3%	4.4%	7.1%	4.8%	1.4%	18.9%
Fourth (4)	1.6%	2.6%	6.4%	10.8%	6.8%	28.2%
Highest (5)	1.1%	0.8%	2.5%	7.4%	22.6%	34.4%
All (6)	10.3%	14.7%	20.0%	23.9%	31.1%	100.0%
Ratio of 1989 Quintile to 1979 Quintile (7)	2.32	1.05	1.06	0.85	0.91	
	D. African-American Men					
	Lowest (1)	Second (2)	Third (3)	Fourth (4)	Highest (5)	All (6)
Lowest (1)	14.0%	0.9%	2.2%	0.0%	0.0%	17.1%
Second (2)	6.0%	8.6%	2.1%	0.9%	0.0%	17.6%
Third (3)	7.4%	2.7%	10.8%	1.4%	0.0%	22.4%
Fourth (4)	1.5%	8.4%	3.8%	13.3%	9.8%	36.8%
Highest (5)	0.1%	0.0%	0.6%	0.8%	4.6%	6.1%
All (6)	29.1%	20.6%	19.4%	16.4%	14.5%	100.0%
Ratio of 1989 Quintile to 1979 Quintile (7)	1.70	1.17	0.87	0.44	2.38	continued

See notes at the end of the table.

TABLE 5. Percent of Individuals from Each 1979 Quintile in Each 1989 Quintile: Prime-Age Adults, by Race and Gender -- continued						
	Quintile in 1989					
	E. White Women					
Quintile in 1979	Lowest (1)	Second (2)	Third (3)	Fourth (4)	Highest (5)	All (6)
Lowest (1)	19.8%	9.8%	2.5%	1.8%	0.2%	34.2%
Second (2)	4.3%	11.1%	9.2%	2.8%	1.2%	28.6%
Third (3)	1.8%	4.4%	7.1%	6.7%	1.0%	21.0%
Fourth (4)	0.5%	0.7%	1.7%	5.1%	2.2%	10.3%
Highest (5)	0.0%	0.0%	0.4%	1.8%	3.8%	6.0%
All (6)	26.5%	26.0%	20.9%	18.2%	8.4%	100.0%
Ratio of 1989 Quintile to 1979 Quintile (7)	0.77	0.91	0.99	1.77	1.41	
	F. African-American Women					
	Lowest (1)	Second (2)	Third (3)	Fourth (4)	Highest (5)	All (6)
Lowest (1)	39.3%	12.1%	2.3%	0.3%	0.0%	54.1%
Second (2)	4.3%	8.4%	2.9%	2.7%	1.1%	19.4%
Third (3)	3.7%	7.1%	8.7%	1.8%	0.6%	22.0%
Fourth (4)	0.1%	0.0%	1.1%	2.5%	0.5%	4.2%
Highest (5)	0.0%	0.1%	0.0%	0.1%	0.0%	0.3%
All (6)	47.4%	27.8%	15.1%	7.5%	2.3%	100.0%
Ratio of 1989 Quintile to 1979 Quintile (7)	0.88	1.43	0.68	1.77	9.30	

Notes: Prime-age adults are persons who were 25 to 54 years of age in 1979. The percentages in table 5 were calculated by CRS using data from the Panel Study of Income Dynamics (PSID). The percentages are based on weighted observations for 1,152 white adults, 557 African-American adults, 649 white males, 229 African-American males, 503 white females, and 328 African-American females. Data on race were missing for 6 individuals, and 26 individuals of other races were excluded from the analysis. Totals may not add because of rounding.

TABLE 6. Summary of Findings on Distribution of Individuals by Wage Class, 1979-89				
	No Change in Wage Class (1)	Higher Wage Class (2)	Lower Wage Class (3)	Total (4)
Table 7: Real Wage Changes, Prime-Age Adults, 1979-89 (1)	48.0%	36.5%	15.5%	100.0%
Table 8: Real Wage Changes, by Gender, 1979-89				
Men (2)	52.8%	27.3%	20.0%	100.0%
Women (3)	42.2%	47.7%	10.1%	100.0%
Table 9: Real Wage Changes, by Years of Education, 1979-89				
16 Years or More (4)	50.1%	39.3%	10.6%	100.0%
Between 13 and 15 Years (5)	44.6%	39.5%	15.9%	100.0%
12 Years (6)	45.1%	37.1%	17.8%	100.0%
Fewer than 12 Years (7)	56.9%	22.4%	20.7%	100.0%
Table 10: Real Wage Changes, by Race and Gender, 1979-89				
White Adults (8)	47.7%	36.8%	15.5%	100.0%
African-American Adults (9)	48.3%	34.8%	16.9%	100.0%
White Men (10)	53.2%	26.9%	19.9%	100.0%
African-American Men (11)	45.6%	31.4%	23.1%	100.0%
White Women (12)	40.5%	49.8%	9.6%	100.0%
African-American Women (13)	50.1%	37.0%	12.9%	100.0%

See the notes to table 1.

TABLE 7. Percent of Individuals from Each Wage Class in 1979 in Each Wage Class in 1989: Prime-Age Adults

Quintile in 1979	Percent of Individuals in Each Wage Class in 1989					
	Lowest (1)	Second (2)	Third (3)	Fourth (4)	Highest (5)	All (6)
Lowest (1)	10.4%	5.9%	2.4%	1.0%	0.2%	19.9%
Second (2)	2.9%	6.2%	7.5%	2.1%	1.3%	20.0%
Third (3)	1.5%	2.4%	7.6%	5.8%	2.8%	20.0%
Fourth (4)	0.9%	1.5%	2.5%	7.6%	7.5%	19.9%
Highest (5)	0.4%	0.3%	1.0%	2.2%	16.2%	20.1%
All (6)	16.1%	16.3%	21.0%	18.7%	27.9%	100.0%
Ratio of Percent of Individuals in Wage Class in 1989 to Percent of Individuals in Wage Class in 1979 (7)	0.81	0.81	1.05	0.94	1.39	

See the notes to table 2. The hourly wage intervals that define the real wage classes (in 1989 dollars) are: lowest quintile, more than $0.00 but less than or equal to $6.70; second quintile, more than $6.70 but less than or equal to $9.22; third quintile, more than $9.22 but less than or equal to $12.35; fourth quintile, more than $12.35 but less than or equal to $15.92; and highest quintile, more than $15.92.

TABLE 8. Percent of Individuals from Each Wage Class in 1979 in Each Wage Class in 1989: Prime-Age Adults, by Gender						
	Percent of Individuals in Each Wage Class in 1989					
	A. Men					
Quintile in 1979	Lowest (1)	Second (2)	Third (3)	Fourth (4)	Highest (5)	All (6)
Lowest (1)	3.6%	1.0%	0.6%	0.4%	0.0%	5.6%
Second (2)	2.5%	4.9%	5.2%	1.1%	0.5%	14.2%
Third (3)	1.3%	2.5%	7.4%	5.5%	2.5%	19.2%
Fourth (4)	1.4%	2.0%	4.3%	10.7%	10.4%	28.8%
Highest (5)	0.8%	0.5%	1.7%	3.0%	26.3%	32.3%
All (6)	9.5%	10.9%	19.2%	20.7%	39.7%	100.0%
Ratio of Percent of Individuals in Wage Class in 1989 to Percent of Individuals in Wage Class in 1979 (7)	1.68	0.77	1.00	0.72	1.23	
	B. Women					
	Lowest (1)	Second (2)	Third (3)	Fourth (4)	Highest (5)	All (6)
Lowest (1)	18.8%	11.9%	4.5%	1.7%	0.5%	37.3%
Second (2)	3.4%	7.8%	10.4%	3.4%	2.2%	27.1%
Third (3)	1.7%	2.3%	7.8%	6.2%	3.1%	21.1%
Fourth (4)	0.2%	0.8%	0.3%	3.9%	3.9%	9.2%
Highest (5)	0.0%	0.0%	0.2%	1.1%	3.9%	5.2%
All (6)	24.2%	22.7%	23.1%	16.3%	13.7%	100.0%
Ratio of Percent of Individuals in Wage Class in 1989 to Percent of Individuals in Wage Class in 1979 (7)	0.65	0.84	1.09	1.77	2.61	

See the notes to tables 3 and 7.

TABLE 9. Percent of Individuals from Each Wage Class in 1979 in Each Wage Class in 1989: Prime-Age Adults, by Level of Education

Quintile in 1979	Percent of Individuals in Each Wage Class in 1989					
	A. 16 or More Years of Education in 1989					
	Lowest (1)	Second (2)	Third (3)	Fourth (4)	Highest (5)	All (6)
Lowest (1)	1.5%	1.8%	1.4%	1.3%	0.5%	6.5%
Second (2)	1.8%	2.3%	4.3%	2.4%	2.1%	12.8%
Third (3)	0.8%	1.3%	6.2%	6.4%	4.8%	19.4%
Fourth (4)	0.2%	0.6%	1.3%	6.4%	14.5%	23.0%
Highest (5)	0.7%	0.6%	0.3%	3.1%	33.7%	38.4%
All (6)	5.0%	6.5%	13.5%	19.5%	55.5%	100.0%
Ratio of Percent of Individuals in Wage Class in 1989 to Percent of Individuals in Wage Class in 1979 (7)	0.77	0.51	0.69	0.85	1.45	
	B. Between 13 and 15 Years of Education in 1989					
	Lowest (1)	Second (2)	Third (3)	Fourth (4)	Highest (5)	All (6)
Lowest (1)	8.8%	5.2%	2.9%	0.6%	0.4%	18.0%
Second (2)	1.7%	5.0%	10.3%	4.5%	2.3%	23.9%
Third (3)	1.7%	2.3%	5.7%	4.8%	3.2%	17.7%
Fourth (4)	0.9%	1.9%	3.0%	9.8%	5.3%	20.8%
Highest (5)	0.0%	0.4%	2.1%	1.9%	15.2%	19.7%
All (6)	13.2%	14.7%	24.1%	21.6%	26.4%	100.0%
Ratio of Percent of Individuals in Wage Class in 1989 to Percent of Individuals in Wage Class in 1979 (7)	0.73	0.62	1.36	1.04	1.34	cont'd

See the notes to tables 4 and 7.

TABLE 9. Percent of Individuals from Each Wage Class in 1979 in Each Wage Class in 1989: Prime-Age Adults, by Level of Education -- continued

Quintile in 1979	Percent of Individuals in Each Wage Class in 1989					
	C. 12 Years of Education in 1989					
	Lowest (1)	Second (2)	Third (3)	Fourth (4)	Highest (5)	All (6)
Lowest (1)	12.0%	8.4%	3.1%	1.1%	0.0%	24.6%
Second (2)	3.4%	7.5%	8.8%	1.2%	0.5%	21.4%
Third (3)	2.1%	3.4%	9.4%	7.5%	1.0%	23.4%
Fourth (4)	0.5%	2.3%	3.6%	9.3%	5.6%	21.2%
Highest (5)	0.4%	0.0%	0.6%	1.6%	6.8%	9.5%
All (6)	18.3%	21.6%	25.5%	20.7%	13.8%	100.0%
Ratio of Percent of Individuals in Wage Class in 1989 to Percent of Individuals in Wage Class in 1979 (7)	0.75	1.01	1.09	0.98	1.46	
	D. Fewer than 12 Years of Education in 1989					
	Lowest (1)	Second (2)	Third (3)	Fourth (4)	Highest (5)	All (6)
Lowest (1)	29.1%	9.7%	1.7%	0.8%	0.0%	41.3%
Second (2)	6.2%	13.5%	6.7%	0.1%	0.0%	26.5%
Third (3)	1.3%	2.6%	8.1%	0.9%	1.8%	14.7%
Fourth (4)	3.5%	0.6%	1.6%	2.5%	0.7%	8.9%
Highest (5)	0.6%	0.0%	2.2%	2.1%	3.8%	8.6%
All (6)	40.7%	26.4%	20.3%	6.4%	6.3%	100.0%
Ratio of Percent of Individuals in Wage Class in 1989 to Percent of Individuals in Wage Class in 1979 (7)	0.99	1.00	1.38	0.72	0.73	

See the notes to tables 4 and 7.

TABLE 10. Percent of Individuals from Each Wage Class in 1979 in Each Wage Class in 1989: Prime-Age Adults, by Race and Gender

Quintile in 1979	Percent of Individuals in Each Wage Class in 1989					
	A. Whites					
	Lowest (1)	Second (2)	Third (3)	Fourth (4)	Highest (5)	All (6)
Lowest (1)	8.3%	5.3%	2.3%	1.1%	0.3%	17.3%
Second (2)	2.9%	6.1%	7.9%	2.0%	1.3%	20.3%
Third (3)	1.1%	2.3%	7.6%	5.8%	3.1%	19.8%
Fourth (4)	1.0%	1.3%	2.5%	7.9%	7.7%	20.4%
Highest (5)	0.5%	0.3%	1.1%	2.5%	17.7%	22.1%
All (6)	13.8%	15.4%	21.4%	19.3%	30.1%	100.0%
Ratio of Percent of Individuals in Wage Class in 1989 to Percent of Individuals in Wage Class in 1979 (7)	0.80	0.76	1.08	0.95	1.36	
	B. African-Americans					
	Lowest (1)	Second (2)	Third (3)	Fourth (4)	Highest (5)	All (6)
Lowest (1)	24.9%	11.1%	3.4%	0.2%	0.0%	39.6%
Second (2)	3.0%	7.7%	4.8%	2.4%	0.8%	18.7%
Third (3)	5.0%	3.6%	7.3%	5.6%	0.7%	22.1%
Fourth (4)	0.1%	2.7%	2.0%	6.4%	5.8%	17.0%
Highest (5)	0.0%	0.0%	0.3%	0.2%	2.0%	2.5%
All (6)	33.0%	25.0%	17.7%	14.9%	9.3%	100.0%
Ratio of Percent of Individuals in Wage Class in 1989 to Percent of Individuals in Wage Class in 1979 (7)	0.83	1.34	0.80	0.88	3.67	cont'd

See the notes to tables 5 and 7.

TABLE 10. Percent of Individuals from Each Wage Class in 1979 in Each Wage Class in 1989: Prime-Age Adults, by Race and Gender -- continued

Quintile in 1979	Percent of Individuals in Each Wage Class in 1989					
	C. White Men					
	Lowest (1)	Second (2)	Third (3)	Fourth (4)	Highest (5)	All (6)
Lowest (1)	2.4%	1.1%	0.5%	0.5%	0.0%	4.4%
Second (2)	2.5%	4.6%	5.4%	1.0%	0.5%	14.0%
Third (3)	0.8%	2.7%	7.6%	5.2%	2.7%	18.9%
Fourth (4)	1.5%	1.6%	4.2%	10.8%	10.1%	28.2%
Highest (5)	0.9%	0.5%	1.8%	3.3%	27.8%	34.4%
All (6)	8.1%	10.5%	19.6%	20.7%	41.2%	100.0%
Ratio of Percent of Individuals in Wage Class in 1989 to Percent of Individuals in Wage Class in 1979 (7)	1.82	0.75	1.03	0.73	1.20	
	D. African-American Men					
	Lowest (1)	Second (2)	Third (3)	Fourth (4)	Highest (5)	All (6)
Lowest (1)	13.7%	1.2%	2.1%	0.1%	0.0%	17.1%
Second (2)	3.4%	9.3%	3.6%	1.1%	0.3%	17.6%
Third (3)	7.1%	1.0%	5.1%	8.5%	0.7%	22.4%
Fourth (4)	0.2%	6.9%	3.4%	12.5%	13.8%	36.8%
Highest (5)	0.1%	0.0%	0.6%	0.5%	5.0%	6.1%
All (6)	24.4%	18.4%	14.8%	22.7%	19.7%	100.0%
Ratio of Percent of Individuals in Wage Class in 1989 to Percent of Individuals in Wage Class in 1979 (7)	1.43	1.04	0.66	0.62	3.24	cont'd

See the notes to tables 5 and 7.

TABLE 10. Percent of Individuals from Each Wage Class in 1979 in Each Wage Class in 1989: Prime-Age Adults, by Race and Gender -- continued						
	Percent of Individuals in Each Wage Class in 1989					
	E. White Women					
Quintile in 1979	Lowest (1)	Second (2)	Third (3)	Fourth (4)	Highest (5)	All (6)
Lowest (1)	16.1%	11.0%	4.5%	2.0%	0.6%	34.2%
Second (2)	3.5%	8.1%	11.2%	3.4%	2.4%	28.6%
Third (3)	1.4%	1.8%	7.7%	6.5%	3.6%	21.0%
Fourth (4)	0.3%	0.9%	0.2%	4.3%	4.6%	10.3%
Highest (5)	0.0%	0.0%	0.2%	1.3%	4.4%	6.0%
All (6)	21.2%	21.8%	23.8%	17.5%	15.6%	100.0%
Ratio of Percent of Individuals in Wage Class in 1989 to Percent of Individuals in Wage Class in 1979 (7)	0.62	0.76	1.13	1.71	2.62	
	F. African-American Women					
	Lowest (1)	Second (2)	Third (3)	Fourth (4)	Highest (5)	All (6)
Lowest (1)	32.1%	17.4%	4.2%	0.3%	0.1%	54.1%
Second (2)	2.7%	6.7%	5.6%	3.3%	1.1%	19.4%
Third (3)	3.7%	5.2%	8.6%	3.7%	0.8%	22.0%
Fourth (4)	0.1%	0.0%	1.1%	2.5%	0.5%	4.2%
Highest (5)	0.0%	0.0%	0.1%	0.1%	0.1%	0.3%
All (6)	38.6%	29.3%	19.6%	9.9%	2.6%	100.0%
Ratio of Percent of Individuals in Wage Class in 1989 to Percent of Individuals in Wage Class in 1979 (7)	0.71	1.51	0.89	2.33	10.46	

See the notes to tables 5 and 7.

Appendix A: Methodology

The analysis of hourly wage mobility in this report is based on data from the Panel Study of Income Dynamics (PSID). The PSID is a longitudinal survey begun in 1968. The survey is conducted each year by the Survey Research Center at the University of Michigan. Information is collected about the members of the original sample, individuals who have moved into families that were part of the original sample, and individuals of families that were part of the original sample but who have split off to form families of their own. The survey collects information on a wide variety of subjects, but the focus is on family income, employment, and demographics.[54]

In 1979, 6,373 families were included in the PSID survey. Because individuals from the original sample of families are tracked when they form their own families, by 1989 the number of families in the PSID survey had increased to 7,114.[55]

The PSID survey collects wage information for the head of household and the head's spouse. Wage information is collected for an individual's main job at the time of the survey (including persons temporarily laid off, on sick leave, or on maternity leave). The measure of wages used in this report is an individual's before-tax hourly wage or salary for regular time.[56] The wage measure does not include overtime pay or bonuses. Individuals are excluded from the analysis if their hourly wage is based solely on income from self-employment, since part of the hourly wage reported by these individuals may represent a return to investments in capital (e.g., buildings or equipment) used in their work.

To be included in the analysis, information on hourly wages had to be available for both 1979 and 1989. Thus, the analysis does not include persons who entered or permanently left the labor force after 1979.[57] The analysis is restricted to individuals who were between the ages of 25 and 54 in 1979 (i.e., prime-age adults). By examining working age adults only, young adults entering the labor force (who may also be attending school) are excluded as are most persons who have reached retirement age (and who may have chosen to work part-time in a lower paying job).

---

[54] Hill, Martha S. *The Panel Study of Income Dynamics*. Newbury Park, CA: Sage Publications, 1992. p. 2-3, 6.

[55] By 1981, almost 40 percent of the original PSID respondents had left the sample. According to one analysis, attrition has had little effect on the representativeness of the PSID sample. Becketti, Sean, William Gould, Lee Lillard, and Finis Welch. The Panel Study of Income Dynamics after Fourteen Years: An Evaluation. *Journal of Labor Economics*, v. 6, October 1988. p. 477, 488-90.

[56] For salaried workers, if salary is given as an annual figure, it is divided by 2000 hours per year. If salary is given as a weekly figure, it is divided by 40 hours per week.

[57] The PSID dataset does not allow an analysis of hourly wages of the family head and the head's spouse for years before 1979.

An individual's hourly wage may be affected by the business cycle. Thus, to examine hourly wage mobility in the 1980s, the analysis in this report begins with hourly wages in 1979 and ends with hourly wages in 1989. The years 1979 and 1989 were selected because in both years the business cycle was at a peak. The civilian unemployment rate was 5.8% in 1979 and 5.3% in 1989.[58] Total industry capacity utilization peaked in both 1979 and 1989 (at 86.2% and 83.7%, respectively).[59]

Inflation adjustments were made using the CPI-U-X1.[60] Unlike the CPI-U, the CPI-U-X1 treats the measurement of homeownership costs consistently over time.[61]

The original PSID included an oversampling of lower-income households. This oversampling resulted in a subsample of black households that was larger than the relative number of black households in the general population.[62] To make the PSID data representative of the United States population, weights are assigned to households and to individuals in the survey. Over time these weights are adjusted to take into account unequal response rates among different groups in the survey. The weights used in this report are the individual weights for 1989.[63]

---

[58] U.S. Department of Labor. Bureau of Labor Statistics. *Employment and Earnings*, v. 43, October 1996. p. 12.

[59] Council of Economic Advisors. *Economic Report of the President*. Washington, U.S. Govt. Print. Off., February 1996, p. 337.

[60] U.S. Bureau of the Census. *Money Income of Households, Families, and Persons in the United States: 1991*. Current Population Reports, Series P-60, No. 180. Washington: U.S. Govt. Print. Off., August 1992, p. B-2.

[61] Before 1983, the measurement of homeowner costs in the CPI-U combined the investment and consumption components of homeownership. To isolate the consumption component of homeownership, in 1983, the method for measuring homeownership costs was revised. The new method uses estimates of the cost of renting equivalent housing. But the historical CPI-U series for years before 1983 was not revised. The CPI-U-X1 series uses a consistent measure (rental equivalence value) of homeownership costs through all years.

[62] The oversampling of lower-income households accounts for the disproportionate number of black men and women in tables 5 and 10.

[63] To help correct for omissions in representing post-1968 immigrants to the U.S., a sample of 2,043 Latino households was added to the PSID survey in 1990. In this report, the individual weights used are from the most recent year that an individual contributes data to the analysis. This approach is recommended in: Hill, The Panel Study of Income Dynamics, p. 2-3, 8-9, 23-24, 64-65.

Appendix B: Findings From Time-Series Data

Most studies of the growth and distribution of wages use cross-sectional time-series data. This appendix describes the findings, summarized in the text, from selected studies that use time-series data.

Real Wage Growth

The Current Population Survey (CPS), conducted by the Census Bureau for BLS, is the source of two income data series. According to data from the monthly CPS outgoing rotation groups, between 1979 and 1989 there was virtually no change in the average hourly real wage among workers in the private sector. Data from the March CPS indicate that, between 1979 and 1989, the average hourly real wage for workers in the private sector increased at an annual rate of 0.3%. According to data from the National Income and Product Accounts (NIPA), the average hourly real wage for all private-sector workers increased at an annual rate of 0.5%.[64] Data from the Census Bureau's Public Use Microdata Sample (PUMS) indicate that, between 1979 and 1989, average hourly wages increased at an annual rate of 0.1%.[65]

---

[64] Data from BLS's Current Employment Statistics (CES) indicate that, between 1979 and 1989, the average hourly real (i.e., inflation-adjusted) wage decreased at an annual rate of 0.6%. But the CES covers a more limited group of workers (production workers in manufacturing, mining, and construction and nonsupervisory workers in other industries) than the CPS and NIPA data series. The CES data series is based on a monthly survey of employers. Establishments that agree to participate in the CES survey typically remain in the sample indefinitely.

The CPS is a household survey, the main purpose of which is to collect information on employment and unemployment. Each month, wage information is collected for individuals in the outgoing rotation group, which consists of one-fourth of individuals in the CPS sample. Wage information for individuals in the outgoing rotation group is for usual weekly earnings, usual hours worked, and, if paid hourly, the rate of hourly pay. The wage information is for the main job of individuals who worked during the week before the survey. The March CPS collects information about wages and weeks worked on all jobs during the previous year. The NIPA data series is based on a quarterly BLS employer survey and is constructed by the Bureau of Economic Analysis at the Department of Commerce. None of the calculations of average hourly real wages includes persons employed in agriculture. U.S. Library of Congress. Congressional Research Service. *Real Wage Trends: An Overview.* Report 95-537 E, by Gail McCallion. April 27, 1995. p. 18-20. U.S. Department of Labor. Bureau of Labor Statistics. *Divergent Trends in Alternative Real Wage Series*. Draft report by Katharine G. Abraham, James R. Spletzer, and Jay C. Stewart. October 19, 1995. p. 4-9.

[65] Schmitt, John, and Lawrence Mishel. *Did International Trade Lower Less-Skilled Wages During the 1980s? Standard Trade Theory and Evidence*. Washington, Economic Policy Institute, July 9, 1996. p. 8-9, 43. The PUMS datafile contains data on individuals in housing units that receive the "long form" of the decennial Census questionnaire. The long form includes questions about age, occupation, and wages.

Gender

Using data from the March CPS, Karoly found that, between 1979 and 1989, the median hourly real wage for all workers increased. But she found that the direction of change was different for men and women. For men, the median hourly real wage decreased, but for women it increased.[66]

Blackburn et al. analyzed average (instead of median) hourly wages and reached the same conclusion as Karoly. Using March CPS data for 1979-88, Blackburn et al. found that the average hourly real wage for men working full-time year-round decreased, but increased for women working full-time year-round.[67,68]

Education

Using data from the March CPS, the Department of Labor found that, from 1979 to 1989, there was an increase in the wage gap between college graduates and individuals with less education. In 1979, the average annual wage of men who had a college education and who worked full-time year-round was 37% greater than the average annual wage of men with a high school education only. By 1989, men with a college education earned 64% more than men with a high school education only. In 1979, women with a college education who worked full-time year-round earned 43% more than women with a high school education only. By 1989, this difference had increased to 61%.[69]

---

[66] Karoly, Lynn A. *The Trend in Inequality Among Families, Individuals, and Workers in the United States: A Twenty-Five-Year Perspective*. Santa Monica, CA., RAND Corporation, 1992. p. 36.

[67] Blackburn, McKinley L.; David E. Bloom; and Richard B. Freeman. An Era of Falling Earnings and Rising Inequality? *The Brookings Review*, v. 9, Winter 1990/91. p. 39-40.

[68] Using March CPS data, Murphy and Welch found that, between 1979-1989, annual average hourly real wages for men increased. However, controlling for changes in age and education among men in the labor force, they found that average hourly real wages decreased. Their sample consisted of white males working full-time who worked at least 40 weeks during the year. Murphy, Kevin M., and Finis Welch. The Structure of Wages. *Quarterly Journal of Economics*, v. 107, February 1992. p. 289-90.

[69] In 1979, the average annual wage of men with a college education who worked full-time year-round was 70% greater than the average annual wage of men with less than a high school education. This gap increased to 119% in 1989. From 1979 to 1989, the wage gap between men with a college education and men with some college (i.e., 13-15 years of education) increased from 28% to 39%. From 1979 to 1989, the wage gap between women with a college education who worked full-time year-round and women with less than a high school education increased from 79% to 111%. From 1979 to 1989, the wage gap between women with a college education and women with some college increased from 26% to 36%. U.S. Department of Labor. *Report on the American Workforce*. Washington, U.S. Govt. Print. Off., 1994. p. 63, 67.

Using data from the Public Use Microdata Sample (PUMS), Schmitt and Mishel found that, in 1979, the average hourly real wage of persons with four years of college was 58.0% greater than the average hourly real wage of individuals with a high school education only. By 1989, this gap had increased to 68.5%. The increased wage gap was due mainly to a decline in the average hourly real wage of high school graduates.[70]

Using data from the March CPS, Bradbury found a widening gap in median (instead of average) wages between college graduates and high school graduates. In 1979, the median annual wage of full-time year-round workers with a college degree or better was 48% greater than the median annual wage of full-time year-round workers with a high school degree. By 1989, the educational wage premium for college graduates increased to 68%. For men, the gap increased from 32% to 60%. For women, the gap increased from 41% to 67%.[71]

Using March CPS data, Murphy and Welch found that, in 1979, the hourly wage for white male college graduates was 37% greater than the hourly wage of white male high school graduates. By 1989, this gap had increased to 58%.[72]

Race

Using data from the March CPS for 1979 and 1989, Card and Lemieux found that in both years, among full-time year-round workers, African-American men had lower average hourly wages than white men and that African-American women had lower average hourly wages than white women. Between 1979 and 1989, the wage gap between black and white men closed slightly, while the wage gap between black and white women increased slightly. Using data from the CPS outgoing rotation groups, Card and Lemieux found that, between 1979 and 1989, the wage gap increased between black and white men and between black and white women.[73]

Using data from the CPS outgoing rotation groups for 1979 and 1989, Bernstein examined the wage gap between black and white adults by educational

---

[70] Schmitt and Mishel, Did International Trade Lower Less-Skilled Wages During the 1980s? Standard Trade Theory and Evidence, p. 9, 43.

[71] Bradbury, Katharine L. The Growing Inequality of Family Incomes: Changing Families and Changing Wages. *New England Economic Review*, July/August 1996. p. 59.

[72] Murphy and Welch, The Structure of Wages, p. 300-301.

[73] Compared to the March CPS, the monthly CPS outgoing rotation groups may underrepresent individuals with less stable employment. Wage information for the outgoing rotation groups is for the main job of individuals who worked during the week before the survey. The March CPS collects wage information for all jobs held during the previous year. Card, David, and Thomas Lemieux. *Wage Dispersion, Returns to Skill, and Black-White Wage Differentials*. Working Paper No. 4365. Cambridge, MA, National Bureau of Economic Research, May 1993. p. 13-14, 29.

level. Bernstein found that, except for high school dropouts, the hourly wage gap increased between black and white men and women.[74]

Using data from the CPS outgoing rotation groups from 1979 to 1989, Bound and Freeman found an increase in the hourly wage gap between young black and white men and that the rise in the wage gap was especially large for college graduates and for men in the midwest with a high school education or less.[75]

Work Experience

Research indicates that real wages are generally higher for older workers (i.e., workers with more work experience) and that, except for college graduates, the return to work experience increased during the 1980s.[76] Using data from the March CPS, Bound and Johnson found that, in 1988, average hourly wages of men with more work experience were greater than the hourly wages of men with less work experience. The relationship held for men at all educational levels. With two exceptions, the average hourly wages of women with more work experience were greater than the hourly wages of women with less work experience. The two exceptions were women with a college education and 10 or more years of experience, and women with some college and 20 or more years of experience.

Bound and Johnson also found that, from 1979 to 1988, except for college graduates, the return to experience increased. This pattern held for both men and women. In large part, the return to experience increased among workers with less than a college education because the hourly real wages of workers with

---

[74] Bernstein's analysis is for individuals between the ages of 16 and 64. Bernstein, Jared. *Where's the Payoff? The Gap Between Black Academic Progress and Economic Gains*. Washington, Economic Policy Institute, 1995. p. 30.

[75] Bound and Freeman studied men with less than ten years of potential work experience. Their study covered the years from 1973 to 1989. For men with a high school education or less, the authors attribute the relative decline in earnings to the loss of manufacturing jobs, the economic decline of inner cities, the fall in the real value of the minimum wage, and the relative drop in union membership among young black men. The authors attribute the largest part of the erosion of wages among black college graduates to a shift to lower-paying occupations. The authors also believe that weakened government pressure to increase minority employment and court decisions that made it harder to prove employment discrimination contributed to the relative decline in earnings among young black men. Bound, John, and Richard B. Freeman. *What Went Wrong: The Erosion of Relative Earnings and Employment Among Young Black Me in the 1980s*. Working Paper No. 3778. Cambridge, MA, National Bureau of Economic Research, July 1991. p. 1-4, 11-12, 24-25, 41.

[76] Gottschalk, Peter, and Robert Moffitt. The Growth of Earnings Instability in the U.S. Labor Market. *Brookings Papers on Economic Activity*, no. 2, 1994. p. 223.

less experience decreased more than the hourly real wages of workers with more experience.[77]

Freeman and Katz reached similar conclusions using data for men from the March CPS. Based on an analysis of hourly wages, Freeman and Katz found that, between 1979 and 1989, the return to experience increased among men with less than a college education but decreased among men with a college education.[78]

The Distribution of Wages

A change in average or median hourly wages does not reveal whether the distribution of hourly wages has changed. In general, research using time-series data has found that, from 1979 to 1989, the distribution of hourly wages became more unequal.[79]

Using data from the March CPS, Karoly found that, between 1979 and 1989, the distribution of hourly real wages among workers 16 years and over became more unequal, and that the increase in inequality occurred among both men and women.[80]

Using data from the March CPS, Freeman and Katz report that, from 1979 to 1989, the hourly wages of full-time workers at the 90th percentile (i.e., workers whose wages exceed the wages of 90% of full-time workers) relative to the hourly wages of workers at the 10th percentile increased by 20% for men and 25% for women.[81]

---

[77] Among workers with less than a college education, average hourly real wages increased among women with some college and 10 or more years of experience. In addition to college graduates, the return to experience decreased among women with less than a high school education and 10-19 years of experience. Bound and Johnson, Changes in the Structure of Wages in the 1980's: An Evaluation of Alternative Explanations, p. 373.

[78] Freeman, Richard B., and Lawrence F. Katz. Rising Wage Inequality: The United States Vs. Other Advanced Countries. In *Working Under Different Rules*, Ed. by Richard B. Freeman. New York, Russell Sage Foundation, 1994. p. 32-36.

[79] Data from the Bureau of the Census indicate that, between 1979-89, there was also a rise in inequality in the distribution of family income. U.S. Library of Congress. Congressional Research Service. *Recent Trends in the Distribution and Growth of Family Income*. Report 96-796 E, by Brian Cashell. September 20, 1996. p. 3-6. Bradbury, The Growing Inequality of Family Incomes: Changing Families and Changing Wages, p. 56, 79.

[80] Karoly, The Trend in Inequality Among Families, Individuals, and Workers in the United States: A Twenty-Five-Year Perspective, p. 32, 35, 42-43, 66-68.

[81] Freeman and Katz, Rising Wage Inequality: The United States Vs. Other Advanced Countries, p. 32.

Using data from the March CPS, Juhn et al. found that, between 1979 and 1989, there was an increase in inequality in hourly wages among men working full-time. They found that the hourly real wages of men at the 10th percentile of the wage distribution fell, but the hourly real wages of men at the 90th percentile increased.[82] Using data from the same source, Topel found that, between 1979 and 1989, the increased gap in hourly real wages between men at the 90th and 10th percentiles was due more to the decline in hourly wages for men at the 10th percentile than to the growth in real wages for men at the 90th percentile.[83]

Some studies have found that, among men, there was a decline in "middle class" jobs during the 1980s. The percentage of men in the middle of the wage distribution decreased (i.e., the middle hollowed out), while the percentage of men at both the top and bottom of the wage distribution increased.[84] Using data from the March CPS, Ryscavage examined the annual wages of full-time year-round workers and found that, between 1979 and 1989, the percentage of men at both the upper ($48,000 or more in 1992 dollars) and lower (less than $24,000) ends of the wage distribution increased, while the percentage of men in the middle ($24,000 to $48,000) of the wage distribution decreased. On the other hand, the percentage of women in the middle and upper end of the wage distribution increased, while the percentage of women in the bottom end of the wage distribution decreased.[85]

---

[82] Juhn, Chinhui; Kevin M. Murphy; and Brooks Pierce. Wage Inequality and the Rise in Returns to Skill. *Journal of Political Economy*, v. 101, June 1993. p. 413-416.

[83] Topel, Robert H. Factor Proportions and Relative Wages: The Supply-Side Determinants of Wage Inequality. *Journal of Economic Perspectives*, v. 11, Spring 1997. p. 56-57.

[84] Levy and Murnane, U.S. Earnings Levels and Earnings Inequality: A Review of Recent Trends and Proposed Explanations, p. 1371.

[85] Ryscavage, Paul. Gender-Related Shifts in the Distribution of Wages. *Monthly Labor Review*, v. 117, July 1994. p. 4-6.

Index